D

2/01

Blake's Visionary Universe

Blake's Visionary Universe

John Beer

Manchester University Press
Barnes & Noble Inc, New York

Published by the
University of Manchester at
The University Press
316–324 Oxford Road
Manchester 13

GB SBN 7190 0390 3

USA
Barnes & Noble, Inc.
105 Fifth Avenue
New York, N.Y. 10003

USA SBN 389 01093 6

Made and Printed in Great Britain by
Butler & Tanner Ltd, Frome and London

Contents

List of Illustrations

Preface

This book grew out of the same work that gave rise to my earlier study *Blake's Humanism*. In many respects, therefore, my debts remain the same.

During the time that I have been preparing the present book for the Press, however, I have been helped by several people in new ways. In particular, a course on Blake arranged by the Cambridge Extra-Mural Department at Madingley in December 1967 enabled me to hear a number of stimulating talks by Blake scholars such as Jack Herbert, Kathleen Raine, Stanley Gardner, Desirée Hirst and T. R. Henn. The contact with an audience representing a cross-section of intelligent readers during this time of final writings and rewritings was also very helpful—particularly in wrestling with the problem of avoiding undue repetitiveness while writing about an artist as obsessive as Blake. The lecture contributed to this course by Mr Herbert and another given shortly afterwards by Professor L. C. Knights to the Cambridge University English Club suggested some additional discussion in my section on *Poetical Sketches*, while the ideas of Stanley Gardner, since printed in his new book, prompted further thought about Blake's London—particularly 'the fields from Islington to Marybone'; I also gained much from one or two supervisions with Mr Andrew Fichter.

In addition to the debts acknowledged to specific writers in my earlier preface I ought to mention the recent editions of 'Tiriel' and 'Vala, or The Four Zoas' by G. E. Bentley, Jnr, the *Blake Dictionary* of S. Foster Damon and the *Blake Concordance* of David Erdman and others—all of which have helped to ease the labours of the final stages. John Danby's book *Shakespeare's Doctrine of Nature* provided unexpectedly relevant parallels for Blake's ideas on Shakespeare as I was reconstructing them. While this book was in page-proof, two further important studies appeared: John Armstrong's *The Paradise Myth*, which has some interesting suggestions concerning the images of Mercury and of the serpent and the tree up to the Romantic period, and Kathleen Raine's *Blake and Tradition*, which gathers up the studies referred to in my notes, along with much more, and places students of Blake still further in her debt.

Once again I owe much to the continual encouragement and understanding of my wife. Mr Malcolm Cormack and Mr E. C. Chamberlain of the Fitzwilliam Museum have again shown kindness and patience in dealing with my enquiries on points connected with the illustrations. The presence of Harold Bloom and David Erdman in London during the summer of 1967 was a double pleasure. A visit to Sir Geoffrey Keynes enabled me both to enjoy his hospitality and conversation and to see his splendid Blake collection. A grant from the University of Cambridge Faculty of English assisted with the typing expenses.

It remains only for me to repeat with undiminished gratitude the names of others, referring the reader to my earlier preface for further details where appropriate: The Master and Fellows of St John's College, Cambridge; the University of Manchester; Professor Frank Kermode, Professor John Jump, Dr Arnold Goldman and Mr Martin Butlin; and the librarians and staffs of the following institutions: Manchester Central Library; the John Rylands Library; the Manchester University Library; the Pierpont Morgan Library; the Harvard University Library; the Fogg Museum; the Cambridge University Library; the Fitzwilliam Museum; the Victoria and Albert Museum; and the Reading Room, Students' Room and Print Room of the British Museum. My final debt, as before, is to the Master and Fellows of Peterhouse.

J. B. B.
Cambridge 1969

A Note on Text and Abbreviations

In general, I have followed the text of *The Poetry and Prose of William Blake*, edited by David Erdman, with commentary by Harold Bloom (New York, 1965). Since most English readers will use the editions edited by Geoffrey Keynes, however, I also give references to three of these: the Nonesuch editions of 1948 (NB) and 1958 (NC) and the Oxford Standard authors edition, in which the pagination is that of NC apart from a few pages of additional text (= o*). (The original one-volume Nonesuch edition, published in 1927 (NA) has a different pagination; a conversion table between this and NB is furnished by A. S. Roe in *Blake's Illustrations to the Divine Comedy* (Princeton, 1953).)

The reader who wishes to consult a text with Blake's own 'illuminations' should ideally have access to the facsimile editions published by the Trianon Press. The most *compendious* edition of the illuminated books is still, surprisingly, the third volume of Blake's *Works* edited by E. J. Ellis and W. B. Yeats (London, 1893).

Additional notes
This is a convenient occasion to correct two points in *Blake's Humanism*. The emmet (p. 200) is not a mole but a dialect word for an ant: Blake is making the same point as in *Thel* but with a slightly different illustration. I also learn that the painting formerly thought to portray Elisha and Elijah (pp. 191–2) has now been identified as 'God judging Adam': the flames are therefore those of twofold vision perverted by the single vision of the moral law, which fits the painting better.

Kathleen Raine's *Blake and Tradition* (1969, I, 274) contains a quotation from Thomas Vaughan's *Aula Lucis* (ed. Waite, 329) which supports my interpretation of 'The Crystal Cabinet' (*Blake's Humanism*, 88–9) and may well have been the germ of Blake's ideas concerning the fall of love into 'vegetation'. With acknowledgments to her I am reproducing it overleaf as an epigraph to the present volume, along with a passage from Blake which illustrates the way in which his advocacy of energized perception adds to—and differs from—the quietist vision of writers like Vaughan.

Matter . . . is the house of light. Here he dwells and builds for himself, and, to speak truth, he takes up his lodging in sight of all the world. When he first enters it, it is a glorious, transparent room, a crystal castle, and he lives like a familiar in diamonds. He hath then the liberty to look out at the windows; his love is all in his sight: I mean that liquid Venus which lures him in; but this continues not very long. He is busy—as all lovers are—labours for a closer union, insinuates and conveys himself into the very substance of his love, so that his heat and action stir up her moist essences, by whose means he becomes an absolute prisoner. For at last the earth grows over him out of the water, so that he is quite shut up in darkness . . .

Thomas Vaughan, Aula Lucis

The cherub with his flaming sword is hereby commanded to leave his guard at tree of life, and when he does, the whole creation will be consumed, and appear infinite and holy whereas it now appears finite & corrupt.

This will come to pass by an improvement of sensual enjoyment.

But first the notion that man has a body distinct from his soul, is to be expunged . . .

If the doors of perception were cleansed every thing would appear to man as it is, infinite.

For man has closed himself up, till he sees all things thro' narrow chinks of his cavern.

Blake, The Marriage of Heaven and Hell

1 Blake's Enterprise

In an era dominated by scientific method, myth-makers are normally forced to take up a defensive stance. Afraid of easy dismissal as 'fantasy-mongers' they often forestall criticism by assuming the rôle of licensed entertainers. A few—and William Blake is prominent among them—refuse to compromise. They offer their own sense of what is real and may even refuse to give more than a rudimentary explanation of what they are doing beyond the myth itself.

Blake's enterprise began from a deep dissatisfaction with the scientific and moral presuppositions of an age which had a more rigid conception than ours of scientific method. The unsatisfactoriness of the contemporary account of man, he felt, had something to do with its genealogy: it was a logical extension to the moral universe set up by orthodox Judaeo-Christian theology, which presupposed a hidden Creator, not only absent from the world but dwelling apart in a blinding cloud of inconceivable and unapproachable holiness. Given this central Being who loved the world but showed his love mainly by giving laws and leaving man to obey them, it was only logical that further rational interpretation of nature should depict it as a vast machine devised in a similar way. The result was the Newtonian world-picture, in which the universe, set in motion by a Supreme Being who was both rational and ultimately benevolent, had been left to run its course according to fixed laws.

Blake's thinking began at every point from the experiment of assuming that the supreme reality in the universe was not, as the Jews, Christians and exponents of natural religion seemed to suppose, a distant, holy and affectionate God but man—man conceived in the fuller nature which was revealed to him by the workings of his energies and his imagination. Seen in this light the mechanisms of physical behaviour were only a partial clue to human nature. If they *were* the full reality man was ultimately left in the universe revealed in *King Lear*, where blind Nature governed all and discreet opportunism was a tempting moral imperative. Man was left to shore up his existence against the inevitable approach of death.

If man was not metaphorically but *literally* the greatest reality in the universe, on the other hand, the universe itself was turned inside out. It was no longer a universe of death and decay but of self-renewing life. If man was the central fact his life was also a central fact: decay and death, the apparent facts of the physical universe at large, became subordinate phenomena. The life and death of the individual, the life and death of the species, would both be seen as part of a larger survival. The fact of individual death would continue, no doubt, to be a matter of fear and struggle; it would no longer be associated with a cosmic despair.

Blake took as point of reference not human perception, which draws the logical consequences of its own observations and assumes the sovereignty of death, but human energy and human imagination, both of which assume their own immortality. In his universe, therefore, the artist is king. From the vantage-point of his creative experience he could mount an independent critique of human society; he could also assure himself that the truth of his creations was validated by the act of creation itself.

Such claims for the artist mark an ultimate form of romanticism, and Blake made them wholeheartedly. At one point in *Milton* the poet cries

> I am inspired! I know it is Truth! for I Sing
> According to the inspiration of the Poetic Genius
> Who is the eternal all-protecting Divine Humanity
> To whom be Glory & Power & Dominion Evermore   Amen

The assurance of this statement is, of course, open to logical objections—if not to clinical observations[1]—but there is little point in dwelling on them. Without this self-justifying faith in his own powers Blake would not have survived as an artist; when possessed by it he could proceed to create with the gnomic brilliance for which he is most praised, as in *The Marriage of Heaven and Hell*.

Blake's larger ambitions seem, in fact, to have sprung less from his moments of assurance than from his moments of doubt. In such moments it became important that he should justify the concept of 'Divine humanity' to men by producing a total, all-comprehending mythology. The common poetic dream of producing an epic often takes this form with the romantic writer. The solidity of the epic structure and the epistemological security of a comprehensive mythology are both needed to back the remainder of his achievement.

For such a task in Blake's time the Bible and *Paradise Lost* were natural starting-points. In them he saw the rudiments of an allegorical interpretation of human nature. He felt, however, that the 'visionary-humanist' mythology which he traced in the Bible had been obscured both by some of the biblical writers and by later interpreters. Milton, likewise, had not had the courage of his own allegorizing insights. Blake's work would take the allegorical method of certain episodes in *Paradise Lost* to its full conclusion and would offer a reinterpretation of the Bible and ancient myths, releasing the visionary-humanist mythology that the ancient prophets and poets had in his view tried to convey.

The rejection of traditional myths as they stood created problems of form, however, which became evident as soon as Blake began writing in this manner. His short works 'Tiriel' and *Thel*, written in pure mythical form, could not carry more than a limited weight of significance. A more extended form was required. Blake went on to experiment with the creation of a new 'Bible' which should consist, like the Old and New Testaments, of a series of loosely related 'books', each conveying some element in the total vision. *The Book of Urizen*, *The Book of Ahania*, the 'Song of Liberty' and *The Book of Los* were attempts to rewrite Genesis and Exodus according to this pattern, but (unless we think of more tangential works such as *The Song of Los* or *The Everlasting Gospel* as contributions to the canon) the effort ceased there.

As part of this 'biblical' mythologizing, however, Blake had produced his own creation story. The account in Genesis of an initial corruption which led to sin and then to the imposition of the moral law as a regulative force, and of an initial 'creation' of the universe from nothing had been replaced by an account in which the Law itself was responsible for man's corruption and the mathematical organization of the universe an act of limitation rather than creation. Both had caused man to fall away from his original state of humanized vision.

Blake now felt himself driven to tell this story in a different manner. With a side-glance at the method of *Paradise Lost* he addressed himself to the creation of an epic poem which should record this lapse of man from his original virtue and prophesy his eventual apocalyptic awakening. As in other allegories this would be seen both as an absolute process and as one which was repeated in many minor patterns of human activity.

The problems of construction—greater than Milton's, since nothing was 'given'—led Blake to adopt the looser form of Young's *Night Thoughts* and to try to organize his poem around an idea—the idea (represented by his figure Vala) that 'nature', seen by eighteenth-century man as the ultimate revelation of creative purpose in the universe, was no more than a partial source of truth. The true energies of the universe, though discernible in the workings of nature, were better revealed in the lineaments of humanity. The plot of the poem would show the disorder among these energies created by the adoption of a false idea of the universe, and their subsequent restoration. The energies would be the 'characters', the 'heroes' required in epic action.

My inverted commas are enough to indicate some of the problems of construction. Blake was in danger of moving away from artistic communication rather than towards it. The poem, begun as 'Vala', became 'The Four Zoas' and was finally left, only partially complete, in manuscript. Instead, *Jerusalem* was engraved, a looser construction which compromises between the 'biblical' and 'epic' methods by adopting a very general plot to give ultimate shape to the poem and presenting only a series of episodes. All of these relate to the general plot and the general shaping ideas, but a fully binding coherence is no longer sought. In the event *Jerusalem* is Blake's nearest approach to solving his problem: even if the poem lacks epic form it achieves epic quality. It also gives Blake the dominating tone for his last phase, in which he devotes himself to illustrations in a similar mode.

A fuller account of Blake's myth-making must follow this process in more detail. It must begin with the acknowledgment that there is no central and sustained point of reference; Blake's many areas of success do not include that sort of coherence. But it will draw attention to the full power of particular passages; it may also offer initiation into the more general vision which haunts Blake and provides the driving-power of all his work. The local successes and the general vision come closer together as a result of more detailed study.

The study of Blake's mythology has an interest of its own as drawing attention to one of the few organized contemporary critiques of the eighteenth-century world-picture. Blake's attack on the Newtonian universe, which he regarded as a machine running down to death and decay, and his substitution for it of a humanized world of life and love that is constantly misunderstood by its inhabitants, has its own value and deserves consideration from the historian of ideas. So far, however, we have spoken as if Blake were simply 'projecting' a new mythology which could be inspected apart from the Prophetic Books and for which his art was largely ornamental. His true purpose was both more revolutionary and more centrally relevant to art: it was to transform his reader's vision of the universe.

In this attempt he was following a modest eighteenth-century tradition to one of its possible conclusions. From the Augustan period onwards poets and artists, looking for relief from the restraints of a dominating rationalism, had found one escape in the concepts of the 'sublime' and of 'pathos'. It was a solution that had the advantage of belonging to the same classical tradition that the Augustans had invoked. Longinus could be appealed to as authority for the terms—even if he might have meant something different by them.

The major disadvantage was that no discipline of usage developed. The cult of the sublime could degenerate only too easily into a sub-Miltonic inflation of imagery, as if in order to create the sublime it were enough to talk about the vast. The cult of pathos, equally, passed all too quickly into an indulgent sentimentality, for which the leisured drawing-rooms were providing a ready audience.

It was difficult, in other words, to escape the disabling effects of eighteenth-century rationalism. In a Newtonian universe the sublime must automatically suggest quantitative distance; under a rationalist view of man, the cult of pathos would be a concession to human weakness, allowing for the activity of the human heart as a complement to, or rest from the more important operations of reason, but strictly subordinate to them.

Wordsworth and Coleridge both saw the problem and discovered partial solutions to it; only Blake was willing to take the radical step of inverting the normal universe and ordering it primarily by sublimity and pathos. The sky of the eighteenth-century astronomers was structured by the north and south poles, matching lights which reduced the universe to a geometrically organized whole. Such an order was inevitably dominated by Law and Death. Blake's universe, on the contrary, was not organized quantitatively at all, nor were its poles poles in space. The opposites of this universe were human extremes: the 'contracting' of a man in the moment of pathos on the one hand, his 'expansion' in the moment of sublimity on the other. Various emblems could express these extremes: the phallus, for example, which in its normal state of contraction is the weakest part of man, a thing of pathos; but which in the state of erection gives him a sense of his own sublimity. The human heart, equally, seen by many as the clock inside the machine, remorselessly ticking away until it eventually runs down, was seen by Blake as an organ that by its perpetual systole and diastole, images and expresses in every moment the human extremes of contraction and expansion.

These 'contraries' are present throughout Blake's work: the *Songs of Innocence*, for example, present emblems of pathos, while the *Songs of Experience* presuppose a sublime (Earth's 'Lord') which human beings fail to accept. The sublimity of the rose is cankered by the destructiveness of a worm that knows nothing of phallic sublimity; the sublimity of the tiger has turned into an energy that, cut off from any fuller human context, rages and destroys in its own isolation.

Blake comes still closer to the heart of his vision in *Milton*, where his hero's genius is consummated in the acceptance of these contraries. Pathos and sublimity are here imaged in the wild thyme and the lark. The thyme concentrates human vision towards the minute particularity of its beauty; simultaneously, its scent contracts the physical senses into a total, unanalysable response. The knowledge that the flower is no static object, that it contains seed within seed within seed for ever, increases one's sense of infinity.

Similarly with the lark. The straining of the eye to follow it into the heavens is matched by an unorganized expansion of the physical senses produced by its song. This again is no quantitative response: to measure the *distance* of the bird's flight would be absurd. The 'infinite' dimension here is measured by the impulse in the bird, not by its capability of ascending to this or that particular height in the sky.

In *Milton* these contraries are also expressed in another way. For the eighteenth-century picture of a clocklike human heart that is matched by the diurnal round of the heavens, Blake substitutes the single globe of blood in the human being which answers to the pulsating energy of the sun itself.

For Blake, man and the universe are not the predictable organizations that are depicted in charts of human anatomy or maps of the sky; they are new and changing in every moment. In the same way his conception of infinity has nothing to do with measurable or immeasurable distance. At any instant ('between two moments') human vision may concentrate on a particular object (a grain of sand or a wild flower) and find in it a total emblem of the infinite; at any moment the operation of his own energy may deliver a human being into a state which is expansive and timeless. This is what Blake means, respectively, by pathos and the sublime, and these are the contraries which structure his visionary universe.

Commentary on the *Prophetic Books*, then, must aim at serving the extremes of Blake's achievement: it must provide an illuminating context for the narrative and it must remove some of the obstacles which stand in the way of the communication of Blake's inward vision. Mythological names like Urizen, Oothoon, Golgonooza have at first sight an uncompromising, even barbaric quality which alienates some readers. But strangeness gives way to familiarity as the names become related to intelligible ideas and as the reader finds himself being initiated into Blake's visionary universe. This unusual universe is peopled by beings who are radiant quintessences of the dancing energies of mankind; it is dominated by an interpretation of nature which sees all other energies and forms as pale by comparison with the imagination and energy of human beings; it is coloured and illuminated by the affirmation that here, rather than in abstract ideals of purity and reason set up by dogmatic theologians and scientists, lies the true source of 'holiness'. Wherever energy expresses itself in living form, there, according to Blake, exists 'genius'; the only acceptable form of religion or worship lies in the open response of a human being to the genius in other men, or beings.

If anyone had attacked his mythology in his presence Blake would no doubt have retorted by enquiring whether his opponent's own 'mythology' was better founded or provided a saner code for men to live by. He might also have pointed out that if his idiosyncratic humanism was more optimistic than eighteenth-century rational benevolence it also made more stringent demands on mankind.

The loose, running form of his poetry, moreover—equally open to criticism by eighteenth-century standards—was a not improper mode for what he had to say. If the form of the sun, or of the human being, was no more than a necessary limitation imposed on a visionary energy which would otherwise be infinite and destructive, it followed that an over-preoccupation with form and rules must be death to poetry and art. True poetry would shine by its own inward light and sing by its own music; its forms would express a self-creating energy unknown to the practitioners of Gothic melodrama and invite a sympathy which surpassed the rational pity of contemporary magazine verses. Blake takes up the available forms but handles them cavalierly.

This is not to say that there are no lapses in diction, or to deny the existence of obscurities in the mythology. It would be hard for anyone to claim unqualified success for Blake's art.

Whatever the obscurities or local failures, however, growing acquaintance makes the total pattern more attractive and illuminating. Blake's myths fall into their proper perspective when they are seen as varying attempts to initiate his readers into a universe where energy responds to energy in endless delight, and where a human being's contractions to pathos and expansions to sublimity interpenetrate the world measured out by his organizing perception, preserving him from falling into cosmic despair and sustaining him in the expression of the energy, the compassion and the imagination which are potentially his noblest resources.

Whether on Ida's shady brow,
  Or in the chambers of the East,
The chambers of the sun, that now
  From antient melody have ceas'd;

Whether in Heav'n ye wander fair,
  Or the green corners of the earth,
Or the blue regions of the air,
  Where the melodious winds have birth;

Whether on chrystal rocks ye rove,
  Beneath the bosom of the sea
Wand'ring in many a coral grove,
  Fair Nine, forsaking Poetry!

How have you left the antient love
  That bards of old enjoy'd in you!
The languid strings do scarcely move!
  The sound is forc'd, the notes are few![1]

So Blake, in a book of verses composed before he was twenty-one, contributed to the eighteenth-century fashion of bewailing in verse the impossibility of writing poetry any more.

Further study of *Poetical Sketches* tells us a good deal about Blake's mind as a young man. It reveals the extent to which he followed contemporary interests, steeping himself in previous 'romantic' literature and art wherever he could find it, and indulging a taste for Gothic sublimity. An examination of his vocabulary suggests borrowings from Spenser, Shakespeare, Jonson, Fletcher, Milton and the Caroline poets.[2] He experiments with a poem of Nordic tyranny, a horrific ballad, and a historical drama entitled *King Edward the Third*. And in the later play, which betrays a desire to imitate the Shakespeare of *Henry V*, there is little or no trace of Blake's later detestation of war. Instead, patriotism is combined with a passion for freedom. Britons are seen as the descendants of Brutus and the Trojans, the future Albion as a bastion of liberty. If war is necessary to defend that liberty, then war must be waged.

The future Blake is only partly discernible in such sentiments: he emerges more clearly in one of the best-known songs:

How sweet I roam'd from field to field,
    And tasted all the summer's pride,
'Till I the prince of love beheld,
    Who in the sunny beams did glide!

He shew'd me lilies for my hair,
    And blushing roses for my brow;
He led me through his gardens fair,
    Where all his golden pleasures grow.

With sweet May dews my wings were wet,
    And Phoebus fir'd my vocal rage;
He caught me in his silken net,
    And shut me in his golden cage.

He loves to sit and hear me sing,
    Then, laughing, sports and plays with me;
Then stretches out my golden wing,
    And mocks my loss of liberty.[3]

In most poems of this early collection the sense is fairly obvious—though an unusual twist in the imagery might sometimes suggest to an attentive reader that the mind behind the poem is not purely conventional. Here the unconventional element is sharper. Even the line, 'And Phoebus fir'd my vocal rage', despite all its antecedents in eighteenth-century poetic diction, conveys a vivid sense. That the imagery as a whole is subtly worked out becomes apparent when one asks who or what is speaking. The theory that it is animal or man is thwarted by the adorned hair and brow of the second stanza; and the resulting image of a maiden is checked by the 'wings' of the third. But a bird will not fit the poem as a whole: one can only conclude that some fairy-like creature is being described.

There is a further difficulty: it is the 'Prince of Love' who imprisons her in a cage. One suspects a bitter irony; yet the action is not easy to reconcile with Blake's devotion to both love and liberty.

In this case, acquaintance with Blake's later work helps to plot a way through difficulties of imagery. In his small collection of engravings entitled *The Gates of Paradise*, there is one which shows a lusty boy chasing flying creatures which he is trying to catch with his cap. The caption reads, 'What are these? Alas! the Female Martyr, Is she also the Divine Image?'. The possessiveness of small boys in trying to catch and destroy butterflies and insects is thus related to the destructive possessiveness of grown men in their sexual relations. In the illustrations of Young's *Night Thoughts* there is a similar drawing, in which a murderer, standing by a female body, sees winged 'joys' flying away.[4] The point is made most explicitly, however, in the well-known couplet,

> He who binds to himself a joy
> Doth the winged life destroy. . . .[5]

If the same idea is being expressed in the poem before us, the effect is muted. The tone is sweet, the pleasures of love are acknowledged; only the reference to the loss of liberty at the end establishes a bitter undertone. At the same time, the very diffuseness of the central image helps to generalize the bitter tone, once expressed. The destruction of joy by possessiveness is made to refer both to the imprisoning of living creatures and, by the feminine beauty of the creature, to sexual greed. The captured bird or the female martyr might see in the enslaver's energy the lineaments of the Prince of Love, which he shares with all human beings; yet the melancholy fact is that, as with most human beings, his 'love' has been twisted out of its proper shape by his possessiveness.

The hint of the later Blake is here no more than a light presence in a pleasing, bitter-sweet poem; the same is true of other poems in the collection. Nevertheless, it is surprising how often an image in them proves, on examination, to carry unexpected power. 'Spring', for example, uses the myth of the Earth as bride, awaiting the sun-god's kiss, in a manner which is, for the eighteenth century, unusually forceful:

> O thou, with dewy locks, who lookest down . . .
> . . . scatter thy pearls
> Upon our love-sick land that mourns for thee.

> O deck her forth with thy fair fingers; pour
> Thy soft kisses on her bosom; and put
> Thy golden crown upon her languish'd head,
> Whose modest tresses were bound up for thee![6]

The image of Blake's Luvah is present in the figure of 'dewy
locks' here, just as his Orc is latent in the 'ruddy limbs and
flourishing hair' of 'Summer' in the next poem and his Urizen,
perhaps, in the 'Winter' that has built his permanent habitation in the North. Later, when he has broken the traditional
symbolic moulds, he is able to use them in more idiosyncratic
paradigms.

The most powerful effect of the poems as a whole, however,
is to remind us that the Gothic of the time had more than one
face. There is typical Gothic melodrama in *Poetical Sketches*,
but far more often the 'Gothic' is really the visionary. The
dominant image in these poems is of the visionary capabilities
of the human being. Images of flesh as 'breathing' or of
'breathing clay' abound, while the militarism of Edward III
is dominated by the idea of glory, mediated by images of
soldiers as shooting stars, or eagles soaring to the sun. The
enemy fight in chains ('Their minds are fetter'd'), but the
soldiers who fight for liberty are made splendid by the sense
of their cause.

Like Coleridge and Keats in youth, Blake was haunted
above all by the sense of Apollo, sun-god and king of poets,
whose inspiration is sun-like in its descent:

> Golden Apollo, that thro' heaven wide
>   Scatter'st the rays of light, and truth's beams!
> In lucent words my darkling verses dight,
>   And wash my earthy mind in thy clear streams,
>   That wisdom may descend in fairy dreams . . .[7]

Blake later modified his view of Apollo, but he did not change
his idea of inspiration: the proper commentary to poems like
these may be found in designs such as those which he executed
much later for Milton's early poems.[8] And although his
mythological figures later achieved a life of their own in his
imagination, independent of their traditional sources, they
always carried the direct and imaginative vividness of these
early poems.

At this stage, however, the symbolic figures still retain much of their conventional significance, the resulting structural rigidity being eased by the illuminative suggestion of the imagery. So far as one can penetrate to the mind behind the poetry one senses a rather dreamy, even dilettante young man with an abnormally strong imagination. When his imagination is fully active it is like a flood of golden light which cannot quite pierce the clouded diction of his verse; when it deserts him he is left impotently raging with an energy that can find no form—'like a fiend in a cloud'.[9]

The elusive visionary dimension (which is liable to disappear as soon as the trained critic grapples with the *verbal* structure) may have been expressed partly by Blake's music. Many of his early poems were, literally, songs: they were written to be sung to the harp, the music now being lost.[10] Music, like the later illuminations to his printed text, could add a generality and depth to indicate the visionary dimension. The importance of such effects seems, in fact, to have deflected Blake from the craftsmanlike concerns of the normal poet. He did not seek mastery of language strictly *as* language; the wonderful verbal effects which are present throughout his work are due rather to his grasp, conscious or intuitive, of the imaginative connotations of words.

The few facts which are known of his youth tell a similar story. The visionary experiences which were a characteristic of his later years were then, if anything, more vivid. At the age of four he was set screaming one day when God 'put his head to the window'. A few years later he saw a tree on Peckham Rye studded with angels—and narrowly escaped a beating from his father on relating the occurrence. When, as an engraver's apprentice, he worked for long hours alone in Westminster Abbey, he one day 'saw Christ and his Apostles among the tombs, and he both saw a great procession of monks and priests, choristers and censer-bearers, and heard their chant'.[11]

These recurrent visionary experiences cannot be ignored in any account of his work. For where one might think of other artists as inspired, one is forced to acknowledge here a 'visitation' which is immediate and direct. What, to his audience, may seem merely an interesting element in a rich personality had for the artist himself the commanding status of full reality. Correspondingly, the attitude of his father after the Peckham Rye vision would come to symbolize for him the common attitude of mankind: blind themselves, they seek to destroy vision in others, particularly the young.

Were this the only fact concerning Blake's inspiration, of course, comment would be restricted. If all his visions had been unpremeditated and unexpected, appreciation of them would necessarily be a hit-or-miss affair, depending partly on similar experiences in the reader. But two further factors must be borne in mind. Many of the visions were preceded, and partly organized, by intense thought. If the visionary experience superseded the previous thinking (as, for example, one suspects that Blake's vision of 'The Ancient of Days' helped to *define* Urizen for him) the earlier process was none the less indispensable. And the vividness of such experiences also helped him to reinterpret many narratives and myths of world literature. In each case he could stress the visionary element and argue that all alike were telling a common story of the decline of Man from original Vision. This enabled him to draw (if somewhat obliquely) on the general imaginative resources of world literature.

Such thinking occupied him from his earliest years. Striking evidence is afforded by a vignette which he executed as part of the illustrations to Bryant's *Analysis of Ancient Mythology*—a work published in 1774–6 when he was still apprenticed to Basire. The engraving (fig. 47), shows the moon as an ark of light, enclosed by an overarching rainbow as it rests upon the surface of the sea.[12]

This design is not a direct interpretation of anything to be found in Bryant's book. It seems rather to be a succinct summary of what Blake took to be important in Bryant's researches. Bryant's main concern was to show the vast extent to which sun-worship and related cults had prevailed in the ancient world. These cults Blake would interpret as representing a world-wide consciousness of lost Vision. And for him three important symbols of that consciousness would be the moon, which reflects the light of a hidden sun, the ark of Noah, which carried mankind over the turbulent waters of the Flood, and the rainbow, which appeared above those same waters as a promise of hope to mankind. His engraving, neatly combining the three, suggests that Vision, the reflection of the forms of Eternity, rests, ark-like, secure above the ever-changing sea of Time and Space, and that the beauty of the rainbow is the guarantee of its ultimate establishment.

These images recur time and time again in Blake's work, always with the same significance. In the same way, he was fascinated by apparent references to Vision among the antiquities of his own country. His enthusiasm for past visionaries of all sorts marched with his enjoyment of Gothic art. The taste for this style was a feature of the age; he also experienced unusually close and prolonged contact with it during the period spent drawing in Westminster Abbey. Gradually, he came to believe that the old Gothic designers had not only been the primitive representatives of true art in British history, but could still stand in judgment upon the forms which were fashionable in his own day.

This belief helps to explain another striking engraving of his youth. In 1773 he copied a figure from Michelangelo's 'Crucifixion of St Peter' (fig. 56) and set it in a landscape of rocks, with the sea in the background. At the head of the engraving (fig. 58) he added, many years later, an inscription,

JOSEPH of Arimathea among The Rocks of Albion

and at the bottom,

Engraved by W. Blake 1773 from an old Italian Drawing.

This is One of the Gothic Artists who Built the Cathedrals in what we call the Dark Ages Wandering about in sheep skins and goat skins, of whom the World was not worthy such were the Christians in all Ages.

Michael Angelo Pinxit[13]

The immediate reference is, of course, to the story that Joseph of Arimathea eventually came to England and was buried at Glastonbury: the description of him as a 'Gothic Artist' is evidently associated with the tradition that he set up there the first Christian church in England. But a further, more important tradition connected with his name was also at work in Blake's mind. Joseph of Arimathea was the man who had provided a sepulchre for the body of Jesus. This would make him, like Noah building his ark in the Old Testament, the guardian of Vision (for in Blake's theology, it is the Vision of man which is constantly submerged or murdered and rises again). Thus the two traditions of Joseph of Arimathea worked together in Blake's mind to forge more closely the link between art and true Vision.

But why 'Gothic' art? For an answer to this question, we need to look at Blake's interest in the 'British Antiquities', and more particularly in Druidism. Sammes's *Britannia Antiqua Illustrata* contained an engraving of a Druid carrying a book, his eyes closed (fig. 57). Stukeley's *Stonehenge*, another well-known volume, opens with a similar but more ornate engraving of a Druid, this time without a book but still with closed eyes. A comparison of either of these with Michelangelo's figure suggests that the strong visual resemblance prompted Blake to see in the centurion standing by the crucifixion of St Peter with eyes closed, a failure of human vision like that of the Druids, and to produce a contrasting figure in the open-eyed visionary of his own design who, like Joseph of Arimathea or the medieval cathedral architects, stands firm by his own vision.

There is strong evidence that Blake saw Stukeley's companion work, *Abury*, in 1773, since his master Basire copied part of one of the plates for an illustration to Bryant's *Analysis*, the first volume of which was published in the following year. Nor is his interest surprising. The accounts of Avebury and Stonehenge, published in the middle of the eighteenth century,[14] had sparked off a current of interest in these ruins which persisted in Blake's time. Stukeley's researches had given rise to the suggestion that the English Druid temples were older than the pyramids in Egypt and might therefore represent the earliest civilization in the world. Could Britain have been the original cradle of civilization, and the Druids priest of a purer religious tradition, dating from a time when mankind lived innocently and at peace in the garden of Nature? To an age which was in any case preoccupied with the relationship between nature and religion, the speculation was more than ordinarily fascinating. Wordsworth, for example, was greatly impressed by such ideas. While walking across Salisbury Plain as a young man he had a visionary experience, which he used in his poem 'Guilt and Sorrow' and later recalled in *The Prelude*:

> a waking dream, a reverie
> That, with believing eyes, where'er I turned,
> Beheld long-bearded teachers, with white wands
> Uplifted, pointing to the starry sky,
> Alternately, and plain below, while breath
> Of music swayed their motions, and the waste
> Rejoiced with them and me in those sweet sounds,[15]

Blake, as we know, was taken by the idea that England might be the site of original paradise and used it in his later poetry. But he was also suspicious of claims that the Druidic traditions represented a purer and more innocent form of worship. John Toland, after all, had given quite a different picture in his *History of the Druids*, claiming that they 'drew the decisions of all Law and Equity to themselves' that they had 'terrible powers of Excommunication' and that they had the 'power of engaging the nation in war . . . while . . . exempted from bearing arms or paying taxes.' 'The History of the Druids', he wrote, 'is the complete History of Priestcraft'—a priestcraft which he defined as the art of 'leading the people by the nose'.[16] Another tenacious tradition said that the Druids had actually practised human sacrifice. Blake evidently drew the natural conclusion that they ought to be seen not as the guardians, but the enemies of Vision; the purer tradition needed to be sought out more diligently.

The stone temple of Stonehenge presented him with a neat emblem of the nature of the Druids as he saw them. Already enamoured of the Gothic, he saw in the Gothic arch, where twin pillars soar to a consummation beyond the height of man, a symbol of true vision. (D. H. Lawrence, in a different manner, was to use the Gothic as a symbol for the vision of one of his characters).[17] And since the eighteenth century found a ready connection between the Gothic arches of the cathedrals and the forests of nature, it is possible that his enthusiasm for the Gothic is also reflected in an early image of the intermingling of trees as a symbol of human love:

Love and harmony combine,
And around our souls intwine,
While thy branches mix with mine,
And our roots together join.[18]

In his later work the Gothic arch appears predominantly as a symbol of vision (see figs. 63–4). Against this, the trilithon of Stonehenge (figs. 61–2) would be the complete antithesis of Vision: whereas the lines of the Gothic arch soar and ultimately blend, the upright pillars of the trilithon remain apart, over-weighted by the third stone. Just so human beings are pre-vented from realizing their true stature by the heavy weight of Law, their vision choked by the pressure of an exclusively analytic Reason.

That Blake's mind worked in this way is evident from a later illustration, the frontispiece to *Jerusalem*, which shows a figure, probably his Los, entering a Gothic doorway (fig. 63). An inscription, later erased from the plate, includes the following:

His Sublime and Pathos become Two Rocks fixd in the Earth
His reason, his Spectrous Power, covers them above[19]

The use of the terms 'Sublime' and 'Pathos', which often bear respectively a male and female connotation in Blake's writings, also supports the view that his idea of Vision is not far re-moved from his idea of human love.

The mention, in the lyric just quoted, of two trees inter-twining their roots suggests a further point. So far we have spoken in terms of Vision and soaring arches, but Blake's ideal man is rooted also in desire. Man in his original state is a visionary being, but he is also of the earth, earthy: the name Adam relates him to the clay of which he is made. Even if he is restored to vision, man must still remember the pit from which he is digged. On the other hand, the pit can also become a trap: he may simply enroot himself further and further in the earth until he is swallowed up completely. And this is likely to happen if he fails to connect his imagination with the earth.

Sexual desire is the activity which can link the two: it is also the one in which man is most exposed to the danger of separat-ing them. Desire, pursued for its own sake, can chain man to the earth; one model for the physical element in sexual relations should be the earth-worm, which acts out its part without fuss or shame, taking its natural place in the order of things.

The true man exists in a constant dialectic between vision and desire, the one nourishing the other. But in his fallen state the two elements fall apart and eventually work against each other as a conflict between Reason and Energy. The light of vision pales to the wan light of analytic reason, the creative work of desire turns into the fiery serpent of destructive energy.

This line of speculation brings us back to Stukeley's theories about Druid remains. The shape of their stone temples, also, suggested an esoteric explanation to him. On examining the stone temple at Avebury, he came to the conclusion that it had originally been more complicated in shape. He thought that he could see traces of two wavy avenues leading away from the main circle (see fig. 59) and argued from this that it had originally followed a design which could also be found in recently discovered Egyptian temple pictures. The design, known as the Uraeon, showed the sun with a pair of wings on either side and serpents emerging below. These serpents, Stukeley decided, corresponded to the wavy avenues: and if no wing-like features could be traced this must be because they had been lost in the processes of time. These stone temples, he thought, were earlier than the Egyptian, and their shape, preserved in the later hierograms, could be regarded as a Druidic prophecy of Christian Trinitarian doctrine. The three elements in the design could be said to represent the Father (as sun or creative Being), the Son (the serpent, or creative energy issuing from the central being) and the Holy Spirit (the wings, or spirit of love relating the created universe back to the creator): together they constituted an esoteric interpretation of the Trinity.[20]

Blake apparently accepted Stukeley's reasoning up to a point, but drew a different conclusion. Having helped to illustrate Bryant's *Analysis* as a young man, he would himself have come across the relevant Egyptian designs (fig. 22).[21] Traditional Christian doctrines were not acceptable to him in their orthodox form, but Stukeley's further theories would be relevant to his growing theories concerning Vision. If the serpent represents energy, the sun reason, the addition of wings would develop the whole design into an image of full, creative visionary man. Without wings, on the other hand, the sun would be merely the spectrous sun of analytic reason, strangling itself with its own energies.

The next step follows naturally. Confronted by Stukeley's findings, Blake drew his own conclusions. Stukeley, he argued, did not discover wings in the temple at Avebury for a very simple reason. They had never existed there. Only the bards and Gothic artists preserved *that* part of the ancient tradition. The Druids, having lost the Divine Vision, worshipped the spectrous Law which resulted in analytic reasoning and cruelty. They had faithfully represented their religion in their temples, where the circle and wavy lines represented reason shut up and constricted by the turning in of energies. The trilitha simply emphasized the loss of soaring vision.

> Then was the serpent temple form'd, image of infinite
> Shut up in finite revolutions . . .[22]

And when, many years later, he concluded *Jerusalem* with an illustration of Los, guardian of Vision, standing before the visionless world of the eighteenth-century, he depicted the latter in the form of a serpent temple from which the wings were absent, and in which the trilitha stretched not only round the central circle but along the serpentine avenues as well (fig. 60).[23]

In the meantime the Druids recurred many times in his poetry, symbolizing the cruelty of the idolaters of Law whom he saw about him on every side. The constituent elements of the symbolism were also to be used again. Rock always symbolized the hardness and opacity which he regarded as the antithesis of true vision, while the simple geometric shapes of circle and trilithon aptly symbolized that reduction to simple order and mathematical design which resulted from the exact thinking of the rationalists. One of the most powerful expressions of the last image can be found in *Milton,*[24] where a giant trilithon dwarfs a human figure on horseback (fig. 62): another appears in *Jerusalem* where, within the rectangle of sky cut out of its enclosing shape, is a waning moon (fig. 61).

The serpent, also, appears again and again as a symbol of energy unrestrained by Vision. Here Blake is concerned with a contemporary theme of considerable importance. The whole

concept of energy had recently become important as a result of
scientific work, particularly on electricity. Blake's interest in
the subject is not confined to his writings. One way in which
his art is markedly different from current forms is in his exploration of modes of representing energy—as compared with the
static, sensitive landscapes and portraits of his contemporaries.
It is no accident that in Sir Kenneth Clark's book *The Nude*, the
section devoted to Blake is entitled 'Energy'.

This preoccupation with the place of energy in human life
emerges particularly in *The Marriage of Heaven and Hell*, where
'The Voice of the Devil' is heard, speaking of the very conflict
which we were discussing earlier:

> All Bibles or sacred codes have been the causes of the following
> Errors.
>
> 1. That Man has two real existing principles Viz: a Body & a
> Soul.
> 2. That Energy. call'd Evil. is alone from the Body. & that
> Reason. calld Good. is alone from the Soul.
> 3. That God will torment Man in Eternity for following his
> Energies.
>
> But the following Contraries to these are true
>
> 1. Man has no Body distinct from his Soul for that calld Body
> is a portion of Soul discernd by the five Senses, the chief inlets
> of Soul in this age
> 2. Energy is the only life and is from the Body and Reason is
> the bound or outward circumference of Energy.
> 3. Energy is Eternal Delight[25]

The statement is central to Blake's thinking. It would be a
mistake, as we shall see, to regard the second set of propositions
as representing the fullness of his own position: but it would be
equally wrong to ignore them. 'Without Contraries is no progression', he had just remarked, and the second set marks a progression from the opposition of Reason and Energy which has
just been set up. He will eventually require a 'marriage' between those contraries, with a place for both; at present he is
content to comment that if it comes to a choice between the
voice of 'Reason' and that of 'the Devil', the Devil's position is
distinctly preferable.

At the same time, Blake's interest in serpent-worship led him to a further subtlety in presenting the symbolism of energy. In Bryant's *Analysis of Ancient Mythology* there were, along with representations of the Uraeon, plates devoted to the Ophites, or serpent-worshippers, and their emblems (see figs. 24–5).[26] These emblems included both the serpents and their eggs. Blake would find here a natural piece of symbolism for his speculations about human beings and their use of energy. The egg would represent the early state of reason, a hardened vision in which energy is easily controlled because it has never known freedom. But this state of reason leads eventually to doubt and despair: the Philosophical and Experimental, left to itself, is soon 'at the ratio of all things' and stands still, 'unable to do other than repeat the same dull round over again'.[27] At this point, therefore, either it deadens, or else the energies which have hitherto been contained by it break out, like the serpent emerging from its shell, and play in unrestrained riot. Finally, the serpent can attack not only by biting but by using its whole physical force to coil round and crush an opponent. With these three images Blake was thus able to represent three separate moments of 'mental' experience: the period of simple reasoning; the breaking of the shell and subsequent exploitation of energy; and the final stage, where visionless man uses his energy to poison others and crush the vision within them.

A reading of Milton

The only detailed account of his early reading which Blake ever gave occurs in a letter of 1800 to John Flaxman:

> Now my lot in the Heavens is this, Milton lov'd me in childhood & shew'd me his face.
> Ezra came with Isaiah the Prophet, but Shakespeare in riper years gave me his hand;
> Paracelsus & Behmen appear'd to me, terrors appear'd in the Heavens above
> And in Hell beneath, & a mighty & awful change threatened the Earth.
> The American War began. All its dark horrors passed before my face
> Across the Atlantic to France. Then the French Revolution commenc'd in thick clouds . . .[28]

The American War broke out in 1776, so that if this is a chronological account we must suppose that Blake read all the authors he mentioned before he was eighteen. It is not altogether clear that it *is* a chronological account (the reference to Shakespeare, in particular, might be a parenthesis referring to a later reading) but it at least indicates, unmistakably, some influences. It also tells us something of the quality of his early major response to Milton and the Bible: the coupling of Isaiah and Ezra suggests an early vision of the building of Jerusalem and of the establishment of peace among all nations, the lion lying down with the lamb. The affectionate terms of his reference to Milton suggest that he was first attracted to the early poems: paradoxically, we are closest to his earliest feeling for Milton when we look at his late illustrations to 'L'Allegro' and 'Il Penseroso'. By the time that he wrote *The Marriage of Heaven and Hell*, however (and possibly much earlier), he had come to adopt his own reading of Milton, which heard in the Voice of the Devil the authentic voice of creative energy.

In my earlier study,[29] I suggested that his preoccupation with the nature of energy led him to read *Paradise Lost* as allegory and to reinterpret the elements of it according to the structuring of his own vision. His belief that the world of energy was of a higher order than that of reason, for example, led him to believe that when Satan fell, the harmonizing unity of Heaven was destroyed and that therefore everyone fell, including God the Father. The only difference was that God the Father fell further, into a sphere where he spoke by reason alone. Satan's world of unrestrained energy might not be the best, but it was at least better than that.

As a result of this reading, Blake seems to have reordered the elements of the universe described in *Paradise Lost* into four states, each being superior to the previous ones:

(1) The so-called 'Hell' of Book One—really the 'Heaven' of Milton's God: with its dens, bogs and darkness it is a fit sphere for the operation of reason in isolation.

(2) The Hell created by Satan's exercise of energy (as when he uses his energy to burst out of the first 'Hell'). This state is shown in his building of Pandaemonium, his pugnacity against Heaven, his heroic journey through space.

(3) Paradise: the state inhabited by Adam and Eve before their fall—the state of innocent sexual love and childhood happiness.

(4) The true Heaven, where reason and energy, no longer at war but raised into a fruitful dialectic, exist as Vision and Desire in the state of 'Genius', and the state temporarily glimpsed in the joys of paradise is made eternal.

To understand why he chose to order Milton's universe in this way, however, we need to look also at his reading of some other authors.

The Tree of the Soul

There can be no doubt of the paramount influence on Blake of Jacob Boehme. Boehme had also been read by Milton; in Boehme's writings Blake could discover doctrines which made sense of the revolt of Satan, conceived allegorically, as an event which is eternally happening in the creation, perverting it from its true ends.

William Law's edition of Boehme's writings, published in the eighteenth century, includes several designs, adapted from those in the German edition, which represent schematically some of Boehme's most important ideas. One of them shows how the eternal soul, translated from its original state, splits into three separate elements: light, fire and darkness.[30] These states, it will be seen, correspond to the Paradise, Hell and ironic 'Heaven of Reason' in Blake's reading of Milton.

In another design (fig. 1)[31] this pattern is worked out more fully. This design, which is entitled 'The Tree of the Soul', shows four states, partly co-ordinated by the structure of a tree which passes through the first three of them. The tree has its roots in a representation of our solar system which is entitled 'Dark World'. Its trunk passes through the flames of a state which is entitled 'Hell', while its branches spread out in a still higher state which is entitled 'Paradise'. Over and above the tree as a whole there appears a fourth circle entitled 'Light of Majesty', which contains symbols representing the Deity.

It is evident that this design expresses more fully the idea shown in the first. If the unfallen soul enjoys the Light of Majesty, the fallen soul exists in descending states, of light, of heat and of darkness (Paradise, Hell and Dark World), each diminished by its separation from the others.

The idea that there exist various states of the soul is of course common in Christian theology, but Boehme differs from the usual tradition at two points. Firstly, he places the 'physical' universe not, as in medieval theology, between Heaven and Hell, but beneath both of them. Secondly, he makes a separation between Heaven and Paradise which suggests that Paradise is itself an inferior state, not to be equated with Heaven. The latter idea falls in with Milton's cosmology, but not with those orthodox conceptions that virtually identify the two states.

Blake takes over these features but differs from Boehme in one important respect; his interest is more in psychological explanation than in pietistic exhortation. The 'dark world' of Boehme is not far removed from the 'vanities of this world' which are rejected by the Christian of conventional piety. Blake, on the other hand, would identify it immediately as the world of 'Reason'—that scientific interpretation of the world set forth by the followers of Locke and Newton which he felt to be the lowest world of all. Again, where Boehme would think of the next stage on the scale as representing the punishing wrath of God, Blake would give it wider significance, regarding it as the sphere where energies operate uncontrolled. The next stage, which Boehme calls 'Paradise', Blake would associate more specifically with the tenderness of married love, while both would agree in seeing the highest state as that of unfallen man, his energies exercised to their fullest extent under the supreme light of Blake's Vision or Boehme's God.

We shall refer back to this scheme of Blake's thought several times in examining his later writings, and it will therefore be useful to comment briefly on some of the ways in which it survived as an important paradigm in his thought.

It should be pointed out that although this scheme is ultimately related to the system of energies (the 'Four Zoas') which Blake later uses, the relationship touches only at certain points. The Zoas are forces; here we are dealing with something more like states, or conditions. In the later thinking, indeed, they are specifically called 'states' and given particular names. Although it may be unwise to read the full development back into works of the 1790s it is clear from *The Marriage of Heaven and Hell* that the general pattern was already at work in his mind as a loose hierarchy of psychical conditions, consisting (in ascending order) of reason, energy, love and genius, each state containing the preceding ones. In the developed thinking these states are further defined as follows:

(1) The state of 'darkness', the 'Dark World', becomes the state of Ulro, which Blake uses to describe the state in which Reason alone holds sway. It is thus also the 'Heaven' of *The Marriage of Heaven and Hell*.

(2) The state of 'Fire' or 'Wrath' is used for the state in which energy is freely exercised. A creative artist, or a lover, purely by exercising his energies, enters this state, which is sometimes called Generation, and is the 'Hell' of *The Marriage of Heaven and Hell*.

(3) The state of 'Light' or 'Paradise' is reserved more particularly for the state of sexual pleasure. Blake often refers to it by the name of 'Beulah', and in so doing displays one of his more clever pieces of symbolic alignment. In Isaiah, Beulah is the name of a country, and is translated by the word 'married'. Thus a symbol lies already to hand for the extending of wedded love into a 'country', a state of the soul, where the energies of Ulro and Hell, now married, produce harmony and pleasure. Another literary reference to Beulah can, however, be found in Bunyan's *Pilgrim's Progress*. There Beulah is a country 'whose Air was very sweet and pleasant':

> In this Countrey the Sun shineth night and day; wherefore this was beyond the Valley of the *shadow of death*, and also out of the reach of Giant *Despair*; neither could they from this place so much as see *Doubting-Castle*. Here they were within sight of the City they were going to: also here met them some of the Inhabitants thereof. For in this Land the shining Ones commonly walked, because it was upon the Borders of Heaven.[32]

This description adds a new dimension to Blake's use of the symbol, linking his concepts of 'light' and 'marriage'. In sexual love there can be a brief revelation of that eternal light which belongs to the state of full vision. It is no more than a temporary revelation, however, and must be accepted as such, with no attempt to possess it permanently. Anyone who tries to remain there merely falls into a permanent sleep, the sleep of 'vegetation'. Nevertheless, the state is of great importance to Blake, being one of the rare moments in which the full vision is glimpsed. As he put it in *Milton*,

> For Golgonooza cannot be seen till having passd the Polypus
> It is viewed on all sides round by a Four-fold Vision
> Or till you become Mortal & Vegetable in Sexuality
> Then you behold its mighty Spires & Domes of ivory & gold[33]

The state of Beulah is also associated with 'marriage' in a less direct sense. The Second Book of *Milton* begins,

> There is a place where Contrarieties are equally True
> This place is called Beulah . . .[34]

In the wars of the world, contraries strive against each other destructively. In this dreamlike state, on the other hand, they are reconciled. It corresponds to the state in *The Marriage of Heaven and Hell* which comes into being when the 'Angel' leaves Blake:

> . . . . I found myself sitting on a pleasant bank beside a river by moon light hearing a harper who sung to the harp, & his theme was, The man who never alters his opinion is like standing water, & breeds reptiles of the mind.[35]

(4) The final state, which reconciles all the others, and allows each to exist in its fullness, is the state of the Eternal Man. We have fallen from this, but it is recaptured in moments of supreme vision—by the Genius, for example, in his moments of inspiration. It can be completely recovered only after death.

A good deal of Blake's thinking becomes clearer when one sees how it exists between these various categories. Much which might appear merely enthusiastic and unorganised turns out to be sophisticated use of a patterned interpretation of human experience. A further run of symbolism (which falls in naturally with the scheme here outlined) concerns the heavenly elements. Interest in Egyptian mythology, coupled with knowledge of Swedenborg's presupposition that the true sun is in this world divided into heat and light, would lead Blake naturally enough to bring the two traditions together and fit them to his ideas. The story of Isis and Osiris, with its figures of Osiris, the lost true sun, Isis the moon-goddess who is constantly seeking to re-create him and Typhon the fallen sun, a sun of heat alone, would fall quite naturally into the Swedenborgian pattern. It would also fit the four levels of vision, the full vision being equivalent to the lost sun, the vision of Beulah being associated with Isis (the moon that reflects the light but not the heat of the sun), the 'Hell' of Blake's Satan being a place of Typhonic heat—wrath and ungratifiable desire—and darkness (or at best starshine) being a state below all three. It is further possible, if not likely, that Blake regarded the four levels of vision in Plato's Myth of the Cave as another traditional version of his pattern.[36]

Despite a tendency to objectify these states, Blake thought of them as basically psychological in nature. He described them on most occasions not as physical states but as levels of vision. Ulro is single vision, Hell is twofold vision, Paradise is threefold vision and the true Vision is fourfold. (The use of the suffix '-fold' emphasizes the fact that each level contains the ones below it.) His most important statement about these levels, which occurs in a letter of 1802, shows how the various types of imagery described play together in his mind:

Now I a fourfold vision see
And a fourfold vision is given to me
Tis fourfold in my supreme delight
And threefold in soft Beulahs night
And twofold Always. May God us keep
From Single vision & Newtons sleep.[37]

One point has still to be dealt with. We know that Blake read Boehme—but are we not, perhaps, taking too much for granted in assuming that he paid attention to diagrams tucked away in William Law's edition?

In this case, we can be certain that we are not, thanks to Crabb Robinson, who kept records of his conversations with Blake. In 1825 he reports:

Jacob Boehme was spoken of as a divinely inspired man. Blake praised, too, the figures in Law's translation as being very beautiful, and Michael Angelo could not have done better.[38]

That Blake knew Boehme very early in his career is clear

from his references in *The Marriage of Heaven and Hell* and in the letter concerning his youthful reading, but explicit accounts of the four levels of vision are not found until writings of the period around 1802. The only further question, therefore, is how far this particular design impressed itself upon him in youth.

My own conclusion is that Blake found in 'The Tree of the Soul' a form against which to structure his vision at an early stage, but did not introduce the specific terms 'single, twofold, threefold, fourfold' or devise names such as Beulah or Ulro till later. During the 1790s, in fact, he seems for a time to have been so attracted by the state of energy that he concentrated on it, exploring it as a means of revelation and a key to genius.

Even in *The Marriage of Heaven and Hell*, however, there is a controlling irony which ensures that we do not listen to the Voice of the Devil uncritically. The suggestion there that the contentions between reason and energy take place at a level *below* the moonlit garden of love and the sunlit heaven of genius guards Blake from Nietzschean extremes. When, soon after 1800, Blake returned to the mental universe of his youth, where imaginative vision remains above energy as a necessary controlling power, the recognition was marked by a return to other images and symbols that had fascinated him as a young man and which find their way into the illustrations of *Jerusalem*.[39] Above all, however, it gave new predominance to Boehme's paradigm. Blake sometimes extended his idea of human 'states' in other directions, as in his discussion of Chaucer,[40] but the descending hierarchy of creative genius, human love, expressive energy and limiting reason now became the unchallenged basic order of his visionary universe.

The Visionary's Bible

Blake's inclination to read the Bible primarily as a visionary document was encouraged by several factors. His work as an engraver's apprentice familiarized him with the emblematic designs which had traditionally been employed by illustrators of the Bible. Antiquaries of the time, correlating the biblical records with the myths and religious forms of other cultures also focused attention on the existence of apparent symbolic structures in the Bible itself. Current interest in Swedenborg-

ianism, finally, gave still further impetus to the search for concealed significances in biblical references. If Blake's enthusiasm
for Swedenborg's interpretations as such was strictly limited,
he was sufficiently impressed by his central insistence on the
'human' nature of God to take that idea a whole stage further,
arguing that the inner meaning of the Bible lay in a revelation not
of 'Divine humaneness' but of the 'divinity' of human nature itself.

A crucial stage in this reinterpretation of the Bible coincided,
I suspect, with Blake's engravings for *The Protestant's Bible*
(published in 1780), which show his early enthusiasm for
Raphael.[41] His engraving 'Joseph's Dream' in that volume is
taken, like others, from Raphael's designs for the Loggie of the
Vatican—which were of contemporary interest, since the Pan-
theon in Oxford Street (opened in 1772) had panels painted
like the Loggie designs.[42] Raphael's designs as a whole
are strongly relevant to Blake's current preoccupations. The
intricate wall-designs contain many emblematic motifs which
recur in Blake's own illustrations: children on the backs of birds,
winged cherubs, serpents. Perhaps Blake actually owned the
volume; if not, it must have made a powerful impression on him
in his youth.

More striking even than these motifs is Raphael's series of
illustrations to the Bible which, as it happens, bear strongly on
Blake's conception of the visionary humanism concealed within
the Judaeo-Christian tradition. The first design, in which God
creates by stretching forth his hand on the heavens and dividing
the clouds, is actually adapted by Blake to his own purposes in
his illustrations to *The Book of Urizen*. Subsequent designs
illustrate biblical events in a way which could be regarded as
illustrating the decline and ultimate recovery of 'human vision'.
First Adam and Eve with their two sons (the 'holy family'
incarnate); then Noah creating his ark (a means of preserving
a human vision above the sea of quantitative measurement
which threatens to engulf it); Abraham welcoming human visi-
tors whom he will only later recognize as 'angelic'; Isaac
warned against descent into Egypt (that state of humanity
according to Blake in which narrowness of vision (symbolized
by the geometric pyramids) gives scope for commercialized
tyranny (the rule of the Pharaohs)); Jacob's Ladder (where

passing human figures gaze at one another as they do in Blake's
later design on the subject); Joseph's Dream (the source of the
engraving just mentioned); the finding of Moses (an incident
used in a later design to suggest rediscovery of the truly human
in a commercial society); Moses showing the tablets of the law
to his followers (which may be compared to Sammes's engraving
of the coming of mathematical law to England (figs. 16, 17));
Joshua conquering a city, accompanied by the 'ark' of the
covenant (depicted by Raphael as a geometrically designed
box, an emblem of the Law as compared with Blake's 'moon-
ark' (figs. 47, 48, 50), which represents vision); a tyrant entering a city while a human figure (slave or bystander) turns
aside from this misuse of human energies; the Judgment of
Solomon (a more optimistic design at last, showing that it is
possible for even legal judgment to avoid the rigidities of the
law and express human wisdom); and, finally, the supper at
Emmaus, where divinity is revealed not in a blinding flash of
destructive light but in the simple action of a man breaking
bread at table.

The particular interest in Joseph, model visionary, which is
shown by Blake's selection of his dream as a subject for *The
Protestant's Bible*, appears also in further paintings of his story,
executed in the 1780s.[43] Other biblical figures are viewed with
the same preoccupation: in the early prose piece 'Samson' he
stresses not the deeds of strength but his inner secret: a secret
which when finally revealed to Delilah is the visionary story of
the angel of light who begot him to be the Deliverer of Israel.[44]

Over the years Blake's interest in specific parts of the Bible
increased. As a result of concentrating on those passages which
concerned visionaries, he began to reverse the orthodox interpretation at certain points. His lines in *The Everlasting Gospel*
are well known:

Both read the Bible day & night
But thou readst black where I read white.[45]

They may be taken in conjunction with a single statement from
Jerusalem:

Los reads the Stars of Albion! the Spectre reads the Voids
Between the Stars . . .[46]

Together, the two passages suggest that Blake read the Bible in an idiosyncratic manner, concentrating on those parts which dealt with Vision (or 'light') and either ignoring the others or subordinating them to his main theme.

Such a reading would reveal a book very different from the handbook of orthodox theology known to Christians of his time. Instead of a constant emphasis on the Law, the covenant between Jehovah and his people, their sin, Christ's sacrificial atonement for that sin, and the establishment of the Church under the new covenant, there would emerge a series of accounts of prophets and seers protesting against the injustices of rulers and looking to an ideal vision of man. By concentrating on such passages it was possible to find an account of humanity which supported the contemporary theory that all men were born innocent and only later perverted from their happiness.

The story of the Garden of Eden would fit readily into the picture created by Blake's other speculations. In his eyes the Fall was not, as in orthodox theology, an act of disobedience but a lapse from Vision. And this account would fall in with the tradition that Satan was originally Lucifer, the light-bearer. When Vision faded the true relationship between man and woman was destroyed: desire forsook its primal function, rising up instead as a consuming flame. This lapse Blake sees as constantly repeated in human experience. Like Prometheus, the lover strives to possess the 'inmost flame', but the possessive act destroys the state which his love has created, leaving him in a world of single vision to which he can only apply the restrictive laws of morality and reason.[47] A conflict is created between man and the serpent of energy; fear of the earth leads in its turn to an unnatural fear of death. The idea of death becomes both terrible and fascinating, with the result that death itself is made to exist, unnaturally, where it did not exist before. The fear and fascination of death cause man to call it into his service in imagined self-defence. Cain, son of Adam, kills his brother Abel.

The loss of primal vision is sealed by the first murder, but its nature is still remembered. The creative activities of the sons of Cain are a blind effort to recreate it; recollection of its nature filters into many of the myths and legends of mankind, which reflect or indicate that initial revelation.

The survival of Vision is emblematized for Blake by the various biblical stories in which an 'ark' survives material threats. The 'ark' of Noah survives on the waters of the Deluge (for Blake an emblem of the 'deluge of the senses'[48] which rushes in to fill the gap left by the failure of vision), though the squared form of the traditional design would be seen by him as of a piece with the legalizing vision which afterwards sees the rainbow as no more than the sign of a formal covenant; the 'ark' of Judah, similarly, is the talisman of the kingdom, though again the geometric design given to it by Raphael is in line with the law-bound obtuseness of those who carry it into battle. From the time that Blake first established his own interpretation by depicting a moon-ark on the waters, surrounded by a rainbow (emblems of vision, not law) the image remained constantly important to him (see figs. 47–50).

Blake's dominant idea gives a new stress to histories such as those of Samuel, a young visionary in an age when 'there was no open vision';[49] Moses, likewise, is seen as a man torn between his universal vision of the glory of God and the solitary urge to impose a code of law upon the people. Samson, the strong man who, having given up the secret of his strength, is blinded, and then turns to destroy those who deprived him of vision, is a prime example of the decline of man (Blake at one point uses him as a symbol for Swedenborg and the perversion of his insight by the Churches).[50] At other times Blake is content to treat the straightforward sense of the Bible more cavalierly. In the Old Testament, Sisera, an enemy of Israel, is slain by the prophetess Deborah who drives a nail through his temples as he lies asleep in his tent;[51] Jonathan, son of Saul, tries to be loyal both to his father and to his friendship with David, who laments over both father and son when they are slain upon the 'high places'.[52] Blake makes more general interpretations. The tent for him is both an emblem of the pastoral and a possible place of withdrawal (as with Achilles). (Deborah's claim 'The stars in their courses fought against Sisera'[53] would suggest the triumph of rationalism in his own time.) The mountain is an equally ambiguous symbol: it is the emblem of sublimity but it can also be a place of dangerous solitary withdrawal, as with Moses. The retreat from human sublimity to worship of the

thundering moral law, and from human pathos to solitary
rationalism is crystallized in a single line describing the sleep of
his Eternal Man which uses these implications of both images:[54]
    Albion was slain upon his mountains & in his tent.

Perhaps the most attractive of all Old Testament visionaries
in the eyes of Blake would be Jacob. At Bethel, Jacob 'took of
the stones of that place and put them for his pillows, and lay
down in that place to sleep. And he dreamed, and behold a
ladder set up on the earth, and the top of it reached to heaven:
and behold the Angels of God ascending and descending on it.'[55]
Blake illustrated Jacob's dream in later years, painting the
heavenly creatures ascending and descending upon a vast
spiral staircase, winding gently away into the distance.[56]
The details of it fitted his general symbolism very neatly. The
rock in his writings is always a symbol of opacity, a complete
resistance to light. Yet Jacob, who sleeps on the stones of the
place, is surprised by vision:

> And Jacob awaked out of his sleep, and he said, Surely the Lord
> is in this place, and I knew it not. And he was afraid, and said,
> How dreadful is this place! this is none other, but the house of
> God, and this is the gate of heaven.[57]

The vision breaks through in spite of unpropitious circum-
stances: when it does so, moreover, Jacob makes an affirmation
concerning the omnipresence of Heaven which is close to
Blake's ideas. No fixed organization or place of worship is
needed. Where Vision is, according to Blake, there is the house
of God; in the visionary experience lies the gate of Heaven.

The schematization of vision which was described in the
previous section could also be paralleled in Biblical traditions.
We are familiar with the ancient division of human history into
four ages: the age of gold, the age of silver, the age of brass, the
age of iron. These four ages would fit without difficulty into
the four levels of vision. Biblical references to these metals
could then be read against the fuller pattern. 'I will make your
heaven as iron and your earth as brass',[58] for example, would
read as the prophecy of a world deprived of wisdom and
innocent love. A still more evocative pattern occurs in the
Book of Daniel, where the king dreams of a man, his head gold,

his breast and arms silver, his belly and thighs of brass, his legs of iron and his feet part iron and part clay.[59] This figure would add to the fourfold paradigm the respective levels of the body: head, breast, thighs and feet; while the last division would give scope for allegorization of the state of man in our own society, set between iron and clay, between the industrial and the pastoral.

Another incident in the Book of Daniel[60] reminds one of the dynamic element in Blake's vision. He was fond of dwelling on the idea that the decline of man from primitive vision eventually became a cyclical phenomenon, a constantly re-enacted vicious circle of non-vision. At the point when the sun of love ought to be born, to restore the full vision, this persistent dislocation prevents the birth and causes a mere re-establishment of the old order. Only occasionally, in the full energy of Vision, is Man glimpsed as he should be. This idea Blake would find symbolized in the story of the three men in the fiery furnace. At the point of greatest heat, the watching king sees a fourth figure 'like the son of God', while the other three survive unharmed. Almost any episode in the Bible involving imaginative incident could be turned to Blake's purpose.

As well as the vision of a 'lost Man', however, the Bible contains the tradition of an adversary of Man: first the serpent in the garden, then Satan—who is later identified with the serpent. Blake saw in the satanic tradition ambiguous qualities. There was on the one hand the Satanic spirit of energy, best typified in the Satan of *Paradise Lost*. But Satan was also Lucifer, who, as a figure of lost Light, would correspond in Blake's eyes to the god of this world, the god of limiting Reason.[61] The two states could be regarded as successive moments in the decline of Man, as he fell, first to twofold, and then to single vision.

One of Blake's most complicated and allusive references to Satan occurs in the Prologue to *The Gates of Paradise*:

Mutual Forgiveness of each Vice
Such are the Gates of Paradise
Against the Accusers chief desire
Who walkd among the Stones of Fire,
Jehovah's Finger wrote the Law
Then Wept! then rose in Zeal and Awe

And the Dead Corpse from Sinais heat
Buried beneath his Mercy Seat
O Christians Christians! tell me Why
You rear it on your Altars high[62]

These lines apparently describe the struggle between a
Jehovah who exists only in single and limited threefold vision
(first making the Law then weeping in pity over the results),
and an Accuser who exists only in the desire and flames of twofold vision. The proper use of his energies would enable man
to walk among the stones of fire like Satan in his unfallen state,
but Jehovah's law ensures that he is consumed by them instead.
Yet Christians, who cannot see this, erect the crucifix, por-
traying the sacrifice of Christ to the Law, upon their altars.
(There is an implication in one of Blake's paintings that they
would do better to follow Moses, who lifted up the brazen serpent as a healing emblem when the children of Israel were sick
—a neat Blakean symbol for the resurrection of energies which
had been crushed by the weight of the Law.)[63]

The mention of 'walking among the stones of fire' serves to
relate Satan to another Biblical passage, as Northrop Frye has
noticed;[64] this is the denunciation of the King of Tyre by Ezekiel:

> Thou hast been in Eden the garden of God; every precious
> stone was thy covering, the sardius, topaz, and the diamond, the
> beryl, the onyx, and the jasper, the sapphire, the emerald, and
> the carbuncle, and gold: the workmanship of thy tabrets and of
> thy pipes was prepared in thee in the day that thou wast created.
> Thou art the anointed Cherub that covereth; and I have set
> thee so: thou wast upon the holy mountain of God; thou hast
> walked up and down in the midst of the stones of fire.
> Thou wast perfect in thy ways from the day that thou wast
> created, till iniquity was found in thee.
> By the multitude of thy merchandise they have filled the midst
> of thee with violence, and thou hast sinned: therefore I will cast
> thee as profane out of the mountain of God: and I will destroy
> thee, O covering Cherub, from the midst of the stones of fire.[65]

For Blake this imaginative account would correspond to the
degradation of Satan as described by Milton.[66] The Desire
which could once walk among the stones of fire is now low and
mean. The serpent that was beautiful and proud, adorned

with gems in Eden, has become the creeping Serpent that moves through the dust.

Yet Desire is still the talisman. The mistake of Satan, according to Blake, is revealed when he tempts Christ in the wilderness. Faced by the incarnation of the Divine Image, the Jesus of the Gospels, he asks him to turn stones into bread. The request reveals his basic inability to distinguish between the dead and the living. And this inability transforms him into his final state as the 'God of this World', unable to distinguish the lineaments of the Divine Image beneath the various incrustations which hide it in each individual man, or to see that this Divine Image is itself neither imposed nor static, but the core of each man's true individuality. Yet even when he has become so hardened as to become the God of Law, the Jehovah who sacrifices Christ as a victim to his own cruel decrees, he still remains at root the representative of fallen Vision, the true 'Man' of whom all men dream, the figure of fourfold genius.

> Truly, My Satan thou art but a Dunce
> And dost not know the Garment from the Man
> Every Harlot was a Virgin once
> Nor canst thou ever change Kate into Nan
>
> Tho thou art Worshipd by the Names Divine
> Of Jesus & Jehovah: thou art still
> The Son of Morn in weary Nights decline
> The lost Travellers Dream under the Hill[67]

The Contraction of Man

Lost Vision is the clue to most of Blake's reading of traditional symbolism and narrative—it is the 'Fall within the Fall'. But how did this loss of Vision itself take place?

In the last resort, Blake could offer no explanation. He could, however, give a further hint as to the process involved in the loss, a process involving Adam rather than Satan. In one of his earliest prose effusions, the one that began with the ominous words, '. . . then she bore pale desire', he gave a long catalogue of human failings which included the following:

> Policy brought forth Guile and fraud. these Gods last namd live in the Smoke of Cities. on Dusky wing breathing forth Clamour

& Destruction. alas in Cities wheres the man whose face is not a mask unto his heart Pride made a Goddess. fair or Image rather till knowledge animated it. 'twas Calld Selflove.[68]

Samuel Palmer described Blake in old age as 'a man without a mask'[69]—a description which Blake would have valued, for in this passage and elsewhere he expresses a firm conviction that all evils ultimately spring from the basic lack of honesty which involves the masking of one's personality. It is a common theme in the mystical writers that the soul falls through falling in love with itself. The first sin is the sin of Narcissus. In *Paradise Lost*, also, one of Eve's first acts on being created is to look at herself in a pool.[70] Milton may or may not have intended an allegorical significance, but later moralists found one: Young used the image of Eve gazing at her own reflection in lines which Blake illustrated:

Like Milton's Eve, when gazing on the lake,
Man makes the matchless image, man admires.[71]

The unified personality is unified by the vision which is allowed to shine through it; self-love is equivalent to the setting up of an inward barrier. It creates a new force, the selfhood, which stands between the vision and its free expression.

As the selfhood begins to assume a life of its own, appropriating to its own use the energies of the individual, it becomes, in Blake's terminology, the 'spectre'; the imagination which remains is called the 'emanation'.

The terms may perhaps be associated with Blake's critique of eighteenth-century mathematical thought as a way of thinking which divided the forces of the universe into two distinct phenomena—the 'spectre' sun, the spherical body which provides a focus for laws of gravitation, and the 'emanation'[72] of vivifying light, which is mysteriously produced by this apparently dead body. If men saw even the sun as a divided image it was not surprising that they should conform to the same pattern, becoming what they beheld: each man became centre of his own mechanically organized little universe, disregarding his imagination as a meaningless accessory except in moments when he wished to relax from the serious clockwork of life. Blake felt, evidently, that if men saw the sun as he saw it, a form which is imposed on that infinite energy of the universe which shouts 'Holy, holy, holy is the Lord God Almighty'[73]—and necessarily imposed if human life is to survive at all—they would see their own humanity in the same light. Spectre and emanation would disappear, their functions being integrated back into a human nature which acted no longer as a moonlit mechanism but as an expressive unity of vision and desire, seeing every thing that lives as holy.

Until such an awakening, the spectre retains power in the individual, permitting his vision to linger on as impotent emanation. In representing the two split forces pictorially, Blake usually gives them both wings: the spectre has the dark sinister wings of the bat (figs. 23, 35 and 44), the emanation the coloured iridescent wings of the butterfly (fig. 51).

He came to feel, however, that the spectre was not wholly evil. If vision was being attacked from outside, as was inevitable once other men had developed their selfhoods, it could act as a powerful defender. In a later verse, it very clearly has this function:

My Spectre around me night and day
Like a Wild beast guards my way
My Emanation far within
Weeps incessantly for my Sin[74]

The ambivalence of the wild beast, indeed, gives Blake a perfect pattern for the two activities of the Spectre. When it has begun to enfold and stifle the true self, it is represented as a serpent or a being with bat-wings. At an earlier stage, however, like the Satan who is its prototype, it is a not ignoble figure, rising up in golden armour with shield and spear. And in this world it can for the man of energetic vision act as a lion to guard his way, a lion which, while fierce against the hypocrite, could yet lie down with the lamb of innocence.

Blake's most detailed treatment of the way in which the spectre is formed is to be found, unexpectedly, in his illustrations to Gray's 'Ode on a Favourite Cat, drowned in a tub of Goldfishes'.[75] The drawings, which are lighthearted throughout, constantly refer to this theme. First the cat is shown gazing into the pool (like Eve before the temptation). She is cleverly

depicted as a cross between cat and woman, while the goldfish
are beautiful spirits of the stream. When a Fate pushes the cat
into the stream she falls in as a woman; the goldfish immediately turn into 'spectres', armed with swords and shields. In
the last illustration, the woman remains submerged and the
goldfish have turned into ordinary, dull fish, devoid of their
former glamour. Blake has employed a gay occasion to re-
create his conception of the Fall: self-love is followed first by
the rising up of the spectre, and then by the disappearance of
Vision in favour of dull everyday 'vision'. The lightness of touch
merely confirms that the conception has a permanent place in
his mind.

Another place in which the awaking of the Spectre is set
forth is in the brief drama entitled *The Ghost of Abel*.[76] Adam
and Eve are shown after the Fall: Adam, now disbelieving even
the voice of Jehovah as a 'Vain delusion of the all creative
Imagination', is obsessed by thoughts of Death. Eve urges that
they should 'believe Vision', and wins him over. But the voice
of Abel continues to be heard, crying aloud for vengeance for
his blood.

> O I cannot Forgive! the Accuser hath
> Enterd into Me as into His House & I loathe thy Tabernacles
> As thou hast said so is it come to pass: My desire is unto Cain
> And he doth rule over Me: therefore My Soul in fumes of Blood
> Cries for Vengeance . . .

At the end of his speech, he actually turns into his own
spectre:

> *Abel sinks down into the Grave from which arises Satan*
> *Armed in glittering scales with a Crown & a Spear.*

Now that his Selfhood has taken possession he makes stronger
demands than before, calling aloud for human sacrifice (with
no possibility of atonement); for the iniquities of the Druid
religion; for the establishment of Cain's city built with human
blood, and for the sacrifice on Calvary.

Jehovah's reply is to demand that he go to Eternal Death—
Satan casting off Satan, self casting off selfhood. Simultaneously
a chorus of angels sings of the establishment of Peace, Brotherhood and Love.

In this way Blake demonstrates that his doctrine of the Spectre and the Emanation, which is so important to him, can cut across one of the earliest stories in the Old Testament and reverse the normal interpretation. Where the orthodox see Cain branded as a victim after his crime, bearing the mark of perpetual divine vengeance, Blake sees in such a supposed vengeance the mark of the eternal Spectre in human affairs: he argues that Satan enters, not into Cain, but into the ghost of Abel as it cries aloud for vengeance. (Shelley's Prometheus voices a similar idea: the very act of cursing Zeus turns the curser into the Phantasm of Zeus.)[77] The terrible thing about the brand of Cain in Blake's eyes is not that it is a punishment, but that it is the mark of divine forgiveness.

One could hardly find a more succinct example of the way in which Blake deals with the traditions that he comes across. As so often, he has not reversed the myth completely; when he comes to create his 'Vision of the Last Judgment', indeed, Abel is set firmly among the Innocents, while Cain, still clutching the flint with which he slew his brother, is falling head downward.[78] Blake cannot approve of murder. But his further conviction leads him to change one vital detail in the normal interpretation in order that a mark of vengeance may be transformed into the mark of divine forgiveness—even for a murderer.

The key to all mythologies

'The Antiquities of every Nation under Heaven, is no less sacred than that of the Jews. They are the same thing[,] as Jacob Bryant, and all antiquaries have proved.' Blake's confident statement in his 'Descriptive Catalogue'[79] reflects the strong contemporary interest in resemblances between the myths and religions of different nations, and in the possibility that they reflected some single original. We have already discussed his interest in the Druids and in ancient hieroglyphs; the available historical accounts of early Britain would suggest some of the possible geographical links. Sammes's *Britannia Antiqua Illustrata* spoke of the Phoenician Hercules who came to Britain and discovered the Cornish tin-mines. He also taught the inhabitants the mathematical arts and, according to Camden, left his imprint in the 'Har' of Hartlow in Devonshire, but was later known as Ogmius, or Og.[80] Lucian had reported that he saw Hercules represented as a little old man, under the name of Ogmius, dragging an infinite multitude of persons by 'extreme fine and almost imperceptible chains: which were fasten'd at the end to their ears and . . . tied to the tip of his tongue.' Toland, recounting this, explained that in Gaul Hercules betokened not Strength of Body but the Force of Eloquence, and that the word Ogmius meant 'secret of Letters'.[81]

The latter rather sinister figure (fig. 17) evidently impressed Blake considerably. Although Og in the later poetry is primarily the giant of Canaan his activities are coloured by memories of Ogmius.[82] Tiriel, in Blake's poem of the name, also has many correspondences with him (Ogmius is 'an old and decrepit Man, Bald Pated, his Hair white, a wrinkled Skin and Sun-burnt, after the manner of Old Sea-men'; Tiriel, depicted with white hair in the illustrations, has a 'poor bald pate' and his head is 'wrinkled like the earth parched with the summer heat').[83] If the 'Har' of Hartlow gave Blake the idea for his own 'Har' (a condition of undeveloped Herculean strength under the law), Ogmius provided an early example of his counterpart, the hypocrisy created by experience under the law. The decline from the Hercules who taught mathematic arts as only one of many creative activities to the Ogmius who elevated compass and sphere as objects of supreme worship seemed to Blake to be the essence of Druidism, the picture being completed by the third deity, Haesus, (the Mars of the Britons) who presided over human sacrifice (fig. 19).[84]

Another linking tradition of this kind was the legend that Britain had been founded by Brutus of Troy. When Blake wrote his 'Edward III' in early youth he could still use this legend, apparently without irony, as a prophetic image of Britain's later supremacy as a nation of liberty and commercial prosperity, succeeding where Troy had failed.[85] Later, however, a less optimistic view of his society coincided with a more searching look at the story of Troy and an attempt to find the inner significance of its fall. His attempt to read Homer as allegory was by no means without precedent; Porphyry's ancient neo-platonic interpretations of the *Odyssey* were being revived and extended in his own time by Thomas Taylor.[86]

If, as Damon suggests, Taylor was the man satirized as 'Sipsop the Pythagorean' in *An Island in the Moon*, it could be argued that Blake found his allegorizings too mealy-mouthed and effeminate, looking instead for an interpretation closer to his own sense of humanity and its failure to combine vision and virility.

He left no ordered account of his own interpretation, but there are strong clues in his writings to suggest that he saw the Fall of Troy, like other ancient traditions, as a veiled account of the eternal process by which humanity is always falling away from its full potentialities. Priam, son of Hercules, failed his kingdom by becoming devoted to the moral law: his highest praise for Hecuba, for example, was that she was 'the chastest of women'. As a result of his self-blinkering, both his greatest sons, Paris the beautiful and Hector the strong, were to fail more disastrously. The failure of Paris, potential visionary, was made evident in the Judgment of Paris (an incident which Blake once painted) [87] when he awarded the apple to Venus, beauty worshipped for its own sake. As always for Blake, a false view of beauty entailed first possessiveness and then destruction: Venus's promise to him of the fairest woman in the world was followed by his seizing of Helen and the consequent outbreak of the Trojan War, in which the more guileful and cunning Greeks took their revenge. Hector was slain and Priam forced to negotiate with the more destructive Achilles, who had Hector's strength without his chivalry. And the downfall of Trojan civilization, which had begun with Priam's false devotion to the moral law, ended with the sacking of Troy and the slaying of Priam himself.

Although Blake makes few direct references to the *Odyssey*,[88] it is reasonable to assume that he read this, too, as an allegorical work, representing the trials of a shrewd and precariously honest human being, finding his way back from Troy through many trials to a proper human existence. The adventures of Ulysses would fall in well with Blake's favourite images. The Cyclops with his one eye would look suspiciously like a creature of single vision; the blinded Cyclops hurling rocks after the boat would suggest the final destructiveness of hardened vision; Circe, enticing Ulysses, would be all too clearly a goddess of Nature, inviting man to 'vegetate'; and the passage between

Scylla and Charybdis would emblematize with considerable
exactitude the two dangers to which Blake felt all men to be
exposed: the hardening of vision into rocky opacity on the one
hand, the exploitation of energy until it became a destructive
whirlpool on the other. Despite his indefensible violence
against the Cyclops, Ulysses eventually wins his way back to
reunion with his feminine counterpart, the weaving Penelope;
his final exploit in bending his bow was to be used by Blake at
the climax of *Jerusalem*[89] to express the reawakening of Albion.

The other great survivor of the fall of Troy was Aeneas,
whose escape was marred by the fact that in listening to his
father Anchises (who had at first refused to come at all) he lost
his wife and was forced to leave her behind. For Blake the
figure of Aeneas, carrying his old father and abandoning his
wife, seems to have been emblematic of a further stage in human
decline, where human strength is burdened by aged hypocrisy;
Aeneas's subsequent actions, betraying Dido in obedience to a
vision of his father and setting out to found a Rome which
would be warlike and imperialistic, showed his father's hypocrisy taking root in the son. Blake's view was summed up in a
marginal comment: 'Every body naturally hates a perfect
character because they are all greater Villains than the imperfect, as Eneas is ... a worse man than Achilles in leaving
Dido.'[90] And his dislike was directed also at Virgil himself,
whose philosophy he thought to be summed up in Anchises' sentiments in the sixth book of the Aeneid as: 'Let others study Art:
Rome has somewhat better to do, namely War & Dominion.'[91]

If Rome was in his eyes a civilization of imperialism wrapped
in a hypocritical moral code, Greece remained what it had
shown itself in the Trojan war: an opportunist civilization
which preserved relics of ancient vision (as in the Farnese
Hercules, the Venus di Medici and the Apollo Belvedere[92])
without understanding them. The Greek Muses were 'daughters
of Mnemosyne, or Memory, and not of Inspiration, or Imagination'[93]; their art and religion were dominated by mathematics.

The same was true of the great Greek writers. Plato was a
great visionary who, like Milton, was in earnest when he
'affirmed his belief in Vision and Revelation'.[94] His most

imaginative conceptions, which had inspired the young Milton, answered to Blake's definition of sublime poetry: 'Allegory address'd to the Intellectual powers, while it is altogether hidden from the Corporeal understanding'.[95] But he was also a devotee of mathematics and, like the later Milton, a servant of the Moral Law, seeking to 'renew the Trojan Gods'[96] and making Socrates 'say that Poets & Prophets do not know or Understand what they write or Utter', a 'most Pernicious Falsehood' in which he confuted himself.[97] Even Homer, who had preserved the history of Troy for humanity, had shown that he did not properly understand it by omitting the story of the Judgment of Paris.[98]

How could this have come about? For Blake the reason was that the Greek artists and writers were not creators but transmitters, reproducing designs and traditions which they derived from elsewhere. 'No man', he wrote, 'can believe that either Homer's Mythology, or Ovid's, were the production of Greece or Latium.'[99] The originals must lie in an Asian source, some lost Eden, from which artists of intermediate civilizations had copied them. Thus he believed that the sources of the great Greek works of art lay in 'those wonderful originals called in the Sacred Scriptures the Cherubim, which were sculptured and painted on walls of Temples, Towers, Cities, Palaces and erected in the highly cultivated states of Egypt, Moab, Edom, Aram, among the Rivers of Paradise . . .'[100]

This was the link between classical and biblical traditions. Just as Priam had encouraged exclusive devotion to the Moral Law in Troy, so in the countries of the Middle East the great hieroglyphic designs of the Cherubim, originally a tribute to Vision and to the great animal energies, had become the 'covering cherubim' of the moral law and a barrier to imagination. The Trojan pattern was repeated. Egypt's devotion to geometric forms matched the Greek obsession with mathematics; Babylon's combination of blind imperialism and hypocritical devotion to the moral law was an earlier form of Rome's (Blake thus gives his version of the traditional association between the two cities). Just as Troy was destroyed by Greece, so Jerusalem was, again and again, threatened and destroyed by Egypt, Babylon and Rome.

At the height of its glory under Solomon, Jerusalem had possessed all the ambiguity of Troy under Priam. The Temple, with its magnificent carvings, could remind men of ancient sublimity, yet the figures were treated as fearful signs of the Law, watching over the priest on his way to the secret Holy of Holies. It was left to Isaiah to see the truth when he looked up at the seraphim and saw that the 'holiness' of the Lord consisted not in moral rebuke but in the fact that his glory filled the earth. Isaiah's initial sense of 'uncleanness', equally, was a result of failed perception: the fire of the seraph need only touch his lips for him to know that his sin was purged.[101] To the transformed eye of vision everything that lived was holy.

This sense of Troy and Jerusalem as equivalent cities, representing the ambiguities of philosophy and religion, became a commonplace of Blake's later thinking. In his etching 'On Virgil' he wrote,

> Sacred Truth has pronounced that Greece & Rome as Babylon & Egypt: so far from being parents of Arts & Sciences as they pretend: were destroyers of all Art. Homer Virgil & Ovid confirm this opinion & make us reverence the Word of God, the only light of antiquity that remains unperverted by War.[102]

The 'Word of God' here is clearly not the Bible as such, since that is by no means 'unperverted by War'. Blake is thinking rather of the 'Word within the Word', as typified, say, by the visions of Isaiah, the songs of David and the sculptures of the Temple.

The assimilation of the Trojan and Jewish traditions occurs elsewhere: at the climax of *Jerusalem*, for example, when all the creatures of the earth 'humanize', they ask in amazement,

> 'Where is the Covenant of Priam, the Moral Virtues of the Heathen . . .?'[103]

It is at its most explicit in the engraving of the Laocoön,[104] executed about 1820. Blake had probably come across the design first in the engraving by Beatrizet,[105] which might well prompt him to depict the one son as beautiful, the other with the curled hair that is for him a sign of dominant energy. The whole design, with its father and two sons struggling against serpents, fitted his speculations perfectly. The strong but

visionless father, by imposing his laws, divided the potentialities of his sons: beauty could not achieve the power of
energized human sublimity, energy could not achieve the
beauty of tender human pathos. Instead of standing clear in
their human forms, they became entangled by irrelevant
reasonings about good and evil. In Eden, humanity eats of the
tree of good and evil, while the serpent remains wreathed
around the tree; but after the imposition of the Law of Jehovah
and the forbidding of the tree, the reasonings of good and evil
turn the serpentine energies of man into hostile powers of self-
strangulation.

The energies evoked by reason take different forms for the
two sons in Blake's design, as his inscriptions show. The left-
hand son, the beautiful one, is Adam, for whom the alliance
between commerce and the Moral Law transforms the tree of
vision into a poison tree: 'Good & Evil are Riches & Poverty a
Tree of Misery propagating Generation & Death'. The right-
hand son, the strong one, is Satan, for whom the serpent takes
the form of Satan's wife Lilith, that false worship of Nature
which turns his powers towards possessiveness and destruction:
'Satans Wife the Goddess Nature is War & Misery & Heroism
a Miser': for him the Tree is degraded by Natural Law
('Science is the Tree of Death'); he must learn that 'Art is the
Tree of Life'. The father is Jehovah himself who, though re-
penting of the divided human image which turns pathos into
rational pity ('He repented that he had made Adam (of the
Female, the Adamah)'), can now do no more than impose the
Law and so create endless serpentine wrestlings with questions
of good and evil.

Although Blake makes so much reference to the Old Testament in his inscriptions, however, there is, as we might expect
from the subject of his design, an equally clear cross-reference
to Troy and the fall of art. Laocoön, the priest of Troy, was in
fact the only man to suspect the trickery of the Wooden Horse:
he threw a lance against it. When he and his sons were later
attacked by serpents who came out of the sea, the people
argued that this was a punishment of his impiety in attacking an
object sacred to Neptune; they therefore hauled the horse into
the city.[106]

Blake would read all this allegorically. The horse is com-
monly for him an emblem of human intellect; the Wooden
Horse with its cargo of armed men, would therefore be an
appropriate image of visionless 'vegetated' intellect and its
destructive consequences. Laocoön, as priest of Hercules, can
sense the falseness but can only use blind strength against it. The
subsequent attack by serpents (seen mistakenly as a punishment) is really a prophetic sign of the fate of energy under the
Law. In Blake's inscriptions the Jehovah figure is labelled
'ὀφιουχος'[107] ('serpent-handler') which associates him with
Hercules, supposed father of Priam. The Adamic son ('Adam
is only the Natural Man and not the Soul or Imagination') may
well be associated with the failure of Paris; while the Satanic
son suggests the thwarted energy of Hector.

The links between Troy and Israel are forged further by
other inscriptions: 'Israel delivered from Egypt is Art delivered
from Nature & Imitation'; 'The Gods of Greece & Egypt were
Mathematical Diagrams See Platos Works'. Just as Egypt and
Babylon 'first spoil and then destroy Imaginative Art For their
Glory is War and Dominion' so Greece and Rome are states 'in
which all Visionary Men are accounted Mad Men . . . Such is
Empire or Tax'.

The concurrence of the two traditions is made explicit in the
assertion that 'The Gods of Priam are the Cherubim of Moses &
Solomon The Hosts of Heaven' and is most striking of all in the
main inscription to the plate, which describes the figures as

> Jah & his two Sons Satan & Adam as they were copied from the
> Cherubim of Solomons Temple by three Rhodians & applied to
> Natural Fact or History of Ilium

The reference to 'Rhodians' presumably means that Blake
saw the ancient Colossus of Rhodes as an elevation of the human
and another of the great visionary emblems which had been
copied from a great original; the words 'applied to Natural
Fact or History of Ilium' show with what sophistication he is
using his mythological interpretations: allegory for him is not
primarily an explanation of particular historical accounts but
a way of finding the significance in all 'natural facts'.

Blake's distrust of Greece and Rome, his belief that despite their preservation of ancient forms they were in themselves hostile to art, was, of course, also related to the popularity of classical art forms in the eighteenth-century: what he said of them could apply to his own age: 'Rome & Greece swept Art into their Maw & destroy'd it; a Warlike State never can produce Art. It will Rob & Plunder & accumulate into one place, & Translate & Copy & Buy & Sell & Criticise, but not Make.' Looking at his own civilization he saw that it suppressed Roman Catholicism (which for all its faults had a strong tradition of art and humanitarianism) yet extolled the classics: 'The Classics! it is the Classics, & not Goths nor Monks, that Desolate Europe with Wars.'[108] The age could be renewed, in fact, only by rediscovering 'the Goths': 'Grecian is Mathematic Form   Gothic is Living Form   Mathematic Form is Eternal in the Reasoning Memory.   Living Form is Eternal Existence.'[109]

If Troy and Jerusalem were alike ambiguous cities, charismatic by reason of the vision which they at once preserved and misinterpreted, the Arthurian legend, like the Book of Daniel, preserved the key to 'Living Form' by its tradition of a lost form of humanity, under whose power the three struggling faculties of the Laocoön design had been integrated into a fourfold harmony. In one of his designs, 'The Ancient Britons',[110] Blake used the paradigm in a different form to describe the three Britons who alone had escaped after the death or sleep of Arthur ('They were originally one man, who was fourfold; he was self-divided, and his real humanity slain on the stems of generation, and the form of the fourth was like the Son of God'), characterizing them as the Strong Man ('the human sublime'), the Beautiful man ('the human pathetic') and the Ugly man ('the human reason').

These three, Blake argued, represented a purer vision of human nature than Greece or Rome had been able to command; he must therefore break free of classical moulds. 'It has been said to the Artist, take the Apollo for the model of your beautiful Man and the Hercules for your strong Man, and the Dancing Fawn for your ugly Man . . .'; but against the classical versions of beauty, strength and reason he asserted his own:

The Beauty proper for sublime art, is lineaments, or forms and features that are capable of being the receptacles of intellect; accordingly the Painter has given in his beautiful man, his own idea of intellectual Beauty. The face and limbs that deviates or alters least, from infancy to old age, is the face and limbs of greatest beauty and perfection.

His Strong man, likewise, is

a receptacle of Wisdom, a sublime energizer: his features and limbs do not spindle out into length, without strength, nor are they too large and unwieldy for his brain and bosom. Strength consists in accumulation of power to the principal seat, and from thence a regular gradation and subordination; strength is compactness, not extent nor bulk.

His Ugly man, on the other hand, lacks both intellect and wisdom: he is

one approaching to the beast in features and form, his forehead small, without frontals; his jaws large; his nose high on the ridge, and narrow; his chest and the stamina of his make, comparatively little, and his joints and extremities large; his eyes with scarce any whites, narrow and cunning, and every thing tending toward what is truly Ugly; the incapability of intellect.

In the background to the design another Briton, a Bard who is perhaps the lost fourth element of humanity, is seen falling, 'singing to his harp in the pains of death'.

This design, with its very explicit doctrine of human nature, is an important key to the nature of Blake's art. When we look at his description of the design *The Canterbury Pilgrims* in the same catalogue,[111] with its assertion that the pilgrims are 'the characters which compose all ages and nations' and that they represent the 'Physiognomies or lineaments of universal human life, beyond which Nature never steps', we can see Blake hovering on the brink of a larger human vision involving the infinite varieties of human behaviour which Chaucer only begins to indicate. He draws back, however, and even insists that the Canterbury Pilgrims represent the full compass of human experience. 'As Newton numbered the stars, and as Linnaeus numbered the plants, so Chaucer numbered the classes of men.'

The reasons for his refusal to go further along the expressionist path are indicated partly by the telling fact, noted above, that he finds no place for the 'Dancing Fawn' in his art. His insistence that the animal energy of man must always be channelled through his visionary capacities automatically excludes any interest in those large areas of human behaviour which are characterized by a more direct engagement between the subliminal animal and the conscious self. These he would probably regard as aberrations from the truly human. The power and limitations of Blake's vision were never better characterized than in his Chaucer design, where each face, despite all the variations of character, has the same underlying lineaments.

This one limitation once created, however, the possibilities for art were endless. It became a human endeavour in which there was no competition or development, only an aspiration towards a vision which Shakespeare and Milton, Michelangelo and Raphael,[112] had already achieved. In this respect 'The Ancient Britons' is closer than his *Canterbury Pilgrims* to Blake's central purposes.

Blake's description of this design, in fact, with its concentration on sublimity, pathos and reason as the three essential human qualities, shows us, in small compass, the real point of his preoccupation with mythology. At first sight the intense and obsessional quality of his mythological studies might suggest George Eliot's Mr Casaubon, and invite a similar censure. But there is a difference. Casaubon's key would simply have established Genesis for ever, locking the traditional scheme of things into a final rigidity; the glory which he was looking for would therefore have been a light of fame directed on himself alone at the centre of the old order. Blake on the other hand searches mythology not to freeze a dogmatic interpretation for ever, but to find some larger field for his own sense of the nature of things. His quest, however mannered, always reflects larger human preoccupations and concerns: his own overwhelming sense that there is a human pathos that has nothing to do with pity but everything to do with beauty, and a human sublimity created by expansive energy, and that if men understood their own visionary and sexual experiences they could not help but see this and so achieve human brotherhood, is the immediate reason for his perplexity that a humanity capable of such experiences should devote itself to anything so mean as war and imperialist commerce. He searches mythology for a key to liberty, not to fixity. Where Casaubon, locking himself in the libraries of Rome and conversing with shadows dire, is a Urizenic figure of darkened single vision, Blake is more like a bolder version of Dorothea Brooke, wandering among the sunlit sculptures of antiquity and seeking some confirmation of her belief that human nature is capable of more dimensions than her own utilitarian society would normally allow.[113]

As a scientific account of comparative mythology Blake's interpretation is largely indefensible; as imaginative fiction it works for everyone who has ever felt that in his moments of energy, or tenderness, or imaginative creation, he is variously different from the self who examines experience by the eye of reason alone.

The ultimate test of Blake's quest for significance lies, of course, in the achieved poetry and art. The pages that follow deal largely with his attempts to create artistic myth on the grand scale, but it must be emphasized throughout that his artistic energy works not only in the larger organization of his art but in the minute particulars as well: that while Blake the architect is creating his larger visionary structures as patterns to interpret human experience, the same artistic energy is also welling up, expressionistically, at each point in the poetry and art, transforming the meanings of common words, renovating conventional images and creating the 'bounding line' of art.[114] Blake's inspiration varies considerably in intensity, but at its best it is always working subterraneanly towards that transfiguration of the human imagination which is, in his eyes, the key to all ancient mythologies and the self-renewing core of his own.

3 Innocence and Experience

Among the records of an early meeting of the Blake Society on
12 August 1912 there occurs the following passage: 'A pleasing
incident of the occasion was the presence of a very pretty robin,
which hopped about unconcernedly on the terrace in front of
the house and among the members while the Papers were being
read . . . Miss Wood, who wrote some verses on the occasion,
makes the robin say of the members of the Society:

> They were friends of the man who loved the lamb,
> And would never do me harm.'

Such is the price that Blake has had to pay for the fact that
his most lucid verses are also those which are most gratifying to
the sentimental. For many readers, still, he is a poet who
expressed with genius sentiments which are worthy but naïve.
He is the poet, above all, of Innocence, and the fact that after
a supposed time of bitter disillusionments he also wrote some
songs of Experience is purely secondary.

Blake, it is true, did not make enough use of his Spectre to
'guard his way'. His portrayals of innocence are often presented
with unambiguous directness: and this unguardedness of vision
led him to be patronized, even in his own lifetime, by men like
Hayley who took it at its face value. The 'Spectre' eventually
retorted vigorously in the composition of a series of epigrams
which even non-visionaries find 'damn'd good to steal from'.[1]
It may seem a far cry from 'Little lamb who made thee?' to

> Of Hayley's birth this was the happy lot
> His Mother on his Father him begot

or

> Thus Hayley on his Toilette seeing the sope
> Cries Homer is very much improvd by Pope.[2]

The connection is that between emanation and spectre, between
innocence and anger at those who mistake innocence for
immaturity.

Once the image of naïveté has been established, however, it is hard to eradicate. A reader readily imposes upon Blake the pattern of his own human development, and supposes that an initial period of 'innocence' must have been followed by a darkening and hardening into a period of 'experience'.[3]

As soon as one begins examining the development of Blake chronologically one is struck by the weight of evidence against such an interpretation. The fact is that Blake wrote poetry and prose *before* the *Songs of Innocence* which was just as sophisticated, in the normal sense of the word, as anything which he wrote after it. Even the poems of his early collection betray something more than a gift for simple melody, as we have seen; and a passage of prose, written before he was twenty, can be quoted to make a similar point.

> then She bore Pale desire father of Curiosity a Virgin ever young. And after. Leaden Sloth from whom came Ignorance. who brought forth wonder. These are the Gods which Came from fear. for Gods like these. nor male nor female are but Single Pregnate or if they list together mingling bring forth mighty powrs She knew them not yet they all war with Shame and Strengthen her weak arm. But Pride awoke nor knew that Joy was born. and taking Poisnous Seed from her own Bowels. in the Monster Shame infusd. forth came Ambition Crawling like a toad Pride Bears it in her Bosom. and the Gods. all bow to it. So Great its Power. that Pride inspird by it Prophetic Saw the King-doms of the World & all their Glory. Giants of Mighty arm before the flood. Cains city. built with Murder.[4]

The style is turgid. It is over-infected by the eighteenth-century taste for personifications. Yet there is also a running wave of enthusiasm to carry it along and, more important, an argument. In one respect, this argument goes plumb against the tradition of eighteenth-century morality. The presupposi-tion of the whole paragraph is that Shame is the original sin: on the one hand bringing out all the qualities that spring from fear to fight on her side—shadowy desire, curiosity, sloth, ignorance, wonder and so on—and on the other hand pride which, not knowing of the birth of joy because it has been hid-den by shame, copulates with Shame to produce Ambition and all the active vices that spring from self-assertion. Thus the one virtue which every eighteenth-century moralist would take for

granted—decent shame, a front of humility—is seen by Blake
as the source of man's evils. An everlasting conflict is precipitated between the forces which spring from fear and those
which spring from pride, because the true ground of both fear
and pride, the energy of joy, has been hidden by shame.

If even a piece of enthusiastic prose contains so much
organized thinking, the longer prose piece entitled *An Island in
the Moon* is positively tuned to the age in its sophistication.
Poetical Sketches had derived some backing from the circle in
which Blake sang its lyrics: revolving round Mrs Mathew, the
wife of a fashionable clergyman, it contained Flaxman, Füseli
and Dr John Hunter, and may also have included figures such
as Mrs Barbauld, Mrs Chapman, Mrs Edward Montagu and
Thomas Taylor.[5] *An Island in the Moon* represents an attitude
towards such figures in which gentle satire is combined with a
touch of impatience. It has been compared to Peacock, and
the resemblances to that satirist are indeed startling. Blake,
however, does not display Peacock's obedience to contemporary canons of taste: he is quite prepared to introduce the
hideous and the nasty. In fact—and this is one of the most
significant facts about the poem, considered against Blake's
later development—it is very difficult to perceive a pattern
which will contain and include everything in it. There is an
element of the outrageous in the satire, probably springing from
a conscious desire to shock. The contributions to the conversation and entertainment of the Islanders range from conversations about the advance of science which are reminiscent of
the third book of *Gulliver's Travels* to songs which are Cockney
in grammar and Swiftian in scabrous wit. Blake, it is true, also
possesses something of the innocence of Swift: he has the same
inability to understand how human beings can be quite as
foolish as they frequently are. But as with Swift, the innocence
is far removed from naïveté.

A good example of Blake's grasp of experience can be seen if
one looks at two or three of the poems which follow in succession
during the party at Steelyard's house. First comes the song
which begins

When the tongues of children are heard on the green
And laughing is heard on the hill

My heart is at rest within my breast
And everything else is still.[6]

This song appears, with a few alterations, in the *Songs of Innocence*. In its first version, however, the 'innocence' is distanced by the fact that the song is put into the mouth of Mrs Nannicantipot, whose very name betrays the element of foolishness that characterizes her other utterances. And if the cynic comments that the 'tongues of children' are very well on a summer evening—so long as you are not near enough to hear what they are actually saying—one can point out that Blake was not unaware of the fact: for the next but one of his songs consists of a transcription of just this sort of speech.

O I say you Joe
Throw us the ball
Ive a good mind to go
And leave you all
I never saw such a bowler
To bowl the ball in a tansey
And to clean it with my handkercher
Without saying a word

That Bills a foolish fellow
He has given me a black eye
He does not know how to handle a bat
Any more than a dog or a cat
He has knockd down the wicket
And broke the stumps
And runs without shoes to save his pumps[7]

In another form, the juxtaposition of the two 'songs' represents the same ability to juxtapose different ways of responding to the same situation that characterizes the *Songs of Innocence* and the corresponding lyrics in *Songs of Experience*. Here, however, the 'realism' which is shown in the second is more directly opposed to the imaginative power of the first: the corresponding piece in *Songs of Experience* is tinged with melancholy about the future of the children but remains a lyric with the same music in its verse—it does not contain the deliberate let-down which here fights against the music itself.

In so far as there is a point of balance in *An Island in the Moon,* it can be found in the gentle mockery of a poem like that which begins,

Hail Matrimony made of Love
To thy wide gates how great a drove
On purpose to be yok'd do come
Widows & maids & Youths also
That lightly trip on beauty's toe
Or sit on beauty's bum[8]

The scabrous element which runs through many of the poems was not unusual in Blake's time. A glance at *The Wits Magazine*, which Blake himself helped to illustrate, shows many examples of the sort. With Blake, however, there is one difference. As sometimes with adolescents, there is a slight desperateness about the humour. Round the corner lurks real disgust: the humour is defensive. To put 'When the tongues of children . . .' into the mouth of Mrs Nannicantipot and 'I say you Joe . . .' into the mouth of Tilly Lally, likewise, is to limit his responsibility for either poem. One feels that Blake's inability to take responsibility for any of the statements made in the work as a whole leads directly to his inability to finish it. He is still too anxious to cover himself: the work lacks a truly binding central statement.

If this appears to be making too much out of an essentially satirical work, one may approach the problem from a different angle. In an article contributed for the Blake Centenary, W. H. Auden wrote as follows:

Blake is the first English example of a dotty artist . . ., a term which applies to many artists in Europe, since his time, including many of the best, such as Mallarmé, Rimbaud and Rilke, all of whom attempted to create their own 'real' world out of nothing. It is better to be dotty than dead, but a lively sanity would be better still. It may be that in this age we can only choose between an art of 'the Land of Dreams' and a 'Land of unbelief and fear' in which there can be no art at all, but such subjectivity remains a defect.
    When I think of any writer whom I really like, I find myself imagining works which I wish they had written. In Blake's case, for instance, I would like to read a sequel to *An Island in the Moon* written when he was fifty; I would give anything to possess a Blake-annotated copy of Goethe's *Theory of Colours*.[9]

Although Auden later defended his use of the word 'dotty' as having an 'affectionate overtone' which words such as 'cranky' and 'eccentric' lack, exception may fairly be taken to it. No amount of affection can render its use other than insular, cosy and patronizing. The desire to have a sequel to *An Island in the Moon* forty years on is more understandable. A work which had the tolerant breadth of the first version coupled with the depth of vision that had come in between would indeed be worth reading. But to think that Blake could have composed such a final volume is to misunderstand the nature of the revolution which overtook his work after he abandoned the first version. From being an uncommitted humorist he turned into a totally committed visionary: and the new commitment automatically excluded some of the old tolerance. In future his satiric gifts were to be sharpened and used in deadly earnest. The comfortable detachment was gone for ever.

When John Middleton Murry was working on Blake, he found that a good deal of the later writing began to yield a meaning only when he examined closely the utterances of the year 1788: although consisting of no more than a few linked aphorisms, they seemed to hold the key to much that came later. Not surprisingly, he turned to ask whether some precipitating event in that year might have caused this new burst of inspiration.[10]

In the event he drew upon his own recent experience and decided that some event in Blake's matrimonial life must have been responsible for the change. His conclusion is all the more astonishing because he was well placed to perceive the truth. Two of the men whom he most admired, Keats and Lawrence, had had the experience of watching by the deathbed of an intimate relative, followed by a period of intense imaginative activity when the strain was removed. In his own life he had been forced to endure the strain of his relationship with Katharine Mansfield, followed by a period of release when he finally came to terms with the fact of her death.[11] The fact that the intense nervous strain caused by the prolonged suffering of a loved person can be followed by a heightened clarity of perception amounting almost to a new vision of the earth, was an essential part of his own experience.

When one looks at Blake's life in the period up to 1788, there is no evidence of any significant disturbance in his relationship with his wife. But we do know that the death of his brother Robert in 1787 was of overwhelming importance to him. He himself related that at the moment of death he had seen his brother rise through the ceiling, clapping his hands.[12] This experience, coming after a period of strain, evidently revolutionized his outlook. Up till now he had cultivated an amused and defensive detachment, allowing the imaginative element in his verse to appear more and more in subjection to that detachment. Now he was to place the visionary experience at the very centre of life as its true controlling and interpretative reality. He proceeded to build all his beliefs upon the assumption that the five senses, so far from being the only organs by which the world could be perceived, constituted a prison in which the visionary faculty of man, his true index of reality, was gradually stifled and killed. The fact that he never returned to complete *An Island in the Moon* and that he now engraved *There is no Natural Religion* are the outward signs in his work of an extensive inner revolution. The dramatic sense which led him to confront Mrs Nannicantipot's children with the actual voices of boys at play would not in future be allowed such wide-ranging play. It would still be exercised, but in subordination to Vision: the musical note would ring through both optimistic and pessimistic statements about the universe. Henceforth, the supremacy of Vision would be his theme and the mode by which men fall from Vision his preoccupation.

Apart from the aphorisms contained in *There is no Natural Religion* and *All Religions are One*, which set out Blake's new tenets in a tantalizingly brief compass, the first fruits of his new outlook are contained in the *Songs of Innocence*, where some of the songs from *An Island in the Moon* are raised to new status, and in a lengthy narrative poem entitled 'Tiriel.'

'Tiriel' ought not to be treated on a level with works which Blake actually engraved and published. It always remained in manuscript and was probably regarded by him as a failure. It is, indeed, unattractive at a first reading. The dominant impression is of incessant mouthing and ranting in a world of starkness and gloom.

So firm is this impression that it comes as a surprise to turn
from it to look at the sepia drawings which Blake made to
accompany the poem. Here, in spite of the passions depicted,
the immediate impression is of calm and dignity. There is even
a 'pre-Raphaelite' quality in some of the figures which goes far
to correct some interpretations of the poem. The critic who
described the man and woman named Har and Heva as
'hideous imbeciles',[13] for instance, would hardly have done so
had he seen them in Blake's portrayal (see fig. 2) where Har is
old but kindly and Heva exists in a perpetual prime of beauty.[14]
After a comparison of text and illustrations the impression is
deepened that whatever effect Blake had in mind, it was not
achieved.

The story unfolded in 'Tiriel', the most *detailed* poetic narrative
that Blake ever wrote, is itself curiously inconsequential. At the
beginning the king Tiriel stands, old and blind, at the gates of
his palace, holding his dead queen Myratana in his arms and
cursing his sons. His sons reply that until they rebelled they
were slaves, and that their later offers of help have been refused.
Tiriel leaves them, and wanders over the mountains until he
comes to the Vale of Har, where he sees the figures just
mentioned:

> And Har and Heva like two children sat beneath the Oak
> Mnetha now aged waited on them. & brought them food &
>   clothing
> But they were as the shadow of Har. & as the years forgotten
> Playing with flowers. & running after birds they spent the day
> And in the night like infants slept delighted with infant dreams

While they are entertaining Tiriel, he disguises his true
identity from them, and explains that he is forced to wander
continually. After a time, disregarding their protests, he leaves
them and goes away into the hills, where he meets his brother,
Ijim. Ijim scorns to attack him but declares that he will make
him his slave instead. Having led him for a time, he carries him
on his shoulders back to Tiriel's palace (fig. 6) and calls for the
sons. He tells them that he has brought the fiend that troubles
him, pretending to be the king Tiriel:

> This is the hypocrite that sometimes roars a dreadful lion
> Then I have rent his limbs & left him rotting in the forest

For birds to eat but I have scarce departed from the place
But like a tyger he would come & so I rent him too
Then like a river he would seek to drown me in his waves
But soon I buffetted the torrent anon like to a cloud
Fraught with the swords of lightning. but I bravd the vengeance
 too
Then he would creep like a bright serpent till around my neck
While I was Sleeping he would twine I squeezd his poisnous soul
Then like a toad or like a newt. would whisper in my ears
Or like a rock stood in my way. or like a poisnous shrub
At last I caught him in the form of Tiriel blind & old
And so I'll keep him . . .

When the sons fail to produce their father, however, Ijim declares that they too are deceivers and goes away in deep gloom. Tiriel now curses his sons, calling on thunder, earthquake and pestilence to fall upon them. As these disasters take place, his five daughters run from the palace and he also curses them—with the exception of Hela. Having explained to her that he and Myratana waited for five years 'in the desolate rock'[15] (presumably, their prison) for calamity to fall upon the sons, he tells her to take him again to Har and Heva. Hela attacks him for his cruelty and says that although she will do as he says, she would be glad if Har and Heva would curse him—

     . . . but they are not like thee
O they are holy. and forgiving filld with loving mercy
Forgetting the offences of their most rebellious children
Or else thou wouldest not have livd to curse thy helpless children.

Tiriel weeps in spite of himself, but at the same time attacks Hela bitterly, accusing her of laughing at him. She replies with the hope that Har and Heva will curse him

     . . . & hang upon thy bones
Fell shaking agonies. & in each wrinkle of that face
Plant worms of death to feast upon the tongue of terrible curses.

Tiriel now curses her: and as he does so, snakes rise from her hair. As she leads him past the caves of Zazel and his sons they come out to throw stones and dirt at him. They are charmed by the 'song' of Hela, but Zazel shouts,

Thy crown is bald old man. the sun will dry thy brains away
And thou wilt be as foolish as thy foolish brother Zazel.

Hela leads Tiriel on towards the mountains of Har and he enters the garden again with her. When he is met by Har and stoops to feel his ankles he exclaims,

> O weak mistaken father of a lawless race
> Thy laws O Har & Tiriels wisdom end together in a curse.

He goes on to explain this 'curse'. From birth, children are deprived of fancies until they are transformed into hypocrites, like himself:

> Such was Tiriel
> Compelld to pray repugnant & to humble the immortal spirit
> Till I am subtil as a serpent in a paradise
> Consuming all both flowers & fruits insects & warbling birds
> And now my paradise is falln & a drear sandy plain
> Returns my thirsty hissings in a curse on thee O Har
> Mistaken father of a lawless race my voice is past

And with these words he stops, 'outstretchd at Har & Hevas feet in awful death'.

What are we to make of this? Clearly the story has little or no importance as a dramatic narrative. If any significance is to be found in the poem, it must lie in some allegorical meaning.*

The ultimate key to the poem lies, I think, in its many references to paradise and the serpent. But the references must themselves be interpreted in the light of Blake's interpretation of Genesis. The real point of the Fall, as he saw it, was not the moral one (that Eve disobeyed), but a psychological one. Vision and desire became separated, so that both forces henceforward existed in isolation as light and energy. In consequence, both sides suffered. His Adam and Eve continued to exist in innocence, but impotent as a result of their loss of energy, while the spirit of energy and wisdom, cut off from true vision, became progressively corrupted.

Thus the real division in 'Tiriel' is between Har and Heva on the one hand and Tiriel on the other. Har and Heva, once glorious as Adam and Eve (Reason and Sense, in Blake's interpretation elsewhere),[16] have lost contact with the dynamic

---

*For a discussion of previous commentaries on 'Tiriel,' see Appendix II.

forces of creation[17] and survive in a pleasant but foolish state of reasonable innocence which recalls Swift's Struldbrugs.[18] Unlike the latter, however, they are still beautiful—Blake's illustration shows them so, gazing past each other with the eyes of vision but without the lineaments of desire.[19]

Tiriel, on the other hand, is a Cain-like figure. He contains within himself the energies which they lack, but his vision has been lost—consumed, as it were, by the very power of his energies. And here we may point to an interesting parallel in the writings of Coleridge. Tiriel's 'once-piercing eyes' remind us that Coleridge too regarded 'piercing eyes' as the sign of a visionary nature. And in Coleridge's 'The Wanderings of Cain', the figure of Cain is curiously like Tiriel. His son Enos is trying to lead him into the moonlight; but when Cain emerges from the darkness, the child is affrighted.

> For the mighty limbs of Cain were wasted as by fire; his hair was as the matted curls on the bison's forehead, and so glared his fierce and sullen eye beneath: and the black abundant locks on either side, a rank and tangled mass, were stained and scorched, as though the grasp of a burning iron hand had striven to rend them . . .[20]

Like Cain, the visionless Tiriel finds himself in a world where heat alone has the power to affect him:

> He wanderd day & night to him both day & night were dark
> The sun he felt but the bright moon was now a useless globe . . .

When he returns to the vale of Har, it is to an effete paradise, where the inhabitants can do no more than rationalize, count and cultivate the arts of memory as taught by their guardian Mnetha. The words of Lear,

> Come let's away to prison;
> We two alone will sing like birds i' the cage . . .

suffer a monstrous actualization in the figure of Har, imprisoning birds and gathering cherries for them, and later singing in his great cage. Unlike Lear, Har has not passed through the fires of experience: his aged innocence therefore lacks power. Har and Heva may not be Struldbrugs, but they are elderly fools. It is not surprising that Tiriel finds himself unable to stay with them.

The encounter with Ijim, which follows, has a Swedenborgian derivation: Tiriel is encountering another form of the dominion of Self.[21] Professor Gleckner's point that he represents honest superstition is also relevant.[22] Ijim's description of himself as a lion establishes him as the highest form of selfhood —the selfhood which has only just lost the divine vision and is more likely to exercise its energies in defence of that vision than against it. He is a figure of honest indignation who can at once sniff out Tiriel's hypocrisy. Lacking the intelligence to perceive its full nature, or even to see that it is Tiriel himself with whom he is dealing, he only recognizes his natural enemy hypocrisy, the corruption by which the visionless self assumes masks of ever-increasing meanness and ends as a rock or a poisonous shrub—an active influence for positive evil.

Tiriel passes on to another state. Effete innocence can do nothing for him, honest superstition has withdrawn from him. Finally, he is to suffer alienation from the earth. The clay from which he sprang becomes a hostile dust, to which he must eventually return, yet to which he is not reconciled.

After cursing his sons and bringing desolation on them, Tiriel sets out with Hela, the last of his five daughters. The commentators may be right in reflecting back from some of Blake's later statements the assumption that Hela is the sense of touch, closely associated with sex.[23] If so, as a promise of continuity with the earth, she is the last hope left him. But now he curses her too, so that she assumes the identity which she possesses in Scandinavian mythology, becoming a goddess of death. Death and the sexual act are closely associated in Blake's mind: he constantly suggests that acceptance of sex helps to destroy the fear of death. When Tiriel curses her, however, Hela becomes Medusa-like; snakes dart from her hair. Har and Heva fell under the same spell as Cadmus and Harmonia; but it is Tiriel, not Har, who suffers the curse of Cadmus the warrior. The hostility which has been voiced in his cursing now returns to attack him as the fear of death.

At this point more might be made of a passage from *Oedipus Coloneus*, quoted by Miss Raine and discussed further in my

appendix, in which Oedipus forbids his daughters to follow
him and cries,

> thou god of shades, great Mercury,
> and Proserpine, infernal powers, conduct me!

It may well have been meditation on this passage which led
Blake to the construction of this scene, in which the volatile
Mercury (Tiriel in the hermetic writings is the name for mercury) and the deathly Proserpine are actually seen wandering
over the earth—a symbol in Blake's mind of that alliance
between dehumanized intelligence and the powers of death
which he saw at work all around him in the eighteenth century,
beneath the benevolent aegis of an effete rationalism.

In any case, it is highly appropriate that at the moment when
death has become fearsome to him, Tiriel once again encounters
the sons of Zazel. The fear of death alienates man from the clay
which is his basic substance and to which he must return. The
throwing of dust by Zazel and his sons, along with the taunts of
madness which they shout at him, alike reflect this alienation:
earth is now no more than a meaningless dust. Tiriel has
moved a long way from the original Adam who walked in
his garden, enjoying the fruits of desire and radiant with
vision.

As Tiriel re-enters the garden of Har, however, he sees, in a
final burst of illumination, the source of all their errors. The
effete Har has tried to live by rational laws; he himself has
ignored vision and tried to live by energy alone. Both modes of
existence are a negation of life as it was meant to be. Where each
individual ought to be perceived in his own identity, men,
animals and other living beings have been reduced to mere
categories. Individuals have been restrained and brought under
regulation in childhood until, 'all youthful fancies' scourged
off, energies make their own way to power under the cloak of
hypocrisy. Hidden, the inward identity has become corrupted;
the plumed serpent who, as Satan, was magnificent in Eden,
creeps upon its belly and licks the dust. All the delights of
Paradise are consumed, and in the midst of the sandy plain
that is left, Tiriel curses Har, 'mistaken father of a lawless
race'. The unholy alliance between unilluminated reason and

tyrannical energy in the eighteenth century stands finally condemned.

The total *poetic* effect of 'Tiriel' is somewhat turgid and crude.
The reason, paradoxically, is that Blake was so possessed by
the power of his inward vision that he took it for granted in his
reader. The events of 'Tiriel' represent the 'negative' of a
radiant state which is elsewhere described more positively.
Blake had so occupied himself in working out the state of man
without vision that he disregarded the monotonous and ranting
effect of some of his poetry. He no doubt perceived this himself,
for he never published the manuscript poem and deleted some
of its best lines for use in other writings.

The ingenuity of the poem, however, is undeniable. It contains, in a highly compressed form, Blake's reading of human
experience. The Paradise and Fall of Milton's poem have been
completely reinterpreted in terms of the energies of humanity.
Yet although the myth is subtle, even more subtlety was required in order to deal with the fullness of the human condition.
He had dealt only with Milton's paradise and serpent; if he were
to do justice to the conflict between God and Satan, some
extension of the field was required. And since 'Tiriel' could not
be added to, any amplification would require a new departure
in myth-making.

The first defect of 'Tiriel', its negative character, Blake remedied
in writing *Thel*, his next poem. It was easier to adapt quiet and
tender verse to his theme than to annex the Gothic sublime,
and *Thel*, by reversing the order of experience and innocence,
achieves just those effects. Thel is young—the youngest
daughter of Mne Seraphim in the Vale of Har, wandering by
the river Adona.[24] Although bound by the laws of Har, she is
still by nature in the state of Innocence: she has not yet had the
chance of accepting or refusing Experience. The Divine Vision
is still active within her, but demands to be made actual. She is
therefore discontented, seeking a further reality.

As she expresses her discontent, voices answer her from the
Vale. A lily of the valley expresses contentment with her lot,
which allows her to blossom and serve in this world before being

transplanted to the fields of Eternity. Thel points out that she herself cannot rejoice in such usefulness—she is more like a transient cloud. At this a cloud intervenes to speak of its own satisfaction at bringing nourishment to the living beings of earth. Thel reiterates her point: she has the transience of a cloud, but not its usefulness. Her only use will be to feed worms. At this she is shown a worm, while a clod of clay speaks of the care with which she nourishes it and the glory which accrues even to her as a result. She invites Thel to enter her domain and return if she wishes to. Won over by this revelation, Thel enters and sees the secrets of the unknown land—the 'fibrous roots of every heart on earth'. But when she comes to her own grave plot, she hears a voice of sorrow breathing from the pit:

> Why cannot the Ear be closed to its own destruction?
> Or the glistning Eye to the poison of a smile!
> Why are Eyelids stord with arrows ready drawn,
> Where a thousand fighting men in ambush lie?
> Or an Eye of gifts & graces, show'ring fruits & coined gold!
> Why a Tongue impress'd with honey from every wind?
> Why an Ear, a whirlpool fierce to draw creations in?
> Why a Nostril wide inhaling terror trembling & affright
> Why a tender curb upon the youthful burning boy!
> Why a little curtain of flesh on the bed of our desire?

At the sound of the voice, Thel starts up, shrieks and flees back into the vales of Har. And with this somewhat bewildering incident, which seems to negate the teaching of the lily, the worm and the clod of clay, the poem ends.

Perhaps the only absolutely clear piece of symbolism in the poem lies in the affinity between the vale of Har and the Happy Valley in Abyssinia. Thel, like Johnson's prince Rasselas, is discontented with a life of perpetual pleasure and longs to enter the world of men. Most critics of Blake have tried to give a fuller explanation, however, none with outstanding success. The immediate explanation if one followed the clue of the Happy Valley would be that Thel, discontented with her use-less existence, seeks to enter the humblest state of all by identi-fying herself with the earth—either literally, by dying, or by assuming humility. But under this interpretation the last section is inexplicable since, after all that has been said in favour of the earth, she finds no greater satisfaction there. Nevertheless, the theme of usefulness is important and was no doubt in Blake's mind. J. G. Davies quotes relevantly from Swedenborg:

> Love and wisdom without the good of use are nothing. . . . Love is nothing without wisdom; for only by means of wisdom does it become really of use; therefore, when love by means of wisdom is expressed in use, it is manifested as something real.[25]

But Blake's conclusion, as Professor Davies points out, registers a dissatisfaction with the simplicity of the Swedenborgian position.

Several other critics have tried to interpret Thel herself more closely. In general, the chief positions are represented by Bernard Blackstone, who declares roundly that 'The theme is the pre-existence of the soul and its unwillingness to enter the living grave of earthly existence,'[26] and by those who see Thel as an adolescent hesitating on the threshold of adulthood. Many critics have felt that the poem also deals in some way with the conflict between innocence and experience.

The objection to the theory that Thel is a pre-existent soul refusing generation is that it involves Blake in an anti-worldly position which is hard to reconcile with his evident delight in living. Moreover, Thel declares that she will in any case eventually enter the earth—which hardly consorts with the supposition that she is being offered the choice of becoming human or remaining immortal. The objection to the idea that she is Innocence facing Experience, on the other hand, is that the state of Experience is represented with such hostility: one feels sympathy with Thel when she flees from it. Yet Blake constantly stresses the importance of experience.

As with 'Tiriel', the problem is to be solved only by moving behind the poem in order to examine the structure of Blake's own philosophy. As we have seen, the basic division which concerned him was not that between pre-existence and existence, or between childhood and adulthood, or even between Innocence and Experience. The basic dialectic lay between Vision and Desire. In Man as he was meant to be this would operate continually to produce generosity and openness. But in the state where most men find themselves, Vision and Desire have separated: Vision has faded into simple Reason and the energies of Desire have been either restrained into impotence or perverted into envy and malice.

If this structure is borne in mind, the meaning of the poem becomes clearer. The fact that Thel lives in the vale of Har immediately identifies her with the world of innocent Reason which Har and Heva inhabited in 'Tiriel'. She has been brought up within that state of faded vision and her discontent reflects an awareness that all is not well in a world where springtime beauties are constantly fading and where she herself is more like a shadow of beauty, a transient rainbow, than a real, existing being. The poetry also gives clues to the reason for her condition. Her complaint is made by the river Adona—in *Paradise Lost* Milton describes how the Syrian maidens lamented over wounded Thammuz

> In amorous ditties all a Summer's day,
> While smooth *Adonis* from his native Rock
> Ran purple to the Sea, suppos'd with blood
> Of *Thammuz* yearly wounded . . .[27]

The river Adona, in other words, is a stream that replaces the river of immortality that flowed through Eden, and the figure of the wounded god, Thammuz or Adonis, symbolizes the fact that Love has fallen. Thel is weeping for a lost lover, the echo of whom can be heard only if she will

> gentle sleep the sleep of death. and gentle hear the voice
> Of him that walketh in the garden in the evening time.

As in Eden after the Fall, the Word is heard only in the evening time, for God no longer walks during the full noonday.

In these various ways, Thel shows herself dimly aware of a lost figure of Love, a lost spring of life, the restoration of which might give her the permanence and reality for which she is seeking. But her awareness is only oblique: when she tries to localize her discontent more specifically she can feel it only as a lack of usefulness.

To her complaints the various figures of the Vale reply. Each one, since it belongs to the natural order rather than the human, finds itself integrated and content with its lot. Where

Thel is half aware of a lost lover, for example, the Lily of the Valley knows only of his presence.

> I am visited from heaven. and he that smiles on all.
> Walks in the valley. and each morn over me spreads his hand . . .

After she has blossomed and played her part she will flourish in eternal vales. When Thel has replied that the Lily is at least of practical use but she herself is like an evanescent cloud, the Cloud takes up the argument. He too is aware of a glorious divine presence:

> O virgin, know'st thou not: our steeds drink of the golden springs
> Where Luvah doth renew his horses . . .

If he dies into rain it is to marry with the virgin forces of earth and produce a sap to nourish the flowers. Thel replies that her only use will be to feed worms, whereupon a Worm is shown to her, looking like a human child, and a Clod of Clay speaks to say that she too is visited by a male presence who praises her for looking after his children and gives her 'a crown that none can take away'.

Finally convinced by her arguments, Thel enters the earth. But, as we have seen, she hears voices of discontent and flees back. It has been suggested that the incident represents Thel passing into the state of Experience, which she can accept until a mention of 'the youthful burning boy' awakens her maidenly prudishness and drives her to flight. This is nonsense. The whole point of the passage is that it is not desire, but the restraints upon desire which frighten Thel. It is the 'tender curb' on the youthful burning boy, the 'little curtain of flesh' on the bed of desire, that make her unwilling to enter this state. We are back to the separation between Vision and Desire. If entering the earth meant enjoying desire in the same way that the lily, the cloud and the worm and clay enjoy their parts, she would accept it willingly. But in man under the law such joy is absent. The lack of vision and the restraint of desire have separated the states of innocence and experience, which in nature are undivided. So when Thel enters the clay she finds that she is not assuming the sort of human body which she wishes for, but a body which is simply a grave-plot, where voices cry in lamentation over the human condition.

The opening lines of their cry represent a reworking of some lines in Young, who in *Night Thoughts*[28] speaks of the insidiousness of Death:

> Behind the rosy bloom he loves to lurk,
> Or ambush in a smile; or wanton, dive
> In dimples deep; love's eddies, which draw in
> Unwary hearts, and sink them in despair.

Young means this literally. Death may come in the prime of life and snatch away a young person—who may even die of love. Blake, on the other hand, thinks in terms of his own ideas. He is more occupied with the idea that sexual attraction may turn into a death-force, by being denied and side-tracked until, if not fatal, it at least results in deceit and destruction:

> Why are Eyelids stord with arrows ready drawn,
> Where a thousand fighting men in ambush lie? . . .
> Why an Ear, a whirlpool fierce to draw creations in?

Under this reading, Thel herself is fully justified throughout; it is the human condition which is condemned. The promise of the blend of innocence and experience that characterizes the creatures of nature has not been fulfilled in man.

The full significance of Thel's motto now becomes apparent. The lines

> Does the Eagle know what is in the pit?
> Or wilt thou go ask the Mole . . .

express her full adventurousness, her desire to face the minute particulars of human existence as well as the sublimities of eternal life. Blake's approval of such an attitude is shown in a couplet from *Auguries of Innocence*:

> The Emmets Inch and Eagles Mile
> Make Lame Philosophy to smile.[29]

Thel's discontent in both spheres, however, is shown in the second couplet:

> Can Wisdom be put in a silver rod?
> Or Love in a golden bowl?

The symbolism here is particularly complex and subtle. The

first clue to an understanding of it lies in two lines of *Jerusalem*, referring to

> The Sexual Death living on accusation of Sin and Judgment
> To freeze Love & Innocence into the gold & silver of the Merchant.[30]

In other words, the first reference in the couplet is to the substitution of material values for human—the dominance of commerce over the glories of true human living. But this substitution is reflected back, also within the presented symbolism, to a more general lapse—the sexual failure. The rod and the bowl have a possible phallic significance which Blake employs in his own way. When he is depicting the decline of fourfold vision in the shape of a man, he depicts the realm of sublimity by a head wearing a crown, the realm of pathos by a sceptre which the man holds near his breast. The sceptre, shaped in the form of a lily, stands for innocence of the heart, the ground of true wisdom; the crown for the golden sublimity involved in true love (even the Clod of Clay is given a crown 'which none can take away').[31] Once again, therefore, the full complexity of Blake's symbolism stands revealed. The golden bowl is a perversion of the golden crown, which is in turn only a symbol of radiance in human love; the silver rod is a symbol of the sceptre, which in turn has to soften to the living form of the lily before it can be regarded as a symbol of true wisdom.

The poise of Blake's symbolism in the poem is thus evident. Critics who try to bind down the meaning to that contained in its traditional or poetic sources are ignoring the amount of thought and organization which has taken place since Blake came across them in their original context.

A good example, not so far touched upon, is that of the earth, entered when the 'northern bar' is lifted. S. F. Damon has pointed out that in the *Odyssey* Ulysses enters the Cave of the Nymphs by the northern gate, and mentions that Porphyry made a long exegesis of the incident.[32] Amplifying the point, Kathleen Raine mentions that in Porphyry the Cave of the Nymphs is a symbol of the entry into Generation.[33] (Damon, on the other hand, thinks that it is the entry into Immortality.) In spite of the fact that there is no specific mention of a cavern in the poem, and despite the existence of a more immediate source to the 'bar' in one of Blake's early poems ('O Winter! bar thine adamantine doors: / The North is thine . . .') [34], there is no reason to believe that he had not read the account of the Cave of the Nymphs and been impressed by it. What is important, however, is that instead of following the traditional account that Generation was simply a fallen state and not a very desirable one, Blake would immediately interpret it by way of his own idea that the cave symbolized rational man, imprisoned by his five senses—a different conception, since it allows for the possibility of permanent escape from the prison even while the body is still alive. His use of the cave as a symbol has therefore only a tenuous connection with Porphyry's and Homer's. To mention the most obvious point, his grave has no nymphs at work. And there is a further suggestion within the imagery, which associates it more directly with the human body. In a deleted line of 'Tiriel', he speaks of 'those whose mouths are graves whose teeth the gates of eternal death'. [35] With this image in mind one immediately has a picture of the 'northern bar' as a gigantic set of teeth, rising to admit Thel to a gaping mouth. [36]

This in its turn suggests a further significance, a firm development beyond the 'mortality' and 'immortality' by which the commentators interpret the two gates of the Cave of Nymphs. If Blake is thinking of the Northern bar as opening to the mouth, he would probably regard the southern gate as that of the sexual organs. Thus 'mortality' and 'immortality' would be given a twist which consorted with Blake's philosophy, where the devouring mouth is deathly, the outgoing sexual organs give a sense of eternity. Such a reading amplifies the impression of restraint as characterizing the flesh in the Vale of Har, yet opposes to the general pessimism of the Neoplatonists a limited optimism. If men could leave the Vale of Har for a world of experience which was dominated not by Reason and restraint but by the interplay of vision and desire, they could achieve satisfaction in this world and see their fear of death swallowed up in their constant awareness of eternity.

Thel is not, therefore, a pessimistic poem, in spite of Thel's continuing discontent. Moreover, Blake does not, as in 'Tiriel', allow gloom to be unalleviated. The voices of the Lily, the Cloud and the Clay stand against Thel's discontent and speak with a lyric quality that makes the poem one of Blake's most memorable. The note of hope is stressed again, visually, at the end of the poem, where Blake reproduces a favourite device of his (cf. fig. 72). Children are playing on the back of a bridled serpent, which responds benevolently to their play. This, in Blake's eyes, is the condition of 'organiz'd innocence' (as David Erdman has suggested).[37] Whereas in the normal human condition the energies of Nature are repressed or distorted, here they are lightly controlled by innocence—a perfect image for that play of energy in a state of visionary desire which Blake regarded as the essence of childhood delight and the secret of adult happiness.

4 The Myth of Creation

In his immediately ensuing works, Blake developed the theme of freedom. *Visions of the Daughters of Albion, The Marriage of Heaven and Hell, Songs of Innocence and of Experience, The French Revolution, America, Europe* and *The Song of Los* all contain a strong political and social reference. Together they contain a wide-ranging critique of the attitudes in his society towards children, sexual relationships and political liberty.

Blake often used his mythology in these works. He may have been partly prompted by motives of expediency: from 1793, when England was at war with France, it became increasingly difficult to publish openly statements which might be regarded by the Government as seditious. These were not his dominant motives, however. An examination of the place of Blake's mythological thinking in these works shows that it often creates a controlling irony within them. Even while liberty is being advocated, political and social forces are shown to be subject to greater laws and to form part of a greater cycle of events, which is working out its own inexorable way. In the case of *America* and *Europe*, each poem is actually preceded by an interpretative 'Preludium', a mythological fragment designed to show the relevant part of the greater pattern that gives significance to the events of the poem and against which they must ultimately be viewed.

At the same time a more profound force was slowly carrying Blake away from immediate political and social issues. After the Reign of Terror in France, it became steadily more difficult for him to identify the forces of Liberty with those at work in the Revolution.

It is unlikely that he had ever been totally in sympathy with the revolutionaries. Like Coleridge, he had seen that the ideals of liberty, equality and fraternity were unlikely to be achieved by mass violence; he probably followed his contemporary still more closely. In a letter of 1798 Coleridge wrote to his brother,

> I have snapped my squeaking baby-trumpet of Sedition & the fragments lie scattered in the lumber-room of Penitence . . . I have for some time past withdrawn myself almost totally from the consideration of *immediate* causes, which are infinitely complex & uncertain, to muse on fundamental & general causes—the 'causae causarum'.

He also made it clear that he was particularly interested in *psychological* causes: 'What our faculties are & what they are capable of becoming.'[1]

In Blake, similarly, a growing interest in patterns of symbolism corresponds to an increasing preoccupation with the 'mental' patterns that underlie the flux of human events. On the one hand he loses interest in revolutionary movements; on the other he works towards a fuller expression of the mythology so far produced. He looks for a total myth which will contain and fulfil the fragments already used in the Preludia to *America* and *Europe*.

The process is not consecutive from the political writings, but contemporaneous with them. Already in 1794 he was producing *The Book of Urizen* and this, in one sense, follows directly upon *The Marriage of Heaven and Hell*. In the latter work he had declared that he had the Bible of Hell, 'which the world shall have whether they will or no'. *The Book of Urizen* is the Genesis of that Bible. And it resembles the *Marriage* particularly in the running line of wit that pervades it. Except on the main title-page, it is called the First Book of Urizen: and the heading of each page is not unlike those in the Authorized Version—for example, 'I Urizen C.VIII'.

The witty presentation is accompanied by a new departure in Blake's mythologizing. In his political works he had produced a range of new characters, many of whom were intended to represent specific forces in the eighteenth-century world. All, however, worshipped the same Supreme Being: Urizen, the fallen prince of Light (Luvah the fallen prince of Love had a more secret following). The visionary radiance of man in his eternal state had shrunk in Urizen to a pin-head of light, the pole-star of a world which was organized solely by Law. Under his reign the natural laws of eighteenth-century science and the moral laws of eighteenth-century divines united in a cruel regime where analysis, doubt and repression were the supreme virtues. In the frontispiece to *Europe* Blake had portrayed Urizen, the god of this rational universe, leaning out of a blank disc of light to extend his compasses into a darkened world.

In the same poem Blake had for the first time evolved a being who could act as a fitting opponent to Urizen. His figure Los, an honest man surviving in a world of hypocrisy and cruelty, contained even in his name (a reversal of 'Sol') the hint of a creative energy which, though serving Urizen's world, could still assert itself against the intellectual tyranny of the analytic reason. In his political books, Blake had described the revolutionary movements by introducing the figure of Orc, a being of untamable destructive energy who, as a result of the failure of Luvah, the Prince of Love in whom energy would be fully humanized, is released whenever energy is reborn. But the confrontation between Urizen and Orc, set up so simply, can never be anything but violent and brief. What Blake also wanted to portray was the eternal struggle between legalism and creative energy. Los could represent this more subtle use of energy: struggling to create and to beat into form but unaware of the proper end of his endeavours, guardian of vision yet powerless to apprehend that vision. The struggle between Urizen and Los might better represent the state of the world before and after the French Revolution.

The Book of Urizen, Blake's first attempt to present this eternal struggle between the basic powers of his world, bears, as its presentation might lead us to expect, a generic relationship to the early chapters of Genesis. The Biblical account, however, begins with a dark and formless void which exists before everything, including light, is created. Blake's universe begins more positively: it is a world where all is initially light and harmony. The so-called 'creation' by Urizen is merely a process of drawing away from eternity and vision in order that matter may be created into forms of solidity and permanence. Such a world can be ordered by Reason in a way that the eternal world of ever-varying identities cannot; but it is also a place of doubt and despair.

The very brief Preludium presents succinctly the argument of the poem:

> Of the primeval Priests assum'd power,
> When Eternals spurn'd back his religion:
> And gave him a place in the north,
> Obscure. shadowy. void. solitary.

The Frontispiece is witty in its use of visual motifs. In the foreground Urizen, his beard flowing and his eyes closed, sits writing with a pen in each hand. He is benevolent but visionless. Behind him stand two stones shaped like those which are often used to depict the Tables of the Law. Their shape is also one occasionally used for twin gravestones—a point which would hardly have escaped Blake's notice. In this case, moreover, the position of the stones against a hillock reminds one of other drawings by Blake representing the entrance to the grave. They are not merely the Law, but the Stone placed against the sepulchre where true Vision lies buried. The top of the hillock is the point of true Vision, to be reached only by acceptance of earth and the grave: to stress the point, Blake shows it as overhung by willow-branches, his symbol for the innocence of paradise.

The illustration of the Preludium depicts once again the counterpoise of twofold and threefold vision. The text is surrounded by the flames of the former; above float a mother and child, dwelling in the latter.[2] The flames are, however, green and foliated, and the design of the opposite page suggests the reason for this. It shows a male running freely through flames, without the manacle that often hinders him in Blake's designs. The freedom and energy of the male is giving life and love to the mother and child.

All this stands in marked contrast to the process that is described in the text. The opening verses describe the growth of 'a shadow of horror' in Eternity,

> Self-closd, all-repelling: what Demon
> Hath form'd this abominable void
> This soul-shudd'ring vacuum?—Some said
> "It is Urizen". But unknown, abstracted
> Brooding secret, the dark power hid.

The nature of the horror is slowly unfolding: it is, essentially,

A self-contemplating shadow,
In enormous labours occupied

This turning in upon himself, away from the harmonizing music of eternity, makes Urizen's world a 'petrific abominable chaos'.

Times on times he divided, & measur'd
Space by space in his ninefold darkness
Unseen, unknown: changes appeard
In his desolate mountains rifted furious
By the black winds of perturbation

For he strove in battles dire
In unseen conflictions with shapes
Bred from his forsaken wilderness,
Of beast, bird, fish, serpent & element
Combustion, blast, vapour and cloud.

Dark revolving in silent activity:
Unseen in tormenting passions;
An activity unknown and horrible . . .

Urizen works in 'vast forests'. His horrors are all anti-human, opposing their darkness, destruction and cold to the warmth, living form and light of human beings. They are thunders; swelling seas; snows, hail and ice.

This is still eternity. 'Earth was not: nor globes of attraction.' The limited order of a Cartesian universe has yet to be imposed. Urizen can still exercise the potencies of an immortal—he 'expanded / Or contracted his all flexible senses.' The hardening of the senses into a single-dimensioned rational vision has not yet occurred. 'Death was not, but eternal life sprung.'

Nevertheless the seeds of destruction are present in Urizen's activities and myriads gather from eternity to see what is happening in this dark world. As thunder rolls over his mountains, words are articulated which reveal Urizen's purposes. In the depths of his dark solitude, in his holiness, hidden and set apart, he has been seeking for a joy without pain, for a solid without fluctuation.

This search for permanence is the key to Urizen's activities:

like all the Immortals, he has a positive purpose, even if it involves a misunderstanding of the nature of things. He cannot
accept the pain that accompanies joy, or kiss delights as they
fly; he cannot see that all things are constantly renewed and
that permanence, paradoxically, is the one thing that kills.
He has even been ready to endure endless pains and struggles
in pursuit of his quest, performing works that out-top those of
Milton's Satan in Chaos:

> First I fought with the fire; consum'd
> Inwards, into a deep world within:
> A void immense, wild dark & deep,
> Where nothing was; Nature's wide womb
> And self balanc'd stretch'd o'er the void
> I alone, even I! the winds merciless
> Bound; but condensing, in torrents
> They fall & fall; strong I repell'd
> The vast waves, & arose on the waters
> A wide world of solid obstruction

Simultaneously, he has been writing down his wisdom, gathered
painfully in his solitude by conflicts with the seven deadly sins
of the soul. He expounds it as his 'Book / Of eternal brass'

> Laws of peace, of love, of unity:
> Of pity, compassion, forgiveness.
> Let each chuse one habitation:
> His ancient infinite mansion:
> One command, one joy, one desire,
> One curse, one weight, one measure
> One King, one God, one Law.

In its opening, this appears to be an attractive programme.
It is only as the hint of disquiet roused by the word 'laws' is
confirmed by the pounding repetition of 'one' in the later lines
that the flaw in Urizen's world is made manifest. Everything
that is valued in eternity—peace, love, unity, pity, compassion,
forgiveness—is to be dealt with by a single yardstick and reduced to a single dimension. In trying to establish permanently
the values of Eternity he is ignoring the one great fact of Eternity
(its only 'law', perhaps) that everything must be apprehended
and reverenced in its own separate identity.

Blake thus achieves the difficult feat of explaining how evil could have been created in Eternity without denying the original goodwill of its author. Indeed, it is Urizen's very benevolence that leads him into error.

> Joy & Woe are woven fine
> A Clothing for the Soul divine[3]

but Urizen in his benevolence wishes to create a world where joy is permanent and woe has no place. Humanity exists by constant self-renewal, but Urizen yearns for a permanence without fluctuation.

Blake here shows his insight into the eighteenth-century mind. He can show how the very 'benevolence' which was a watch-word of the age could, by trying to make itself into a Law, become stultified. Wordsworth's later 'Ode to Duty' shows the same eighteenth-century bias towards permanence, even if the expression is 'romantic':

> Me this unchartered freedom tires;
> I feel the weight of chance-desires
> My hopes no more must change their name,
> I long for a repose that ever is the same.

Urizen's proclamation provokes an immediate and violent reaction from the 'enormous forms of energy'. In 'rage, fury, intense indignation', the unbridled powers of twofold vision pit themselves against Urizen's solitude. With a crash, Eternity rolls apart, leaving a void in which the fires of energy pass over Urizen's self-begotten armies. But because of the limitations of twofold vision there is

> no light from the fires, all was darkness
> In the flames of Eternal fury

In his headlong flight to hide from the flames, Urizen rears mountains and hills against them (as the damned wish to do in Revelation). At last he constructs a vast cavern:

> . . . a roof vast petrific around,
> On all sides He fram'd: like a womb;
> Where thousands of rivers in veins
> Of blood pour down the mountains to cool
> The eternal fires beating without
> From Eternals; & like a black globe

> View'd by sons of Eternity, standing
> On the shore of the infinite ocean
> Like a human heart strugling & beating
> The vast world of Urizen appear'd.

Los now makes his first appearance in the book. As the watchman and guardian of Eternity, he is waiting for the moment when this obscure separation can in some way be confined. Being the great Former, he wishes to give it form. At present Eternity is cut off, shining apart like the stars above the earth: Los is therefore also in agony. The separation of Urizen means that he himself is divided; without Urizen he has only

> a fathomless void for his feet;
> And intense fires for his dwelling.

(The illustration shows the Eternals falling, wreathed round by snaky selfhoods). There is no healing of Urizen's breach, however. He continues to exist apart and the Eternals conclude that Death (which they can imagine only as 'a clod of clay') has been created. Urizen, for all his aspirations to permanence, has no form, only continual change. Eventually, therefore, Los, 'affrighted / At the formless unmeasurable death', sets to work to give it form. As fast as Urizen changes, he binds the change, gradually producing a total body. The changes, like the days of Creation, are seven in number. But there is a further subtlety. Such is the mutual interexistence in Eternity that in giving form to Urizen, Los is actually creating a form for himself; this form turns out to be the limited human body as we know it.

First the Eternal Mind, bounded, begins to roll round in eddies of wrath, until the sulphureous foam thus created settles into a white cold lake. Working on this, Los creates a skull ('a roof, shaggy wild inclos'd / In an orb, his fountain of thought') and a Spine with ribs,

> And bones of solidness, froze
> Over all his nerves of joy.

Next the Heart is created:

> From the caverns of his jointed Spine,
> Down sunk with fright a red
> Round globe hot burning deep
> Deep down into the Abyss:

> Panting, Conglobing, Trembling
> Shooting out ten thousand branches
> Around his solid bones.

Thirdly, his nervous brain shoots branches round the branches of the heart and creates two little orbs sheltered in caverns—his eyes. And now in succession the other senses are created—two Ears, two Nostrils and finally, to appease the 'Hungry Cavern' in his ribs, a Throat and 'a Tongue of thirst & of hunger'. Unlike the God of the Old Testament who on the seventh day saw all that he had made in satisfaction at its goodness and rested, the figure now created spends the seventh Age in an agony of frustration, stamping the nether Abyss 'in trembling & howling & dismay'.

At this point, Los's own creative urge slackens, for now he too endures the limitations to which he has given form, being one with Urizen.

> A nerveless silence, his prophetic voice
> Siez'd; a cold solitude & dark void
> The Eternal Prophet & Urizen clos'd
>
> Ages on ages rolld over them
> Cut off from life & light frozen
> Into horrible forms of deformity

The greatest horror for Los lies in the fact that in giving form to Urizen and himself, he has totally destroyed their freedom. In their predicament assistance could come only from a division of the soul, painfully, towards a new creation; eventually, such a division begins to take place. Seeing what has happened, Los is divided by pity and, following his eternal nature, immediately sets to work to give form to his pity. A globe of life-blood is separated from him and is gradually given female form. The Eternals watching these events (which are a parody of the creation of Eve from Adam and an image of the first separation between the Sublime and Pathos) are seized by wonder and fear. They order that a tent be spread around them to shut them off from sight. This tent is called Science.

We now begin to approach events recorded in the Preludia to *America* and *Europe*. Los begins to make love to the newly created female, who is named Enitharmon. She flees from him in perversity and cruelty, but eventually yields to his embrace. A creature is formed within her which exists first as a Worm (the residual element of threefold vision), then as a serpent (the residual element of twofold vision) and finally as an infant form in the darkness of single vision. This 'human shadow' issues in flames from her. At the same moment the closing of the tent is completed, so that Los can see Eternity no more. The child is given the name of Orc, and fed with the milk of Enitharmon.

Los begins to be oppressed by the pangs of jealousy, symbolized by a series of girdles around his bosom. These eventually link together to form a chain, which Los uses to bind Orc to the top of a mountain(cf. fig. 16). But the voice of the child awakens all dead things, so that Urizen too is revived and begins to explore his dens. He measures out the Abyss with various instruments and plants a garden of fruits, while Enitharmon, cut off from the sight of both Urizen and Orc, bears 'an enormous race'.

Urizen takes a globe of fire (symbolizing perhaps the twofold energy which the voice of Orc has created in him) and uses it to explore his visionless world. The enormities which he finds are reminiscent of the creations of Hieronymous Bosch:

And his world teemd vast enormities
Frightning; faithless; fawning
Portions of life; similitudes
Of a foot, or a hand, or a head
Or a heart, or an eye, they swam mischevous
Dread terrors! delighting in blood . . .

He sees his sons, who resemble the figures representing air, water, earth and fire (though not in that order) in successive plates of *The Gates of Paradise*.[4] They are here given the names of Thiriel, Utha, Grodna and Fuzon respectively. The last-named, as representative of fire, recalls that Satanic figure who, in *The Gates of Paradise* breaks out of the world of Reason. He is described as 'first-begotten, last-born': for energy is at the heart of creation, but exists in its pure form (such is its destructive force) only at the end of creation. The illustration on the opposite plate shows all four figures in their respective elements.

As Urizen wanders on he sees his race enclosed in darkness,

and understands that none can keep his iron laws. Like Lear on the heath, he is confronted by the starkness of physical reality, and as he perceives that all life feeds on death

> he wept, & he called it Pity
> And his tears flowed down on the winds

Wherever he wanders, a web stretches out, created by the sorrows of his soul. This web, which has meshes 'twisted like to the human brain' and is called the Net of Religion, is evidently a product of reason mingled with pity. In all human beings who dwell beneath this net the limiting of the senses is repeated, not now as a binding but a shrinking. Becoming what they behold, their perceptions shrink until they do not even perceive the 'woven hipocrisy' of Urizen's net, but are reduced to reptile forms. The seven ages of binding are reproduced in seven days of shrinking:

> And on the seventh day they rested
> And they bless'd the seventh day, in sick hope:
> And forgot their eternal life

Their thirty cities divide in the form of a human heart (the shape of Africa) and in bondage to their perceptions they build tombs in the desolate places, forming laws of prudence which they call the eternal laws of God:

Their captivity in Africa paves the way for a new use of the Exodus *motif*. Their senses being hardened (as the hearts of Pharaoh and later of the children of Israel were 'hardened'), Fuzon arises to play the part of Moses.

> So Fuzon call'd all together
> The remaining children of Urizen:
> And they left the pendulous earth:
> They called it Egypt, & left it.

Blake's version of Genesis thus ends with a parody of the Exodus story. He probably intended to go on from this version of the Creation as a falling from Vision and contraction from true humanity to write his own version of other biblical incidents—that 'Bible of Hell' which he had promised to the world.

In the event, he added little to what he had done. *The Book of Urizen* is by no means an unsuccessful volume, however. Blake manages both to produce a vivid version of the Creation in his own terms and to develop the Miltonic idea of a fallen Immortal who transmits his fall to humanity. The rhetoric of the volume though occasionally bombastic is more often convincing, while the illustrations are fine. For some of them he produces clever adaptations of Raphael's Creation-designs. The figure of Urizen, taking his globe of fire to light him on his journey while regarded balefully by a lion (who stands in judgment on this misuse of twofold vision) has the austerity and grandeur of Raphael's creator-God (fig. 15) but not his energy, which is reserved for a figure elsewhere representing desire running through flames.

If there is a defect in the volume it lies in a certain negative quality. No light breaks upon the scene. And despite skilful use of language there is at times a dragging effect: one wishes for livelier rhythms to break through the etiolated falls of phrase.

The Book of Ahania follows naturally upon *The Book of Urizen*. It continues the Exodus-theme from the end of that book and stresses the identification of Fuzon with Moses in his fiery prophetic character.

> Fuzon, on a chariot iron-wing'd
> On spiked flames rose . . .

This confrontation between Fuzon (Moses/Elijah) and Urizen (Pharaoh/Ahab) is amplified by use of a myth from the beginning of *Paradise Lost*. Blake was stirred by Satan's exit from Hell and his meeting with Sin and Death: he illustrated it more than once.[5] In *The Book of Ahania* we again have three characters: Fuzon, who has the rebellious energy of Milton's Satan, Urizen, who is a figure of anti-vision and of Death, and a new figure, Ahania, who is specifically identified by Urizen with Sin:

> He groand anguishd & called her Sin,
> Kissing her and weeping over her . . .

With this addition, we see that Blake's version, while belonging neither to the Old Testament nor to Milton, draws upon the resources of both. The basis of the polarization is the contrast between twofold vision and single vision, represented respectively by Fuzon (Moses/Elijah/Satan) and Urizen (Pharaoh/Ahab/Jehovah). So Fuzon, at the outset, raises his voice against 'this Demon of smoke . . . this abstract non-entity', and shakes the globe of wrath (= fire without light) against him. But when he throws it, and it lengthens into a beam, it meets resistance:

> Oppos'd to the exulting flam'd beam
> The Broad Disk of Urizen upheav'd
> Across the Void many a mile.

> It was forg'd in mills where the winter
> Beats incessant; ten winters the disk
> Unremitting endur'd the cold hammer.

> But the strong arm that sent it, remember'd
> The sounding beam . . .

This last statement introduces a new note. Why should Fuzon 'remember' the sounding beam? The clue seems to lie in the well-known conclusion to *A Vision of the Last Judgment*:

> What it will be Questioned When the Sun rises do you not see a round Disk of fire somewhat like a Guinea   O no no I see an Innumerable company of the Heavenly host crying Holy Holy Holy is the Lord God Almighty . . .[6]

The act of energy in throwing the globe has induced within Fuzon a recollection of fourfold vision and Eternity, where light and music are one. But the loss of Eternity makes the globe more wounding to Urizen: incapable of love, he is awakened by a sterile lust, and seizes Ahania 'on his mountains of Jealousy' while simultaneously calling her 'Sin'. She, who might have existed in renewing threefold vision, is reduced to the status of a faint shadow circling Urizen as the moon circles the earth, a death-shadow. The world is left between the ineffective light of Ahania and the pillar of fire created by Fuzon's fiery beam, until eventually Los takes the latter and beats it 'in a mass / With the body of the sun'—thus ensuring that it retains some form.

Meanwhile Urizen slowly prepares his revenge. The Egyptian

imagery is continued, his thoughts being likened to the Nile
of popular tradition:[7]

> For his dire Contemplations
> Rush'd down like floods from his mountains
> In torrents of mud settling thick
> With Eggs of unnatural production . . .

Of the monsters that are hatched, the most striking is an enormous horned serpent, a 'lust form'd monster', which Urizen
smites and puts away, using its nerve as a string for the bow of
the clouds of black secrecy. With this he launches a poisonous
rock at Fuzon, just when the latter imagines that Urizen has
been slain and left him as sole God. Fuzon, as he dies, is revealed as a young and beautiful figure, like Absalom or Adonis,
left 'deform'd / And outstretch'd on the edge of the forest.' The
rock falls upon the earth as Mount Sinai, mountain of the Law.[8]
This is a symbolic representation of the Doctrine of the Atonement, which presupposes a Jehovah so devoted to law that he
requires death (even if it is his own son who must die) in order
that it may be satisfied.

Now Urizen dresses his own wound and lifts the corpse of
Fuzon to find a proper place for it. Just as the body of Christ
is worshipped on the Crucifix, Fuzon's body is nailed to the
Tree of Mystery, which is described as a growth from the rock
on which Urizen sat when he wrote his book of iron. Like the
tree to which Adam and Eve retire in shame in *Paradise Lost*,[9]
this tree once rooted spreads quickly, so that Urizen soon finds
himself surrounded by a forest. Meanwhile Fuzon's corpse
nailed to the tree becomes a centre of pestilence; the energies
of man, isolated, turn into single horrible forces:

> The shapes screaming flutter'd vain
> Some combin'd into muscles & glands
> Some organs for craving and lust
> Most remain'd on the tormented void:
> Urizens army of horrors.

While these perverted energies plague the sons of Urizen,
the voice of his lost bride, Ahania, is heard, weeping on the
verge of Non-entity, and complaining that she has been cast out
from the joyful presence of Urizen into a World of Loneliness.

As her complaint swells, she recalls the joys of Eternity—the golden palace, the sons of eternity singing to awaken Urizen to mountain sport. In a threefold vision that is devoid of jealousy she recalls how Urizen would take the daughters of love into her chambers of love:

> When I found babes of bliss on my beds.
> And bosoms of milk in my chambers
> Fill'd with eternal seed
> O! eternal births sung round Ahania,
> In interchange sweet of their joys.

And now she recalls Urizen himself in his lost glory, when his self-absorption was replaced by generosity, his constricting analytics by true science:

> Then thou with thy lap full of seed
> With thy hand full of generous fire
> Walked forth from the clouds of morning
> On the virgins of springing joy,
> On the human soul to cast
> The seed of eternal science.
>
> The sweat poured down thy temples
> To Ahania return'd in evening
> The moisture awoke to birth
> My mothers-joys, sleeping in bliss.

With that figure she contrasts Urizen's present state. Like Earth in *Songs of Experience*, who addresses her captor as 'Cruel, jealous, selfish fear!' she calls Urizen

> Cruel jealousy! selfish fear!

and complains that her delight cannot renew in the chains of darkness, on the bleak and snowy mountains where she now finds herself.

Ahania's vision, which ends the poem, gives a welcome relief to the horrors of Urizen's struggle with Fuzon. Blake is here feeling his way towards a fuller scheme which will allow him to develop his mythology more extensively: his later 'Zoas' will each possess an 'emanation' like Urizen's Ahania. Nevertheless, the chief fault of the book is that arbitrariness persists in the symbolism. The world of law and mystery which is symbolized in the rock and the dark forest is credible but lacks the further symbols which would give it full life. Instead, we sink towards straight allegorizing—the rock that becomes Mount Sinai, or the 'Just So Story' touch of

> The ointment flow'd down on the void
> Mix'd with blood; here the snake gets her poison.

At such points Blake is led astray by his own delight in invention. Greater stringency and a more fully worked out scheme were called for if he was to produce work of the wholeness and magnitude that he evidently wanted.

Blake's final work in this *genre* was called *The Book of Los*. It does not fall into clear sequence with the other two, but simply tells the same myth in a new framework, setting Los instead of Urizen at the centre. It begins with the song of 'Eno aged Mother, / Who the chariot of Leutha guides, / Since the day of thunders in old time'. She, like a Delphic priestess recalling the lost wisdom of the earth, dwells on that theme of generosity, the expression of which always brings out Blake's best poetic gifts. She recalls a time when the various sins associated with selfishness—covetousness, envy, wrath and wantonness—could not find existence, because love and joy refused to regard them as impure and ministered to them until they were transformed into forms of generosity and innocence:

> But Covet was poured full:
> Envy fed with fat of lambs:
> Wrath with lions gore:
> Wantonness lulld to sleep
> With the virgins lute,
> Or sated with her love.
>
> Till Covet broke his locks & bars,
> And slept with open doors:
> Envy sung at the rich mans feast:
> Wrath was follow'd up and down
> By a little ewe lamb
> And Wantonness on his own true love
> Begot a giant race . . .

But her song finds no echo in the earth, where the flames of desire, though intelligent and organized, minister not to life but to death, armed with destruction and plagues. Los, creator of forms, has no part in their activity but is compelled to watch Urizen's shadow. In his bondage he can only rage with curses and fling his limbs about in the vacuum where he exists, 'in the void between fire and fire'. From these fires there is no light—not even heat, for heat is bound into fiery spheres away from his fury. He experiences only coldness, darkness, obstruction:

A vast solid without fluctuation,
Bound in his expanding clear senses . . .

In the end Los's impatience and fury are too much for his bondage: with a mighty effort he rends the 'vast solid', which

With a crash from immense to immense

Crack'd across into numberless fragments.

His action is like that of Milton's Satan breaking out of Hell. Once outside the dark cavern, he finds himself in the infinite. Unlike the Satan of *Paradise Lost*, however, he has no wings to fly with and no destination. He can only fall. The description of his fall shows Blake's powers in full control.

Falling, falling! Los fell & fell
Sunk precipitant heavy down down
Times on times, night on night, day on day
Truth has bounds. Error none: falling, falling:
Years on years, and ages on ages
Still he fell thro' the void, still a void
Found for falling day & night without end.
For tho' day or night was not; their spaces
Were measur'd by his incessant whirls
In the horrid vacuity bottomless.

At first he can only throw out his limbs in wrathful gestures, with the vigour and helplessness of a young baby. But the void is a mental void and his falling the result of the state of his mind. As he comes to and as his mind begins to be organized, therefore, the Vacuum turns into element and Los becomes

pliant to rise,
Or to fall, or to swim, or to fly:
With ease searching the dire vacuity

The Lungs heave incessant . . .

There begins again the story of the Binding of Urizen, told now

in a different form. Los can exist neither within the captivity of
Urizen, nor in the void outside Urizen's domain. He must therefore compromise with the solid world, and this compromise takes
the form of the human body, conceived now on a cosmic scale.

At first the human body consists of a pair of lungs, all other
parts being as yet formless,

> Dim & glutinous as the white Polypus
> Driv'n by waves & englob'd on the tide.

As the branchy forms weave out into an 'immense Fibrous form',
he thrashes out in the deep, separating the heavy from the thin.
The heavy sinks down into the solid, the thin rises round the
fierce fires that glow in the expanse. And this provides an
element through which the fires, till now dark, can give forth
light. But as soon as light appears he recognizes the presence
of Urizen.

> Los beheld
> Forthwith, writhing upon the dark void
> The Back bone of Urizen appear
> Hurtling upon the wind
> Like a serpent! Like an iron chain
> Whirling about in the Deep.

Accordingly, he sets to work to bind Urizen. His ultimate, if
unconscious aim, evidently, is to re-create the Eternal Man: to
unite the form of Reason with the flames of Energy and thus
re-marry Vision with Desire. He therefore takes the infinite
fires that burn in the expanse and begins to beat them into a
mass, which takes the form of an immense 'Orb of fire'. After
nine ages the work is complete, the mass is cast down into the
deeps and the sun stands self-balanced. Los smiles with joy at
the sight and then binds the vast spine of Urizen down to the
'glowing illusion'.

But this well-meaning attempt to bring together the two
elements in Eternal man is unavailing, for the true binding
forces are absent. He has simply brought together darkness
and heat:

> But no light, for the Deep fled away
> On all sides, and left an unform'd
> Dark vacuity: here Urizen lay
> In fierce torments on his glowing bed. . . .

Urizen sets to work to cut himself off from the energy with
which he is unwillingly involved. He creates a paradise-garden
for his heart which so far from being, like Eden, centred in a
sun-fountain of love, sends forth four rivers to obscure the
infinite energy. And this private garden, along with the rock-
enclosed brain, ensures that the Orb of fire is obscured:

> Till his Brain in a rock, & his Heart
> In a fleshy slough formed four rivers
> Obscuring the immense Orb of fire
> Flowing down into night: till a Form
> Was completed, a Human Illusion
> In darkness and deep clouds involvd.

Blake's satiric point does not fully emerge until these last
lines. All this limiting, binding, breaking out and fresh creation
has finally resulted in the human form as we know it—not the
Eternal Man, however, but a 'human illusion'. Fearing the
concurrence of Vision and Desire, it devotes itself to the pursuit
of analytic reason and the cultivation of its own private garden.
Man has been created in the image of Voltaire; only in the
final illustration to the poem, which shows Los jumping for joy
above the orb of the sun, do we catch a glimpse of what he
might be.

The Book of Los is more tightly woven and more intricately
thought out than its predecessors. It gains at a first reading by
the fact that it contains only a few references to history or
literature. Yet one feels, even here, that Blake regarded it as
simply another sketch for the longer poem which he wanted to
produce. The illustrations have a perfunctory air. There is
some wit in the title-page, which shows Urizen imprisoned in
the egg-shaped O of LOS, cobwebbed and spreading out his
web to cover man and woman, but little further attention is
given to design.

Blake's mind was evidently running toward the construction
of a more massive poem, an epic form which would be for his
day what *Paradise Lost* had been for the seventeenth-century.
For such an achievement to be possible the various schemes
which he had so far worked out must be extended into a

broader pattern. But the short cosmological prophetic books that we have looked at so far indicate the ambiguities which made this difficult. He might try, following Milton, to offer an account of the process by which the world had arrived at its present state, but he could not escape the fact that where Milton could still hold a precarious balance between cosmology and psychology, his own myth must inevitably find its centre in a critique of the nature of man. He might attack current social injustices; he might reach further and attack the dominance of law which made these injustices possible; but he would always be driven back to account for the condition of man which made it impossible for him to appreciate his own enslavement.

This problem, which is crucial in Blake's extended myth-making, had preoccupied him from his earliest writings. Even in *Poetical Sketches* he had written, 'I am wrapped in mortality, my flesh is a prison, my bones the bars of death'.[10] His sense that this enslaving power was a necessary consequence of current rationalism had brought him (in *The Marriage of Heaven and Hell*), to the assertion that the creation which appeared to be finite and corrupt was really infinite and holy and to the further affirmation that

> If the doors of perception were cleansed every thing would appear to man as it is, infinite.[11]

This was not a sudden insight. In a deleted passage of 'Tiriel' he had made an early attempt to give an account of the individualities of men which would also suggest the latent power of man's senses to perceive the infinity in all things:

> Dost thou not see that men cannot be formed all alike
> Some nostrild wide breathing out blood. Some close shut up
> In silent deceit. poisons inhaling from the morning rose
> With daggers hid beneath their lips & poison in their tongue
> Or eyed with little sparks of Hell or with infernal brands
> Flinging flames of discontent & plagues of dark despair
> Or those whose mouths are graves whose teeth the gates of
>   eternal death[12]

It is a sinister vision, fitted to Tiriel's condition, which makes it inevitable that if he does see the individuality of all men he will see it through the various types of evil which they practise. But the imagery of the morning rose and the sparks of fire provides a hint that a more optimistic account of men's individualities might also be possible.

Blake's deletion of the lines may well have been due to a fear that his irony had become too complicated at this point: if he wished to express the ambiguity of the senses it might be better to do so on the lips of a character who did not labour under Tiriel's disabilities. Certainly the similar speech at the climax of *The Book of Thel* makes the implications of infinity far more explicit. Here each sense is described at a point when it is most likely to glimpse the infinity of all things: the tongue at the moment of eating honey, the eye when a generous look is expressing the abundance of the human personality behind it, the nostril in the moment of sharp awareness induced by terror, the phallic organs when they are fired by desire:

> Why cannot the Ear be closed to its own destruction?
> Or the glistning Eye to the poison of a smile!
> Why are Eyelids stord with arrows ready drawn,
> Where a thousand fighting men in ambush lie?
> Or an Eye of gifts & graces, show'ring fruits & coined gold!
> Why a Tongue impress'd with honey from every wind?
> Why an Ear, a whirlpool fierce to draw creations in?
> Why a Nostril wide inhaling terror trembling & affright
> Why a tender curb upon the youthful burning boy!
> Why a little curtain of flesh on the bed of our desire?[13]

But if Thel's innocence gives her the power to perceive the potentialities of the senses, it also precludes her from knowing the answers to her questions. She cannot know that it is the imposition of the Law which has inhibited perception and placed a tender curb upon the youthful burning boy.

The event which is hidden from her is in fact described in *Europe*, where Blake describes the moment when the eyes changed from infinite organs of light into sheltered receptors, the ears from Jacob's ladders, ascending to music of the spheres, into winding, hardened shells[14] which could find no nearer emblem of infinity than the fearsome whirlpool of *Thel*, and the other senses from gateways into barriers:

> when the five senses whelm'd
> In deluge o'er the earth-born man; then turn'd the fluxile eyes
> Into two stationary orbs, concentrating all things.

The ever-varying spiral ascents to the heavens of heavens
Were bended downward; and the nostrils golden gate shut,
Turn'd outward, barr'd and petrify'd against the infinite.[15]

The process is examined more closely in *The Book of Urizen*
where, as we have seen, Blake actually tries to depict the hardening of perception into the forms of the senses as we know
them, the initial solidification of the spine being followed by the
formation of the red round globe of the heart, the retreat of
vision into two cave-bound orbs, and the petrifaction of the
infinite volutions of the whirlpool into the finite shell-like volutions of the inner ear. This process once complete, the chemical
senses mediated by nose, mouth and phallus—which have the
power to link man closely to the external world by direct contact with air, liquid and food, and even more directly to another body in the act of sex—find themselves cut off from any
larger context of connection. As a result they express only an
impotent craving, bringing the mind to the margin of non-
existence and inciting the body to impotent gestures of an
ultimate despair.

One other passage, the preface affixed to some copies of
Europe, presents even more explicitly Blake's belief in the
potential sublimity of the senses. The note here, despite the
pessimism, is one of gaiety:

Five windows light the cavern'd Man; thro' one he breathes the
     air,
Thro' one, hears music of the spheres; thro' one, the eternal vine
Flourishes, that he may receive the grapes; thro' one can look
And see small portions of the eternal world that ever groweth;
Thro' one, himself pass out what time he please, but he will not;
For stolen joys are sweet, & bread eaten in secret pleasant.
So sang a Fairy mocking as he sat on a streak'd Tulip . . .[16]

The passage is important not only as giving Blake's clearest
picture of perception with its doors cleansed, but also because
the very need to place it where he does shows Blake's problem
of construction. To the main action of *Europe*, which has a
historical framework, he had already prefixed a 'Preludium'
which gave the relevant segment of his larger mythology;[17] but
even this was not enough. He must now preface that, in its
turn, by a picture of sense-experience in the state of perfection

to counterpoise the pattern of decline and non-vision which governs both other statements.

It was for Blake a recurring problem, exacerbated by the fact that the necessary rendering of the perfection of the senses could not by its nature be expressed directly except in short passages. However 'visionary and dramatic' the state, it could not be turned directly into drama or narrative: though energetic and dynamic in Blake's imagination it lacked the necessary possibilities of suspense and development. Yet the creation of an epic poem demanded dramatic narrative.

There was, however, one pattern in Blake's visionary universe which could be conceived dramatically: the pattern of decline itself. The central idea of a creation-process which had started by division away from an ideal state, was the possible basis for a long narrative. Indeed, it enabled him to go further and turn some of the most static symbols of Western art into emblems of a more active process. The crucifix, for example, familiar to Christian tradition as an icon of redemption through submission, could provide a suggestive picture of the process by which law-worshipping Druids had destroyed humanity. Their presentation of the world under the domination of law had hidden from man his true potentialities. Under their blind tutelage his head was crowned with the thorns of a doubting rationalism, his heart pierced by tyranny, his genitals covered by the winding sheet of shame and his hands and feet nailed to the fixities of a law-bound universe.

This enslavement was brought about by the mutually reinforcing power of natural and moral law. The natural law prevented the head from wearing its golden crown of visionary reason; only when released from it would the heart melt the fixed forms of the quantitatively measured universe in its furnaces and allow them to emerge as the ever-changing forms of imaginative vision; the hands and feet, no longer constrained to the limiting functions of ordering the world by geometric patterns and exact symmetries could then give expression and shaping outline to the running forms of a liberated imagination. Released from subservience to a fixed moral law, equally, the phallus would cease to be hidden by the cloths of shame and become instead the sceptre of an organized innocence. It would release the energy of the heart and the creative power of hands and feet. Its expansions and contractions would become the poles of a universe far removed from the Newtonian—a humanized universe, dominated by expansions to sublimity and contractions to pathos. In this universe, the circumscribed sun of the reasoners, hanging in their sky like a golden guinea, would be transformed into an emblem of the sublimity of desire, infinite in its own energy and irradiating its own universe in every human being.

The double failure of man under the law is for Blake the source of a vicious circle which ensures its continuance. Imposition of the moral law, by cutting man off from the wisdom of the heart and genitals and from the world of sublimity and pathos to which they are the ancient key, leaves him at the mercy of reason, his only other light, which tells him to create a permanent civilization as a defence against his fear of extinction. The cult of natural law, equally, dominated by the quantitative measurement of time and space, must, whenever it measures the size of man against the size of space, or the life-span of man against the age of the world, impress upon man the significance of death. Rational man, made aware of his helplessness and of the brevity of his life, will protect his own existence by pushing the rule of law to the point of tyranny.

The sense of this self-perpetuating situation became for Blake the master-idea for his extended myth-making. It gave him the sense of human faculties trapped in a recurring cycle which underlies his conception of the Zoas. Urizen, the former king of Vision who has lost his inner illumination, has turned into a fading old man, leaning out of a blank sun-disk to stretch circumscribing compasses over a darkness that he can no longer comprehend. Luvah, the former prince of the heart, who has laid aside his sceptre of desire to become a creature of blood, now reflects the blood's ambiguities: he is alternately a murderer and a sacrificial victim. Tharmas, the sexual energy who once dwelt in pastures of organized innocence, now finds himself raging in a sea of rationally organized sense-perception which has rushed in upon his lost Atlantis, submerging all but a few rocks (its former mountain-tops) and allowing a fallen light to filter through to the rational self which still, unawares, sits on the ocean bed intent on geometric activities. Los, the creative power that remains, is left to give what shape and form he can to matter in a universe that is deprived of its ultimate vision and desire.

Some of the Zoas had already been present in earlier works: this new scheme suggests their status in the greater cosmic drama that Blake was now planning. The drawback, in dramatic terms, was that they did not have full significance in either of Blake's universes. Rather, they moved in a shadowy region between the two spheres of his experience: his own society, moving into a technological era which would give the rule of law a new and subtler power; and the world of his own imagination and energy. The best way to understand the mythology which he created, therefore, is to see it stretched between these two universes and to trace the areas of its operation *across* the dramatic action of his poem: from the points at which it offers a direct critique of his own society to the points at which it attempts, by the power of its own poetry, to effect that transformation of human perception which is for Blake the one and final key that can rescue man from the circular eddyings of a law-bound world.

5 A Developing Mythology

The first sketch of Blake's extended myth-making occurs in a fragment of verse which is sometimes printed at the end of *The Four Zoas*:

Beneath the veil of Vala rose Tharmas from dewy tears
The eternal man bowd his bright head & Urizen prince of light
Astonishd lookd from his bright portals. Luvah King of Love
Awakend Vala. Ariston ran forth with bright Onana
And dark Urthona rouzd his shady bride from her deep den
Pitying they viewd the new born demon for they could not love
Male formd the demon mild athletic force his shoulders spread
And his bright feet firm as a brazen altar, but the parts
To love devoted, female, all astonishd stood the hosts
Of heaven, while Tharmas with wingd speed flew to the sandy
    shore
He rested on the desert wild & on the raging sea
He stood & stretchd his wings &c[1]

Several points deserve mention. To begin with, this is the first time that we have met with Ariston, Vala or Tharmas in Blake's text. The mention of 'dewy tears' in the first line recalls other uses of this image in Blake and suggests that the rise of Tharmas beneath the veil of Vala takes place at approach of evening in that dewy garden where man first knows himself in his fallen human condition.

This fact helps to suggest another point. 'The eternal man bowd his bright head.' It is no subsequent event: on the contrary, it tells the reader in what the fall consisted. The creation of Tharmas resulted directly from the loss of vision in the Eternal Man. Moreover, the four daemons who now appear have not until now existed in separation. They are the faculties of Man—only now, in this loss of vision, separated and left to pursue their own ends. In *The Marriage of Heaven and Hell*, Blake characterized man thus:

The head Sublime, the heart Pathos, the genitals Beauty, the hands & feet Proportion.[2]

From the lines before us it seems evident that a similar scheme is still at work in his mind. Urizen, prince of light, is the head of the Eternal Man; Luvah his heart; Ariston his genitals; Urthona his hands and feet and also the earth with which his feet are in contact (with his 'shady bride', he reminds us of Pluto).

Once the Eternal Man who should hold them in harmony bows his head, these four are separated. Moreover, they observe with fascination the birth of a new daemon, Tharmas, who is a hermaphrodite. Blake is evidently thinking here of the female domination which he sees as a characteristic of the Christian era: Tharmas has the wings and feet of the masculine sublime, but no positive sexual force—he is not altogether unlike Enitharmon, the dominating female.

This piece of writing may well have been undertaken before the composition of most of the prophetic books that we have so far examined. Certainly, Blake changed his organization of the figures in various ways. The original scheme was neat, but contained little scope for extension into a longer poem. What sort of myth could one construct from it?

As he thought about the nature of revolution, moreover, other figures had emerged. He had, for instance, created Orc[3]— like Tharmas, a new-born demon, but otherwise very different. He was the force that was unleashed when the moment came for the Eternal Man to be reborn to his true glory. Since Luvah was now only the fallen shadow of that glory, providing no dynamic form in which infinite energy could live, it burst forth instead as the raging fire of Orc.

At the same time, Blake had probably decided that the hermaphroditic figure of Tharmas did not express fully enough the concept of masculine failure and feminine domination. In *Europe* he produced the figure of Enitharmon,[4] who contains part of Tharmas's name at her heart, and who represents feminine domination in clearer form. He had also given her, in Los, a male counterpart who was more dynamic than Tharmas: deprived of the vision, but seeking to re-create it; jealous but also honest; bound to Urizen's shadow yet seeking to give form even to the darkness of single vision.

With Los and Enitharmon, Blake had created two figures to

represent the best creative energies of his time; in Orc a figure
for revolutionary energy. The next step was not a difficult one.
Orc was to be the son of Los and Enitharmon—the object of his
mother's love and the victim of his father's jealousy.

  Once these relationships are introduced into Blake's scheme,
it begins to take a different form. So far we have suggested the
scheme:

Urizen	head
Luvah	heart
Ariston	genitals
Urthona	hands and feet

This scheme, which contained little internal dynamics, is now
radically altered. Ariston drops out of Blake's mythology for
ever, and Tharmas, originally intended to be the new-born
demon, takes his place, representing the privation of sex which
follows on the Fall. Urthona, too, retires into the background,
to be replaced by Los and Enitharmon, who represent his
energies as they exist under the dominion of Urizen.

  A further important modification takes place. The birth of
Orc seems to have introduced the idea of a cycle which is
constantly being enacted. This cycle does not pass through the
four energies in that order, however. Instead of the cycle

  Urizen—Luvah—Tharmas—Urthona (Los)—Urizen (Orc)

Blake adopts a subtler idea. He supposes a particularly intimate relationship between the energies of the heart and
those of sex, so that his scheme of the ideal man would be as
follows:

Urizen (head)

Luvah (heart) *in union with* Tharmas (genitals)

Urthona (hands and feet)

The true failure of the Eternal Man lies not in the head, but at
some profounder level. This failure reacts upon the head, however, depriving it of its true vision. At one and the same moment,
the link between heart and genitals is broken, so that instead of
the unity of man portrayed above, where the interplay of Luvah
and Tharmas acts as a link between Urizen and Urthona, man

is inverted. Communication between his energies can now take place only in a cyclical fashion, thus:

```
        ┌──────►4. Urthona (Los and Enitharmon)──────┐
        │                                            ▼
3. Tharmas (fallen sex)      1. Luvah (heart)┐      5. Orc
        ↑_____2. Urizen (head) ◄──────┘
```

This rearrangement immediately gives scope for a new run of geographical symbols, with all their implications. The associations of the East with the rising of the sun and the resurrection make it the natural domain of Luvah and the birth of Orc. The associations of the west with decline make it the natural dwelling-place of Tharmas. In Eternity, Urizen would give light to the north and Urthona would beat out the vital rhythms of southern countries; now they are reversed, so that Urizen dwells on a rock in the far south while Urthona is confined to the dark caverns of the north. The scheme becomes

                    Urthona (north)
    Tharmas (west)   Luvah/Orc (east)
                    Urizen (south)

The point which needs to be stressed repeatedly, however, is that this cycle exists only because of the failure of the Eternal Man. If he were to rise again in the east, the cycle would immediately be abolished, and the various separate energies would resume their natural functions as harmonizing and interacting parts of his reunited humanity.

The story of the cycle is therefore intimately related to the story of the Fall and the efforts of man towards recovery. And this, as we have already hinted, is not a simple event but one involving several disasters—which all happened at one and the same moment, when the energies of Man became separated.

The main disaster is in the heart: it is Luvah who is most involved. There has been a conflict between the heart and head, between Luvah and Urizen, in which they changed functions, so that the energies of light and those of love have become interchanged. Luvah is reduced to ineffectual light, Urizen to darkness. Moreover, since Luvah is cut off from Tharmas, his energies can only act by the intervention of reason. Sexual love turns into a sterile lust.

This dislocation of function is, however, related to another disaster, only hinted at. Luvah has in some sense, it seems, 'murdered' Tharmas, who, in his innocence, formerly gave a surrounding and protecting vision to him. All four energies are affected by the disaster, and the only spirits who can now act positively are Los and Enitharmon, left in the north, visionless but still guarding the remnants of the primeval Vision. They strive to re-create it and give it new birth but because they cannot escape the dominion of Urizen, they can only bring forth Orc. The other action open to Los is to contend with Urizen himself and seek to bind him in the way that Blake described in *The Book of Urizen*.

Already, it will be observed, a complicated pattern has been introduced; it is made more intricate by the fact that these 'psychological' events were backed by a hinterland of speculation on Blake's part, derived from his reading of visionary authors. In particular, his meditations upon the Fall as related in the Old Testament had played a great part in shaping his mythology. We have already seen how he was haunted by the idea of Eternal Man as a spirit walking in the garden and of the Fall as a break within this primitive unity of Vision and Desire. The decline of the Eternal Man into Luvah and his associates obviously bears a strong relation to the story of fallen Adam. And the sinister outcome of the break, the 'murder' of Tharmas by Luvah, can be matched in the murder of Abel by Cain.

The story of Cain and Abel was one which exercised a peculiar fascination in England at the end of the eighteenth century. Gessner's *Death of Abel*, in translation, had an enormous sale and ran into many editions. Blake would, moreover, be aware that several writers, including Jacob Boehme, had regarded the story as an allegory of the origin of evil in man.[5] Several statements in the Old Testament assisted attempts at allegorical interpretation of the story, including the references to Cain as a 'tiller of the earth' and Abel as a 'keeper of sheep'. This hint that not merely two men but two types of civilization were involved was supported by the further fact that after the murder the earth was no longer fruitful for Cain. Instead, he built a city east of Eden and his sons, particularly Tubal-Cain, became masters in all kinds of metal-work. (The name Cain means 'a smith'.) We may add here that the persistent traditions that Cain's creative activities after the Fall were all due to a desire to re-create the glory of the Lord which was now no longer visible to him fits the nature of Blake's Los, who is also striving to recreate a lost vision. Now, therefore, we have a further pattern at work in the cycle:

Luvah	Cain
Urizen	—
Tharmas	Abel
Los	Tubal-Cain.

There was also another tradition of the Fall. Etymologists of the eighteenth century thought that a connection could be traced between Cain and the Ham, or Cham, who was the rebellious son of Noah. Ham, the son who made his father drunk and uncovered his nakedness, was often regarded as a figure of lust. If Cain was the son of Adam who realized the Fall by the creation of Death, Ham was the son of Noah who realized the Fall as a decline from light and love into lust. We have already seen how Blake identified Urizen with Noah, and this further piece of evidence can be related to the conflict between Luvah and Urizen. The rise of lust and the intervention of death are features of the Fall which Blake finds it difficult to separate: they are related perversions of human energy.

Luvah	Cain	Ham
Urizen	—	Noah
Tharmas	Abel	—
Los	Tubal-Cain	—

In his evolution of the cycle, Blake has constructed a mythological pattern by which he can tell the story of the Fall in full, showing the intimate relationship between the rise of lust and the beginnings of murder. A further range of symbolism lay open to him. The story of Cain and Abel was sometimes read as an allegory of the ages of civilization. The tillers of the soil, steadily seeking to extend their lands, had gradually encroached upon and destroyed the pastures of the wandering herdsmen and then used their new gains for the building and enrichment of cities.[6] Such traditions gave Blake the cue for a further development. So far his figures, being no more than functions of the human body, had a shadowy existence. What better than to give them solid flesh and blood by making each the representative of a form of human industry?

For Luvah, the choice of occupation was clear. Since he was related both to Cain, the shedder of human blood, and to Ham, the son who made his father drunk with wine, he should be a vine-dresser. Wine, by its association both with human blood and with sexual energy, was a natural symbol for the ambiguity of the energies of love. And if Luvah was to be associated with Wine, it was appropriate for Urizen to be associated with Bread. The symbolism could be extended to all the stages of its production, moreover, Urizen being made the ploughman of Eternity (giving scope for byplay both with the constellation of the Plough, which points in the sky to the starry Pole, and with Blake's own 'horses of Reason'); the Reaper who puts in his sickle to gather the harvest; and finally the Baker who kneads and makes the bread of human wisdom. The functions of Tharmas and Urthona were already suggested by the Cain story. Tharmas was quite naturally the Shepherd, symbol of pastoral innocence; while Urthona was the Smith (the lame smith of many traditional myths) and Los his representative, a worker in metals.

At about the time that he began work on his epic Blake was illustrating Young's *Night Thoughts*, arranging the actual pages of poetry within his visual design, so that vast figures emerged around the printed text. In the same way his picturing of the Energies as Cosmic Workmen gave them an immediate reality and grandeur which they had not previously possessed:

Luvah	Cain	Ham	Vine-dresser
Urizen	—	Noah	Ploughman
Tharmas	Abel	—	Shepherd
Los	Tubal-cain	—	Smith

The four Energies, or Zoas, as Blake was to call them, were now both rooted in biblical tradition and given flesh and blood as cosmic Workmen. Other speculations of Blake's are still at work, relating them both to tradition and to his own thought. They can be related to the four levels of vision: for if Urizen already exists in single vision and Los in twofold, Tharmas's murdered pastoral landscape is clearly the landscape of threefold vision, while the domain of Luvah is that of the lost fourfold vision. And the whole cycle is reminiscent of the story in Daniel where the three men of God, flung into the fiery furnace, were seen as four, the fourth being 'like unto the son of God'.[7] Only the rebirth of Man in the fires of fourfold vision can re-harmonize his warring energies. The other organization of the Zoas, in terms of parts of the human body, is also related to the Book of Daniel. In that book there appears the vision of a man, his head of gold, his breast of silver, his thighs of brass and his two feet of iron and clay respectively.[8] The paradigm introduces yet another run of symbolism into Blake's scheme: that of Love as gold, Wisdom as silver, fallen sexual love as brass and mere physical creativity as iron. The additional touch that one foot is iron, the other clay, suggests the double rôle of Los, half in touch with the earth, half cut off from it by his devotion to the binding of matter. (Urthona, on the other hand, is wholly in touch with the earth.) So the Fall can be related to the four traditional ages of humanity—the ages of gold, silver, brass and iron—leaving Los dominant in the Age of Iron as the only positive creative energy. Our scheme can now be produced still further, therefore:

Luvah	Cain	Ham	Vine-dresser	Heart	Gold
Urizen	—	Noah	Ploughman	Head	Silver
Tharmas	Abel	—	Shepherd	Thighs	Brass
Los	Tubal-Cain	—	Smith	Feet	Iron

At this point, however, even while one is admiring the neatness with which various traditional patterns have all been fitted to a single scheme, one observes the presence of stresses and strains. The interchange of gold and silver to represent heart and head respectively may be justified by the fact that head and heart themselves exchange functions at the Fall, but there are ways in which the various patterns of symbolism do not march happily together. All the symbolism fits together at some point, but whereas some parts fit organically and completely, others are held in place by the poet's wit. To make Luvah a wine-dresser, for example, is to symbolize brilliantly the part of love in Blake's Fall-drama, whereas to make Urizen a ploughman is rather to show ingenuity in the working out of parallels between the production of wheat and bread and the workings of Reason. Similarly, whereas the parts of body associated with Luvah, Urizen and Tharmas do in fact have an actual psycho-physical relevance, each being the site of a specific function, the association of the feet with Los is less convincing.

Blake's myth-making did not stop there. More traditions could be invoked and brought into the picture, particularly the heathen myths associated with the Fall of Man. The story of Isis, Osiris and Typhon, for example, could be regarded as another version of the tradition behind Abel and Cain. Osiris, god of the true sun, slain by a usurping Typhon and then sought endlessly by the moon-goddess who is trying to re-create him, provides a perfect parallel with the lost Man, dimly remembered and yearned after by the four Zoas, but now existing only in destructive heat. So also with the story of Cupid and Psyche: Psyche seeks her lost, winged lover who to the cold eye of her rational sisters is no more than a destructive serpent.

These traditions no doubt helped with the formation of another element in the Zoa-cycle, so far hardly touched upon. We have already examined the *Book of Ahania*, in which the woman rejected by Urizen utters her complaint as she remembers him in his glory. Now Blake gives *each* of his Zoas a female counterpart, or 'emanation'. Each is cut off from her Zoa, but in each case the relationship is slightly different. It is with Ahania that the separation is most complete. Tharmas has an emanation called Enion; from this point in the cycle the concept of the spectre and emanation becomes active. As Isis seeks Osiris (or Psyche Cupid), Enion continually seeks her lost lover, only to be rebuffed by the wrath of Tharmas, who acts the rôle of Typhon. And the other part of the myth, the idea that Isis actually creates her lost lover, as the moon continually 'creates' the lost sun only to lose it again as it wanes, seems partly to account for the nature of Enitharmon. Her very name suggests Tharmas in the arms of Enion, even as Osiris is said to grow within the arms of Isis: she has the same longing to bring forth the lost sun or Osiris of fourfold vision. So while Enion and Tharmas are somewhat shadowy figures, constantly seeking each other, Los and Enitharmon play the rôles respectively of creating sun and moon.

The 'emanation' associated with Luvah is particularly important. In the moment of separation caused by the Fall, Luvah finds himself confronted by her: she is called Vala. She too bears a resemblance to Isis, the goddess of all nature. Nature was regarded by the ancients as the 'veil of Isis': those who could lift the veil would understand the inmost secrets of the universe. Vala represents a similar ambiguity of Nature.

> A man that looks on glasse,
> On it may stay his eye;
> Or if he pleaseth, through it passe,
> And then the heav'n espie.[9]

George Herbert's stanza gives the clue. A man can see Nature as an end in itself, the ultimate revelation of truth, or look through it to see the reality which it half reveals, half veils. To those who have lost Vision, Nature is the ultimate; the visionary, on the other hand, looks through nature and sees it as the 'signature of all things', revealing the true nature of humanity and reconciling man's inward nature with the inward nature of the universe.

The idea of Vala was of great importance to Blake at this time: his epic was originally named after her. In the beginning, evidently, he regarded the idea which she represented as the controlling one of his poem, giving shape to all lesser myths of the loss of Vision. He also introduced one or two other myths. The myth of lost Atlantis, for example, provides a source for the disaster which overtakes Tharmas. His pastoral landscape is flooded by the ocean—a symbol of the 'deluge of the senses' which swamps true Vision and deifies Vala, leaving the tops of the sublime mountains as desolate rocks in the sea. Again, the myth of the Fall of Chronos may have helped to shape the Urthona segment in the cycle. There is a suggestion that, with the retirement of Urthona, Eternity is transformed into a world where Time and Space are necessary mercies. Los's binding of the sun is used to represent his control of time, the beating of his hammer the steady pulsation of days, seasons and years. Enitharmon, on the other hand, takes charge of space. As moonlight creates a unity of tone in the landscape which it illuminates, so she reduces space to a unity. In the background can be sensed one of Blake's most interesting ideas. Instead of the dead sun of Urizen's world, he projects the idea of a sun which exists to contain and conserve energy, and which is constantly created by the 'hammer of Los' in order that the lost energy of Vision may not be altogether dissipated. Similarly, space is constantly being woven by Enitharmon as an act of mercy, that human spirits may have existence. What to the eye of single vision seems a dead mechanical world is really an exciting universe of creation, in which Eternity constantly grants to man a regulated Time and Space so that he may exist in his limited person, neither utterly consumed by the force of cosmic energy nor shrinking away into non-existence through lack of a place in which to extend himself. Time and Space are the mercy of Eternity. Moreover, these truths are reiterated in the sexual lives of men and women, where the hammer-beat of the male sexual force and the opening of female tenderness into new creation are constant emblems of the four-fold and threefold vision in which human beings were intended to walk.

Los and Enitharmon have thus advanced to the centre of Blake's stage. But by now he has also constructed behind them a great pattern of mythological ideas, all intended to play their parts in the great epic which he plans. It is easy to see how the curious homogeneity of these various patterns would fascinate and even obsess him as he worked: it would be hard to resist the conclusion that he was not just building a particularly happy mythology, but reconstructing the hidden truth of things.

Yet massive problems also faced him. First of all lay the difficulty, experienced by many modern writers of metaphysical fiction, of creating a narrative which could reveal an under-lying mythological pattern without doing violence to the mechanics of the story simply as a story. The pattern behind the story, moreover, was not simple. It consisted of the running together of schemes standing for quite different strands of human experience: the faculties of the human body; the points of compass; the Ages of mankind; the forms of human industry; the biblical accounts of the Fall; and finally Blake's own version of the moments of the Fall of Man, and the stages of his re-demption. To have run together some of these strands might have resulted in an interesting psychological myth. To run them all together and at the same time hope to produce a narrative poem was a feat of wild and hopeless ambition. Nevertheless Blake, fired by the power of his own vision, excited by the ferment of his ideas and spurred on by the weight of mythological tradition that seemed to support what he had to say, set to work.

Throughout his labour, moreover, he could sustain himself with the conviction that in one sense the labour of the imagina-tion carried its own divine self-justification—a self-justification that had been argued for by Christian writers more orthodox than himself. When, for example, he writes of one of his female figures that 'her bright eyes behold the Abyss' and that as a result she wanders, 'repelld on the margin of Non Entity',[10] his language sounds like a direct reflection of the seventeenth-century platonist, John Smith, who wrote that God

> would not raise up (the soul) to such *Mounts of Vision*, to shew it all the glory of that Heavenly *Canaan* flowing with eternal and unbounded pleasures, and then tumble it down again into that deep and darkest Abyss of Death and Non-entity.[11]

In that sense, Blake might reflect, what his imagination created for other men must, by its very sustaining power, be a form of truth.

This was not all. In other prophetic books and notebook writings he makes many references, some oblique, some direct, to the importance of the liberated phallic consciousness for the artist. He even personified it in the form of his Antamon whose 'soft hands . . . draw the indelible line: / Form immortal with golden pen.'[12] This phallic consciousness, moving back and forth between fiery sublimity and tender pathos, would be a central presence in his epic poem: it is creative of the world which Urizen has lost. The illustrations to the manuscript of *Vala*[13] bring this out very strongly: they fill out the significance of the text, making it clear that the apocalypse towards which the poem is moving is not a Last Judgment at the end of time, but a self-realization available to man at every moment. Blake's movement towards a conjunction of mythologies, in the same way, always falls back towards his own human experience and his desire to make it universal. Others might interpret their lives as they wished; for him there was no doubt that at those moments when his phallic awareness harmonized his perceptions or fired his imagination to create human forms of visionary tenderness or glory he was delivered into a world more real than that world of space and time, under the changeless face of Destiny, which the eighteenth-century rationalists inhabited.

6 Towards a Supreme Fiction

To read *The Four Zoas* now is like walking through an ancient city which has seen several civilizations. Here a group of pillars indicates a temple, there a frieze survives in isolation, elsewhere we enter a Christian basilica. It is only by taking thought that the traveller can see the various visions, the different shaping forces, that were felt in the city at one time or another. Yet this does not prevent him from stopping and admiring, at this point or that, the finished piece that meets his eyes. And behind all these fragments there may still lurk the haunting sense of a unifying *genius loci*.

Blake never published his poem. The manuscript version which survives is full of corrections, rewritings and marginal insertions which indicate his frequent dissatisfactions and changes of plan (see Appendix Three). In plotting a way through it we become aware of his constant gropings towards an organizing pattern, palimpsests of imagination in which one piece of mythologizing after another is brought into prominence for the purpose of giving an over-riding coherence and unity.

Certain organizing themes remain constant, however. The theme of 'levels of vision' is no longer an important organizing force. Instead, the scheme of energies that we have seen Blake evolving is used to provide a landscape and an activity of epic scope.

For the form of his work Blake had looked in the past to Milton and the Bible: a more recent book now seemed to offer a looser, more flexible structure for his visionary epic. At the time when he set to work on the first version of the poem he was, as we have seen, busy with a scheme to illustrate the whole of Young's *Night Thoughts*, providing an 'illumination' for every page; he now took over Young's division of his poem into 'Nights' as a suitably open structure for his own work. He also shared some of Young's preoccupations. Young is firmly in the tradition of eighteenth-century moralizing wisdom, but his central, obsessive theme is that since death is ever-imminent, man in time is always 'about to be judged'. There were enough apocalyptic preachings abroad in the air during the 1790's to give the theme contemporary relevance. Blake, in his customary manner, cut through the moralizing to the central preoccupation and then gave it the impress of his own views. Eternity for him was not something evermore about to be, but something that is constantly being revealed in the whole process of human history. Men may dimly remember Eternity; they may dimly foresee it: so far as they are possessed by vision they also live in Eternity at this moment. So Blake is concerned not with the morality of living each day as though it were the last, but with the morality of living each day in the light of the Eternity that is always here. His point of difference from Young is epitomized in the fact that he at first called his poem *Vala*. The veil that can either hide men from eternity or reveal it to them is for him the great fact in the world, the one which explains all other problems of good and evil.

In the construction of the poem two forces were to dominate. Since it was to be a *Paradise Regained* as well as a *Paradise Lost*, it was important that positive forces should be at work as well as negative. Materials for these were already to hand in the mythological sections of the political books and works such as *The Book of Urizen*. An important element in the unravelling of the action would be the binding of Urizen, followed by the birth of Orc, the consequent stirring of Urizen, and the final apocalypse.

Behind these struggles, however, there would lie a further pattern, to explain how the participants arrived at their present situation. The various characters in the drama are set one against the other because they have all lost the primal unity which formerly possessed them as members of one body. None is fully aware of what has happened, for in isolation none can put together the original picture. Only in moments of prophetic insight will one or another recall a primeval catastrophe, which he will try to describe in the terms available to him. These moments constitute a series of 'flash-backs', by means of which the nature of the Eternal Man will be recalled.

This basic factor in the construction must be borne in mind if the poem is to make sense at all. Critics often write of the Eternal Man as though he were another character in the story, instead of being the one character in which all the others find their original unity.

Originally Blake seems to have intended to give Vala the chief position in his story, since the idea which she embodies, that of a Nature who could either be worshipped as the ultimate order in the universe or looked 'through' by the penetrating eye of human imagination, was to him a key to all human decline. But this idea, however central, was essentially undramatic in nature. One cannot create a proper dramatic struggle out of a fading. Accordingly Blake widened the scope of the action to include all the human forces that were disrupted by the decline. The beginning of the poem as finally formulated ('The Song of the Aged Mother') declares the theme in terms of the Four Zoas:

Four Mighty Ones are in every Man: a Perfect Unity
Cannot Exist. but from the Universal Brotherhood of Eden,
The Universal Man. To whom be Glory Evermore Amen
(I, 9-11)

Many of Blake's hesitations and over-writings in the poem were due to the problems created by this much more complex plot, and they can be mentioned in their place. Other problems were created by the growth of mythological and schematic significances, as outlined in the last chapter. The most profound problems, however, were only reflected in these technical difficulties: they arose from the interworking of various ideas in Blake's mind: his desire to present an epic poem which would be immediately relevant to his time; his preoccupation with the deleterious effects of devotion to natural and moral law; his sense that such devotion reflected some further disorder in the psyche as it had developed in human civilization; and his related conviction that the human failures of his time were intimately related to the failure of artists to exercise imagination to the fulness of its power. Although these themes are working together throughout the poem, the nature of its success and failure will become clearer if each is examined in turn.

I Contemporary relevance
Since *The Four Zoas* incorporates segments from the Preludia to
America and *Europe*, with their direct reference to political and
social events, it is natural to look for similar references in this
longer poem. One cannot look at a poem which concludes in a
massive apocalypse without asking oneself whether the whole
story of the poem may not be a veiled account of England in
the 1790s, with all its apocalyptic rumblings.

In one sense it is, of course; but it is a mistake to look for too
many contemporary references or for 'prophecy' in the popular
sense. Blake never claimed to foretell the immediate future.
Although he spoke of many of his works as 'prophetic books',
he was careful to define his view of prophecy:[1]

> Prophets in the modern sense of the word have never existed
> Jonah was no prophet in the modern sense for his prophecy of
> Nineveh failed Every honest man is a Prophet he utters his
> opinion both of private matters Thus If you go on So the result
> is So He never says such a thing Shall happen let you do what
> you will. a Prophet is a Seer not an Arbitrary Dictator.

The passages in the poem which are directly relevant to the
1790s come at a late stage in the plot: the revolutionary activities of the late eighteenth-century are seen as final stages in a
long process. They have come about because the 'decline of the
Zoas' has reached its lowest point: it is only when Urizen's
success in creating an isolated universe has also locked him in
despair that the fire of revolutionary energy reaches flashpoint.

This moment of despair comes in Night the Sixth, an expanded version of the chapter in *The Book of Urizen* which described Urizen exploring his dens. Tharmas, hearing Urizen's
curses, feels an urge to bring all things to death. The incident,
evidently modelled upon the briefer exploration of Hell by
Satan in *Paradise Lost*, also bears a distinct resemblance to the
wanderings of Tiriel. Urizen meets three women at a river who
prevent him from drinking enough water to slake his thirst.
The first is filling an urn and pouring it forth, the second is
drawing all into a fountain of attraction, the third is dividing
the current into four. The reference here is evidently to the
exclusive cult of sense-perception: the fountain and river of
life in Eden have here been brought under rational control.

(Blake once suggested that the four streams that flowed through
Eden represented the four senses[2]). Urizen, in another speech
of reminiscence, recalls their former glory, adorned with jewels
and flowers, and making music. In words like those of Tiriel[3]
he curses them, that they in their turn may curse Tharmas
and Los:

> Go forth sons of my curse Go forth daughters of my abhorrence
> (VI, 46)

Tharmas (by now a sea-god figure) hears Urizen's voice and
meets his progress by freezing his waves solid. He proposes to
Urizen a pact of death. Since he wishes to die, he will withhold
food from Urizen if Urizen will withhold light from him. In
this way both may hope to die. Urizen takes no notice, but
continues his exploration, struggling with horrible monsters of
the deep. He sees many visions of suffering humanity: columns
of women marching over deserts, multitudes shut up in mountains and rocks, their senses limited, self-enclosed:

> Oft he stood by a howling victim Questioning in words
> Soothing or Furious no one answerd every one wrapd up
> In his own sorrow howld regardless of his words, nor voice
> Of sweet response could he obtain tho oft assayd with tears
> He knew they were his Children ruind in his ruind world
> (VI, 126–30)

In the East, Luvah's realm, all is void, so that Urizen finds
himself constantly either falling or struggling upwards. His
attempts to find a way by creating a world of abstract science
meet with no success: he has created only a point of reference,
not a firmament. The consequent nightmare state is described
in surrealist terms:

> Creating many a Vortex fixing many a Science in the deep
> And thence throwing his venturous limbs into the Vast unknown
> Swift Swift from Chaos to chaos from void to void a road immense
>
> For when he came to where a Vortex ceasd to operate
> Nor down nor up remaind then if he turnd & lookd back
> From whence he came twas upward all. & if he turnd and
> viewd
> The unpassd void upward was still his mighty wandring. . . .
> (VI, 187–93)

Urizen laments his lot, the loss of the old world of innocence on the plains and laughter under the oaks. Eventually he determines to use the Mountains of Brass as a foundation for his rebuilding. He continues to create 'Vortexes' which operate on all the sons of men, cutting off their vision of eternity; these Vortexes form no palace but a mighty spider's web dragging behind him in the darkness, and torn by the shrieks of the human beings whom it enslaves.

Finally he comes into the darkest world of all, the world of Urthona, where he is greeted by Urthona's shadow, Los:

> A spectre Vast appeard whose feet & legs with iron scaled
> Stampd the hard rocks expectant of the unknown wanderer. . . .
> (VI, 298–9)

Los summons his own armies, 'his fifty two armies / From the four Cliffs of Urthona'—the forces, in other words, of Time organized into weeks and seasons; seeing his warlike gestures, Urizen retires into his web. The scene recalls the incident in *Paradise Lost* where Satan retires after facing Gabriel's forces:

> th' Angelic Squadron bright
> Turn'd fierie red, sharpning in mooned horns
> Thir Phalanx, and began to hemm him round. . . .[4]

Here, however, the squadrons of Urthona, a more sombre band, help Urizen on his way:

> Slow roll the massy Globes at his command & slow oerwheel
> The dismal squadrons of Urthona. weaving the dire Web
> In their progressions & preparing Urizens path before him

With these lines (which show, incidentally, that he can handle rhythm in rolling sequences as well as in vital bursts of energy), Blake brings to a close the sixth Night. The next Night follows in ordered sequence, with Urizen descending finally to the Caves of Orc. There he sees the energies which he has handed over to Luvah, no longer harnessed to true Vision but rearing in the rage of twofold vision:

> the horses of Urizen
> Here bound to fiery mangers furious dash their golden hoofs
> Striking fierce sparkles from their brazen fetters. fierce his lions

Howl in the burning dens his tygers roam in the redounding
  smoke
In forests of affliction . . .

(VIIa, 6-10)

Urizen has passed through several regions, but his confrontation now with Orc is final and absolute. It is the revolutionary
situation: the confrontation, inherent in many of the prophetic
books, between dominating Reason and unfettered Energy.
So, while the limbs of Orc cast forth smoke and fire, Urizen
sends forth snows and storms to cool the flames, meeting the
pulses of energy with the carefully spelled out laws of his book
of iron. Subsequently the root of Mystery produces a Tree
which spreads rapidly until Urizen is shut in.

Urizen addresses Orc. His weary reproaches are remarkably
like those of Milton's God the Father concerning Satan:[5]

Image of dread whence art thou whence is this most woful place
Whence these fierce fires but from thyself . . .

(VIIa, 44-5)

He recalls his own selflessness in coming to help Orc:

Pity for thee movd me to break my dark & long repose
And to reveal myself before thee in a form of wisdom. . . .

(VIIa, 57-8)

To his surprise, he has found that Orc laughs at all tortures.
Is it, he asks, that he is moved by visions of sweet bliss, of rivers
of delight and verdant fields, so lovely that they urge him on in
rage to rend his chain; or is his joy founded on the torments
which others bear for him?

Orc replies in scorn and contempt, telling him to go and
scatter his snows elsewhere. If he rages, it is because his feet
and hands are nailed to the rock: otherwise Urizen would feel
the effects of his enmity and hate. Urizen, unable to grasp that
the desire for liberty should be so strong in anyone, replies
calmly, urging Orc to learn of his books and science: his sons
will teach him how to make war scientifically, his daughters
how to knead the bread of sorrow without raging. At his command, his daughters show themselves, kneading the bread of
Orc while singing the words of Urizen's book of iron. When at
last they ask for rest, Urizen replies by reading them a lecture of

his 'Wisdom', on the theme, 'Let Moral Duty tune your tongue. / But be your hearts harder than the nether millstone.' At this point his principles show themselves to be, explicitly, a means to domination by the impoverishment of man.

> Compell the poor to live upon a Crust of bread by soft mild arts
> Smile when they frown frown when they smile & when a man
>   looks pale
> With labour & abstinence say   he looks healthy & happy
> And when his children sicken let them die there are enough
> Born even too many & our Earth will be overrun
> Without these arts. . . .
>
> (VIIa, 117–21)

The argument continues in this vein, concluding with a picture of the growing race of Los, and the danger that they will devour all.

Orc remains defiant in his revolutionary energy, however, and Blake brings in the part of his myth which he first used as a Preludium to *America*. The Nameless Shadowy Female, now called the Nameless Shadowy Vortex, stands before Orc, who tears himself free from the rock and rends her. As he does so, the Elemental Gods sing a song of battle, recalling the former battle which resulted in the death of Luvah (parallel in many of its features with the death of Christ):

> They give the Oath of blood they cast the lots into the helmet,
> They vote the death of Luvah & they naild him to the tree
> They pierced him with a spear & laid him in a sepulcher
> To die a death of Six thousand years bound round with desolation.
>
> (VIIb, 165–8)

Orc and Luvah are, of course, complementary figures of the human heart. If the energy of Luvah is nailed to the tree, as in the crucifixion of Christ, its resurgence, in the shape of revolutionary energy, is bound to take place in the course of time. Yet it is Jesus, not Orc, who has the true human form, so that the divine humanity, however etiolated, is evident in the human Christ of the gospels rather than in any figure produced by revolution.

The slow reawakening of the Eternal Man, here prefigured, is outwardly expressed by Los and Enitharmon, with their creative works of compassion and love: Los declares that he can see the Divine Vision in Enitharmon's broken heart and she that she can see the Lamb of God. While the dead in Beulah continue to be drawn down by the attraction of the Shadowy Female into the darkened single vision of Ulro, Los and Enitharmon stand ready, as before, to give them forms. Enitharmon weaves them in her looms while Los stands by her, able to unite himself with her again by means of her broken heart. So the Divine Hand is at work and the Divine Countenance shines forth in their city of Golgonooza. The daughters of Beulah, looking down, see there the Divine Vision and the 'Human form', Jesus.

Urizen is mystified by this new incarnation of Luvah as the Lamb of God, since he already exists as the serpent Orc. Orc, moreover, is rearing in greater and greater pride, fed by the Shadowy Female on the fruit of his Tree of Mystery, which is kneaded into food by his daughters. However, Urizen gives the signal for war against the world of Los. As it progresses, he sees, to his astonishment, that it is taking the unexpected form of a shadowy hermaphrodite (the degradation of Orc and the Shadowy Female—the unholy union of war and religion as the Beast and the Whore). So the hermaphroditic form (which had belonged, in the earliest brief draft, to Tharmas[6]) at last appears in the poem.

As the terrors unleashed by Urizen approach the world of Los and Enitharmon, however, they are compelled by the power of the forces at work there into human forms and begin to rend one another: eventually, they fall back into the forms of animals and retire in meanness to await new warfare or to practise secret religion. Urizen creates still more inhuman forms of warfare in order to pervert all the senses and establish his dominion, 'even at the cost of every thing that breathes'. The Night ends with a description of Los and Enitharmon building the sepulchre for the Lamb, while in the synagogue of Satan a decision is taken to burn down the tree of Mystery with fire and form another from her ashes. This is to be a new form of Deism, or Natural Religion, the re-incarnation of Mystery in the eighteenth-century.

All is now ready for the final Apocalypse, which happens in the end simply. At the beginning of Night the Ninth, which opens with a brief mention of Los and Enitharmon building Jerusalem 'over the Sepulchre and over the Crucified body', Los, terrified at Non Existence, suddenly stretches out his hands and tears down the Sun and Moon, cracking the heavens across. The incident includes a Resurrection *motif*: Man, after imprisonment in the Sepulchre of the senses, is, by rending the fixities of the Newtonian universe, rolling away the rock at the door of his cave.

At the moment of Los's action, the fires of Eternity fall, while the sound of a trumpet is heard calling the dead to waken and come to Judgment from the four winds. Blake's poetry rises to new heights as he describes the heavens shaken and the earth removed. The poor and the slaves rise up at last against their oppressors, for whom there is no escape. In the distance the spectre of Enitharmon and the spectre of Urthona embrace like two shadows beneath the ruins of the universe.

The books of Urizen and the serpent of Orc are alike consumed and there is a long description of the ensuing destruction. At last not one of Mystery's tyrants is left on earth and the flames begin to enter the Holy City:

> living flames winged with intellect
> And Reason round the Earth they march in order flame by flame
> From the clotted gore & from the hollow den
> Start forth the trembling millions into flames of mental fire
> Bathing their Limbs in the bright visions of Eternity
>
> (IX, 86–90)

This is a repetition of the situation in Blake's *America* where, despite their destructiveness, the flames of revolution were to the men and women whom they engulfed a revelation of the living potencies of energy.

When, finally, Urizen sees his error, the whole universe explodes. The vast destruction that results is also a new birth in which all existing things retain their lineaments, though not in any idealized form: the victims still have the marks of their sufferings, the tyrants the marks of their dominance:

> And all the marks remain of the slaves scourge & tyrants Crown
> And of the Priests oergorged Abdomen, & of the merchants thin
> Sinewy deception & of the warriors outbraving & thoughtlessness
> In lineaments too extended & in bones too strait & long
>
> (IX, 246–9)

A 'Cold babe' stands in the 'furious air', denouncing the warriors and tyrants who have been responsible for the deaths of infants through the ages. As the flames roll more strongly, the innocent prisoner stands before the Judge while the Judge pleads forgiveness for his error.

The moment of exposure and revelation is followed by the completion of the Apocalypse in the form of a great Harvest, and this in turn by a harvest Feast at which the Eternals sum up the lessons learnt from the human experience:

> . . . divided all
> In families we see our shadows born, & thence we know
> That Man subsists by Brotherhood & Universal Love
> We fall on one anothers necks more closely we embrace
> Not for ourselves but for the Eternal family we live
> Man liveth not by Self alone   but in his brothers face
> Each shall behold the Eternal Father & love & joy abound
>
> (IX, 636–42)

So far as the social content of the poem is concerned, it is the final summing-up. The Feast itself reflects many references in the Christian gospel to the 'kingdom of heaven' as a great feast, and the vision presented in these lines reflect Blake's belief (based also, perhaps, on certain gospel sayings) that the kingdom of heaven exists whenever brotherhood exists. 'Where two or three are gathered together in my name there am I in the midst of them': in Blake's interpretation the lineaments of the Father are made visible when men look at the faces of one another with a penetration that sees the divine image in each.

At the end of the harvest Urizen rises with his flail, Tharmas with his winnowing fan, to thresh out the nations, the stars from their husks. In a newly humanized world Mystery goes down to be destroyed while slaves and prisoners are released to walk in liberty. A passage from *America*[7] is brought in to express their feelings as they walk through a world which seems more like a dream:

> How is it we have walkd thro fires & yet are not consumd
> How is it that all things are changd even as in ancient time

> The Sun arises from his dewy bed & the fresh airs
> Play in his smiling beams giving the seeds of life to grow
> And the fresh Earth beams forth ten thousand thousand springs of
>   life

The lines illustrate the place of Blake's social concern throughout the poem: injustice and tyranny are passionately condemned, but are always seen as part of a larger human failure.
It is the nature of that fuller failure that is his major concern.

II   Establishment of the Moral Law

If the contemporary reference of *The Four Zoas* is most evident
in the second half of the poem, where despair is followed by
revolution, revolution by Urizen's attempts to contain the
feared energy, and the resulting tyrannical wars by a final
apocalypse renewing all things, that is because the poem as a
whole has a further aim. Contemporary events are to be given
an interpretative context; they are to be shown as late elements
in a process which had been set in motion by other forces,
notably the establishment of moral and natural law.

The materials for expressing these two forces were already
available in Blake's developing mythology. The imposition of
natural law was a part of Urizen's aspiration to a permanent
universe, while the imposition of moral law could be represented in the decline of Tharmas from a delight in beauty
openly displayed to the hiding of his bride in secrecy and shame.

Which of these events should come first in the poem, however?
Many of the hesitations and over-writings in the early books
seem to be due to changes of mind on this question. At first
it seemed right that the failure of light should be given precedence, that the 'Let there be light' of Genesis should find a
counterpart in a gesture of decline at the beginning of Blake's
epic. This opening gesture is to be found in the lines at the
beginning of Night the Second which were at one point intended to open the whole poem:

> Turning his Eyes outward to Self. losing the Divine Vision
> Man calld Urizen & said. Behold these sickning Spheres . . .
> Take thou possession! take this Scepter! go forth in my might . . .[8]

Presumably, however, Blake realized that this decline of light
did not provide enough drama for the opening of his epic. It

was also important to bring in Los and Enitharmon at an early stage, since they were the most truly positive characters in the poem. He therefore decided to begin the work not with the darkening of Urizen but with the other prong of the human decline—the failure of genital beauty in the person of Tharmas, and its replacement by a cult of shame and jealousy. We hear at the beginning the voice of Tharmas, lamenting the loss of his Emanations. He declares that he has hidden Enion in jealous despair and that he will build her a Labyrinth (the story of Minos, king of Crete, is clearly in Blake's mind here as an archetypal story of jealousy and its eventual overthrow). Enion replies in words which are to be echoed in various forms by the other Emanations, complaining that she is threatened with non-existence by the new order, which changes values and puts Sin where she would formerly have seen joy.

> All Love is lost Terror succeeds & Hatred instead of Love
> And stern demands of Right & Duty instead of Liberty
> Once thou was to Me the loveliest son of heaven—But now
> Why art thou Terrible and yet I love thee in thy terror till
> I am almost Extinct & soon shall be a shadow in Oblivion
> Unless some way can be found that I may look upon thee & live
> Hide me some Shadowy semblance. secret whispring in my Ear,
> In secret of soft wings. in mazes of delusive beauty
> I have lookd into the secret soul of him I lovd
> And in the Dark recesses found Sin & cannot return.
>
> (I, 36–45)

Tharmas's answering counter-accusations show his resentment at the analytic attitude which she has taken over from Urizen.

> Why wilt thou Examine every little fibre of my soul
> Spreading them out before the Sun like Stalks of flax to dry
> The infant joy is beautiful but its anatomy
> Horrible Ghast & Deadly nought shalt thou find in it
> But Death Despair & Everlasting brooding Melancholy . . .
>
> (I, 47–51)

His is the torture of a vision that is being slowly strangled: he declares that he sees her sometimes as a flower expanding, or a fruit breaking from its bud in pain, while he remains an atom, a nothing—yet conscious still of possessing an identity. He sinks down into the sea as a pale corpse and simultaneously his

Spectre issues from his feet as a flame of fire. As it does so, Enion begins to create it, weaving it with analytic care. Eventually it is completed and springs up like Satan in *Paradise Lost* and *The Gates of Paradise*:[9]

> . . . in masculine strength augmenting he
> Reard up a form of gold & stood upon the glittering rock
> A shadowy human form winged   & in his depths
> The dazzlings as of gems shone clear, rapturous in fury
> Glorying in his own eyes   Exalted in terrific Pride. . . .
>
> (I, 125-9)

When his narcissistic rapture has continued for some time he seeks out Enion, who sees that she has murdered all the secret loves and graces of Tharmas; the spectre replies by announcing that from now on she will be held in bonds of jealousy. They join their bodies in a burning anguish and Enion brings forth two infants, a fierce boy and girl. As they grow up, these two wander away her and repel her into 'Non Entity'. They are revealed as Los and Enitharmon, possessing something of the vanished glory of Adam and Eve, but limited by the fallen world in which they find themselves and aware of an opposition between themselves and their parents. Enitharmon declares that their parents weary themselves in feeding them with delights, while they can return nothing but scorn—for if they were to show gratitude the parents would immediately withhold their love, which can only feed on thorns and bitter roots. In saying this she reveals their fallen state. Their passions move only by opposition—in Eden the passions would be freely expressed, freely accepted. Deprived of that freedom her scorn is bound to grow and direct itself against Los himself; and soon she is calling on Urizen to descend with horse and chariot to face Los. He does so, but then behaves according to his own laws rather than her expectations, offering a bargain. After they have eyed each other for some moments, he offers to deliver Luvah, 'the prince of Love', 'the murderer' into Los's hands; the starry hosts of Urizen will be the servants of Los if he obeys his law.

Los replies to Urizen in an equally unexpected manner, declaring that one or other must be master and that they should therefore try their arts against each other. Urizen, surprised at this directness and vigour, enquires suspiciously whether Los is 'a visionary of Jesus the soft delusion of Eternity'. He inveighs against the idea that man should war against his own spectre (which is what Los would in effect be doing in taking up arms against Urizen) and declares roundly

> The Spectre is the Man the rest is only delusion and fancy
> (I, 341)

As Urizen speaks, all his forces gather on the wind and sky to celebrate his victory, while Los and Enitharmon, having healed their quarrel, partake of the feast and enjoy all the delights of Urizen's world. Only in the distant bloody sky is the other side of their condition reflected: Luvah and Vala continue to sit lonely and in fierce jealousy, while above them Eternity appears as a single Man, suffering in the shape of Luvah.

The ambiguity of their condition continues in the next Night, where Enitharmon can sing to Los that 'every thing that lives is holy' and revive him by this momentary glimpse of vision and of the delights of desire, yet show even in the midst of her inspiration her will to dominate. Other stanzas show how she uses the delights of desire to achieve her purpose:

> The joy of woman is the Death of her most best beloved
> Who dies for Love of her
> In torments of fierce jealousy & pangs of adoration.
> The Lovers night bears on my song
> And the nine Spheres rejoice beneath my powerful controll . . .
> (II, 349–53)

In the world of Enitharmon that is here established, the delights of love are all harnessed to the one end of female domination. There can be no generous response from the woman, for her delight in the exercise of power is accompanied (and caused) by a fear of non-existence if she yields to the power of her lover:

> O I am weary lay thine hand upon me or I faint
> I faint beneath these beams of thine
> For thou hast touched my five senses & they answerd thee.
> Now I am nothing & I sink
> And on the bed of silence sleep till thou awakest me.
> (II, 374–8)

The negative implication in her song of joy is immediately brought out and given positive form in a further song. The singer is Enion, the empty womb, the woman deprived of sexual love, who expresses the very emptiness in Enitharmon which has caused her desire for domination. Her song of Experience is one of the finest that Blake ever wrote. As always, his powers are brought out to the full when he exposes the sorrows and injustices of men; in addition, his gift for writing in the style of proverbial wisdom is given full play:

> What is the price of Experience do men buy it for a song
> Or wisdom for a dance in the street? No it is bought with the price
> Of all that a man hath   his house his wife his children
> Wisdom is sold in the desolate market where none come to buy
> And in the witherd field where the farmer plows for bread in vain
>
> (II, 397-401)

There is no need to quote the whole of this hymn, which is one of Blake's best-known and most universal poems. The ease with which men look at sufferings of all kinds when they are not personally affected is indignantly and sadly described. In two lines of it Enion refers briefly to the central symbolism of the poem, picturing the universe in which she lives as a place where the dialectic between the sun of fourfold light and the moon and garden of threefold light exists no more, giving place to lower worlds of twofold energy and single vision:

> My heavens are brass   my earth is iron   my moon a clod of clay
> My sun a pestilence burning at noon & vapour of death in night
>
> (II, 395-6)

Such is the world of Urizen, a world of strictly controlled energies, in which Enion finds herself deprived of her true life and love. And when she sings, Ahania, the emanation of Urizen, hears her voice, which, by starting an uneasy echo in her own breast, disturbs her peace.

The misgivings grow, and Ahania tries to express them to Urizen. He will not listen; instead he is angered by what she says and casts her out. By the laws of Blake's universe, however, the fall of one is the fall of all: Urizen and his hosts plunge into the ocean. The visionary form of the human is thus submerged: and when it struggles to emerge again it can rear itself only in helpless wrath. It is Tharmas, figure of genital energy, that now rears himself as an impotently raging old man of the sea:

> Fury in my limbs. destruction in my bones & marrow
> My skull riven into filaments. my eyes into sea jellies
> Floating upon the tide wander bubbling & bubbling
> Uttering my lamentations & begetting little monsters
> Who sit mocking upon the little pebbles of the tide
> In all my rivers & on dried shells that the fish
> Have quite forsaken. O fool fool to lose my sweetest bliss
> Where art thou, Enion . . .
>
> (III, 162–9)

For Tharmas the fall of Urizen means the loss of Atlantis: he does not, in fact, see it as a fall at all: he experiences only an irruption into his settled world. His garden of delights has been flooded; his perception of the infinite has been destroyed by the 'deluge of the senses'. But of the process or cause he understands nothing—his phallic existence can deal only with an actual situation and begin from there.

The more Tharmas gives vent to his positive rage, the more Enion feels herself negated: while he roars to the heavens, she wanders 'like a cloud into the deep / Where never yet Existence came'. The separation between the two is now as complete as could be imagined; Enion's shadowy existence is indeed taken over by Ahania, who 'wanders in Eternal fear of falling into the indefinite', afraid to sleep lest she lose her precarious hold upon 'the margin of Non Entity'.

Blake at some point thought of putting Night the First immediately before Night the Fourth, the beginning of which could fittingly follow directly from a number of the 'final' lines in Night the First, including those where Los and Enitharmon

> . . . wanderd long, till they sat down upon the margind sea.
> Conversing with the visions of Beulah in dark slumberous bliss . . .
>
> (I, 245–6)

The fourth Night begins,

> But Tharmas rode on the dark Abyss. the voice of Tharmas rolld
> Over the heaving deluge. he saw Los & Enitharmon Emerge
> In strength & Brightness from the Abyss his bowels yearnd over
> them . . .

The important point, however, is that the new Night follows on equally from the separation between Tharmas and Enion *and* from the creation of Los and Enitharmon. Tharmas, continuing in his rage, sees the rise of Los and immediately hopes that he will prove an obedient son who will rebuild the universe without Urizen and Luvah and according to his own limitations:

> The all powerful curse of an honest man be upon Urizen & Luvah
> But thou My Son Glorious in brightness comforter of Tharmas
> Go forth Rebuild this Universe beneath my indignant power
> A Universe of Death & Decay.
>
> (IV, 25–8)

Los refuses the invitation. Recognizing in Tharmas only the contracted image of 'man', he rejects the death and decay which are implicit in this lowest form of human existence affirming his faith in Urizen. Urizen, however, is now fallen into the deep,

> And Los remains God over all.   weak father of worms & clay
> I know I was Urthona keeper of the gates of heaven
> But now I am all powerful Los & Urthona is but my shadow . . .
>
> (IV, 41–3)

(The irony here is complicated. It is one of Blake's deepest beliefs that humanity, when possessed by the Vision and Desire of which Urizen and Luvah are fallen shadows, accepts death and decay as natural processes. But when Vision and Desire fall apart into Reason and Energy, such acceptance ceases: death and decay then become, indeed, positively repulsive and terrible, while the universe itself is seen as a universe of death and vehemently rejected. So it is with the visionless Los. Instead, he puts his faith in the impersonal permanence and stability of Urizen's order. But the world which he is thus rejecting, the world of threefold vision, is still implied in his description of Tharmas as 'weak father of worms & clay' and in his defensive explanation of the fact that he is no longer Urthona, 'keeper of the gates of heaven'.)

While Tharmas and Los face one another, ready to destroy each other, Enitharmon cries out with a memory of the world that has been lost, blaming Tharmas for its overthrow. Tharmas replies by seizing Enitharmon and cutting her off from Los, so that the two of them are finally split into Spectre and Emanation. The Spectre, however, being that of earthy Urthona, still recognizes Tharmas as his former companion. From his position at the end of the cycle of the Zoas he cannot know the full story of the catastrophe that has overtaken them, only the part that affected pastoral Tharmas, the Zoa nearest to him. He asserts that Tharmas, once the mildest son of heaven, is now a rage and a terror to all living things; and recalls the day of his flight and fall, when he drew all the sons of Beulah into his vortex. It was then that Los protected Tharmas as he lay 'rotting on the rocks'.

These words rouse Tharmas to limited remembrance. The rough honesty which characterizes him again comes to the fore as he half-recognizes the Spectre:

> Art thou Urthona My friend my old companion,
> With whom I livd in happiness before that deadly night
> When Urizen gave the horses of Light into the hands of Luvah
> Thou knowest not what Tharmas knows. O I could tell thee tales
> That would enrage thee as it has Enraged me even
> From death in wrath & fury. . . .
>
> (IV, 111–16)

In this moment of recognition he offers to restore Enitharmon to the Spectre and urges him to aid Los in the binding of the fallen king, Urizen, so that he may not rise to power again. Like all the other Zoas, he imagines that he is now God. Yet as soon as he has said so, he recognizes the separation in his life which is caused by the loss of Enion, a separation which makes his state of power valueless:

> Is this to be A God far rather would I be a Man
> To know sweet Science & to do with simple companions
> Sitting beneath a tent & viewing Sheepfolds & soft pastures. . . .
>
> (IV, 146–8)

Turning from this reflection, he urges Los to set to work and rebuild his furnaces, setting before him the choice between death and life. He then leaves him to his work.

Los finds himself in the midst of a void, looking down upon the Chaos which is Urizen's ruined world,

A horrible Chaos to his eyes. a formless unmeasurable Death
Whirling up broken rocks on high into the dismal air
And fluctuating all beneath in Eddies of molten fluid

(IV, 162–4)

(One is reminded vividly of the mighty fountain of deadly
energy which Coleridge's Kubla Khan saw.[10]) Los immediately sets to work to tame the energy, and the story of the rebuilding of his furnaces and the creation of chains of hours, days
and years leads into the story of the Binding of Urizen, transferred almost verbatim from *The Book of Urizen*. The Night
concludes with a picture of Los (who in binding Urizen has
bound himself) responding to all the movements of Urizen and
Enitharmon ('his pallid lips / Unwilling movd as Urizen
howld . . . he lookd / With stony Eyes on Urizen') and existing
mainly as a pair of legs, his bones

dancing & howling   stamping the Abyss.

This image of Los dancing 'on his mountains high & dark as
heaven' (which recalls Satan's 'gestures fierce . . . and mad
demeanour' on Mount Niphates in *Paradise Lost*[11]) is carried
over directly into the opening of Night the Fifth. The Fall of
Man has now reached its lowest point; Los retires from the
furnaces, contracted to the limits of Man, and leaves Urizen,
cold and bound, opaque and lifeless. It is a scene of desolation,
relieved only by sounds of music which Enitharmon hears; even
these are constantly drowned by her groans.

At this point, however, a new, dynamic force is introduced
into the desolation of the scene. Enitharmon's groans are the
accompaniment of labour-pangs and she brings forth a terrible
child. The cycle of the Zoas being completed, Demons of the
Deep think they recognize the child as Luvah, formerly king of
Love, but now returned as king of rage and death. They demand
the return also of Vala: once the queen with a bow and arrows
of light, but now about to draw a black bow and release arrows
of secret fires; once a 'fair crystal form divinely clear', but now
a dark wife producing serpents in the ribs of the male.

This deathly form of Vala does not, however, appear, for the
child is not Luvah but Orc. Enitharmon nurses him, and as
Los looks on in anguish and gloom, afraid that Eternal Death

will intervene, the chain of jealousy which he produced for Urizen appears again. Having assimilated some of the attributes of Urizen, Los is afraid that the new born boy, who embraces his mother but looks with malignant eyes at his father, will plot his death: and so, as in the *Book of Urizen*, the child is taken to a high mountain and there bound by the chain of jealousy to a rock (cf. fig. 16).

The final effect of the moral law is now apparent. What was begun between Tharmas and Enion had grown into a struggle for domination between Los and Enitharmon; the jealousy of Enitharmon has in turn been given form by Los in the shape of the chain which binds Orc down.

The universe of jealousy is now complete, therefore, and must remain so. Even the action of Orc in tearing away from his roots and rending his manacles cannot heal the separation between spectre and emanation. The spectre of Los understands this better than Los himself, and his awareness that in all his ugliness and ill-doing he is still trying to reunite himself with Los's emanation leads him to try to bring Vala to the embraces of Orc, in the hope that their union, reflecting the union with Enitharmon that he himself desires, may help restore the state of Man to its former harmony: for even in his present brutish form he still knows where his true happiness would lie:

> Thou knowest that the Spectre is in Every Man insane brutish
> Deformd that I am thus a ravening devouring lust continually
> Craving & devouring but my Eyes are always upon thee O lovely
> Delusion & I cannot crave for anything but thee . . .
>
> (VIIa, 304–7)

The conferences between the Spectre and Enitharmon have one immediate result. A cloud is born, who awakens many of the dead into enmity, hatred and war. This is the Nameless Shadowy Female, destined to be Orc's emanation and to be embraced by him. Meanwhile, however, Enitharmon recounts to Los the story which the Spectre has told her, and Los begins to feel pity and then to humanize, giving up the lust for domination which has hitherto possessed him. The Spectre then reveals that he is Los's real self. Los formerly subdued him because he saw him as cruel lust and murder; he was right to condemn these qualities, but in casting them out so completely he was also depriving himself of his most important inward energies. Let him reunite with his Spectre and he will find himself existing not in one dimension but in three, which will, by mutual interaction, turn into four:

> . . . another better world will be
> Opend within your heart & loins & wondrous brain
> Threefold as it was in Eternity & this the fourth Universe
> Will be Renewd by the three & consummated in Mental fires . . .
>
> (VIIa, 353–6)

Los answers that he is a being who can be persuaded by reason, and that something within himself is responding to the Spectre's assertions.

> . . . Even I already feel a World within
> Opening its gates & in it all the real substances
> Of which these in the outward World are shadows which pass away . . .
>
> (VIIa, 364–6)

At this point, therefore, a complete reconciliation between Los, Enitharmon and the Spectre is possible. But now it is Enitharmon who runs away and hides under the Tree of Urizen. Even while Los is being reconciled to the Spectre and setting out upon the construction of Golgonooza, the new city founded upon the three energies of man, Enitharmon is speaking to him of the fruit of Urizen's Tree, by which she has come to know good and evil. She now knows, she says, that life feeds upon death and that she cannot be saved from Eternal Death without ransom. Her exposition of the Doctrine of the Atonement (a dogma abhorrent to Blake) is followed by a plea that Los will eat the same fruit and give her proof of life Eternal if he can.

Los obeys her injunction and finds himself also in danger of eternal death; but at this point the Spectre helps him. He, too, sees the need for ransom and redemption—but from the state of separation. He urges that counterparts be created for all the spectrous males who exist without a concentring vision. Simultaneously, Los has a vision of Luvah's other form: as the Lamb of God he complements Orc, the tiger of twofold vision:

> Turn inwardly thine Eyes & there behold the Lamb of God
> Clothed in Luvahs robes of blood descending to redeem . . .
>
> (VIIa, 415–16)

To Enitharmon he points out that this figure will be the ransom for which she is looking; to the Spectre, that Forgiveness will heal all divisions and separations.

Enitharmon replies that she sees the Lamb of God descending but is afraid that he will punish them with Eternal Death. She is filled with the guilt of Urizen's world; Los, on the other hand, still possessed by the sense of brotherhood which he has gained from his reunion with the Spectre, sees the whole situation differently. Ignoring her fears altogether, he tells her that their function is to serve as sacrificial victims on whose life the victims of war may feed—

> To form a world of Sacrifice of brothers & sons & daughters
> To comfort Orc in his dire sufferings . . .
>
> (VIIa, 443–4)

He sees the Lamb of God not as a condemning judge but as an example of self-giving humanity. Enitharmon in turn takes up the theme and develops it, urging Los to give forms to the piteous spectres:

> . . . if thou my Los
> Wilt in sweet moderated fury. fabricate forms sublime
> Such as the piteous spectres may assimilate themselves into
> They shall be ransoms for our Souls that we may live . . .
>
> (VIIa, 452–5)

Los follows her advice, drawing immortal lines upon the heavens, and Enitharmon releases the spectres, who assimilate to the forms. The first two forms to be created are Rintrah and Palamabron, the prophet and priest who for all their limitations are the only available agents for the energy of Orc and the tenderness of the Lamb of God in the eighteenth-century world. To his surprise, moreover, Los finds that it is Urizen that is delivered into his hands. Once assimilated to a form, he is no longer hostile to Los:

> . . . he wonderd that he felt love & not hate
> His whole soul loved him he beheld him an infant
> Lovely breathd from Enitharmon he trembled within himself
>
> (VIIa, 497–9)

This, however, is no more than a momentary enlightenment. The next Night begins with a return to Urizen beneath the Tree of Mystery, where he is planning the final stages of his design to take complete control of the heavens. He develops Trade and Commerce until slave-labour produces a groaning Universal Empire. He builds a temple in the image of the human heart and there involves all the works of love in secrecy.

The sun is forced to descend into the temple in order that it may give light to the abyss of Urizen, a world devoted to war by day and secret lust by night.

At the opposite extreme from this dark world lies the world of uncontrolled energy, where the rape of Vala by Orc has turned into endless destruction between them. As fast as Orc rends her his human form is consumed in his own fires. When nothing remains but his serpent form on the Tree of Mystery, this is removed to become a constellation in Urizen's heaven. While Orc has rent her life into a formless indefinite, she has ensured that this form of her vanished lover shall itself be vanquished.

The only force that can break into this remorseless logic of mutual destruction is that of rough honesty. When Tharmas, still searching for his lost Enion, encounters the Nameless Shadowy Female and learns who she is, he tells her of his loss, when Enion and how she turned away from him in the garden of delight. The Female replies that her loved one is hidden in the outrageous form of Orc, who torments her for her secret sins. Tharmas, in his honest innocence, perceives that something is wrong with her argument: he attacks her for wishing to keep her secret actions hidden and blames her for the curse which has overtaken all the Zoas, swearing that he will never depart from his present wrath until he can bring love into the light of day. His openness affects the Female, who goes abroad, seeing in Nature the presence of Luvah and reading everywhere the promise inscribed by the daughters of Beulah on all objects associated with death: 'If ye will believe your Brother shall rise again.' The daughters (with their echo of Mary and Martha)[12] are waiting with patience for the fulfilment of that promise, guarding their region against the rise of doubt from the Clouds of the Shadowy Female. In a world dominated by shame and jealousy, this guardianship is the only available resource: the bonds themselves cannot be broken without a more radical change, which will replace the alternating presences of Luvah and Orc by a reintegration of Luvah into his full human form, where the energy of Orc is at one with the compassion of Luvah, and Vala is restored to a world of organized innocence.

This is in fact the change that takes place in the last Night of the poem. Vala ceases to be the Namelesss Shadowy Female, tortured by her destructive relationship with Orc; she becomes a Psyche whose Cupid is no longer visualized in the form of a serpent but has been revealed in his full winged stature. The revelation restores her to the world of threefold innocence where she falls asleep on the fleece of a ram; while she sleeps, Luvah causes a house to be built for her (corresponding, as Miss Raine has pointed out,[13] to the house built by Cupid for Psyche).

In her sleep Vala sees Luvah 'like a spirit stand in the bright air'. When she awakes she is aware (like the Cloud who spoke of Luvah as the god of its universe in *Thel*) that he is the guardian of her flocks, which she leads down to the waters. The power of the moral law is not yet broken: Tharmas sits by the shore, still mourning for Enion, his limbs wrapped round by the weeds of death. As he lays down his head, Vala's voice, calling to Enion, comes echoing back to her as her own former cry to her lord:

> Where is the voice of God that calld me from the silent dew
> Where is the Lord of Vala dost thou hide in clefts of the rock
> Why shouldst thou hide thyself from Vala from the soul that wanders desolate
>
> (IX, 500–2)

In the world of Urizen it is not Adam but the Lord who hides. Vala's cry has its effect, nevertheless: reviving innocence begins to break the bonds of the moral law. When she goes back into her garden she finds Enion and Tharmas playing there as a girl and boy; she lets them sleep in her house. They are not yet reconciled, however. Enion still turns away from Tharmas, who fades into watery death as a result. It is only when Vala coaxes her into greater confidence that she consents to take his hand. They begin to learn through infant play, sorrow and joy alternating.

These glimpses of Enion and Tharmas, growing into human

form as the power of Urizen disintegrates, suggest something of
the nature of morality in Blake's visionary universe. When the
shame and separation created by consciousness of the law have
disappeared, man is left as a newborn child, needing to undergo
his moral education again from the beginning.

> Man was made for Joy & Woe
> And when this we rightly know
> Thro the World we safely go
> Joy & Woe are woven fine
> A Clothing for the Soul divine
> Under every grief and pine
> Runs a joy with silken twine[14]

This, the lesson that Enion and Tharmas are learning in their
new childhood, is, according to Blake, the lesson that all men
must learn when they release themselves from the Law. The
concurrence of vision and desire liberates a 'silken twine' of
imaginative energy which reveals joy as the ultimate binding
force in human nature and enables it to give a form to all grief
and woe, however pressing. Learning to live within this
dialectic between joy and woe men gradually discover the full
implications of their own human nature and its relationship
with others.

III   Establishment of the Natural Law

In Blake's view the establishment of moral and natural law
were inter-related developments in the decline from full vision.
The two stories must sometimes proceed in parallel, however,
or even develop separately. Since Night the First initiates the
reader into the dramatic contentions created by jealousy, for
example, Night the Second is largely devoted to setting in
motion the story of Urizen. This is the more literal 'loss of
vision'—it begins, indeed, with an account of the eternal Man
'turning his eyes outward to Self, losing the Divine Vision', and
handing over his rule to Urizen. As he gives him the sceptre
he hints at a conspiracy which has led to his weariness and
sleep:

> Thy brother Luvah hath smitten me but pity thou his youth
> Tho thou hast not pitid my Age   O Urizen Prince of Light
>   (II, 7–8)

Urizen at first exults at his new power, but his exultation turns to dismay when he sees beneath his feet the horrors of Death advancing upon the Eternal Man and the Abyss where Enion wanders. Against this danger of 'Non Existence' there can be only one remedy. Milton's Satan ordered the building of Pandaemonium;[15] Urizen orders a similar vast feat of construction. But as his various ministers set to work, the tigers of wrath, for example, harnessing the horses of instruction, the Human Imagination is petrified into rock and sand, and sounds of chaos and cruelty are heard. Furnaces are set up, into which Luvah and Vala are cast. Luvah's voice is heard from the furnaces, lamenting the change in his fortunes: the earth-worm which he nurtured has changed first into a serpent, then into a winged dragon, and finally into an infant whom he guarded jealously but who has now been taken from him. He himself was love, but hatred has awakened in him; Urizen, 'who was Faith & certainty is changd to Doubt'. And all has come about because he wished to deliver the sons of God from so-called 'bondage' of the Human form.

In this speech of Luvah's one of the most important points of the poem is made. The disharmony of the Zoas has come about because they wished to be delivered from the bondage of the Human, to become as 'gods'. But it is Luvah that is cast into bondage: his bulls pull the plough of Urizen and instead of the true light a fierce sulphur sun of heat gives illumination to the world. Devoid of Vision, the children of men set to work to measure the course of the sun and engage in commerce.

The Lions of Urizen continue the same work. making pyramids and dividing up the great deep with compasses. Other energies hang out vast curtains across the deep until the fabric of a palace is constructed. Three domes encompass the Golden Hall of Urizen where reposes the Shadowy Female Semblance —all that remains of his emanation (presently to separate from him completely and become Ahania).

At this point (and here the value of having already established their identity is evident) Los and Enitharmon descend to see the labour and sorrow of the operation. Meanwhile the voice of Vala is heard, a slave labourer like the children of Israel under Pharaoh, lamenting the afflictions of the workers:

> Our beauty is coverd over with clay & ashes, & our backs
> Furrowd with whips, & our flesh bruised with the heavy basket
> (II, 225–6)

The symbolism of the Zoas as parts of the human body appears for a moment as she sees Los:

> I see not Luvah as of old I only see his feet
> Like pillars of fire travelling thro darkness & non entity.
> (II, 229–30)

She does not even recognize Luvah now, despising him as he brings his love to her. Yet in the midst of all the sorrow the great work of Urizen arises in its beauty—

> a Golden World whose porches round the heavens
> And pillard halls & rooms recievd the eternal wandering stars
> (II, 241–2)

Heaven permits the work, for fear that man should perish altogether, while Jesus puts on the robes of blood to take the place of Luvah for the time being (a reference perhaps to the place of pietistic Christianity in the world of Reason: a mistaken form yet keeping alive certain values until a fuller revelation is possible).

The transition from Night the Second to Night the Third is facilitated by this incident. Urizen's establishment of supremacy over the world of Luvah and Vala is to be followed by a further assertion of absolute power on his part. The new development is introduced by the entrance of Ahania. Under the influence of Enion's song of desolation, she comes to plead with him to abandon his dark musings, which destroy the possibility of present joy. She points to the power that he enjoys over all things. Is it not enough?

Urizen, however, is by now becoming the traditional tyrant, who feels his dominion constantly threatened. As Herod feared the birth of a rival, who should be king in his place, Urizen is disturbed by the knowledge that

> . . . a Boy is born of the dark Ocean
> Whom Urizen doth serve, with Light replenishing his darkness.
> (III, 14–15)

The boy is of course Orc: his birth is the rebirth of Luvah—
'Luvah in the loins of Los a dark & furious death'—that will
complete the cycle of the Zoas. Urizen has overcome Luvah
but he fears that the new birth will be of dark power to destroy
him. Ahania pleads with him not to think of such issues and to
resume his fields of light: she contrasts his present uneasy
stability with his former state of liberty and science, and blames
him for listening to the voice of Luvah:

> They call thy lions to the field of blood they rowze thy tygers
> Out of the halls of justice, till these dens thy wisdom framd
> Golden & beautiful but O how unlike those sweet fields of bliss
> Where liberty was justice & eternal science was mercy
>
> (III, 37–40)

Urizen refuses to listen. Determined to keep some sort of
identity and reality at all cost, he throws her out into a world
which his work has deprived of reality:

> Into the Caverns of the Grave & places of Human Seed
> Where the impressions of Despair & Hope enroot for ever
> A world of darkness. Ahania fell far into Non Entity
>
> (III, 142–4)

This is another element in the human fall; and in the vast
chaos created by the event there eventually emerges the voice
of Man, the struggles of a broken creature to reassume human
features and human limbs. When he has achieved this as far as
he can, the figure which emerges from the chaos is that of
Tharmas, standing upon the ocean. Rage at his present condition is mingled with annoyance and sorrow at his loss of Enion
(which is implicit in Urizen's casting-out of Ahania). The
separation between spectre and emanation, which is a tragic
but uncomprehended fact in the worlds of Tharmas and Los,
is here shown to be a result of the operation of Urizen's laws.
The same laws, by separating Vala from Luvah, have removed
the visionary dimension from nature. Under the domination of
Urizen, indeed, she is persuaded to deceive her lord, Luvah,
and prevent him from rising to his true stature. Where nature
is not understood, moreover, energy is misapplied: the struggle
for power between Luvah and Urizen in Urizen's world, the
major theme of subsequent Nights, gives Blake the opportunity

for a long, savage satire on war and industrialism. The implements of peace are first turned into weapons of war, and then replaced by machines; the simple hour glass and water wheel are destroyed,

> And in their stead intricate wheels invented Wheel without wheel
> To perplex youth in their outgoings & to bind to labours
> Of day & night the myriads of Eternity. that they might file
> And polish brass & iron hour after hour laborious workmanship
> Kept ignorant of the use that they might spend the days of wisdom
> In sorrowful drudgery to obtain a scanty pittance of bread
> In ignorance to view a small portion & think that All
> And call it Demonstration   blind to all the simple rules of life
> (VIIb, 179–86)

The main battle, however, takes place around the limbs of Vala; the Elemental Gods call on her, a melancholy Magdalen waiting by the Sepulchre of Luvah, to go down into it and exercise all her arts of charm and deception there, in order that the glorious king may not rise but perish.

For a time she can do so, but she is not altogether devoid of memory of her former condition and when, as the 'shadowy female', she carries out Urizen's commands and sees the resulting destruction, she is moved to action. As Urizen sits in his tyrannic temple of the Sun, reading his books of law, she approaches his terrible presence and speaks to him of his works —works of dread, falling snows, the lash of the blast—and declares that she will yet face him, for in him she now beholds the murderer of her Luvah.

> Where hast thou hid him whom I love   in what remote Abyss
> Resides that God of my delight   O might my eyes behold
> My Luvah then could I deliver all the sons of God
> From Bondage of these terrors & with influences sweet
> As once in those eternal fields in brotherhood & Love
> United we should live in bliss as those who sinned not . . .
> (VIII, 155–60)

Having now seen that Luvah was the source of all the joys which now exist only allegorically, in the fruit of Urizen's Tree of Mystery, she longs for their renewal.

The effect of her plea is to bring the power of Orc into contact with the Web of Religion, so that its energies stir into a hungry desire and lust. Urizen finds hinself entangled in his own net, 'in sorrow, lust, repentance'.

The main hope for humanity now lies in the work of Los and Enitharmon. A female form is created, to be called Jerusalem, the counterpart of the Eternal Man: Simultaneously, the sons of Eden begin a long song of rejoicing, because the Lamb of God is beginning to put off the Satanic body. They look down into the war which is raging and see its vast hermaphroditic form labouring like an earthquake, until from it bursts Satan, visible at last (now that the Lamb of God is also revealed) in his true nature:

A male without a female counterpart a howling fiend
Forlorn of Eden & repugnant to the forms of life
Yet hiding the shadowy female Vala as in an ark & Curtains . . .
(VIII, 253–5)

The Lamb of God stands before Satan, 'to put off Mystery'. Urizen's reply is that of Caiaphas faced by Christ:

Urizen calld together the Synagogue of Satan in dire Sanhedrim
To judge the Lamb of God to Death as a murderer & robber . . .
(VIII, 272–3)

The assembly which meets is pictured as the twelve rocky forms of a druid circle, 'cold dark opaque'. In their midst stands Vala, the 'nameless shadowy female' now visible only as Rahab, the great Whore. She and her daughters begin to bind and wound their victims (though singing a song of tenderness and pity as they do so) for fear that their own life will flee away if their beloved is not bound upon the stems of Vegetation. Rahab's companion Tirzah, who is usually associated in Blake with the cruelty of the flesh, makes her first appearance in the poem as the inspiration of the songs of the women, who now proceed to nail the Lamb of God to the Tree of Mystery.

At this final attempt to destroy the Divine Vision, Jerusalem, the female counterpart of the Eternal Man in his true glory, also appears, voicing her fears at the sight of Eternal Death and begging Los and Urizen to create a sepulchre where Death can be worshipped. Los does so; meanwhile the death of the Lamb and the removal of the robes of Luvah reveals Rahab in all her despicable Mystery. Los, seeing her, also reveals himself:

> I am that shadowy Prophet who six thousand years ago
> Fell from my station in the Eternal bosom . . .
>
> (VIII, 351-2)

He tells the story of his life, with many references to biblical lore, and finally orders Rahab to set Jerusalem free. Instead, burning with pride and revenge, she goes to Urizen; and the long story of the Fall from vision to 'Mystery' concludes as Urizen, embracing the shadowy Female, is turned into an enormous monster, his tail lashing the Abyss. By the usual laws of the Zoas, his 'stony stupor' is at once transmitted to Tharmas and Urthona, who yield up their powers to Los.

The voice of Ahania is heard once again, mourning the folly of men, who pursue Death with such sureness, who 'seek pleasure from the festering wound', who in their possessiveness 'marry for a Wife / The ancient Leprosy'. She describes the Eternal Man, his faded head upon the rock, his limbs exposed to the destructive power of the elements, while the Eagle waits to devour him once he is completely corrupted (cf. fig. 42).

Enion replies with a message of hope. She too, has wailed like Ahania, but now she has a vision of future happiness. She has heard the ploughed field tell the grave that soon it shall cease to exist; she has also heard of new happenings in the caverns of the grave:

> The Lamb of God has rent the Veil of Mystery soon to return
> In Clouds & Fires around the rock & the Mysterious tree.
>
> (VIII, 556-7)

Enion's prophecy is to be fulfilled, but it is left to the Eternal Man to take the decisive steps. Beyond all the havoc and confusion there remains the rock in the far south where his faded head rests, while he mourns over the consuming universe and the destruction of all the joys which he formerly knew. Impotent to intervene directly in the struggle which he senses within his members, he calls to Urizen to resume the position which he once held as Prince of Light, stepping forth in the fields of Eternity with harps and songs, and so to resume his human form:

> Schoolmaster of souls great opposer of change arise
> That the Eternal worlds may see thy face in peace & joy

> That thou dread form of Certainty maist sit in town & village
> While little children play around thy feet in gentle awe
> Fearing thy frown loving thy smile O Urizen Prince of Light
> (IX, 131–5)

He calls again to Urizen, telling him to shed his dragon form or else be cast out into the indefinite for ever. His anger is greater against Urizen than against Luvah, for Luvah's war is at least a form of energy, even if of energy enslaved; whereas Urizen's religion is no more than a detestable deceit. Sin can be redeemed, as Rahab the harlot was redeemed when she hung her scarlet across the window in the Old Testament, but Error can never be redeemed. He ends by crying, 'Wake, thou dragon of the deeps!' (In the background of the imagery here there is evident play with the fact that 'Rahab' in the Old Testament is used both for the harlot and for a great monster[16]—Blake is also identifying Urizen and Vala with the Beast and the Whore of Revelation.)

Urizen remains in his stony despair, however, and his immediate response is to invite more destruction. It is only when the Eternal Man finally reproaches him, speaking of a new birth, a new spring, that Urizen acknowledges his error—his belief that the 'river of light' can be controlled by a lock or 'the infinite & unbounded' by a limiting chain. But when he does so the effect is overwhelming: the universe finally explodes and all things appear in their own identity, recharged with the infinite.

This is by no means the first time that Urizen has recognized his fallen status. When the roots of the chain of jealousy which bound Orc stretched down into the earth, they transmitted the sound of his struggles to the deep dens where Urizen lay, causing him to remember his own former state and to chant his woes in a song which included reminiscence of his lost glory:

> Once how I walked from my palace in gardens of delight
> The sons of wisdom stood around the harpers followd with harps
> Nine virgins clothd in light composd the song to their immortal
> voices
> And at my banquets of new wine my head was crownd with joy
> (V, 198–201)

Now, however, reminded again by the Eternal Man of this

former self, he is finally enabled to see the nature of his error—
his fear of death and the enslavement to the time process which
resulted from that fear, producing in its wake all the evils of a
technologically orientated society. He has sought eternity as an
endless possible extension of the time-process instead of seeing
that Eternity exists essentially in the present:

> . . . O that I had never drank the wine nor eat the bread
> Of dark mortality nor cast my view into futurity nor turnd
> My back darkning the present clouding with a cloud
> And building arches high & cities turrets & towers & domes
> Whose smoke destroyd the pleasant garden & whose running
>   kennels
> Chokd the bright rivers burdning with my Ships the angry deep
> Thro Chaos seeking for delight & in spaces remote
> Seeking the Eternal which is always present to the wise
> Seeking for pleasure which unsought falls round the infants path
> And on the fleeces of mild flocks who neither care nor labour . . .
>
> I cast futurity away & turn my back upon that void
> Which I have made for lo futurity is in this moment . . .
>   (IX, 164–73; 182–3)

When Urizen has discovered the secret of true wisdom the
transformation is total: he is no longer a snowy tyrant but a
monarch of wisdom; no longer the law-giver but the light-
bearer. He shakes the snows from his shoulders, scatters his
white robes, and rises into the heavens 'in naked majesty / In
radiant youth'. He can now enter into the harvest and then,
with Urthona, 'arisen in his strength', take his full part in a
civilization where the only war is 'intellectual War' and the
only armour science. After all the hard words that have been
spoken against the dominance of analytic 'reason' in Blake's
poems it is notable that the final words of this poem stress his
belief in the virtue of true knowledge: 'The dark Religions are
departed & sweet Science reigns.'

The abolition of law (whether moral or natural) is, nevertheless, a negative act. The ultimate positives of the poem are
mediated though the Eternal Man himself, and his story,
though tangential to the intricacies of the full plot, must inevitably be central in the poem as a whole.

IV The phallic lapse

Taking the stories of Orc, of Tharmas and of Urizen in turn, we have seen Blake treating, in more detail, themes which he had already used in previous prophetic books, setting the contemporary theme of revolution in the context of a tyrannical moral and natural law which were in their turn created by the analytic eye of Urizen. We are still left facing ultimate questions, however. How could Urizen's vision have achieved such dominance in the first place?

In *The Book of Urizen* Blake had opted for the simple method of making Urizen a nuller version of Milton's Satan, a being who had not rebelled, but simply turned away from the inward harmony of heaven to establish a permanent universe for himself. Urizen's failure was never explained; it was simply recorded as a doleful fact. In his longer account Blake felt the need for a more complicated explanation, which would throw less of the blame on Urizen and suggest further human relevances.

It was also part of his larger purpose that this more complicated story of the human decline should not be told immediately. Instead *The Four Zoas* becomes a mystery story, in which each of the four main characters is aware of a sinister act (which he suspects to have been a crime of some sort) and looks for the culprit. Their search gives the plot some of its force.

If Blake learnt a great deal about the handling of allegory from Spenser and Milton, he probably drew for this dramatic element in his poem on his reading of Shakespeare. I have suggested in an appendix the reading of Shakespeare which Blake seems to have adopted, as though each of the great tragic heroes were taking part in a larger cosmic drama which none of them fully understood. The four Zoas of this poem are characters in a similar cosmic tragedy. Urizen, devotee of law on his snowy mountains, is the equivalent of Lear at the beginning of the play; Luvah, who, through misapplied energy of the heart, has destroyed instead of creating, is a version of Macbeth; Tharmas, raging over his lost emanations, corresponds to Othello raging over a Desdemona whom he has slain through stupid devotion to the moral law; Los, honest and creative but destined through lack of vision to see his actions miss their ends, is another Prince Hamlet. From the beginning of the epic there

is continued suggestion of a sinister event, normally associated
with Luvah. The Eternal Man, for example, delivering his
power into the hands of Urizen, says

> Thy brother Luvah hath smitten me but pity thou his youth
> Tho thou hast not pitid my Age   O Urizen Prince of Light
>
> (II, 7–8)

In his distress this cosmic man reminds one both of Job, smitten
with boils by Satan, and of King David, asking that the young
man Absalom be spared in spite of his insurrection against the
established order (both of which stories Blake would have read
allegorically). In terms of the plot they arouse a suspicion about
Luvah which is also voiced by some of the other characters.
When Tharmas and Los recognize one another in Night the
Fourth, nevertheless, and begin to discuss the original disaster,
Tharmas, speaking in the accents of Prince Hamlet after his
interview with the Ghost, suggests a more complex crime,
involving Urizen as well as Luvah:

> . . . Art thou Urthona   My friend my old companion
> With whom I livd in happiness before that deadly night
> When Urizen gave the horses of Light in the hands of Luvah
> Thou knowest not what Tharmas knows.   O I could tell thee
>   tales
> That would enrage thee as it has Enraged me even
> From Death in wrath & fury.
>
> (IV, 111–16)

This too is an incomplete account. We approach the truth more
closely in some of the 'dreams' and 'songs' which intersperse
the poem. It is Enitharmon, in Night the First, who gives the
first of these versions, which, in her unenlightened state, she
calls 'a Song of Death':

> Hear!   I will sing a Song of Death!   it is a Song of Vala!
> The Fallen Man takes his repose: Urizen sleeps in the porch
> Luvah and Vala woke & flew up from the Human Heart
> Into the Brain; from thence upon the pillow Vala slumber'd,
> And Luvah siez'd the Horses of Light, & rose into the Chariot of
>   Day
> Sweet laughter siezd me in my sleep! silent & close I laughd
> For in the visions of Vala I walkd with the mighty Fallen One
> I heard his voice among the branches, & among sweet flowers. . . .
>
> (I, 260–7)

In the first part of this description she has recognized dimly the events of the Fall—the Eternal Man falling asleep and the resulting conflict of his energies. The passions of the breast have seized control of the head—Phaethon has tried to guide the sun-chariot of his father—and the energies of light have subsequently been usurped by those of fire. Then, as she recalls the subsequent words of the Fallen Man, Enitharmon smiles at her new sense of power. Although he had refused to look on the Universal Vision he begged her not to slay Los, who is devoted to her, by driving the female emanations away from him.

As she delightedly recounts all this, Los sees the import of what she is saying. He replies in indignation (though masking it in smiles):

> I die not Enitharmon tho thou singst thy Song of Death
> Nor shalt thou me torment   For I behold the Fallen Man
> Seeking to comfort Vala,   she will not be comforted
> She rises from his throne and seeks the shadows of her garden
> Weeping for Luvah lost, in the bloody beams of your false morn-
> ing . . .

(I, 283–7)

Los's reply continues an intricate run of imagery from Enitharmon's speech. She had said that the Fallen Man asked her, 'Why dost thou weep as Vala & wet thy veil with dewy tears. . .?' Her image of Vala as a fallen Eve, an Earth weeping in the dew of evening, is countered by Los's image of Vala as a Magdalen, seeking for her lord in the garden at break of day and not finding him. The two women weeping in the garden, the one at the Fall, the other at the Resurrection, are linked in Blake's mind as complementary images of the loss and recovery of Vision.

Los is retorting to Enitharmon's oblique prophecy of his death by claiming that woman will be no better off by it: she will simply weep the tears of a Magdalen for a lost lord who is slain. He goes on to prophesy the form of the loss. The Lamb of God will be drawn into a mortal form and will be destined to destruction from his mother's womb:

> I see, invisible descend into the Gardens of Vala
> Luvah walking on the winds.   I see the invisible knife
> I see the shower of blood: I see the swords & spears of futurity. . . .

(I, 299–301)

Just as Enitharmon has denied the hope of fourfold vision
for Los, he in his turn is denying the hope of threefold vision
for her.

> Thou neer shalt leave this cold expanse where watry Tharmas
>   mourns
>
> (I, 305)

Later in the poem, Ahania describes another vision of the
disruption which brought about the present disorder. Her vision goes further back than Enitharmon's: she not only recalls
the fact of the Eternal Man's sleep but also the manner in which
his loss of vision operated. In his weariness of vision, a shadow
was produced, a vision of man existing in purity, perfection and
holiness—'a sweet entrancing self delusion'. This Shadow so
absorbed the energies of the Man that he fell prostrate before
it, declaring his complete unworthiness in the face of such perfection.

At this point the illustrations to the manuscript (discussed in
an appendix) are integrally important, showing that the 'sleep'
of the Eternal Man is also a phallic failure. Although the exact
nature of the failure is not made clear, there is the strong suggestion of a sexual climax during his sleep which was a response
not to a real woman (or even the image of one) but to a false
self-created image, the 'delusion' mentioned in the text, which,
like the Lilith of ancient lore, weakened and drew off his
virility. As a result the operation of his sexual consciousness
through the blood, creating the rhythmic alternation between
heart-expanding creation and heart-piercing tenderness, was
lost: he turned away from Vala, even though a dismal prophetic
voice made him aware that in doing so he was turning her into
the deprived figure of Enion, and followed instead the image
of his dream.

It is this pursuit of false holiness and delusory perfection, we
learn, that brought about the disorder of the Zoas in the Eternal
Man. Once the 'love & life & light' which formerly possessed
him were deprived of their central, binding 'life', love and light
were left at war. Immediately the energies of love turned in
upon him in self-destruction. The scene is immediately linked
with Blake's interpretation of the Book of Job[17], where the

smitings of Satan are seen as a similar assertion of energy against holiness:

> And Luvah strove to gain dominion over the Ancient Man
> They strove together above the Body where Vala was inclos'd
> And the dark Body of Man left prostrate upon the crystal pave-
>   ment
> Coverd with boils from head to foot, the terrible smitings of
>   Luvah
>
> (III, 79–82)

The reaction of the Eternal Man was to put forth Luvah, his own heart, from his presence, telling him to 'go & die the Death of Man for Vala the sweet wanderer'. And this 'Death' turns out to be the very disorganization of the senses that has recurred in previous works of Blake's, its cause now finally revealed as loss of that harmonizing imagination which is created by full sexual consciousness:

> I will turn the volutions of your Ears outward; & bend your
>   Nostrils
> Downward; & your fluxile Eyes englob'd, roll round in fear
> Your withring Lips & Tongue shrink up into a narrow circle
> Till into narrow forms you creep.
>
> (III, 86–9)

The effect of this curse directly recalls Adam and Eve leaving paradise. Instead of a flaming sword, however, the symbol of the serpent is brought in, emphasizing that it is energy that is cut off. In their new restricted form, they would no longer be one with Nature, but would see it with an analytical vision; its energies would remain apart from them:

> . . . Luvah & Vala
> Went down the Human Heart where Paradise & its joys abounded
> In jealous fears in fury & rage, & flames roll'd round their fervid
>   feet
> And the vast form of Nature like a Serpent play'd before them
> And as they went in folding fires & thunders of the deep
> Vala shrunk in like the dark sea that leaves its slimy banks
> And from her bosom Luvah fell far as the east & west
> And the vast form of Nature like a Serpent roll'd between.
>
> (III, 94–101)

As Ahania concludes her account of the catastrophe which gave
rise to their present condition, Urizen's anger mounts steadily
until, when she ends, he asserts his own authority ('Am I not
God?') and declares that she has become like Vala. He cannot,
of course, recall the original state of the Eternal Man and Vala,
but he can dimly remember that Ahania was once to him a
repose,

> A sluggish current of dim waters. on whose verdant margin
> A cavern shaggd with horrid shades. dark cool & deadly. where
> I laid my head in the hot noon after the broken clods
> Had wearied me . . . .
>
> (III, 121–4)

Even that diminished vision is now mainly lost to him, however:
he sees her, like the scornful Vala who is separated from Luvah,
trying to drag him into Non Entity.

So long as he remains enclosed by his own legalism, this
cavernous vision is the only one that is available to Urizen. In
a later Night, however, he is stirred by an encounter with Orc
to a momentary glimpse of the world that he has lost. The
energies of Orc inevitably remind him of his own former delights—delights which have vanished because, like Milton's
Satan[18], he refused to acknowledge the son of Man (Luvah)
and withheld his own energies from him. This was a revolt of
Light against the Humanity which was its true source:

> O Fool to think that I could hide from his all piercing eyes
> The gold & silver & costly stones his holy workmanship
> O Fool could I forget the light that filled my bright spheres
> Was a reflection of his face who calld me from the deep
>
> I well remember for I heard the mild & holy voice
> Saying O light spring up & shine & I sprang up from the deep
> He gave to me a silver scepter & crownd me with a golden crown
> & said Go forth & guide my Son who wanders on the ocean
>
> I went not forth   I hid myself in black clouds of my wrath
> I calld the stars around my feet in the night of councils dark
> The stars threw down their spears & fled naked away
> We fell.
>
> (V, 214–25)

In this song of Urizen we approach still more closely to the heart of the myth. Up till now we have been aware of a primeval catastrophe, seen in various lights—sometimes as the weakness of the Eternal Man, sometimes as a sinister murder on the part of Luvah, sometimes simply as a deluge of the senses. Here we see that the cause of the fall was a disharmony like that in *Paradise Lost*. But whereas in Milton's poem it is pride that revolts against a new honour to the Son of God, in Blake's poem it is mere meanness that withholds service to the 'son of Man'. The allegorical implications of this are worked out as fully as in Milton's poem. In *Paradise Lost* pride, once asserted, is cast into Hell with all its energies, leaving God and his Son supreme in Heaven. In Blake, on the other hand, the withholding of Urizen's light from the son of Man means that *the Son* becomes the rebel. Deprived of Vision, his Desire is uncontrolled and riots into destruction. Like Cain, he murders innocence; like Phaethon he falls into the sea. And while the energies of desire are reeling to destruction, vision, its energies cut off from their source, loses all its power. As Urizen in his egoism calls his chariots of light round him instead of sending them to aid Luvah, they turn into the cold shining stars of the world of Reason. The stars of the world of Vision have thrown down their spears in nakedness and despair, while the innocence of Desire has turned into the destructive rage of the Tyger.

Urizen goes on to recall the former glory of Luvah and Urthona, who in the unfallen world guarded Vision and Desire: Luvah being the beautiful cup-bearer and keeper, with Urthona, of the gates of heaven. He confesses that he made himself drunk with the wine which Luvah gave him for his steeds, giving the steeds instead to Luvah (another way of symbolizing the establishment of a dominion of pure reason, in separation from human energies and human love).

All these events are now recalled to him by the renewed presence of infinite energy in the distant pulsations which reach him from Orc. These in their turn remind him of an ancient prophecy which seems to promise a re-uniting of light with love:

> I will arise Explore these dens & find that deep pulsation
> That shakes my cavern with strong shudders.   perhaps this is the
>   night

> Of Prophesy & Luvah hath burst his way from Enitharmon
> When Thought is closd in Caves.   Then love shall shew its root in
>   deepest Hell
>
> (V, 238–41)

Orc responds to the exploration by cursing the cold hypocrisy of Urizen. Yet from his words it is clear that he, too, fails to understand his own nature. So long as he is content to be a worm, he says, he can rise in peace; when he rages, his fetters bind him more. He is not a worm, and he prefers to rage. That he should say this is understandable, given the universe in which he lives: but his remarks are to be counterpoised against an ideal state of man, in which the interaction of Vision and Desire would ensure that he accepted his own dual nature as angel of light *and* worm of the earth. That even Orc dimly recognizes a truth beyond the one for which he is contending is shown in the next lines when, recognizing that the figure beyond him may be the 'cold attractive power' who holds him enchained, he goes on,

> I well remember how I stole thy light & it became fire
> Consuming. Thou Knowst me now O Urizen Prince of Light
> And I know thee is this the triumph this the Godlike State
> That lies beyond the bounds of Science in the Grey obscure
>
> (VIIa, 147–50)

The other side of the coin is now before us, revealing that, as Blake asserted concerning *Paradise Lost*, the Fall involved not the crime of one principle against another, but a mutual crime in which each contender sinned against the other[19]. While Urizen was stealing Luvah's wine to make himself drunk (the drunkenness of Noah), Luvah was stealing his light—which immediately became a consuming fire.

Orc is willing to accept the position. He

> begin to Organize a Serpent body,
> Despising Urizens light & turning it into flaming fire. . . .
>
> (VIIa, 152–3)

Urizen replies by making Orc in his serpent form entwine himself round the Tree of Mystery.

The focus of the narrative moves to Los and Enitharmon. Los laments the separation between them.

> Once how I sang & calld the beasts & birds to their delights . . .
>
> (VIIa, 199)

But he is now no longer an Adam in Eden, naming the beasts, or a sun-god calling forth the dawn chorus[20]. Instead, he says, Enitharmon exists for him only as a land that no longer rejoices in fertility, her fruits drooping in sickness and decay.

Enitharmon does not hear. Her Shadow, descending from the tree of Mystery, has met with the Spectre of Urthona, who prepares for her the 'poison of sweet Love'. Fascinated by him, she asks whether he is set as a guardian of Orc and offers to reveal to him 'Secrets of Eternity'—which turn out to be yet another version of the primeval catastrophe, taking the story still further back.

> Among the Flowers of Beulah walkd the Eternal Man & Saw
> Vala the lilly of the desart. melting in high noon
> Upon her bosom in sweet bliss he fainted Wonder siezd
> All heaven they saw him dark. they built a golden wall
> Round Beulah There he reveld in delight among the Flowers
> Vala was pregnant & brought forth Urizen Prince of Light
> First born of Generation. Then behold a wonder to the Eyes
> Of the now fallen Man a double form Vala appeard. A Male
> And female shuddring pale the Fallen Man recoild
> From the Enormity & calld them Luvah & Vala. . . .
>
> (VIIa, 239–48)

This version not only makes it finally clear that Luvah did not exist until the Eternal Man had begun to divide, but adds something to the account of that division. Initially, it was a lapse into permanent threefold vision, a weakness which caused Man, no longer able to suffer the power of full fourfold vision, to want to remain, like Coleridge's Kubla Khan, within the restful delights of threefold vision as in a walled garden. Cut off from his full energies, he dwelt happily enough in the 'holy Tent of Man'; but the lost energies of vision and love soon conspired against him as reason and murder, and his Beulah fell in dark confusion. Between this event and the birth of herself and Los, she can remember nothing: but now she finds herself enslaved to vegetative forms according to the will of Luvah, and hopes that the Spectre will find some way of punishing Vala— ' . . . To bring her down subjected to the rage of my fierce boy.'

The Spectre replies with a monologue of his own. In spite of his horrible and ghostly form, he has a more vivid remembrance of Eternity than any of the Zoas, for he is the only being who still stands in an organic relationship with the Eternal Man. So he recalls to Enitharmon her former happiness with him,

> Where thou & I in undivided Essence walkd about
> Imbodied. thou my garden of delight & I the spirit in the garden
> (VIIa, 271–2)

Of the catastrophe he can remember only that the tender passions, instead of retaining their embodiment within the Eternal Man, became isolated as a Female; and that this division of manhood resulted in all the later confusion, during which he himself was swept away down to his present state.

The slow process of revelation culminates in this vision of an ultimate phallic reality where humanity was the Spirit of sublimity walking in the Garden of pathos. The Apocalypse must restore humanity to that state through liberation from the 'false delusions of holiness'.

But how is that liberation to be achieved, and what is its positive form? In asking this we find ourselves discovering the points of the poem where myth and poetic achievement are most closely united.

V   The renewal of human perception

The inner myth of *The Four Zoas* is something more than a clever scheme to bind the plot together. We are familiar with the type of mystery-story in which the successful detective at last holds up the clue which sets all the events of the narrative in a new light for us. In such stories the final explanation is often of the same sort as the earlier ones: it simply exposes a hitherto unsuspected criminal or demonstrates the unexpectedly subtle method by which the crime was committed. Blake's method, working through the 'flashback' technique involved in the dreams and songs, actually changes the whole interpretation of his poem: it shows that the struggle between the Zoas was part of a mistaken reading of experience. There had in fact been no crime, no criminal, rather a failure of the full visionary and phallic consciousness pictured in the simple image of the Eternal Man bowing his head in the noonday heat.

The Four Zoas, then, emerges as a long poem with a basic structure which is allegorical, a plot which is that of a mystery-drama and a further, visionary dimension which first directs the reader to see the struggles of the Zoas as black and white dramatic movements and then reduces them to flickering shadows by comparing them with the bold colourings of a lost reality where man walks in his garden in a state of radiance and generosity. The function of the allegory, in other words, is to transpose one mode of seeing action into another, to initiate the reader who habitually interprets human life as struggle into another order where each spring of action is traced back to its good and naturally harmonious source.

To say this is to suggest a division between the main action of the poem, on the one hand, which is organized according to the rules of time and space and contains its own rational momentum, and the 'inner myth' which is organized by the imagination.

Such a division is not without its truth, but it needlessly simplifies the poetic achievement of the poem. For the inner myth here is not simply an autonomous achievement of the imagination, a useful fantasy: its human and artistic relevance is more direct. Blake is arguing that all human warfare springs from a central failure of imagination.

The fashioning of his inner myth, however, made him aware of certain defects in the original structure. The first lay in the fact that the Eternal Man, as ultimate containing figure, would, on his awakening into unity, become isolated. The Zoas could be described, resuming their proper activities in a paradisal landscape, but the Man himself must appear as a super-Urizen, without context and therefore without possibilities of brotherhood.

It was also difficult to see why the Eternal Man, if so isolated, should ever wake at all.

To meet these difficulties Blake introduced the idea of a council 'of God', in Great Eternity, presiding over the whole scene. In some late additions to the poem they actually meet to create the Fallen Man, so that he awakens on the couch of death and (like the Shunammite's son raised by Samuel)[21] sneezes seven times.

Lines added to Night the First describe the activities of the Council more closely. Like the daemons of *Paradise Lost*[22] they have the powers of contracting and expanding—though in Blake's poem the power is exercised perceptually.

> Then those in Great Eternity met in the Council of God
> As one Man for Contracting their Exalted Senses
> They behold Multitude or Expanding they behold as one
> As One Man all the Universal family   & that One Man
> They call Jesus the Christ & they in him & he in them
> Live in Perfect harmony in Eden the land of life . . .
>
> (I, 469–74)

On news of the disharmony within the Eternal Man, which is reported (rather like the story of the conspiracy of the rebel angels in *Paradise Lost*[23]) as being the result of a plot between Urizen and Luvah, the council proceed to elect seven 'Eyes of God', concentred in the Lamb, to watch over Man.

The introduction of this new framework for the plot witnesses to the stresses and strains which were becoming evident. They could not in fact be resolved by patching on such simple devices, but when Blake came to write his last two long poems, he was able to learn from his experience here, and to include the 'Eternals' from the beginning as an essential ordering force.

Although a rather unsatisfactory 'framing' device so far as the plot is concerned, however, the account of the Council of God is important as showing Blake's growing sense of what he was actually doing in the poem. The ability to contract or expand the senses, ascribed to the members of the Council, is in fact the essential element in the quality of Vision, and plays a more profound part in the poem than any piece of mythological machinery. When it is in operation it has the great virtue of working poetically as well as descriptively, so that poetry and action are brought intimately together.

Although the importance ascribed to this non-quantitative vision will have been evident in many passages already quoted, its importance as a unifying factor merits separate discussion.

It·is responsible, for example, for the very striking success of the early passages describing Los and Enitharmon:

> Nine Times they livd among the forests, feeding on sweet fruits
> And nine bright Spaces wanderd weaving mazes of delight
> Snáring the wild Goats for their milk they eat the flesh of Lambs
> A male & female naked & ruddy as the pride of summer
>
> Alternate Love & Hate his breast; hers Scorn & Jealousy
> In embryon passions. they kissd not nor embrac'd for shame & fear
> His head beamd light & in his vigorous voice was prophecy
> Hé could controll the times & seasons, & the days & years
> She could controll the spaces, regions, desart, flood & forest...
> (I, 233–42)

The curious contrast between their shrinkage towards mean human passions and their surviving power of visionary perception comes to a climax in their wedding celebration, where the bride and bridegroom look on in discontent and scorn, despite the grandeur and beauty. The description of the feast shows Blake's gifts at their nervous best, his mastery of rhythm complete.

> For Elemental Gods their thunderous Organs blew; creating
> Delicious Viands. Demons of Waves their watry Eccho's woke!
> Bright Souls of vegetative life, budding and blossoming
> Stretch their immortal hands to smite the gold & silver Wires
> And with immortal Voice soft warbling fill all Earth & Heaven.
> With doubling Voices & loud Horns wound round sounding
> Cavernous dwellers fill'd the enormous Revelry, Responsing!
> And Spirits of Flaming fire on high, govern'd the mighty Song.
> (I, 377–84)

The verse-writing here, with imaginative light constantly glancing from one word to another, is perhaps the best in the whole poem. It leads directly into the first of the 'hymns'. This one, the hymn for the feast of Los and Enitharmon, describes how the whole landscape of the world is revolting against peaceful cultivation of its fields and vineyards: preferring that its rivers should run with human blood, that the energies of warfare should ride supreme over desolated cities, and that the Human Image should be finally destroyed. Then Luvah and Vala, under whose aegis the warfare has been carried out, will them-

selves be brought low by the full power of the forces which they
have unleashed; in their destruction Los and Enitharmon will
be brought forth, giving form to that destruction in the shape
of rugged wintry rocks 'justling together in the void, suspended
by inward fires' which will replace the cities, cornfields and
orchards, the sun, the moon and the stars of former times. In
the final verse of the hymn, the spirits turn on Luvah, who has
brought about this chaos and who will come forth again as a
howling fire from the loins of Enitharmon when he is reborn as
Orc:

> Bursting forth from the loins of Enitharmon, Thou fierce
>   Terror
> Go howl in vain, Smite Smite his fetters Smite O wintry hammers
> Smite Spectre of Urthona mock the fiend who drew us down
> From heavens of joy into this deep. Now rage, but rage in vain
>   (I, 430-3)

The bride and groom sit on in the midst of the feast, hearing
this hymn, which directs the energies of the sublime towards
aggression. In the midst of all the pleasure their discontent remains. And since this discontent marks a failure within themselves, a craving which remains unsatisfied, it is only natural
that this craving should be given separate, autonomous expression. What is no more than a sullenness on their faces receives
a life of its own in the voice of Enion, heard from far away. She
becomes the witness and spokesman for all those who suffer
from the cruelties of the universe. Her song replaces the expansive energy of the previous descriptions by a lyrical form
which contracts towards pathos:

> Why does the Raven cry aloud and no eye pities her?
> Why fall the Sparrow & the Robin in the foodless winter?
> Faint! shivering they sit on leafless bush, or frozen stone
>
> Wearied with seeking food across the snowy waste; the little
> Heart, cold; and the little tongue consum'd that once in thought-
>   less joy
> Gave songs of gratitude to waving corn fields round their nest.
>   (I, 445-50)

Her song, reminiscent of the best of the *Songs of Experience*, mutes
the gaiety of the golden Feast. Unlike, say, the fable of the

Grasshopper and the Cricket, with its prudential morality and worldly wisdom, it jolts the reader from his vantage point of comfort and insists that he enter the actual world of the victim, where the desolations of suffering create an entire universe. The foresight of those who have escaped (so satisfying to themselves) is largely irrelevant to those who actually inhabit such a world.

Despite the shortcomings of Los and Enitharmon, however, the creation of Urizen's golden palace in Night II leaves their essential existence untouched. Whatever their failings, Urizen's need for permanence is not one of them. Their senses, still humanized, enable them to walk abroad on the dewy earth and enjoy the harmony of the Elemental Gods all about them—

> Contracting or expanding their all flexible senses
> At will to murmur in the flowers small as the honey bee
> At will to stretch across the heavens & step from star to star. . . .
>
> (II, 296–8)

But they themselves are still in a state of jealousy towards each other. They may have escaped the petrifaction of the senses which is the curse of Urizen, but they cannot escape the other curse, that of Luvah and Vala, which has caused a permanent separation between energy and vision, between spectre and emanation. So Los finds himself forever pursuing without attainment, like the river-god Alpheus pursuing the fountain-goddess Arethusa:

> I grasp thy vest in my strong hand in vain. like water springs
> In the bright sands of Los. evading my embrace. . . .
>
> (II, 304–5)

Enitharmon argues that his love is false. He rebukes her for her secrecy; while she affirms that she will maintain her jealousy, the instrument by which, in her weakness, she can dominate his strength. When Los dies under her cruelty she revives him by singing her song of joy. As with everything that concerns this pair, the incident is to be interpreted ironically, for she at once sings the delight of female joy and the triumph of female will.

Hardly aware of the potentialities of their humanized vision, Los and Enitharmon continue to be fully occupied by the contentions of jealousy, which leads to the binding of their son Orc.

But the account of Orc on the mountain, a Prometheus, an Eternal in spite of his bonds and therefore able to exercise the energies of eternity in the midst of his captivity, shows him with senses which, like those of Los and Enitharmon, are not limited to quantitative perceptions:

> His eyes the lights of his large soul contract or else expand
> Contracted they behold the secrets of the infinite mountains
> The veins of gold & silver & the hidden things of Vala
> Whatever grows from its pure bud or breathes a fragrant soul
> Expanded they behold the terrors of the Sun & Moon
> The Elemental Planets & the orbs of eccentric fire
>
> (V, 121–6)

The limited contractions and expansions afforded to human beings by the use of microscope or telescope are here superseded by a vision which sees the infinite beauty and energy in all things, and the description passes into a picture of all nature, seen in the delight of its manifold energies.

> His nostrils breathe a fiery flame. his locks are like the forests
> Of wild beasts there the lion glares the tyger & wolf howl there
> And there the Eagle hides her young in cliffs & precipices
> His bosom is like starry heaven expanded all the stars
> Sing round. there waves the harvest & the vintage rejoices. the
>   Springs
> Flow into rivers of delight. there the spontaneous flowers
> Drink laugh & sing. the grasshopper the Emmet & the Fly
> The golden Moth builds there a house & spreads her silken bed
>
> (V, 127–34)

As the struggles initiated by Orc's rebellion reach the point of open warfare, however, these energies and perceptions become turned more and more towards destruction. Los shouts aloud, looking forward to the carnage. Tharmas looks to him for revenge after all the sufferings which he and his daughters have been made to suffer. Orc rages with all his furies; Enitharmon, hearing and seeing him, is terrified at his power, calling for the watchman to awaken. As she does so, many of the trees in the earth about her force their way into existence, their energies longing for a part in the vast war which is about to take place in her world. Animals arise also: the sheep is sullen, the bull, the lions and tigers, the serpent and the scorpion rage in their various energies. The Prester Serpent (the word Prester denoting a union of priestly and kingly functions, as in 'Prester John') runs along the files, claiming his right to lead the warriors into battle.

These are not the only energies to be aroused, nevertheless. Enion has no hope of renewal but her Isis-nature makes her sense that her Osiris, the Eternal Man, is recreating his scattered body, however sorrowful the process:

> As the seed waits Eagerly watching for its flower & fruit,
> Anxious its little soul looks out into the clear expanse
> To see if hungry winds are abroad with their invisible army
> So Man looks out in tree & herb & fish & bird & beast
> Collecting up the scattered portions of his immortal body
> Into the Elemental forms of every thing that grows . . .
> (VIII, 558–63)

She describes the sorrows of Man as he works in Creation, seeing all its agonies and waiting to reassume his bliss.

Since the fall is a fall from phallic awareness, however, interconnected with the bondage of law, the work of restitution must begin with the restoration of vision to Urizen himself. The action begins to pass into its final stage only when his voice is at last heard in the dark deep, acknowledging his errors—his building of industrial cities at the expense of pleasant gardens and bright rivers, for example. These particular errors, he now recognizes, all resulted from the single, more general error of seeking Eternity and pleasure in some future state, yet to be constructed, and not perceiving that it was his own vision that needed renewal. As a result of his new understanding he decides that he will no longer restrain the raging of the other Zoas. His decision is accompanied by a casting off of his snows and aged mantles as he rises up 'in naked majesty, / In radiant Youth'. Ahania dances from the east to meet him and, in her excess of joy, dies.

The Eternal Man speaks. With the self-renewal of the Lamb of God and Urizen's recantation he is himself reviving, and perceives that all things can renew themselves: Ahania will be restored to Urizen, 'a Self renewing Vision'. Instead of existing between excesses of joy and sorrow, she will in future awaken to spring and summer and sleep again in the winter, while

Urizen prepares to receive her in the regeneration of the next spring:

> Immortal thou. Regenerate She   & all the lovely Sex
> From her shall learn obedience & prepare for a wintry grave
> That spring may see them rise in tenfold joy & sweet delight
>   (IX, 216–18)

So male and female shall live the life of Eternity.

The vision reaches its climax in the descending of the bride to the Lamb and her revelation as Jerusalem—not merely a woman, but a city within which all may live in happiness.

At this revelation Urizen sheds the last vestiges of his error by accepting the fact that it consisted in trying to impose bonds on those forces of eternity which are by their nature illimitable:

> What Chain encompasses in what Lock is the river of light confind
> That issues forth in the morning by measure & the evening by
>   carefulness
> Where shall we take our stand to view the infinite & unbounded
> Or where are human feet for Lo our eyes are in the heavens
>   (IX, 226–9)

Urizen has at last recognized that whereas human eyes are incapable of taking in the infinite, conceived spatially, true human Vision recognizes the infinite as part of its own nature. His recognition is so apocalyptic that the whole universe explodes, giving place to a scene in the midst of which roll on the Wonders of the Almighty,

> Four Starry Universes going forward from Eternity to Eternity.

Beholding the Vision, the fallen Man tries to rise and meet it but finds that he is still unable to endure the flames or to enter the Consummation which they offer. More must happen before he will have the necessary strength.

The new process is initiated by the sons of Urizen, who seize his plough and polish it, beating their weapons of war into tools of husbandry and summoning all the fierce energies to service. Urizen arises as the mighty Ploughman and passes with his plough over the whole of civilization in cities and villages, mountains and valleys, graves and caverns of the dead. Next he comes as the great Sower sowing the seeds of men everywhere. Finally he rests with his sons, while they watch the human

harvest springing up. Ahania comes forth again, casting off her
death-clothes, and appears as the harvest moon.

When Orc has quite consumed himself in his mental flames,
the Eternal Man, now called the Regenerate Man, stoops down
to take up both him and the shadowy female, 'the flaming Demon
& Demoness of Smoke' in his hands, and gives them to Urizen.
They are diminished to Lilliputian dimensions at a stroke; and
Urizen is able to lecture them as Luvah and Vala (their original
names) and tell them to return into their proper place, which
is the place of seed and not the brain (Urizen's dominion) or
the Heart (now the heart of the Regenerate Man). As they
descend into the Gates of Urthona, they find themselves in a
country far from the 'wracking universe'. This is, in fact, the
world that Thel was longing for, or Earth, in the 'Introduction'
to *Songs of Experience*, when she lay amid the 'dewy grass'. Luvah,
in the early morning, calls,

> Come forth O Vala from the grass & from the silent Dew
> Rise from the dews of death for the Eternal Man is Risen . . .
>
> (IX, 388–9)

Vala hears him and rejoices—but, like Psyche listening to Cupid,
she is at a loss to know where he is: she only knows that the
rising sun is closely associated with him. The creating voice
which she can hear tells her that a rhythm will be given to her
by the sun and that she will fold up like a flower at sunset. Like
Thel, she laments the brevity of such an existence and weeps
that she has been brought to life at all: but the voice tells her
that in spite of this rhythm she shall survive:

> The fruit shall ripen & fall down & the flowers consume away
> But thou shalt still survive arise O dry thy dewy tears . . .
>
> (IX, 420–1)

Vala hears with new rejoicing and sings a hymn of joy to the
sun. She is now in the land of 'organized innocence', that
world of pathos and threefold vision which reconciles the energies of lesser levels of vision and which is symbolized, as before,
by the ram, with its harmless horn:[24]

> So spoke the Sinless Soul & laid her head on the downy fleece
> Of a curld Ram who stretchd himself in sleep beside his mistress
> And soft sleep fell upon her eyelids in the silent noon of day
>
> (IX, 455–7)

Meanwhile the human harvest has finally come to fruition in groans of woe, and Urizen has arisen as a mighty Harvester to gather in the sheaves. When they are all gathered into barns to the accompaniment of music, a great feast is spread, at which the Regenerate Man sits down, while the wine of Eternity is served by the flames of Luvah. The voice of Enion is heard again. Like Ahania, she casts off her death garments and rises to embrace Tharmas, who humanizes as he embraces her. He carries her off into the heavens, where they are welcomed to the Feast by the Eternal Man. The assembled Eternals shudder at the sight of a female form separated from Man, drinking up his powers stead of giving him rest and pleasure: and one of the Company rises to discourse on the results of this separation. Man, having lost the Vision which should illuminate and fire his flesh, has become no more than a worm: as a result he has enclosed his threefold vision and shuts himself up in selfishness, cultivating abstract science instead of brotherhood:

> Man is a Worm wearied with joy he seeks the caves of sleep
> Among the Flowers of Beulah in his Selfish cold repose
> Forsaking Brotherhood & Universal love in selfish clay
> Folding the pure wings of his mind seeking the places dark
> Abstracted from the roots of Science . . .
>
> (IX, 627–31)

The remedy of the Eternals is to cast the selfish terror into the earth and reopen his threefold vision by giving him life in a family.

With the birth of a new world, even the slaves begin singing, and their song rises to the Golden feast; the Eternal Man, hearing, foresees in the coming harvest the re-establishment of organized innocence:

> Let the Bulls of Luvah tread the Corn & draw the loaded waggon
> Into the Barn while children glean the Ears around the door
> Then shall they lift their innocent hands & stroke his furious nose
> And he shall lick the little girls white neck & on her head
> Scatter the perfume of his breath while from his mountains high
> The lion of terror shall come down & bending his bright mane
> And crouching at their side shall eat from the curld boys white lap
> His golden food and in the Evening sleep before the door.
>
> (IX, 701–8)

As the families of men are thrust into the wine-presses, it becomes evident that their sufferings are not the deadly sufferings of war but the pangs which accompany the birth of joy. Odours of life rise round the presses, singing of this terror and joy:

O trembling joy excess of joy is like Excess of grief

And while in the presses all seems to be cruelty, around the presses all the wise creatures of earth rejoice. Blake describes delicately the individuality of each one, suggesting also the innocence of all human emotions when seen in their nakedness:

> Timbrels & Violins sport round the Wine Presses   The little Seed
> The sportive root the Earthworm the small beetle the wise Emmet
> Dance round the Wine Presses of Luvah. the Centipede is there
> The ground Spider with many Eyes the Mole clothed in Velvet
> The Earwig armd the tender maggot emblem of Immortality
> The Slow Slug the grasshopper that sings & laughs & drinks
> The winter comes he folds his slender bones without a murmur
> There is the Nettle that stings with soft down & there
> The indignant Thistle whose bitterness is bred in his milk
> And who lives on the contempt of his neighbour there all the idle weeds
> That creep about the obscure places shew their various limbs
> Naked in all their beauty dancing round the Wine Presses.
> (IX, 755–66)

This vintage in joy and woe, the final stage in the redemptive process, is a counterpart to the original sexual lapse and Blake's version of the redemption described by Christian writers, who quote the words of Isaiah: 'Who is this that cometh from Edom? ... I have trodden the wine-press alone.'[25]   Blake's Redeemer, the Eternal Man, calls on Tharmas and Urthona to resume their former state, Tharmas with his shepherd's crook, Urthona the limping smith with his hammer. They are followed by the emanations of all four Zoas, who rise to their looms. Luvah and Vala are put upon the earth for dung, and the Wine of Ages is taken away; Urthona finishes Urizen's work by grinding the corn of Wisdom in his mills and baking it as bread in his ovens. Fourfold vision is re-established.

At the end of the poem, therefore, because the phallic ex-

tremes of innocence and desire are restored, vision is renewed
and humanized. Man walks abroad, no longer at the mercy of
Urizen's laws but perceiving the world in its true nature, where
sublimity alternates with pathos. Light comes not from the
distant, cold stars of Reason but from nightly fires of energy,
replaced in the daytime by a Sun who resembles a Man. The
long visionary passage describes the pastoral innocence of
Tharmas and the steady beat of desire from Urthona's caves;
it concludes with the astonishment of men that they are not
consumed, but liberated, by the fires of this vision.

> The Expanding Eyes of Man behold the depths of wondrous
>   worlds
> One Earth one sea beneath nor Erring Globes wander but Stars
> Of fire rise up nightly from the Ocean & one Sun
> Each morning like a New born Man issues with songs & Joy
> Calling the Plowman to his Labour and the Shepherd to his rest
> He walks upon the Eternal Mountains raising his heavenly voice
> Conversing with the Animal forms of wisdom night & day
> That risen from the Sea of fire renewd walk oer the Earth
>
> For Tharmas brought his flocks upon the hills & in the Vales
> Around the Eternal Mans bright tent the little Children play
> Among the wooly flocks   The hammer of Urthona sounds
> In the deep caves beneath his limbs renewd his Lions roar
> Around the Furnaces & in Evening sport upon the plains
> They raise their faces from the Earth conversing with the Man
>
> How is it we have walkd thro fires & yet are not consumd
> How is it that all things are changd even as in ancient time
>   (IX, 830-45)

In this apocalyptic state Urthona is left as the commanding
figure, a warrior whose warfare is mental, not physical. And
by Urthona's 'mental fight' those analytic techniques which
when employed exclusively, whether by scientists or others,
lead to the destruction of Vision are now kept in subordination,
leaving Science free to appear in its true glory.

> Urthona rises from the ruinous Walls
> In all his ancient strength to form the golden armour of science
> For intellectual War   The War of swords departed now
> The dark Religions are departed & sweet Science reigns
>   (IX, 852-5)

Despite its thematic coherences, *The Four Zoas* is clearly not the fully articulated epic which Blake intended. In fact, when one takes into account the complexities of symbolism involved, it is surprising that the poem is as successful as it is. There are certain failures of plot, resulting mainly from three central problems of construction:

(1) The difficulty of presenting as an inter-related sequence a fourfold Fall, in which all the energies supposedly fell at one and the same time.

(2) The limited scene of action available in Nights Five and Eight, where the struggle between Urizen and Los necessarily takes place against a shadowy, negative landscape.

(3) The difficulty of gearing this middle part of the story to a satisfying Apocalypse and Judgment in Night the Ninth.

There are also failures of allegory, due partly to swift alternations of mode between witty, emblematic writing and a more organic symbolism. The general difficulty of conveying allegorical significances without spelling out the significance at each point is created by the originality of the ideas involved. Previous allegorists would take some shared mythic structure (the Bible, say, or Greek mythology) for granted. Blake's myth must necessarily be recreated at every point by the reader in the act of reading.

Nothing of this is to be construed as a criticism of Blake himself, of course, for he did not publish the poem and presumably regarded it as unsatisfactory. The direct successes of the poem lie in individual, coherent passages, particularly those suggesting the expansions and contractions of liberated vision, which impress the imagination and stay in the memory. Blake's powers were always at their best in the short concentrated vision, and his achievement would have been greater could he have used more often the method of his *Songs of Innocence and of Experience*. Isolated visions, each with its own impetus and form, may present only a fragmented picture of reality, but the immediate result is more satisfactory.

That he did not is matter for ironical contemplation. Blake, the opponent of Urizen and the asserter of individual identity, the man who believed that 'Everything that lives is holy', had succumbed for a time to the very curse of Urizen which he described so vigorously. In trying to write an epic which should contain within itself a complete view of truth he had leaned out with his compasses to circumscribe, in nine or ten books, a universe which could never be organized so simply. But his epic intent is also a witness to the urgency which he felt in trying to transmit his central ideas.

The passages which remain in the mind are the lyric laments of the wandering emanations, the visions by which the Zoas strive to recall their lost harmony, and the episodes of the last Night—which all give something of the cosmic suggestion that Blake wished to communicate. In such an interwoven tissue of success and failure, however, it is not possible to separate the wheat from the chaff in a decisive manner, for the effect of the poem grows continuously in the mind during successive readings: the reader can best approach the poem by first grasping its general shape and then reading steadily through it. It is not difficult to linger over the best passages and enjoy them without the hindrance caused by intrusions of an unfamiliar symbolism. The curse of Urizen is lifted, so far as each passage is approached in its own identity: each identity helps to interpret the others, so that the reader's imagination moves increasingly in harmony with the poet's. Bewilderment, however justifiable, gives place to admiration of Blake's multifarious invention, his power to show forth the different countries of his imagination in their varying colours and lights. Attempts to deal with the poem as a linear narrative, equally, are replaced by a sense that the importance of *this* story lies in other dimensions of significance, to which the confluence of visionary and phallic elements in the drawings are as important a guide as the extraordinary assimilation of light and energy into the actual language of the poem.

7 Intimations of Sublimity

The Romantic writer who takes as his theme the ultimate meaning of human existence is likely to find his work falling into one or other of two separate patterns. On the one hand he will be concerned with the sense of 'visitation'—the experience which some human beings have of receiving impulses from a world not immediately present to the eye of reason. On the other, he will be concerned with the sense of 'yearning'—the reaching out for another existence more satisfying than the mortal, decaying human condition. So Kafka found that his most important works were *The Trial*, a record of visitation from an unknown order, and *The Castle*, a record of search for an unattainable one.

Blake's late work betrays similar preoccupations. In *Milton*, he wrote of the visitation of the poet which we call inspiration; in his final long work, *Jerusalem*, he is concerned with mankind's incessant yearning for eternity. *Milton*, which had been planned to exist in twelve books was completed in two, and it is clear that he finally intended *Jerusalem* to be his long-desired epic poem. But to order the latter poem was more difficult than to order *Milton*; it needed a pattern which would succeed, where *Vala* had failed, in presenting a mythological interpretation of human experience.

So difficult did this task prove to be that a new method of composing becomes evident as we examine the final text. In composing *Milton* Blake had added several plates after he had completed the first version of the engraved book. The plates which he added were more or less self-contained, expressing some idea which he wished to emphasize at that point: in introducing the new plate he made little or no adjustment to the context. In writing *Jerusalem* he went a stage further, engraving sequences of plates on particular themes, which he probably intended finally to incorporate into a single binding action.

But the task which had been overpoweringly difficult in *Vala* proved again to be intractable. The theme was clear enough, as it had always been; the problem of producing a heroic action from it was wellnigh insoluble. In the end, Blake evidently realized this, for he produced a more artificial shape for his poem by creating four sections, each consisting of twenty-five plates and carrying its own preface addressed to the class of men who seemed most concerned with its contents: the Public; the Jews; the Deists; and the Christians, in that order. This symmetrical ordering of the sections gives rise to a suspicion of arbitrariness which is confirmed when one examines the plates in detail. While the poem has a firm beginning and end, and a roughly shaped structure between, it consists for the most part of juxtaposed sequences: in some cases a whole sequence has been broken up, the plates being scattered at random through the book. For example, the reader who cares to read plates 16, 72, 59 and 73 in that order will find that they interlock neatly and may well have been originally engraved in that sequence. But since they contain some of Blake's least inspired symbolism, he probably thought it best to break them up. Between making two copies of the final work, also, he took a whole section of four plates and transferred its position: evidently, then, the general order of the poem is not absolutely determined or sacrosanct in his mind. This piece-meal composition throws more importance upon the individual plate, which, while always in loose relation to the general theme of the poem, will often be found to be relatively self-contained.

At the same time, Blake evolved for this poem certain new runs of imagery. The process of change can already be seen in action in the pages of *The Four Zoas*, where some of the later revisions serve to give concreteness to more general images. He deletes references to 'the Man', for instance and inserts 'Albion'; he replaces vague references to 'mountains' by using specific names such as 'Gilead' and 'Hermon', or 'Snowdon' and 'Plynlimmon'—holy mountains of the Israelites or the Druids respectively. The fact that the substitutions could be made so easily proves that there is nothing esoteric in the use of these particular names beyond their traditional numinous quality. Blake had found the task of producing his psychological epic intractable partly by reason of the difficulty of discovering a final framework to contain everything. If all things existed within one Man, what contained him? By setting him in landscapes used by the Hebrew and English writers, Blake could at least give him a context—a context which was familiar, and already vivified by poetry such as the Book of Isaiah or Drayton's *Polyolbion*. And the mythological references of these names carried further creative implications for Blake. The possible significance of the 'British Antiquities' had long fascinated him —even in youth he had engraved a figure from Michelangelo in order to picture Joseph of Arimathea wandering among the rocks of Albion. Now he used the parallels between Jewish and British history more widely, in an attempt to give greater definition to his poem.

The Druidic tradition furnished the necessary link. Blake once declared that Abraham and Noah were Druids[1]—by which he meant *pure* Druids, before the cult declined. These original Druids walked through nature in complete liberty of spirit, reconciled to the earth and possessed by vision. But when vision faded, some set themselves up as priests and ruled by law. Their symbols were the trilithon, a product of useless labour which was also an image of the worship of geometry in art, and the Wicker Man—in which travesty of human form human sacrifices were carried out.

A similar decline from an ideal state could, according to Blake's ideas, be traced through Hebrew history. From Adam in his garden or Noah upon his mountain there had been corruption, imaged in Cain or Ham respectively, towards a visionless state where priests ruled by law. The story of Joseph, which Blake illustrated as a young man,[2] was itself an allegory of the process. Joseph, the dreamer and visionary, conspired against by jealous brothers, was matched at the other extreme by Reuben, whose gathering of mandrakes in the Old Testament narrative symbolized his nature as a 'vegetative' man: full of natural kindness and striving to save Joseph from being killed, but devoid of energized vision. Between the extremes was Judah, who did save Joseph's life—but only for the money to be gained by selling him to the Midianites. So Joseph was sold into Egypt, whose Pyramids, meaningless and antivisionary products of the forced labour exacted by the Pharaohs, were apt symbols of a tyrannical commercial civilization.

Turning back to early British history, Blake found this pattern duplicated there. On the one hand of Arthur one might see Merlin the magician, guide of his imagination; on the other the earlier figure of Bladud, father of Lear and founder of Bath, a man of natural kindness. Arthur himself held a precarious position: his name reflected the glory of Arcturus, keeper of the pole, but he was liable to become enslaved by the frosty formality of reason. When this happened, Merlin was rejected in favour of Blake's Urizen and Bladud replaced by the foolish 'vegetative' Lear, facing cruel daughters of his flesh. Bath, from being a place of healing springs, turned into a city where artificiality and hypocrisy poisoned humanity.

The pattern is by now familiar. Vision degenerates to pure analysis, and a pursuit of non-visionary sexual fulfilment turns humanity into mere 'vegetation'. To describe the Man who has split into these varying entities Blake also took over, probably from Spenser,[3] the name Albion. Albion is the Eternal Man of *Vala*: not just another character in the drama but *the* character, who once included all the others and whose darkening is responsible for their various distresses. In terms of Hebrew cabbalistic tradition he would be Adam Kadmon; but Blake does not make this identification by name. Instead, he chooses to wed British and Hebrew tradition, giving to Albion Jerusalem as his emanation. Thus he can draw upon all the resources of the Old Testament love for the Holy City, together with the later significance of Jerusalem as the city where Christ was crucified and its final reappearance as the New Jerusalem in Revelation. She is always, of course, to be identified with London: but the feminine associations of the Hebrew capital, culminating in her descent from heaven 'as a bride adorned for her husband' gives Jerusalem a peculiar relevance to the inner structure of Blake's mythology.

His particular preoccupations are also evident in the landscape of the poem. As previously, the Man walking in the Garden is diminished by the withdrawal of light and by the hardening of earth into rock, so that the typical scene in the poem is of Albion's rocky shore illuminated only by the distant, ineffectual, even cruel light of the pole star. The points of relief in the scene are the fitful appearances of the moon and the presence near the pole-star of a constellation, picked out in points of light, in the shape of a Man. But Arcturus, like Arthur, is only a dim intimation of a lost glory.[4]

Once these central ideas are grasped, the poem gains in intelligibility. The main task is to separate the wheat from the chaff in Blake's symbolism—to decide, for instance, which are the important names and which the unimportant. It is a paradoxical result of the poem's initial obscurity that the reader in quest of firm ground is most likely to seize on one of the long lists of counties of England and Wales—which in fact yield less meaning a line than any other passages in the poem. Blake's 'statement' here is very general indeed: he is simply demonstrating that an English poet can have the sort of feeling for the towns of England that a Hebrew poet had for the towns of Palestine. He is also trying to suggest that each has its own visionary identity, its own creative possibilities. Passages like this derive the way that they should be read from the rest of the poem, not vice versa.

The poem as a whole depicts struggles and contentions which are, in the same way, part of a larger pattern, the travails of creation to find its true nature. As before, the dominant myth is that of the sleep of the Eternal Man and the consequent disorder of various forces which would otherwise be harmonized within his activity. Blake has by now moved away from his attempt to describe the struggle between the Zoas in detail. As a theme for poetry, it had proved too negative in final effect. Instead, Blake seizes on Los, the major positive force in his cycle, and makes him the central figure in the poem. Albion being darkened, Los is automatically without vision also, but by his continuing use of his energies in desire and creation, he does act as the guardian of vision. He continues his labours, blindly creating and forming, binding down and giving shape, in order that things may appear as they are, in their true nature, and be dealt with accordingly. In the background, meanwhile, Albion continues to darken.

In the second book, addressed to the Jews, the theme is the growth of Law, which results in the tyranny of the politicians, the harsh moral judgments of the priests and the abstract reasonings of the scientists.

In the third book, Blake rounds on the rationalists. One might have expected to find him on the side of Voltaire and Rousseau, protagonists of liberty, but his attitude proves to be more subtle. Looking more closely into the so-called Enlightenment, he decides that it was really a darkening, a setting up of abstract reason as god. And so, far from destroying the tyrant, it plays into his hands, enabling him to argue that law is inherent in the natural creation. At best, it is true, as in Greek religion and philosophy, the vegetative man is exalted—but still at the expense of vision.

In the final book, addressed to the Christians, the reawakening of Albion is foretold. The work ends with an account of the renewal of creation: as the faded Man is reunited with his Emanation, Albion and Jerusalem become the Spirit and Bride of Revelation, the restoration of Man in his true glory.

But if the outline of the poem is clear, its general run is much more difficult to deal with. More than in any preceding work, Blake veers between arbitrary symbolism and passages of heightened insight. For the shape of the poem, in fact, we turn rather to the themes which help to organize *The Four Zoas*. The incidents of the new poem can only very loosely be described as a 'plot': rather they offer a series of occasions for developing these themes still further. And although, as a result, the themes are more difficult to isolate, it will be useful, in view of the general narrative diffuseness, to make several readings of the poem as before, directing attention to each in turn. To do so will provide a better focusing-point for discussion than to pursue an illusory plot-structure where only a large framework exists; it will also bring out something of the real shape of this poem, which revolves again and again on the insistence that social, moral and intellectual problems alike can find solution only in a renewal of the human imagination itself. The renewal, as before, is imaged in the yearnings of the participating characters and enacted in the poetry—but now more consistently and pervasively than in the earlier attempt. It is this achievement of imagery and language, working through a series of acute social, moral and intellectual judgments, that gives *Jerusalem* its true unity and coherence.

I   *The social relevance*

The greater prominence of Los in *Jerusalem* assists Blake to render the contemporary scene more satisfactorily. In previous works there were no suitable spokesmen for criticism of the eighteenth-century apart from Rintrah and Palamabron, so that such references were often made obliquely or ambiguously. The positive character now given to Los endows him with a particular status also as social critic. Previously, as Urthona's spectre, he could never completely achieve a life of his own; now, though still called the spectre of Urthona, he is more like a representative, humanity's prophet: he is even endowed with a 'spectre' of his own. If the mythological machinery is put under strain by this, the artistic gain is clear. We no longer see Los primarily as a jealous father, binding Orc to the natural world; instead we see him first and foremost as the builder of Golgonooza, the limited earthly city. The creative force which characterized him at times as smith in *The Four Zoas* is now his dominant activity.

Orc, on the other hand, is named only once. He lies coiled in the south—a threat, but a distant one. Instead, more is said of Los's 'sons', who correspond to the twelve tribes of Israel, and the most important of whom are Hand, Hyle and Skofeld. The fact that the names of people who participated in Blake's trial (such as Schofield, the Soldier who originally touched off the incident) are used for sons of Los is interesting but need not detain us unduly.[5] It is a mild form of revenge on Blake's part, enabling him also to comment obliquely on the state of contemporary justice in England. In the poem, the sons are not real people: as always, they are the representatives of particular states. Between them they represent various aspects of Orc as his energy declines. Thus Hand represents impotent desire, burning in isolation; Hyle the decline of man under domination by the female will; and Skofeld (the captive of his lusts) the completed degradation of man. All are earthbound, 'vegetated', cut off from Vision.[6]

Viewed against Los's impulse to create, the world that we

know is seen largely as a world of death. Its dominant features are those of the world of Urizen in previous poems: darkness, snow, hail and earthquakes. Meanwhile, Los walks around the walls of his city of Golgonooza, surveying his creations. And since creation is not in itself good, but serves simply to bring all things to the point where they can be seen for what they are, the works which he notices are works of cruelty—those looms, mills, prisons and workhouses which hardly seem to exist to those who are outside them, but which are, for those who have entered them, the only world:

> For every thing exists & not one sigh nor smile nor tear,
> One hair nor particle of dust, not one can pass away.
>
> (13. 66–14.1)

He also sees the familiar regions of Blake's mythology: in the east the cherub preventing access to the Tree of Life; in the south Orc lying coiled as a serpent or as the dragon Urizen—for energy may either break out in revolution or, linked with reason, inform tyranny—and Tharmas, who is seen as the devouring vegetated Tongue:

> a false brain: a false heart:
> And false bowels: altogether composing the False Tongue . . .
>
> (14. 5–6)

The failure of Tharmas, the sexual in man, is not restricted to itself but is part of an expressive failure at all three levels, including the failure of the heart and the restriction of the head's activity to works of reason.

Los continues to look at his sons and daughters and perceives that each of them is beautiful and has the three regions of Childhood, Manhood and Age: but because the 'western gate' is closed in them the secret of immortality is lost, and they are made false in each of the three remaining regions. Only in the distance he sees, faintly, Jerusalem the emanation, protected by the daughters of Beulah. The illustration (fig. 51) portrays his state: emaciated, but still aware of vision.

At one stage in the poem's evolution, Chapter One ended at this point; the next few plates seem to have been included primarily to make up the number of plates to the required twenty-five. Although there is no ordered development, however, these plates expand our sense of the contemporary scene and enable Blake to speak in his own person—another new feature of this poem.

The first consists of a vision of Albion sleeping, while his spectral sons enroot into every nation, becoming a giant polypus. The power of Bacon and Newton is everywhere: Blake finds that reasonings like 'vast serpents' enfold about him, constantly destroying the 'minute articulations' of his imaginative powers (cf. figs. 28–30). And as he surveys the schools and universities he sees them as a monstrous dark mill of analysis, in which the Loom of Locke is washed by the water-wheels of Newton to create a black cloth of reason. The wheels of analysis move like cog-wheels, mutually fitting and turning each other; they are the opposite of the wheels of Eden which, like the wheels described by Ezekiel, move in harmony, each within the other, an emblem of true human relationships (cf. fig. 38).[7]

As Blake looks at London he sees Los and his sons working in metals, while Reuben and his followers take refuge in 'vegetation' (—a covert reference, perhaps, to the idea that after Cain's crime there was a division between the artificers and the pastoral tribes).[8] In contemporary London he sees the powers of Bromion, Theotormon, Palamabron and Rintrah repeating the same pattern: Bromion's law creating 'furnaces' in the suburbs, while Theotormon's doubts lead to 'vegetation'. The run of imagery culminates in

> The Soldiers fife; the Harlots shriek; the Virgins dismal groan
> The Parents fear: the Brothers jealousy: the Sisters curse . . .
> (16. 6–7)

The work of the Spectre in the furnaces is here carried on by Palamabron, while Rintrah is the hammerer. This reference to the work of pity and indignation is followed by a description of Los's halls of the imagination, decorated by many stories of the pathos resulting from 'Hate or Wayward Love'.

> & every sorrow & distress is carved here
> Every Affinity of Parents Marriages & Friendships are here
> In all their various combinations wrought with wondrous Art
> All that can happen to Man in his pilgrimage of seventy years . . .
> (16. 64–9)

The preface to the next chapter includes a long piece of verse in four-line stanzas which, like the corresponding passages in other prefaces, shows Blake's lyric gifts at their best. London has become Jerusalem, seen with a light that springs from the visionary eye of childhood—though the nostalgia is perhaps a nostalgia for the future rather than the past:

> The fields from Islington to Marybone,
> To Primrose Hill and Saint Johns Wood:
> Were builded over with pillars of gold,
> And there Jerusalems pillars stood.
>
> (27. 1–4)

The place-names are bathed in nostalgia of a different sort for the modern reader: there are now no fields between Islington and Marylebone. In Blake's time, however, the view from Hampstead and similar high spots was still a pastoral one: these stanzas suggest a sweeping view of this landscape, after which Blake focuses on a particular small area well-known to him from boyhood: the area north of Oxford Street, soon to be developed as Regent's Park, which contained the Jews-harp tea house and Willan's Farm (a contemporary painting of which has recently been reproduced by Paul Miner):[9]

> The Jews-harp-house & the Green Man;
> The Ponds where Boys to bathe delight:
> The fields of Cows by Willans farm:
> Shine in Jerusalems pleasant sight.

Beyond this innocent, gilded landscape, however, Blake is aware of the city, with all its visionlessness and cruelty:

> Where Albion slept beneath the fatal Tree
> And the Druids golden Knife,
> Rioted in human gore,
> In Offerings of Human Life . . .

The two hints of Albion's sleep and human sacrifice are brought to bear upon the London of the day in the next stanza:

> They groan'd aloud on London Stone
> They groan'd aloud on Tyburns Brook,
> Albion gave his deadly groan,
> And all the Atlantic Mountains shook . . .

The images refer to familiar themes. The tyranny of Natural Law is suggested by London Stone—a true rock of anti-vision since it marked the point from which all distances were measured and was thus a point of reference for the world of abstract calculation. Tyburn, similarly, is the place where criminals were executed, human offerings to the Moral Law.

These laws are responsible for the growth of Albion's spectre and the fall of Jerusalem. The Spectre, or Satan, spread his power over all lands:

> He witherd up the Human Form,
> By laws of sacrifice for sin:
> Till it became a Mortal Worm:
> But O! translucent all within.

On the other hand, the translucence of the divine Vision is not always imprisoned: the human form has been seen in Jesus who, though 'weeping in weak & mortal clay', gave the clue and the example to be followed:

> Create my Spirit to thy Love:
> Subdue my Spectre to thy Fear.

As he imagines this process of assimilation, Blake points out that it involves not the destruction but the reclamation of the Spectre—('My Selfhood! Satan! armd in gold'[10]). And the restoration of Satan is the key to the restoration of vision, for the gold of which his armour is made will be the gold of 'mental fight' and visionary Jerusalem. As the self rises into its true, generous pride once more, it sees the errors that have been committed by the Spectre—particularly in cultivating that extension of the Self, the Family:

> Is this thy soft Family-Love
> Thy cruel Patriarchal pride
> Planting thy Family alone,
> Destroying all the World beside.

Instead of this vicarious selfishness (—which can itself become a curse when a man's own relations turn against him) Blake sets his vision of a state where human beings live by constant 'exchange':

> In my Exchanges every Land
> Shall walk, & mine in every Land,

> Mutual shall build Jerusalem:
> Both heart in heart & hand in hand.

The new chapter presents the opposite of such a visionary England. In a prophetic speech Los describes the groaning of England's cities now that the divine countenance is no longer seen on her hills: the labourers are oppressed, and cunning humility ensures that the poor shall live on a crust of bread. Above all, he condemns the tyranny of sexual distinctions:

> Humanity knows not of Sex: wherefore are Sexes in Beulah?
> In Beulah the Female lets down her beautiful Tabernacle;
> Which the Male enters magnificent between her Cherubim;
> And becomes One with her mingling condensing in Self-love
> The Rocky Law of Condemnation & double Generation &
>   Death.
>
> (30. [44]. 33-7)

The imagery brings together the humanizing idea of the 'fleshly tabernacle' and the artistic idea of the Temple, with its Cherubim. The magnificence of Solomon's temple is made an emblem of true sexual relations, whereas the pomp of the Hebrew priest going up into the secret place becomes an emblem of sexual relations under the Law. Los cries aloud for a rending of the veil and an awakening of the dead to generation.

Since Albion does not heed his words, Los takes his globe of fire (as Urizen had done in *The Book of Urizen*) and proceeds to examine the interior of Albion, to prevent him, if possible, from finally turning his back on the Divine Vision. Desolation is everywhere, but he cannot see the destroyer. The 'minute particulars' are being destroyed and turned into bricks for the construction of graceless pyramids, but the Pharaoh who commands these useless labours—the spirit of Analysis—is hidden. He walks through the surrounding villages into London, where a dirty and despicable landscape corresponds to the degradation of the human body. The Isle of Dogs is the 'Isle of Leuthas Dogs' (in Blake's thought the dog is a constant symbol for the animal lust in man which, if separated from full humanity, becomes degraded). Everywhere the tale is the same: sublime jewels and ornaments are made into hard objects and opaque rocks, the beauties of human feeling are turned into filth and mire. The Tower of London stands, an abiding symbol of separateness; instead of Bethlehem, centre of humanity, he finds only Bedlam, where mentally tormented humanity asks for bread and is given a stone.[11]

Los sees the crimes, not the criminals: being a creature of positiveness he cannot conceive a state which is purely negative. He sees, too, that anything which he might do to punish or avenge would simply make matters worse, for everything there is a victim and degraded. In Westminster and Marylebone alone, some elements of beauty (or Gothic form) speak faintly of Jerusalem; and when he sits down in despair upon the symbolic London Stone, he hears the voice of Jerusalem herself, complaining that she cannot be the wife of an Albion who is wholly devoted to 'demonstration' and who does not see the holiness of 'minute particulars'. Vala, too, has become simply a figure of mourning. Existing for herself alone, no longer translucent of eternity, she weaves a net and a bondage for the visionary human being. (The illumination to plate 31 shows the resulting state.)

Albion himself, who perceives the truth but only in a fading form, senses that something is wrong with the scene and Los takes up his distant reproaches in a more primitive form, returning to his favourite theme. The legally imposed dominance of woman has led to the enslaving of man—who ought to be the servant only of God (An echo of the Miltonic doctrine, 'He for God only, she for God in him'.) Instead of the woman perceiving the Divine Vision by reflection from the man, the man has become captive to the will of the female:

> What may Man be? who can tell! but what may Woman be;
> To have power over Man from Cradle to corruptible Grave.
> There is a Throne in every Man, it is the Throne of God
> This Woman has claimd as her own & Man is no more!
> Albion is the Tabernacle of Vala & her Temple
> And not the Tabernacle & Temple of the Most High . . .
>
> (34. [30.] 25–30)

Seeing this absurd exaltation of Law, some of the Eternals laugh:

> Have you know the Judgment that is arisen among the
> Zoa's of Albion? where a Man dare hardly to embrace

His own Wife. for the terrors of Chastity that they call
By the name of Morality. their Daughters govern all
In hidden deceit! they are Vegetable only fit for burning:
Art & Science cannot exist but by Naked Beauty displayd.
                              (36. [32.] 44–49)

Others, more serious, see that this state, where what seems to be
is taken for the reality, can be redeemed only by reassumption
into the 'Body of Jesus', when length, breadth and height will
again find proper subordinate positions within a humanized
whole.

In a later plate, the sick Albion cries out to Los, reproaching
him for his cultivation of mercy and demanding justice and
righteousness. Los replies in one of the most important speeches
of the poem, explaining that he is willing to give justice and
righteousness but must also give mercy, so as to contain Albion's
vengeance. He asserts himself as a practical energy:

Thou art in Error; trouble me not with thy righteousness.
I have innocence to defend and ignorance to instruct:
I have no time for seeming; and little arts of compliment,
In morality and virtue: in self-glorying and pride.
                              (42. 25–8)

His energy is superior to the deathly powers of Hand and
Hyle, who try to seize him, calling for the building of Babylon
and the establishment of Rahab (the moral law in all her
glory): for inwardly they are themselves groaning for salvation.

Oh when shall the morning of the grave appear, and when
Shall our salvation come? we sleep upon our watch
We cannot awake! and our Spectres rage in the forests
O God of Albion where art thou! pity the watchers!
                              (42. 71–4)

They look on in despair as the Zoas plot poisonously against
Albion. Once again, it is Los who sounds the practical note:

Then Los grew furious raging: Why stand we here trembling
        around
Calling on God for help; and not ourselves in whom God dwells
Stretching a hand to save the falling Man . . .
                              (43. [38.] 12–14)

He denounces the activities of the other Zoas,

> Brooding in holy hypocritic lust, drinking the cries of pain
> From howling victims of Law: building Heavens Twenty-seven-
>   fold.
> Swelld & bloated General Forms. repugnant to the Divine-
> Humanity, who is the Only General and Universal Form
> To which all Lineaments tend & seek with Love & sympathy . . .
>
>   (43. [38.] 17–21)

Everywhere he sees hypocrisy: a pretence of liberty which destroys liberty, a pretence of religion which destroys religion, the generalizing of Art and Science until Art and Science are lost. The true warfare, in which men contend for truth, is replaced by physical warfare, in which they kill one another.

Across the landscape is heard, very faintly, the distant voice of Bath (the illustration shows her as a spirit rising from vegetation). Appropriately and amusingly, her speech has one or two touches of elegant sensibility:

> Brothers of Eternity: this Man whose great example
> We all admir'd & lov'd, whose all benevolent countenance, seen
> In Eden, in lovely Jerusalem, drew even from envy
> The tear: and the confession of honesty, open & undisguis'd
> From mistrust and suspition. The Man is himself become
> A piteous example of oblivion . . .
>
>   (45. [40.] 4–9)

She goes on to point the lesson. However great and glorious an individuality may be, it has only to shrink into Selfhood to be reduced to nothing, fading away in morning's breath. There is a brief reference to a previous near-disaster which, although not explicitly described elsewhere in Blake, was clearly an attempt by the energies of twofold vision to take the place of threefold and fourfold, as represented by the moon and sun.

>   When Africa in sleep
> Rose in the night of Beulah, and bound down the Sun & Moon
> His friends cut his strong chains, & overwhelm'd his dark
> Machines in fury & destruction, and the Man reviving
>   repented. . .
>
>   (45. [40.]19–22)

But Albion's sleep is not like Africa's—it is the darker sleep of single vision: 'his machines are woven with his life'.

The other Gothic cities of England combine with Bath to plead with Albion that instead of remaining in Ulro he should repose in Beulah's night until his error is cast out. He refuses their comfort and they mourn towards one another. The plate continues with the reflection.

> Alas!—The time will come. when a mans worst enemies
> Shall be those of his own house and family: in a Religion
> Of Generation, to destroy by Sin and Atonement, happy Jerusa-
> lem.
> The Bride and Wife of the Lamb. O God thou art Not an
> Avenger!
>
> (46. [41.] 25–8)

The illumination to this page (fig. 34) is striking. Two horned tyrants with animal bodies, on the backs of which mean little winged creatures are busily writing, are harnessed (rather like the kings of Asia in *Tamburlaine*) to a chariot consisting of snakes, whose tails are coiled into wheels. Above the snakes, in the flames, sit Albion and Jerusalem, fading and distressed. This design is not, as has been claimed, 'the Chariot of Inspiration'; the sufferings portrayed relate it to the lines just quoted, which appear immediately above it. It is a witty commentary on them, showing tyrannical and visionless creatures whose energies, instead of harmonizing into a chariot of fire, have become intractable serpents. The little recording angels on their backs enact a profitless moral judgment of their many sins, while the tyrants themselves struggle to drag forward an effete Albion and a fading Jerusalem. This is Blake's verdict on the Doctrine of the Atonement.

The next plate, equally striking, shows the souls of the dead lost in clouds of abstraction. The text describes the agonies of cruelty now that Luvah has broken loose and become a spirit of war.

Albion finally loses hope and is received into the arms of the Saviour to repose upon the Rock of Ages. His grave, however, is ornamented and will become those books of the Bible which, though normally interpreted according to the Law, can also be read as visionary documents: the five books of the Decalogue (the first five books of the Bible, dominated by the Mosaic law), Joshua, Judges, Samuel, Kings, Psalms, Prophets, the four-fold gospel (fourfold in vision as well as number) and Revelation ('the Revelations eternal'). The omission of St Paul's writings is perhaps the most significant feature of Blake's list: it seems that in spite of their exaltation of charity (cf. fig. 75) he finds no truly visionary dimension in them.

Meanwhile Jerusalem awakens in Beulah and goes forth to create a vestige of Vision in the world. She takes a moment of time and draws it out into a rainbow, she takes an atom of space and opens a centre of beauty in it. The other Daughters of Beulah mourn over her, and Erin speaks to them all, explaining that Albion, who has always stood for sacrifice, is in danger of abandoning the true sacrifice, undertaken by friend for friend, in favour of the false, which immolates victims to the Law. Even child-offerings may result. She describes the consequences of growing into the state of vegetation:

> The vegetating Cities are burned & consumed from the Earth,
> And the Bodies in which all Animals & Vegetations, the Earth & Heaven
> Were contain'd in the All Glorious Imagination are witherd & darkend. . .
>
> (49. 12–14)

They sing the virtues of the positive: it is better to prevent misery than to release from misery, to prevent error than to be forced to forgive the criminal. Everything must be brought to the light, that the Reasoner may be compelled to demonstrate without merely analysing ('with unhewn Demonstrations'); those who pretend to good must show their goodness in detailed activity:

> General Good is the plea of the scoundrel hypocrite & flatterer:
> For Art & Science cannot exist but in minutely organized Particulars . . .
>
> (55. 61–2)

In lines which recall Milton's refusal to praise the 'fugitive and cloistered virtue',[12] they demand the establishment of truth in the only proper form of infinity—in a definite and determinate identity created by the destruction of falsehood.

The Eternals ask for a champion and Los offers himself, singing bitterly of the separation between man and woman.

Looking at female domination, he decries the power of woman
over man from the cradle to the grave. Instead of being a son
of the morning with the earth in subjection under his feet, man
is a phantom, living only by the mercies of calendar time and
geographical space, vegetated.

> This World is all a Cradle for the erred wandering Phantom:
> Rock'd by Year, Month, Day & Hour; and every two Moments,
> Between. dwells a Daughter of Beulah. to feed the Human
>   Vegetable. . . .
>
>   (56. 8–10)

Only by the tenderness of woman can the human phantom
accept life in the first place, in a world where the sun, instead of
imaging the chariot of the morning, appears as a scythed war
chariot, and the moon, instead of imaging the Ark of Vision, is
'a Ship in the British Ocean!'. Los also attacks St Paul, whose
moral law creates the separate female will, with its secrecy and
shame:

> Look back into the Church Paul! Look! Three Women around
> The Cross! O Albion   why didst thou a female Will create?
>   (56. 42–3)

The three Maries around the cross include Mary Magdalen:
the harlot is there as well as the virgin. This thought is taken up
by the Gothic cities of England who cry over the rocky Druid
temples and their consecration to the moral law,

> What is a Wife & what is a Harlot? What is a Church? & What
> Is a Theatre? are they Two & not One? can they Exist Separate?
> Are not Religion & Politics the Same Thing? Brotherhood is
>   Religion
> O Demonstrations of Reason Dividing Families in Cruelty &
>   Pride!
>
>   (57. 8–11)

The decline continues, however, Luvah's power turning more
and more to cruelty, exemplified in the victims of Tyburn. Los,
meanwhile, lives between cloud and fire, the prophet in the
wilderness. Since the cloud hides the light of vision from him,
he can only apprehend Vision through the heat of his furnace.
So long as he is making, or shaping, or even simply desiring,
Vision is present; but when he sits down and ponders on Death
Eternal, the Vision is lost and his return to the furnaces painful.

The illumination to the page (partly shown, fig. 36) displays the full state of Man at this point. His visionary head lolls despairingly at the top of the page, coiled round by a rope and cut off from the wings of love, which exist outside it. Apart from his clutching hands, his body is imprisoned in rock down to the feet, where the rock turns into flames of unrestrained energy. In front of him stands a diminutive figure—perhaps suggesting the shrunken 'man' who results from this condition of Man. The illumination as a whole represents the agonies of humanity, torn between the bonds of reason and the flames of unorganized energy.

The next plate describes this condition more fully. Jehovah is said to stand among the Druids (the visionless righteous god amid the priests of his law). The Zoas, meanwhile, stand before a corresponding vision of enslaved reason,

> the Spectre in the starry Harness of the Plow
> Of Nations.

> (63. 3–4)

Albion is no longer a sublime ploughman, but a beast who drags the plough of the Law. The reflection brings Blake sharply back to the events of his own time:

> Luvah slew Tharmas the Angel of the Tongue & Albion brought him
> To Justice in his own City of Paris, denying the Resurrection
> Then Vala the Wife of Albion, who is the Daughter of Luvah
> Took vengeance Twelve-fold among the Chaotic Rocks of the Druids . . .

> (63. 5–8)

Blake's eternally recurring myth is here seen at work on the events of the French Revolution, when the agents of revolutionary energy turned on the representatives of the truth. They themselves were subsequently brought to justice, but the power of justice itself remained unenlightened. The result of its action was to establish the rule of law more firmly than before, with sacrifices of humanity. So the world of Urizen looms large, a universe where fruitful earth is replaced by rock, where heavens imaging the divine beauty have lapsed to a mathematically plotted sky.

The sons of Urizen complete the human sacrifice by turning

their ploughshares into swords and fitting their instruments of song for martial music. Rustic arts are replaced by industrial machinery, described in the long passage, already used in *The Four Zoas*, which constitutes Blake's most detailed critique of contemporary technological developments:

> The hour-glass contemnd because its simple workmanship.
> Was like the workmanship of the plowman, & the water wheel,
> That raises water into cisterns: broken & burnd with fire:
> Because its workmanship was like the workmanship of the shepherd.
> And in their stead, intricate wheels invented, wheel without wheel . . .
>
> (65. 17–21; see above, p. 143)

This is followed by a lengthy song from the Spectre sons of Albion, describing the torments of Luvah (humanized energy) in the furnaces of war. The last plate of the section brings us to the nadir of the eighteenth-century world. Rahab, Babylon the Great, has destroyed Jerusalem. She, embodied in Bath, has split into the three figures of Merlin (fallen imagination), Bladud (fallen desire, like Reuben), and Arthur (fallen heart). She is the antitype of the city of vision, possessing twenty-seven heavens in delusive light of time and space, compared to Jerusalem's twenty-eight. The missing twenty-eighth is the moment when the lark mounts, that union of time with eternity which by comparison renders invalid and delusory all other moments. Los can draw out the twenty-seven and create them, but he lacks the final heaven which would recreate the cycle, and make a health-giving fountain of what is now a poisonous stream. Blake describes the twenty-seven heavens; he draws on Boehme for his nine hermaphroditic giants of the first world:[13] eleven 'female males' begin with Noah; he ends with seven 'male females' from Abraham onwards. These last are grouped together because they support the formulation of law, or the cult of war, or both, in the name of religion: they are Abraham, Moses, Solomon, Paul, Constantine, Charlemagne, Luther:

> . . . thus Rahab is reveald
> Mystery Babylon the Great: the Abomination of Desolation
> Religion hid in War: a Dragon red & hidden Harlot
>
> (75. 18–20)

The illumination to this page (fig. 30) counterpoints the theme. Benevolent dragons of energy are depicted, together with women who control them, stroking their heads. 'Organiz'd innocence' resolves human energies into melody and outline. The necessary condition of such re-organization is, however, the descent of vision from the lost twenty-eighth heaven:

> But Jesus breaking thro' the Central Zones of Death & Hell
> Opens Eternity in Time & Space; triumphant in Mercy
>
> (75. 21–2)

Without that imaginative intervention, the other heavens can only continue 'in Eternal Cycle', preserving the hope that Luvah will one day be reborn as Albion, but powerless to achieve that end.

In the gloomy world that remains, Los is humanity's one great hero; so long as his creativity can turn abstractions into positives hope remains. Yet this is no easy task; it involves control of his spectre who labours at the furnaces while Los watches all night. Because of his separation from Enitharmon, he is accompanied also by the Dogs of Leutha, the physical desires which threaten to break out into an independent and destructive existence. Nevertheless Los's faithfulness to his task gives him a growing grasp of truth. When the Giants of Albion hide their scepticism by setting themselves up as Deists, he castigates their hypocrisy. Through his Spectre he tells them to obey their Humanities, and not to pretend Holiness when in fact they are murderers; he proceeds to unfold the gospel of Humanity, which is also the Gospel of Genius and of delight in the Genius of other men.

> Go, tell them that the Worship of God, is honouring his gifts
> In other men: & loving the greatest men best, each according
> To his Genius: which is the Holy Ghost in Man; there is no other
> God, than that God who is the intellectual fountain of Humanity;
> He who envies or calumniates: which is murder & cruelty,
> Murders the Holy-one . . .
>
> (91. 8–13)

The passage, one of the best in all the prophetic books, continues with the argument that friends can only be made by spiritual gifts, not by corporeal, by 'severe contentions of friendship & the burning fire of thought'. He goes on to reinterpret the words of Jesus 'Where two or three are gathered together in my name, there am I in the midst of them.' God can be seen only in his children ('He that hath seen me hath seen the Father') and so

> He who would see the Divinity must see him in his Children
> One first, in friendship & love; then a Divine Family, & in the
>   midst
> Jesus will appear . . .
>
> (91. 18–20; cf. p. 124 above)

This sublime principle of Humanity is then applied to all other forms of thought. Visions must be seen in their Minute Particulars, not described in vague generalities:

> You smile with pomp & rigor: you talk of benevolence & virtue!
> I act with benevolence & Virtue & get murderd time after
>   time . . .
>
> But General Forms have their vitality in Particulars: & every
> Particular is a Man: a Divine Member of the Divine Jesus.
>
> (91. 25–6; 30–1)

Los's affirmation of the relation between perception of the 'minute particulars' and true brotherhood is crucial to the end of the poem. Because of them Albion sees in his turn that his selfhood is constantly marching against Jesus: he is reluctant to let him know this, but Jesus affirms that this is a process of Eternity, and that his own self-giving in forgiveness is equally Eternal—a work of 'Friendship and Brotherhood':

> for Man is Love:
> As God is Love: every kindness to another is a little Death
> In the Divine Image nor can Man exist but by Brotherhood . . .
>
> (96. 26–8)

As in *The Four Zoas*, therefore, Blake's social thinking culminates in the urging of a new, redefined brotherhood. But the elevation of Los in *Jerusalem* makes possible an actual brotherhood between himself and Albion to express, in this poem, the realization of Blake's social ideal.

II *Forgiveness and moral law*

In constructing his final long poem Blake profited from the dramatic lessons that he had learnt earlier and concentrated from the beginning on the struggles created by the existence of the moral law. He also made Los chief protagonist in the struggle, which he associated with the separation between spectre and emanation.

This tightened the structure considerably; it also followed a change of emphasis in Blake's own attitude. In the 1790s he had thought in terms of an apocalypse which would also be a restoration of human liberty and could be expected to include sexual liberty as part of the general renovation. The jealousy of Los had been no more than a prelude to the rise of Orc. But in the early years of the new century, as we have seen, he became less happy with the cultivation of twofold vision, seeing such exploitation of energy as a feeding of the selfhood. The shift back to emphasis on vision can be seen enacted in the poem 'William Bond', where true love is located not in the fire of twofold energy but in the shining of threefold vision:

> I thought Love livd in the hot sun shine
> But O he lives in the Moony light
> I thought to find Love in the heat of the day
> But sweet Love is the Comforter of Night

In another poem of the same period, 'My Spectre around me . . .', the final plea is not (as in *Visions of the Daughters of Albion*) for the granting of sexual liberty, but for an ending to the struggles of love and the replacement of them by a love springing from vision:

> Let us agree to give up Love
> And root up the infernal grove
> Then shall we return & see
> The worlds of happy Eternity
>
> & Throughout all Eternity
> I forgive you you forgive me
> As our Dear Redeemer said
> This the Wine & this the Bread

Again it is light and vision which are emphasized; liberty is now seen as a by-product of the liberating power of vision and

aspirations after liberty are seen as mistaken when directed
towards political ends: they really represent the yearning of the
spectre towards its emanation.

From the beginning of the poem, therefore, Blake is concerned
to keep the relation between spectre and emanation before the
reader as an important theme. On the second plate of his text
he describes the sons and daughters of Albion, separated from
each other and hardened into their separated functions:

> The Male is a Furnace of beryll; the Female is a golden Loom . . .
> (5. 34)

The implications of this 'hardened' beauty are explored in
the descriptions which follow. Los may labour in creation at
his furnaces, but his sons are constantly drawn away into the
'starry wheels' of analysis—until they threaten to destroy the
furnaces themselves. And the daughters of Albion,

>   now contemn'd as fictions!
> Although in every bosom they controll our Vegetative powers . . .
> (5. 38–9)

become devoted to maternal love alone. So they weep and find
their weeping vain, for they nurse the immortal form of
humanity only to find that

> all within is open'd into the deeps of Entuthon Benython
> A dark and unknown night. indefinite. unmeasurable. without
>   end.
> Abstract Philosophy warring in enmity against Imagination
> (Which is the Divine Body of the Lord Jesus. blessed for ever) . . .
> (5. 56–9)

Meanwhile, Jerusalem is led away in a pillar of cloud with Vala,
as the moral law begins to take on its full force; simultaneously,
we turn from Albion to Los, who finds both his spectre and
emanation dividing away from him. The illustration (fig. 44)
shows Los at his furnaces, surrounded by bellows and tongs,
symbols of energy, holding his hammer before him like an erect
phallus, and looking up at his spectre. His separation from his
emanation is directly bound up with his readiness to listen to
the spectre, who is suggesting murderous thoughts against
Albion. As true sexual love disappears, brotherly love also is
destroyed.

The spectre talks cleverly with Los in an attempt to undermine his faith in Albion. He describes incidents which have also appeared in *Vala*—the sealing of Luvah in the furnace, while Vala watched in cruel delight and Urizen in fear; the weaving of webs of war and religion.[14] In doing so he is recalling only the disastrous results of Albion's sleep, but Los does not know this. Los's reply, however, does show a limited insight: he declares that the wrath which has called up these events must be matched by a corresponding pity to heal their results. In particular, he calls on 'holy Generation Image of Regeneration' (Blake's theme that sexual love is not a bar to virtue, but a key to its very nature, is thus re-emphasized). He rounds on his Spectre, ordering him to help in destroying 'hypocritic Selfhoods'. The Spectre promises to do so, but merely out of fear, watching for a chance to attack him. Los continues his speech, declaring that the Spectre is in fact his own pride and self-righteousness which must be destroyed—his 'Uncircumcised pretences to Chastity must be cut in sunder.' The illustration to plate 8 looks like a commentary on this point: it shows a woman harnessed to a moon which she is dragging in misery across the clouds—an image presumably of the burden created for woman by such 'pretences to Chastity'. It forms a companion to the design showing Los at his anvil.

Los now compels the Spectre to labour with him. But because Los remains a separate male their labours together result only in cruelty. 'Infant thoughts & desires' are turned into 'cold, dark, cliffs of death', and Los's labours result only in the creation of weapons of war. The Emanations are buried alive to the accompanying pomp of religion; inspiration is denied; genius forbidden. As Los labours, he finds constantly that the soft affections condense under his hammer into forms of cruelty. He continues to create and bind, however, still hoping that by the process evil will at least be shown for what it is—that those who will not defend Truth may find themselves compelled to defend a lie.

The illuminations to the plate set it in a broader background. Two vignettes of states of innocence—a shepherd piping to his flock and a woman playing with a serpent (unorganized and organized innocence respectively)—contrast with a larger design at the bottom in which daughters of Beulah mourn the body of the fallen Albion, from which the stars of genius and inspiration are passing away.

The next plate continues the justification of Los. By compelling the Spectre to labour, he hopes to rescue the sons and daughters of Jerusalem from the spectres of Albion and bring them into his own sphere. So long as they remain under the spectral influence they are inhibited from creation, for they take the Contraries of the human soul, the states between which creative man constantly exists, and stultify them by labelling them as 'good' and 'evil'. They are left with an abstraction: the reasoning power which in its negative judgments recoils to murder all that is divine and visionary in man. Los, alone in his creative task, continues to compel his spectre and to build the city of Golgonooza. He justifies his actions:

> I must Create a System. or be enslav'd by another Mans
> I will not Reason & Compare: my business is to Create . . .
>
> (10. 20–1)

If the first line is an expression of Blake's own faith (as has sometimes been claimed) it must be read with an awareness of the limitation involved. The creation of a system is a defensive operation, undertaken to protect one's own freedom.

Since the Spectre curses everything on earth, Los continues his speech, commanding him not to show himself to his children, lest they be tempted by doubt and despair, and declaring that he will break the fetters of 'strong & mighty Shame'. The Spectre counter-attacks, asserting that Los's children are themselves his sins and Enitharmon his 'Great Sin'; that God is a being of Righteousness, not of compassion: and that he himself is Despair.

He weeps, and Los wipes the tears from his face (for the face is his own: they are alternate beings vicariously inhabiting the same body). The building of Golgonooza continues; eventually there come forth from the furnaces not only Los's children but 'Erin' and 'the daughters of Beulah'—beings who now replace the daughters of Jerusalem as protectors of the tender and affectionate. Even as they emerge, however, they are aware of their enemies: figures such as cruel Ragan and vegetating Skofeld. Against such threats Ignoge and Sabrina muster the only forces available to them—they

> . . . sharpen their beamy spears
> Of light and love: their little children stand with arrows of gold . . .

(11. 19-20)

If family love imprisons, it is a cruel substitute for such true and complete human love. The feminine will to power is imaged in the illustrations. A figure at the top combines wittily the features of woman and swan (Blake may have read the story of Leda and the Swan as another version of the Fall).[15] The swan's neck leans down on the waters, suggesting not the innocence of the snakebird that carries children through the night in *America*, but the cruel force of the natural swan. The water continues to the foot of the plate, where a woman is seen swimming, her ornaments and dress caricaturing the dress of Jerusalem on the title-page. She is like a chrysalis, but with none of Jerusalem's translucent beauty. Her attractiveness is intended to draw attention to itself: she is Vala.

The fears of the daughters of Beulah at these threats are matched by the despair of Los as he feels his own emanation drawing away from him. In his despair he devotes himself to his spectre, the only positive force available to him, and urges it on to greater and greater efforts:

> His Spectre divides & Los in fury compells it to divide:
> To labour in the fire. in the water. in the earth. in the air.
> To follow the Daughters of Albion as the hound follows the scent
> Of the wild inhabitant of the forest, to drive them from his own:
> To make a way for the Children of Los to come from the Furnaces
> But Los himself against Albions Sons his fury bends. for he
> Dare not approach the Daughters openly lest he be consumed
> In the fires of their beauty & perfection & be Vegetated beneath
> Their Looms. in a Generation of death & resurrection to forget-
>   fulness
> They wooe Los continually to subdue his strength; he continually
> Shews them his Spectre: sending him abroad over the four points
>   of heaven
> In the fierce desires of beauty & in the tortures of repulse! He is
> The Spectre of the Living pursuing the Emanations of the Dead.

> Shuddring they flee: they hide in the Druid temples in cold
>> chastity:
> Subdued by the Spectre of the Living & terrified by undisguised
>> desire.
>
> (17. 1-15)

The limitations of Los are here laid bare. Alienated from
his emanation, he fears beauty lest it root him to the earth.
Any communication with the Daughters of Albion must be left
to his Spectre. But they, frightened by the Spectre, flee away
and hide in the 'Druid temples in cold chastity'. So is set up
the eternal cycle of a darkened desire pursuing terrified beauty.
Vision would reconcile the two; instead there is only

> The Spectre of the Living pursuing the Emanations of the Dead.
> (17. 13)

Los declares that he will continue to compel his spectre to
obey him for the sake of Enitharmon. The beauties of Albion
he sees as a threat to her: he suspects feminine love, as masking
an urge to destroy.

> Vala would never have sought & loved Albion
> If she had not sought to destroy Jerusalem; such is that false
> And Generating Love: a pretence of love to destroy love:
> Cruel hipocrisy . . .
>
> (17. 24-7)

Similarly, as he looks at Vala's love (love under the law) he
sees that its devotees are mistaken,

> Calling that Holy Love: which is Envy Revenge & Cruelty
> Which separated the stars from the mountains: the mountains
>> from Man
> And left Man, a little grovelling Root, outside of himself.
> (17. 30-2)

Behind such images loom the lost visionary mountains of
Atlantis, on which the palaces of light stood eternally to give
illumination to man. Once they cease to be a part of Man, his
status is diminished to that of a mere root in the earth.

Los goes on to associate the separation directly with the
Spectre. He is the shadow of the sublime, the Negation. By
the Negation, Los and his emanation are prohibited from
achieving full humanity, but they at least remain Contraries,

whereas the Spectre does not even exist. He is the one thing that will never be organized by Los, remaining for ever a figure of Non Entity. In him the fiery Cain and the pastoral Abel stay continually unreconciled, so that anyone falling under his power will fall apart into the separate elements of man, his spirit raging in the Hell of closed twofold vision, of insatiable desire, while his vegetative human body is left to despair in the cell of enclosed threefold vision, no more than a worm in the ground. This is evidently Blake's interpretation of the 'flame' and the 'undying worm' of Hell as described by Jesus.[16]

> And if any enter into thee, thou shalt be an Unquenchable Fire
> And he shall be a never dying Worm, mutually tormented by
> Those that thou tormentest, a Hell & Despair for ever & ever . . .
>
> (17. 45–7)

Los's speech here is heroic but also unenlightened. Enitharmon, hearing it, recognizes the accents of prophecy and is comforted; but there is no beam of vision to reconcile her to him: he persists as a globe of blood hanging over her while his Spectre is a darkness at his back.

They cannot help themselves because their state is the result of a much deeper disorganization. Enitharmon, as emanation of Los, is no more than a reflection of Jerusalem, emanation of Albion; it is only when Jerusalem and Vala see the fallen Albion, and begin to glimpse that the separation between them is essentially false, that there can be any solution to the dislocation. Then Jerusalem becomes conscious that she has been cut off from the regions of youth and virgin innocence; Vala, replying in her own terms, speaks with the accents of experience, weeping with sympathy not merely for Jerusalem but for all the outcasts of human life—the hungry, the wanderers, the slaves, the victims of forced labour. She sees that Jerusalem's shame is her own.

Jerusalem then penetrates to the heart of the matter by speaking of shame itself and questioning Vala's fear of sin:

> What is Sin but a little
> Error & fault that is soon forgiven; but mercy is not a Sin
> Nor pity nor love nor kind forgiveness!
>
> (20. 23–5)

In asking for forgiveness she recalls a 'time of love' when she was the bride of the Lamb of God and Vala was given to Albion without either feeling jealous. Illuminations inserted between the lines illustrate this theme of jealousy: desire is a row of flowers which have been turned into a flaming vehicle, drawn with great effort by bearded old men; a female figure floats helplessly in the flames, grasping at fallen stars.

Responding to her insight Vala acknowledges that something has been wrong: that she has been dedicated to the purposes of war in an order where love has been replaced by hatred, liberty by ideals of right and duty. Her old relationship with Albion has been destroyed.

> Once thou wast to me the loveliest Son of heaven; but now
> Where shall I hide from thy dread countenance & searching eyes
> I have looked into the secret Soul of him I loved
> And in the dark recesses found Sin & can never return.
>
> (22. 12–15)

Albion, still rapt by the 'delusions of holiness', declares that he has brought love into the light of day, 'to pride in chaste beauty' —and 'fancied Innocence' is no more. Jerusalem cries out against such exposure. To number every little fibre of the soul is to destroy its very life—it is like spreading them out in the sun to be dried: joy is beautiful but its anatomy horrible. Albion, rounding on her, tells her to hide herself; he invites Vala to the rites of knife and cup (see fig. 21), calling on her to drain his blood to the last drop and hide him in her Scarlet Tabernacle. The last lines, in which he declares that in his spectre he sees Luvah whom he slew, and in Vala Jerusalem, suggest an explanation for this unexpected behaviour. The knowledge of his guilt is still hardening him away from objects which remind him of it, while also inducing a masochistic desire to be hurt by them.

Jerusalem makes one final plea:

> Why should Punishment Weave the Veil with Iron Wheels of War
> When Forgiveness might it Weave with Wings of Cherubim . . .
>
> (22. 34–5)

The illumination (fig. 38) makes the point neatly by contrasting the interplay of cogwheels, engaging each other's teeth, with the interplay of angels leaning to touch one another. War is here contrasted with the 'exchange' of imaginative vision.

Albion denounces Jerusalem, declaring that she has rewoven more beautifully the 'Veil of Vala' which he rent in previous times. (He is confusing her truly natural beauty, translucent with the light of eternity, and the specious attraction of Vala.) When Jerusalem protests that pity is not a sin and that she ought not to be hidden in remoteness from the Divine Vision, Albion replies in despair that he has erred and is ashamed. Since his error has resulted in such cruelty the only course for him is to die.

This is not an awakening to truth but despair: he remains convinced that

> God in the dreary Void
> Dwells from Eternity. wide separated from the Human Soul . . .
> (23. 29–30)

and that his sufferings, together with those of his children, result from a divine vengeance. He ends by cursing mankind, with the hope that all humanity will be drawn after him into the abyss of sorrow and torture. Yet, even as he does so, the curse recoils upon him and he senses its power. He sees 'two bleeding Contraries' which witness against him, as he recalls how with Vala he tried to bring Love into the full light of Day —dancing naked around mighty stones—until they were suddenly seized by shame. In the same moment the universe which until then had been contained in their bodies fled away.

Loss of the inward universe, which is here revealed as the key to Albion's decline, is seen by Blake as a universal human phenomenon. In the beginning to his next chapter, dedicated to the Jews, he is able to see it mirrored in their ancient cabbalistic tradition of Adam Kadmon,[17] the 'tradition that Man anciently contained in his mighty limbs all things in Heaven & Earth', and to urge them to leave their preoccupation with the moral law and revert to this more sublime conception. The traditional humility of the Jews would then find its proper form: not the false humility resulting from a rejection of human passions (as symbolized in their former animal sacrifices), but

the humanized humility which accepts both the animals and
the human passions to which they correspond.

> If Humility is Christianity: you O Jews are the true Christians; If
> your tradition that Man contained in his Limbs, all Animals, is
> True & they were separated from him by cruel Sacrifices: and
> when compulsory cruel Sacrifices had brought Humanity into a
> Feminine Tabernacle, in the loins of Abraham & David: the
> Lamb of God, the Saviour became apparent on Earth as the
> Prophets had foretold? The Return of Israel is a Return to
> Mental Sacrifice & War. Take up the Cross O Israel & follow
> Jesus.

Through the sacrifices of the moral law and the binding of the
passions, humanity was delivered into the state of sexual
bondage which releases its energy by cruelty in wars. Eventually, however, the Lamb of God arises to sacrifice himself—and
this annihilation of Self is the true redemptive force. It provides
the 'mental' sacrifice and war which are the proper exercise of
human energy.

Chapter Two opens with an illumination showing a man and
woman embracing within the petals of a flower like a water-
lily, which rises above the sea. This glimpse of the state of
Beulah, which raises man and woman above the Sea of Time
and Space, giving them a momentary glimpse of Eden, is
followed by a description of the jealousy which has now overtaken the scene.

> Every ornament of perfection, and every labour of love,
> In all the Garden of Eden. & in all the golden mountains
> Was become an envied horror. and a remembrance of jealousy:
> And every Act a Crime, and Albion the punisher & judge.
>
> (28. 1–4)

In Eden the garden is pathos, the golden mountains are the
sublime. But everything in the world of the passions has now
been bound down as an object of jealousy, while the once
sublime intellect occupies itself with elaborations of the moral
law. Albion is not creating intimacy between man and man
but separating them; intellectually, meanwhile, he hardens
vision into the rocks of 'demonstration'. Like Urizen in the
earlier prophetic books, he becomes cold and hard: he plants

the tree of a moral law which at once goes on enrooting itself in all directions, creating a labyrinth where once was a garden.[18] Sacrifice of Self, 'mental' sacrifice, is replaced by sacrifice of one's enemies as an imagined atonement for wrongs committed. Albion sets up altars of so-called Justice and Truth. His sons, recognizing that they will be early victims of his sacrifices, flee away and fortify themselves, setting up shame and jealousy against the Divine Mercy and Humanity.

The decline of Albion continues unchecked throughout the chapter. It is only at the end, when he has finally lain down on the Rock of Ages, that Jerusalem's vision appears again in the form of Erin to warn the Daughters of Beulah that what they see in process is not eternal but only a transitory state:

Learn therefore O Sisters to distinguish the Eternal Human
That walks about among the stones of fire in bliss & woe
Alternate! from those States or Worlds in which the Spirit travels:
This is the only means to Forgiveness of Enemies . . .

(49. 72–5)

She is now revealed as the rainbow which has been created by Jerusalem, containing the true 'wheels' of the sons of Albion. The Daughters of Beulah reply with a song of forgiveness which repeats the main theme of the poem:

Come O thou Lamb of God, and take away the remembrance of
    Sin
To Sin & to hide the Sin in sweet deceit. is lovely!
To Sin in the open face of day is cruel & pitiless! But
To record the Sin for a reproach; to let the Sun go down
In a remembrance of the Sin; is a Woe & a Horror!
A brooder of an Evil Day, and a Sun rising in blood
Come then O Lamb of God and take away the remembrance of
    Sin

(50. 24–30)

In the next chapter, dedicated to the Christians, their cry begins to be answered in a new version of the story of Joseph and Mary. Joseph, who has just discovered that Mary is with child, speaks with the accents of the scrutinizing moral law, Mary with the new voice of forgiveness springing from vision.

She replies to his reproaches by asking whether he claims to

be more pure than his Maker, who forgives and calls again her
that is lost. If she were pure, she says,

> never could I taste the sweets
> Of the Forgiveness of Sins! if I were holy! I never could behold the
>   tears
> Of love! of him who loves me in the midst of his anger in furnace
>   of fire.
>
> (61. 11–13)

Joseph replies in the full spirit of forgiveness, which, he now
recognizes, must be unconditional—'without Money & without
Price'. In a phrase which looks forward to the Lord's Prayer,
he recognizes the true, generous covenant of Jehovah: 'If you
Forgive one-another, so shall Jehovah Forgive You. . . .'

Hearing Joseph's words of forgiveness, Mary breaks into song
and her tears of joy merge into an imagery of fertile gardens and
villages; as they do so, the voices of Jerusalem are heard,
recognizing her new-found liberty. Jerusalem, finding herself
no longer regarded as an adulteress, responds to the Mercy of
God with joy: her words repeat on a universal scale the words
of Mary just quoted—even employing the words of Mary's
Magnificat:[19]

> O Forgiveness & Pity & Compassion! If I were Pure I should never
> Have known Thee; If I were Unpolluted I should never have
> Glorified thy Holiness. or rejoiced in thy great Salvation.
>
> (61. 44–6)

After this outburst of joy, however, Jerusalem sees the Crucifixion and Burial of Jesus and hears a voice which comments on
this submission to the Roman penal code, seeing in it the fore-
shadowing of a Christianity which will obey the law and
dominion of the Roman empire and base its view of man on
moral law rather than insight into his humanity:

> Wilt thou make Rome thy Patriarch Druid & the Kings of
>   Europe his
> Horsemen? Man in the Resurrection changes his Sexual Garments
>   at Will
> Every Harlot was once a Virgin: every Criminal an Infant Love!
>
> (61. 50–2)

Jerusalem responds to the appeal of the Divine by proclaiming her own pollution and unworthiness. As she recalls

various women of the Old Testament, however, she suspects
that she has a different status—even a particular privilege:

> These are the Daughters of Vala, Mother of the Body of death;
> But I thy Magdalen behold thy Spiritual Risen Body . . .
>
> (62. 13–14)

Yet her doubts recur, linking her with two 'hopeless believers'
of the Bible: Martha, who could believe in a Resurrection, but
not until the end of time; and Job, who knew that he would see
God, but could not tell how:[20]

> Shall Albion arise? I know he shall arise at the Last Day!
> I know that in my flesh I shall see God: but Emanations
> Are weak. they know not whence they are, nor whither tend.
>
> (62. 15–17)

Jesus, named for the first time in this sequence, replies to her
doubts and questionings in a speech which points to the essen-
tials of Blake's interpretation of Christianity. It is necessary for
Luvah and Vala to be created (in Blake's universe, everything
must be created before it can be judged, as in the parable of the
Wheat and the Tares).[21] Nevertheless, the Divine Vision will
always be with her, as the Lord was with the Israelites in the
Wilderness:

> Tho thou art taken to prison & judgment, starved in the streets
> I will command the cloud to give thee food & the hard rock
> To flow with milk & wine, tho thou seest me not a season
> Even a long season & a hard journey & a howling wilderness!
> Tho Valas cloud hide thee & Luvahs fires follow thee!
> Only believe & trust in me. Lo. I am always with thee!
>
> (62. 24–9)

In these lines, Blake's language is saturated with Biblical
echoes, uniting the cloud, fire, manna and rock-fountain of the
wilderness with the land flowing with milk and honey and with
all the biblical associations of the word 'wine'. Christ's teaching
is established in these lines as a vision to guide humanity as the
cloud and fire guided the tribes in the wilderness. But in the
wilderness itself, meanwhile, the Druids establish their power
more fully, exacting human sacrifice and demanding obedience
to the laws of reason and chastity.

Los lifts up his voice in protest against them. Like Mary
earlier, he maintains that true chastity can be gained only by

continual forgiveness: otherwise all men and women must exist under constant accusation of unchastity. The only worthwhile chastity, that which involves *seeing* the essential purity of others, is gained in a state of Vision which brings with it constant forgiveness. His final plea recalls the story of Abraham, prevented from offering his son by the late intervention of Jehovah and instructed to replace him by a ram caught in a nearby thicket.[22] Characteristically, Blake is interested not in the 'obedience' of Abraham (as approved by the biblical writers and orthodox theologians), but in the Divine intervention to prevent human sacrifice:

> O when shall Jehovah give us Victims from his Flocks & Herds
> Instead of Human Victims by the Daughters of Albion & Canaan
> (63. 30–1)

At this, however, Gwendolen, the fierce princess of England gives vent to a reverberating laughter which hints war. Wild animals sport on the Thames and Medway, centres of Britain's naval power, while London and Canterbury, cities of vision, weep. Yet Los regards all this, including the sight of Vala with her knife of revenge and poison cup of jealousy, as a mere 'Poetic Vision', until Canaan is actually torn away from Albion and Reuben flees into caverns of the Mundane Shell. In such a time-ridden world, the web of Ages and Generations wavers between moments of sublimity and moments when the spectrous rational power is in control. Vala stands forth, terrible amid the disasters which she portends, proclaiming female dominance. Since the human being is no more than a worm, woman, who creates human beings, has complete control. At best, the male is a source of seed for her; the so-called Human Divine is a transient shadow created by her. Man is invited to assume 'Papal dignity' or kingly status—a shadow of authority which is nothing compared with her own, overwhelming power.

Los asks her why man cannot live in her presence, yet his very words show that her dominance is created by the hegemony of reason.

> All Quarrels arise from Reasoning. the secret Murder, and
> The violent Man-slaughter. these are the Spectres double Cave
> The Sexual Death living on accusation of Sin & Judgment

> To freeze Love & Innocence into the gold & silver of the Mer-
> chant
> Without Forgiveness of Sin Love is Itself Eternal Death.
>
> (64. 20–4; c.f. p. 124 above)

Blake's mythology is here tightly condensed. All evil springs
from twin sources: the secret Murder (the replacement of open
love by shame and secrecy; the fall of Adam, which destroyed
the Sublime) and the violent Man-slaughter (the subsequent
destruction of innocence, Cain killing Abel, which destroyed
pathos). Henceforth Love and Innocence are hardened into
the non-human forms of gold and silver—the silver rod and the
golden bowl where love and wisdom are sought in vain. Human
intercourse has solidified into the network of commerce.

The protests of Los are unavailing. The Spectre of Reason
and Vala the spirit of Nature only draw closer. The Spectre
takes command of the plough (now a Juggernaut which destroys the human beings who drag it along) and Vala spins the
web of human miseries. Their intercourse creates the 'dark
Hermaphrodite', Natural Man. In the absence of sublimity
and pathos, this composite creature exists in the contraries of
wrath and pity—pity for the sleeping Albion and wrath against
Luvah, who is condemned to be nailed to the vegetation which
is at once fostered and feared by the spectrous lovers.

> They cast the lots into the helmet: they give the oath of blood
> in Lambeth
> They vote the death of Luvah, & they naild him to Albions tree
> in Bath. . . .
>
> (65. 7–8)

The crucifixion of Luvah seems a final blow to humanity's
hopes. Such a crucifixion cannot, in Blake's view of the world,
be efficacious as a sacrifice: belief in human sacrifice is a form
of Druid cruelty. Yet Blake does find a virtue in the story of
Christ's crucifixion—not in the act itself, but in the power of
Jesus to retain his vision in spite of everything that is done to
him. For him the great and unique quality of the gospels lies
in their teaching of forgiveness through vision, a teaching
which reaches a climax in the events of Christ's death. Accordingly he ends this chapter with a full-plate picture of man
standing before Christ on the cross. This Christ is not an

obedient son, offering himself to his Urizenic father as a ransom for man's supposed guilt; he is humanity in its sublimest form, suffering everything that the forces of tyranny and unenlightenment can do, yet still asking 'Father, forgive them, they know not what they do'. In Blake's illustration between chapters 3 and 4 the light of that visionary forgiveness streams from the body of Jesus.

Christianity, so interpreted, contains its own answer to the tyrannical power of priests and law-givers and becomes the voice of Jerusalem herself. Of the many voices which Christianity adopts it is this one which nullifies the effects of the moral law and which will eventually do most to awaken Albion.

III Imagination and natural law
Although Blake found an answer to the demands of the moral law in the Christian teaching of forgiveness, his conception of forgiveness made this a more complicated solution than it seems at first sight. Forgiveness is often viewed as a simple moral act, one more code-word in the book of law: the making of a bargain or the exercise of a prerogative. For Blake forgiveness, if it were to mean anything, must be an act of the total human psyche, springing naturally from a full imaginative understanding of the human being who was forgiven. Failure to forgive in this way was part of a larger failure of human vision, intimately interinvolved with the analytic scientific method which dominated contemporary intellectual life.

This further failure is expressed in the poem largely in the person of Vala, whose limited view of nature constantly exacerbates the strife. In the second chapter, for example, there is a discussion between Vala and Jerusalem in which Jerusalem declares that she cannot be the wife of an Albion who devotes himself to demonstration and not to faith, thus destroying, rather than valuing, the 'minute particulars'. Vala's reply shows that she has failed to appreciate the attitude of generous self-giving which prompts Jerusalem's declaration, since she thinks purely in terms of separateness and possessiveness. She argues that Albion is hers, having been given to her by Luvah, and that Albion is now fighting to retain her, his champion being Urizen. The meaning is largely allegorical. Nature has been reduced to a mere bone of contention: men, instead of enjoying her freely and equally, seek to bind her to their own uses, whether by physical force or, more obliquely, by rational analysis. True nature, with its free and generous availability to all men, has been turned into a 'harlot'. (The symbolism echoes both the Trojan War, where Greeks and Trojans alike fought for possession of a harlot, and the captivity of Jerusalem in Babylon.) Vala watches the struggle and gloats over the prospect of war.

Los, hearing these contentions between Jerusalem and Vala, is urgently alarmed by the inward-turned energies of Albion which they reflect and calls for divine help to re-create him. Instead, however, the twelve sons of Albion remove their father to a place where he can be guarded by a ring of Druid temples.

The theme of destructive intellectual analysis is then taken up in the main narrative. The Spectre of Albion (whom Los is unable to see) is heard informing Albion that he is his 'Rational Power'. He tells him that the human form which Albion regards as divine is no more than a worm, nearly six feet long, which 'creeps forth in a night & is dried in the morning sun'. Echoing the famous phrase 'a fortuitous concourse of atoms', he describes the human body as a 'fortuitous concourse of memorys'.[23] He is described by Blake as 'the Great Selfhood'. Instead of the sublimity symbolized by Albion's lovely mountains and the pathos symbolized by Jerusalem's curtains, the world is filled with jealousy and cruelty. Los calls for action.

In an access of love, the Zoas respond and surround Albion, to carry him back to Eden. The illumination (fig. 49) images their action, showing the Ark of Vision wafted by wings upon the sea of Time and Space. But despite their kindly efforts, Albion's own condition forces him back towards Non-Entity: they find themselves labouring against a lack of vision which turns everything into difficulty:

> That every little particle of light & air, became Opake
> Black & immense, a Rock of difficulty & a Cliff
> Of black despair; that the immortal Wings labourd against
> Cliff after cliff, & over Valleys of despair & death ...
>
> (44 [39]. 10–13)

The undertaking of this hopeless task is reflected by a process which is taking place elsewhere. The 'spectrous vegetation'

which is visionless man now subsists in Ulro, one of the functions of Ulro being that it allows life to things that are essentially negative. So the vegetating spectres create a monster of
sexual darkness,

> a Sexual Machine: an Aged Virgin Form.
> In Erins land toward the north, joint after joint & burning
> In love & jealousy immingled & calling it Religion . . .
>
> (44 [39]. 25-7)

Sensing that this form of love and jealousy contains death,
however, they set a guardian spirit against it. Los is chosen to
be this Spirit of Prophecy, named Elijah. But where Elijah was
sustained by ravens, they themselves, smitten by Albion's
disease, remain in the deep like a stationary ark to which no
dove or raven returns:

> Their Emanations return not: their Spectres rage in the Deep
>
> (44 [39]. 34)

The next paragraph contains an exposition of the doctrine of
the emanation, that power which enables man to expand
vestigially and so links one man with another.

> Man is adjoind to Man by his Emanative portion:
> Who is Jerusalem in every individual Man: and her
> Shadow is Vala, builded by the Reasoning power in Man
> O search & see: turn your eyes inward: Open O thou World
> Of Love & Harmony in Man: expand thy ever lovely Gates.
>
> (44 [39]. 38-42)

The cry is at present unheeded, however, and the section closes
with an illumination showing Albion on a green rock in the
Atlantic (this being the crest of one of the Atlantic mountains—
and all that remains of its sublimity). His body now has three
tyrant heads, from which proceed delusive feminine figures.
In the background, to the right, a group of suns is setting, while
to the left the sublimity of vision is dissolving into a spectre
(broken into forked lightning), a falling cross and a pallid moon-
like orb (symbols of human authority outside the state of
Vision).

At this nadir of the poem's action, a full-page plate further
illustrates the situation. Three figures are shown who, in
another version of the design, are labelled Vala, Hyle and

Skofeld.[24] The first figure, who is bowing his head, clutching in one hand the crown of fourfold vision solidified and in the other a sceptre (the lily of threefold vision hardened), represents the first stage in the loss of vision. The second, shut up so that only his knees and bowed head are visible, represents a further contraction. The third is the captive of law, chained and diseased, slouching through flame. The negative moral vision of the one and the rational self-enclosure of the other have, in him, emerged into corruption.

Book Three begins with a dedication to the Deists. The core of Blake's argument against their beliefs is presented at the head of the page: 'The Spiritual States of the Soul are Eternal. Distinguish between Man & his present State.' It is his old distinction between Eternal Humanity and its successive states —each of which, if lingered in, becomes Error.

Natural Religion, he says, is itself one of these states, the state Rahab. To preach that there are in Nature laws of morality and laws of religion is to play directly into the hands of tyrants and corrupters, who can use these very same arguments to keep mankind enslaved. They are following the Greeks who, preaching that Nature was in itself good, worshipped the human body. While Blake believes in the beauty of the human body, the cult of the natural man alone is the cult of a 'vegetated spectre'. Man being so born must be changed continually into his contrary, his selfhood kept in perpetual flux, if the Eternal Human within him is to be renewed. He needs a religion that will present him with changing and living images of eternity: the religion nurtured by Deism is no more than the cult of a 'permanent' natural world and therefore of Satan.

Blake also argues, from his central position, that the Deists are wrong to accuse Christians of hypocrisy. If a Christian sets up his standard and fails this is not hypocrisy, for he has not claimed that he himself *is* righteous. The true hypocrite is rather the actor or artist who preaches that the self is righteous —and so denies the facts of his own nature. Nor can Blake accept the idea that monks and religious men are responsible for wars: it is the tyrants—the Caesars, Alexanders and Fredericks —who are to blame. He concludes his homily with a lyric in

which he imagines Gibbon and Voltaire chastising a monk of
Charlemagne's time and causing him to be bound in his cell by
war. This cultivation of a moral law extracted from the gospel, without an accompanying acceptance of the forgiveness
preached in the gospel, is equivalent to the behaviour of the
Pharisees, who condemned Christ by the moral law and
finally crucified him.

> When Satan first the black bow bent
> And the Moral Law from the Gospel rent
>   He forgd the Law into a Sword
> And spilld the blood of mercys Lord.
>
> $(52.\ 17\text{--}20)$

The true warfare is 'mental strife', against which the supporters
of natural religion and physical war are powerless:

> For a Tear is an Intellectual thing;
> And a Sigh is the Sword of an Angel King
>   And the bitter groan of a Martyrs woe
> Is an Arrow from the Almighties bow!

The book proper begins with a splendid illustration of Vala
brooding (fig. 52). Her throne is a sunflower on the waters of
Time and Space, her folded wings contain representations of
the sun, moon and stars. The sunflower, as in Blake's earlier
poem, 'Ah! Sunflower',[25] images the human desire which
hungers for the fullness of the Divine Vision. Vala, likewise,
possesses the ambiguity of a Nature which is wrongly worshipped
in itself by men, yet is still the only substance from which
Jerusalem can be re-established. The relevance of a false
vision of Nature to the fall of Albion is succinctly illustrated by
a further design which shows the daughters of Albion mourning round a single rocky lump. The Humanity which should
mount to the sublimity of Vision from the roots of desire,
encompassing on its way the contrary states of wrath and pity,
has hardened to a rocky mass which is labelled 'This World'
and, in its separate regions,

> Reason
> Pity   Wrath
>   Desire

At the foot of the plate lies fallen man, troubled by winged
insects, (the assaults of his spectrous reason). In the text the

Spectre speaks in frosty triumph, revealing his identity as the 'Rational Power'.

> Am I not Bacon & Newton & Locke who teach humility to Man!
> Who teach Doubt & Experiment & my two Wings Voltaire:
>   Rousseau.
>
> (54. 17–18)

He goes on to speak with the words of Satan in the Wilderness, demanding that, since Jesus rebels against his laws by teaching Belief and 'an unknown Eternal Life', he shall come forth into the desert and turn stones to bread.

> Vain Foolish Man! wilt thou believe without Experiment?
> And build a World of Phantasy upon my Great Abyss!
>
> (54. 22–3)

Yet there is a sign of hope. Albion tries to draw England into his bosom and although she responds by stretching out abysses of darkness against him a vision appears there, sketched out in pricks of light from the stars, which consists of familiar elements: the serpent of energy, the wings of love and, in the midst, the human sun of light and generous energy which should reconcile them. From this version of the Uraeon, the Divine Vision is shadowed forth:

> A long Serpent, in the Abyss of the Spectre which augmented
> The Night with Dragon wings coverd with stars & in the Wings
> Jerusalem & Vala appeard: & above between the Wings magnificent
>   cent
> The Divine Vision dimly appeard in clouds of blood weeping.
>
> (54. 29–32)

Such visions are fragile and short-lived. The Uraeon finds its unenlightened and permanent form in the Druid serpent-temples that are built everywhere. A plate soon after this is dominated by the picture of a trilithon and stars—the rocky temple and starry wheels of Urizen. Opacity and abstraction, the negatives which these symbolize, are now shaping themselves into positive menace: clouds at present, they will harden into torments of physical cruelty. Meanwhile, the Divine Vision appears among the hills of Albion in the shape of a shepherd gathering in his arms the children of Jerusalem and reproaching her. He tells how he gave her liberty and life,

spreading into many gardened cities; but she in return has
sought to dominate him, to bind him down 'upon the Stems of
Vegetation', building the Babylon of natural religion and
sacrificing in secret groves. His language throughout draws
strongly upon the invocations of Jerusalem by Isaiah and the
Hebrew prophets; as always, however, her captivity is interpreted according to Blake's own ideas. The despoiling of her
cities and the loss of her beauty is related directly to her action
in building a secluded place of rest and 'a peculiar Tabernacle
to cut the integuments of beauty'. Nevertheless, the Divine
Vision prophesies the end of those who have misled her: he will
lead her through the Wilderness to the rediscovery of her
former beauty.

Jerusalem can see him only faintly from her bondage as a
slave in the Mills of analysis, where her reason revolves like a
wheel. Vala triumphs over her

> In a Religion of Chastity & Uncircumcised Selfishness
> Both of the Head & Heart & Loins, closed up in Moral Pride.
>
> (60. 48–9)

These 'Mills' are the work of the Sons of Albion. Like the
devils in *Paradise Lost*, who found themselves turning into
creeping serpents, embodiments of the evil to which they
earlier announced their devotion,[26] they become what they
behold and build rocky temples of law:

> They build a stupendous Building on the Plain of Salisbury; with
>   chains
> Of rocks round London Stone: of Reasonings: of unhewn Demon-
>   strations
> In labyrinthine arches. . . .
>
> The Building is Natural Religion & its Altars Natural
>   Morality. . . .
>
> (66. 2–4; 8)

While this work is in progress, destroying the visionary power
of man, the daughters of Albion are at work perverting his
senses to create a body of cruel sufferings. Once again, all who
look on become what they behold. Their own senses are shut up;
simultaneously the Divine Vision removes into an appearance
first of fire, then of blood.

> The Divine Vision became First a burning flame, then a column
> Of fire, then an awful fiery wheel surrounding earth & heaven:
> And then a globe of blood wandering distant in an unknown night:
> Afar into the unknown night the mountains fled away. . . .
>
> (66. 41–4)

As the perceptions of humanity are made indefinite, men wither
into darkness and separation: their love, in turn, becomes
hatred, so that they exist in a monstrous caricature of eternity—
paradoxically bound more closely together by their mutual
hatred and separation, a large 'vegetation' which replaces
the light and harmony of eternity.

> As the Misletoe grows on the Oak, so Albions Tree on Eternity:
> Lo!
> He who will not comingle in Love. must be adjoind by Hate
>
> (66. 55–6)

In this image a further piece of Blake's Druid lore becomes
apparent. The Oak expresses an original part of the Druid
religion: its wisdom and innocence. Their sacred mistletoe, on
the other hand, is an emblem of the perversion of reason,
sucking a parasitic life from the full organism.

Against such war and cruelty all efforts at visionary redemption are impotent. The dove of light and threefold vision,
the raven of darkness and single vision, are alike powerless; the
serpent of energy and twofold vision, even the eagle and lion
of fourfold vision, all fail:

>   In vain
> They send the Dove & Raven: & in vain the Serpent over the
>   mountains.
> And in vain the Eagle & Lion over the four-fold wilderness . . .
> They return not; but build a habitation separate from Man.
>
> (66. 70–2; 74)

The fourfold sun becomes a globe of blood, the moon turns
leprous as snow (like Gehazi when he tried to turn the Divine
Vision to his own gain[27]) and positive corruption sets in, the
moon

> Scattering her leprous snows in flakes of disease over Albion.

As the stars flee and the worlds of gold, silver and brass disappear, there remains a world of iron and shrinking vegetation

(the last reminiscent of Jonah's gourd, which withered at the assault of a worm).[28]

> The Stars flee remote: the heaven is iron, the earth is sulphur,
> And all the mountains & hills shrink up like a withering gourd,
> As the Senses of Men shrink together under the Knife of Flint. . . .
> (66. 81–3)

Finally the Daughters of Men create a world of 'natural' men,

> Calling the Rocks Atomic Origins of Existence; denying Eternity
> By the Atheistical Epicurean Philosophy of Albions Tree
> (67. 12–13)

And they themselves thus become devoted to men of war—

> Ashamed to give Love openly to the piteous & merciful Man
> Counting him an imbecile mockery: but the Warrior
> They adore: & his revenge cherish with the blood of the Innocent
> (67. 19–21)

Always they aim at more power over the human form. They remember the delights of eternity, but, reflecting now the cruelty of the warriors, seek to bind the human form (which is shown at the foot of the plate, racked with torture). The warriors delight in the cruelty of the women; a few lines near the end of the next plate suggest that their behaviour is a natural result of unconsummated sexual love:[29] the warrior cries,

> . . . I am drunk with unsatiated love
> I must rush again to War: for the Virgin has frownd & refusd
> Sometimes I curse & sometimes bless thy fascinating beauty
> Once Man was occupied in intellectual pleasures & energies
> But now my Soul is harrowd with grief & fear & love & desire
> And now I hate & now I love & Intellect is no more:
> There is no time for any thing but the torments of love & desire
> The Feminine & Masculine Shadows soft, mild & ever varying
> In beauty: are Shadows now no more, but Rocks in Horeb
> (68. 62–70)

The next plate works out the implications of this world, in which a former acceptance of sexual delights has given place to analytic separation, and a consequent alternation between love and hate. The illumination (fig. 21) shows two cruel women, with knife and cup, dancing round the fallen body of Man. The only hope now lies with Los, who has enough self-knowledge to stand up as Albion's champion. The vast scene of cruelty before him in England makes him appeal that London may be founded as a city where the 'little ones' may be laid as on the bosom of a parent and that Surrey and Sussex (favourite counties of Blake's) may become both a place of repose for Enitharmon and a labyrinth in which she may be hidden.

In this work Oothoon is his natural ally: she, he finds, has been hidden in Oxford with Antamon. Their relationship is the antithesis of his own with Enitharmon—for Oothoon consummates woman's bliss and gives to Antamon the lineaments of gratified desire. Blake's mention of Oxford here suggests a tribute to the tradition of intellectual liberty in the English universities. Various deceits are organized in them; truth is wrapped in graceful error for fear of the civil power; yet their encouragement of free speculation opens the way for exercise of imagination and discovery of truth. So the analytic Cambel and her sisters are pictured as freed from the blinkers which reduce the universe to a compendium of the Copernican system. Their new, manifold vision ranges from the accuracy of strict analysis to an awareness of the imaginative sublime:

> And sometimes the Earth shall roll in the Abyss & sometimes
> Stand in the Center & sometimes stretch flat in the Expanse.
> According to the will of the lovely Daughters of Albion.
> Sometimes it shall assimilate with mighty Golgonooza:
> Touching its summits: & sometimes divided roll apart.
>
> (83. 40–4)

Oxford (perhaps Eton also—the Eton of Gray's poem[30]) is viewed, representatively and indulgently, as a place where the sons of Albion may suffer the inevitable separation from their emanations more gently than elsewhere, retaining some feelings of Humanity:

> Separate Albions Sons gently from their Emanations,
> Weaving bowers of delight on the current of infant Thames
> Where the old Parent still retains his youth as I alas!
> Retain my youth eight thousand and five hundred years.
> The labourer of ages in the Valleys of Despair!
> The land is markd for desolation & unless we plant
> The seeds of Cities & of Villages in the Human bosom
> Albion must be a rock of blood . . .
>
> (83. 49–56)

'Humanity' will at least save England from bloody revolution;

<blockquote>
for the rest!
It must lie in confusion till Albions time of awaking.
</blockquote>

(83. 57–8)

The contentions between Los and his Spectre continue, Los responding to the sublimity of the starry heavens while the spectre reduces them to matter for analysis:

> Los reads the Stars of Albion! the Spectre reads the Voids
> Between the Stars . . .

(91. 37–8)

The Spectre forms Leviathan and Behemoth, the forces of war on sea and land; Los, undismayed, brings down his hammer on the pyramids of this visionless civilization and shows that to the eye of imagination such delusions of grandeur are a very little thing: the pyramids grains of sand; the pillars dust on the wings of a fly; the starry heavens a moth of gold and silver which flutters in beauty, yet always eludes the grasping hand which tries to possess it.

> I care not whether a Man is Good or Evil; all that I care
> Is whether he is a Wise Man or a Fool. Go! put off Holiness
> And put on Intellect: or my thundrous Hammer shall drive thee
> To wrath which thou condemnest: till thou obey my voice . . .

(91. 55–8)

Just as the light of Jesus's forgiveness helps to awaken Albion from moral opaqueness so the energy of Los's indignant creativeness stimulates his intellect to expand from its shrunken torpor and reassume a wisdom that is not confined to abstract calculation.

IV   Albion as Eternal Man

Although the cycle of the Four Zoas is only a sub-theme in *Jerusalem*, the 'sleep of the Eternal Man' remains as central mythological theme, the introduction of Jerusalem giving him both a permanent emanation and a home. Instead of the Four Zoas the chief allegorical rôles are played by personages representing the decline of man into his vegetative form and his loss of imagination: Bladud triumphing over Merlin, for example, and Reuben over Joseph. Within the vegetated state the monstrous triumph of the moral law is exemplified in the person of Rahab, that of the natural law in Tirzah.

These simple divisions help to explain some of the more outlandish lines in *Jerusalem*. At an early point, for example, Los commands his Spectre:

> Go thou to Skofeld: ask him if he is Bath or if he is Canterbury
> Tell him to be no more dubious: demand explicit words . . .
>
> (17. 59–60)

This strange imagery reflects a central dialectic in the poem. The contrast between Reuben and Joseph, or Bladud and Merlin, as separated Nature and Vision, gives rise to this contrast between 'Bath', Bladud's city now corrupted, and 'Canterbury', city of true, Gothic Vision. In his quest for positiveness Los demands that the spectral Skofeld should declare himself for one or the other, in order that contraries may be created.

A good deal of the inner action of the poem is carried out by groups of representative characters, such as the 'Sons of Albion' or 'Daughters of Beulah'. Immediately after Los's demand to his spectre, for example, the darkened sons of Albion meet in the penumbra of Negation, gathering, like the demons of *Paradise Lost*, in solemn conclave. Their place of assembly is more like Milton's Hell than his Pandaemonium—'An orbed Void of doubt, despair, hunger, & thirst & sorrow'. They demand that Jerusalem should be cast forth as a harlot daughter and that the lost World of Albion with all its 'sinful' pleasures should be finally destroyed:

> But father now no more!
> Nor sons! nor hateful peace & love. nor soft complacencies
> With transgressors meeting in brotherhood around the table,
> Or in the porch or garden. No more the sinful delights
> Of age and youth and boy and girl and animal and herb,
> And river and mountain, and city & village, and house & family,
> Beneath the Oak & Palm. beneath the Vine and Fig-tree.
> In self-denial!
>
> (18. 13–20)

One notices a characteristic Blakean touch here. 'Self-denial' is usually associated in Christian thought and practice with asceticism and with particular, detailed actions—a denying of something to oneself. But Blake's usage follows the letter of the New Testament: one denies *oneself*. It is strictly secondary (though none the less a necessary consequence), that this denial cannot be separated from an outgoing in tenderness and generosity.

The Sons of Albion determine to replace their father's world by a world of hatred and suspicion, with the object

> That the Perfect.
> May live in glory, redeem'd by Sacrifice of the Lamb
> And of his children, before sinful Jerusalem. To build
> Babylon the City of Vala, the Goddess Virgin-Mother.
> (18. 26–9)

Again the individuality of Blake's attitude to orthodox Christian doctrine is apparent. Sacrifice, in the sense of self-giving, is not the object of his attack; instead, he criticizes the idea that sacrifice of the innocent can ever provide an 'atonement' for sin. Indulgence in such beliefs, however 'spiritual' their form, is a concession to commerce, a building of Babylon, a setting up of the Virgin-mother as goddess.

It is not unnatural, therefore, that Hand and Hyle, who have been joining in the cry, now set out to destroy the Divine Saviour (whom they call contemptuously 'the Friend of Sinners') and to build castles and fortifications in desolate places. The illustration to the page shows the Eternal Man and his emanation falling apart from each other, while their children still reach out to embrace each other in tenderness. The next plate is illuminated by a design showing the setting sun and the fallen body of Albion, mourned over by two figures while his children weep above. The text describing his condition, is taken almost entirely from *Vala*:[31]

> His Children exil'd from his breast, pass to and fro before him
> His birds are silent on his hills, flocks die beneath his branches
> His tents are fall'n! his trumpets, and the sweet sound of his harp
> Are silent on his clouded hills, that belch forth storms & fire,
> His milk of Cows, & honey of Bees, & fruit of golden harvest,
> Is gather'd in the scorching heat, & in the driving rain:
> Where once he sat he weary walks in misery and pain:
> His Giant beauty and perfection fallen into dust:

Till from within his witherd breast grown narrow with his woes:
The corn is turn'd to thistles & the apples into poison:
The birds of song to murderous crows, his joys to bitter groans!
The voices of children in his tents. to cries of helpless infants:
And self-exiled from the face of light & shine of morning,
In the dark world a narrow house! he wanders up and down,
Seeking for rest and finding none! and hidden far within,
His Eon weeping in the cold and desolated Earth.

(19. 1–16)

His bosom hardens away from his friends; or (another way of saying the same thing) his Circumference is closed. The outgoing of Albion is energy, his inwardness is light: so that as his outgoing ceases, his inwardness ceases to radiate the full light of the sun and becomes a moonlit night:

his Center began darkning
Into the Night of Beulah, and the Moon of Beulah rose
Clouded with storms: Los his strong Guard walkd round beneath
the Moon
And Albion fled inward among the currents of his rivers.

(19. 36–9)

Albion's flight carries him towards the lost paradise from whose fountain all rivers flow: there in the moonlight (which can still harmonize and unify a landscape, however diverse[32]) he has a vision of Jerusalem and Vala assimilated into one form—'the Lilly of Havilah'.

He cannot escape his new state, however, in which the 'disease of Shame' possesses him. Sins cover him like the boils which covered Job. He has been assailed first by doubt (disease of the natural law) next by shame (disease of the moral law). His family, animals and possessions have all become separated from him. His whole kingdom is distressed by doubts, accusations of sin and, finally, war.

In a last burst of vision, he laments the fate of his children and regrets the loss of Jerusalem with her courts and pillars, her pavements and walls, her gates and windows. Instead of this sublime palace (the feminine body before it was seized by shame) he sees only 'the wastes of Moral Law'. Babylon is built in the Waste. Where Jerusalem included thanksgiving and praise and blessing, Babylon is constructed out of miseries,

destruction and death. Yet Babylon (the city of Vala) was
herself once pleasing.

> Yet thou wast lovely as the summer cloud upon my hills
> When Jerusalem was thy hearts desire in times of youth & love.
> Thy Sons came to Jerusalem with gifts. she sent them away
> With blessings on their hands & on their feet, blessings of gold,
> And pearl & diamond: thy Daughters sang in her Courts:
> They came up to Jerusalem; they walked before Albion
> In the Exchanges of London every Nation walkd
> And London walkd in every Nation mutual in love & harmony
> Albion coverd the whole Earth. England encompassd the
>   Nations.
> Mutual each within others bosom in Visions of Regeneration . . .
> $(24. 36-45)$

In the concluding ironic contrast, the 'exchanges' of contemporary London, the seats of commerce, are compared with the
'exchanges' of love, where men and women meet one another
face to face, without masks. Albion continues to be puzzled by
the fact that this vision has been lost. The Lamb of God who
was its innocent centre has gone and is 'closd in Luvah's
sepulcher', yet this surprises him. How can so mild a Zoa as
Luvah have become destructive?

The reason has been revealed to Blake's reader, but not to
Albion. 'God out of Christ is a consuming fire';[33] the burial of
the Lamb of God, by depriving Luvah of his former controlling
innocence, has turned his energy into a destructive flame. And
even while Albion is declaring that Luvah's destructiveness is
irreconcilable with God's mercy the Lamb appears—wearing,
to Albion's distress, a merciful look. (His resulting cry, 'Look
not so merciful upon me!' is a counterpart to Dr Faustus's 'Look
not so fierce on me!'[34]—for Blake the divine mercy is more
awesome than the divine retribution). Albion dies, utterly
despairing, in the arms of the Lamb, while Beulah laments over
him, deploring the advent of cruelty and vengeance, imaged in
the growth of oak groves of mystery (compared with the single
oaks of innocent man) and the spread of rocky serpent temples
(as opposed to Gothic cathedrals). Everything done to Luvah
has been done to 'the Divine Lord & Saviour', who suffers even
in the sufferings of a sparrow. They pray that the Lamb of God

may descend and judge states instead of individuals: only then will the concept of sin disappear from the earth. The illumination shows the daughters weeping over Albion's fallen body (adorned with images of the heavenly bodies in the universe) and striving to wind into a ball the rope that comes from it. The action is ambiguous, but suggests the growth of analysis, since rope is often an emblem of reason and a later plate, perhaps intended to contrast with it, shows fruits and foliage being drawn from his body instead.

A full-page design follows showing Hand (who has some of the qualities of Orc) walking in the flames of twofold vision before the eyes of Jerusalem, who watches in wonder and anxiety from the light of threefold vision. Hand suffers the torments of youthful energy when removed from the organizing context of Albion's love, liberty and vision. He is tormented by a sense of lost liberty, political and sexual, but the true source of his sense of loss lies in his separation from his emanation, with the consequent results in these spheres. The dual significance is well brought out in the inscription to the design:

> SUCH VISIONS HAVE APPEARD TO ME
> AS I MY ORDERD RACE HAVE RUN
> JERUSALEM IS NAMED LIBERTY
> AMONG THE SONS OF ALBION

Although it is necessary to explain the decline of Albion, Blake carries out the explanation as economically as possible in this poem. Four plates (which he actually moved forward in certain copies, feeling, presumably, that the information they carried should be given as soon as possible to the reader) concentrate a good deal of the central mythology from *Vala*, concerning the sleep of Albion and the rise of the Zoas. The Divine Vision appears, in the form of a sun, and a prophetic voice is heard mourning over Albion, who was elected to possess the whole earth but who in his jealousy reacted against the Divine Vision and fell into a profound sleep. In spite of the resulting desolation, it is promised that Albion shall rise again. The prophetic words are followed by repetition of an incident from *Vala*, as two awestruck messengers come from Albion to report on what has happened—the now familiar story that the

sublime Albion became converted into the Reasoning Man and
then, having created a form of holiness, prostrated himself
before its judgment. Several concentrated lines tell the story:

> Albion walkd on the steps of fire before his Halls
> And Vala walkd with him in dreams of soft deluding slumber.
> He looked up & saw the Prince of Light with splendor faded
> Then Albion ascended mourning into the porches of his Palace
> Above him rose a Shadow from his wearied intellect:
> Of living gold, pure, perfect, holy: in white linen pure he hoverd
> A sweet entrancing self-delusion   a watry vision of Albion,
> Soft exulting in existence; all the Man absorbing!
>
> (29 [43]. 33–40; cf. pp. 151–2 above)

Subsequent lines describe Albion's prostration before this
image, the rise of Luvah to fill the vacuum caused by his self-
abnegation and the rejection of Luvah and Vala.

The fugitives who have been telling the story are now identified as Los's Emanation and his Spectre. As in his earlier lyric,
Blake describes them as necessary figures, complementary to
each other now that Albion is fallen. (The Spectre is not here
sinister, but appears in his alternative, prophetic rôle as the
positive voice of Urthona.) As Albion's children vegetate,
however, these two flee away. They are not deceived: they see
that friendship based upon common interest is not friendship
but leads in the end to patronizing benevolence—

> Being not irritated by insult bearing insulting benevolences
> They percieved that corporeal friends are spiritual enemies
> They saw the Sexual Religion in its embryon Uncircumcision . . .
>
> (30 [44]. 9–11)

The 'ark of vision' motif reappears momentarily: they are like
the birds who were let loose on the face of the deep to find dry
ground after the Deluge. Then the Spectre is praised for
keeping watch over the Vision which he cannot possess.

> And the Divine Hand was upon them bearing them thro darkness
> Back safe to their Humanity as doves to their windows:
> Therefore the Sons of Eden praise Urthonas Spectre in Songs
> Because he kept the Divine Vision in time of trouble.
>
> (30 [44]. 12–15)

Los takes them into his bosom. This cannot bring about the

re-creation of Albion—all three still remain separate—but the action does cause a temporary renewal of the Divine Vision.

A similar moment of vision is given expression by Albion's emanation, who has been hidden in jealousy but now appears in the form of Vala. With the insight, modified by self-centred interest, which marks several of the figures in this poem she recalls her former state, when she was Jerusalem:

> I was a City & a Temple built by Albions Children.
> I was a Garden planted with beauty I allured on hill & valley
> The River of Life to flow against my walls & among my trees
> Vala was Albions Bride & Wife in great Eternity . . .
>
> (33 [29]. 36-9)

For a moment she wonders how it has come about that she who loved and was one with Jerusalem plotted with Albion and hid the Divine Vision, but returns to an emphatic insistence on her present beauty and its exclusiveness.

> . . . I alone am Beauty
> The Imaginative Human Form is but a breathing of Vala
> I breathe him forth into the Heaven from my secret Cave
> Born of the Woman to obey the Woman O Albion the mighty
> For the Divine appearance is Brotherhood, but I am Love . . .
>
> (33 [29]. 48-52)

Her assertion, with its self-damaging suggestion that she is a higher reality than the 'brotherhood' which she refers to slightingly as a 'divine appearance', is followed by a dismayed speech from Albion. With ambiguous vision, he senses what Vala ought to be—a feminine being of light, emblematized by the moon, and complementing the male power of the sun. He is even aware of the existence of Jerusalem (the true figure involved) but concludes that she must be Vala's daughter, since Vala seems the more important.

> Is not that Sun thy husband & that Moon thy glimmering Veil?
> Are not the Stars of heaven thy Children! art thou not Babylon?
> Art thou Nature Mother of all! is Jerusalem thy Daughter . . .
>
> (34 [30]. 7-9)

He perceives that Nature has been turned inside out—her measurable substance taken for the reality and her visionary beauty regarded merely as something created by certain moods

of the observer; in the same reversal, peace has been turned
into war, the ploughshare into weapons of destruction. He
quotes the words of Jesus, 'In Eternity they neither marry
nor are given in marriage', against the possessiveness which
accompanies these disruptions in man's nature.

The loss of Vision means that Man enters the shadowy world
of Reason, where he is divided into the vegetating man who
clings to the earth (fallen Reuben) and the disembodied mind
which loses itself in abstract calculations (fallen Merlin):

> O Albion why wilt thou Create a Female Will?
> To hide the most evident God in a hidden covert, even
> In the shadows of a Woman & a secluded Holy Place
> That we may pry after him as after a stolen treasure
> Hidden among the Dead & mured up from the paths of life
> Hand! art thou not Reuben enrooting thyself into Bashan
> Till thou remainest a vaporous Shadow in a Void! O Merlin!
> Unknown among the Dead where never before Existence came
> Is this the Female Will O ye lovely Daughters of Albion. To
> Converse concerning Weight & Distance in the Wilds of Newton
>   & Locke
>
>   (34 [30]. 31–40)

Reuben, 'cut off from Albions mountains & from all the Earths
summits', loses all sublimity and is bound completely to the
earth. When they see him, men are overtaken by the fate of
Har and Heva: becoming what they behold, they contract,
their world becoming smaller as their perceptive organs change.
Los creates a state for them to exist in:

> Consider this O mortal Man! O worm of sixty winters said Los
> Consider Sexual Organization & hide thee in the dust
>   (34 [30]. 57–8)

Since man is in danger of disintegrating completely into
vegetative root and blind rock, however, the Divine Hand goes
forth to save him from complete contraction and opacity. Just
as, in the Book of Daniel, a fourth figure was seen in the Fiery
Furnace, 'Like the Son of God',[35] so now 'the appearance
of a Man' is seen in the furnaces. The limits of humanity are
created. Adam is the limit of contraction, for the creation of
Eve from his side (the illumination shows this happening)
ensures that his physical form will be continually reproduced.

Satan, as the Self, is equally the limit of opacity, ensuring a basis of reason upon which Man may always rest—so that his Vision will not be finally lost. The divine voice is heard from the furnaces, proclaiming that the state of Satan (minimal vision, maximal analysis and condemnation) has been created in order that Albion may enter it, pass through and rise again, his energies being renewed at the springs of life.

The fate of the vegetated part of man is also traced. Reuben is pictured in Ulro, searching for his vegetative complement, Tirzah—but by now too contracted to find her. Los, on the other hand, tries to construct the Vision even in Ulro. Blake's old image is of Vision as both Moon and Ark, a light riding the waters of Time and Space, but Los cannot create more than a limited version, corresponding to Noah's ark, or Jonah's whale:

> And Sixty Winters Los raged in the Divisions of Reuben:
> Building the Moon of Ulro. plank by plank & rib by rib
> (36 [32]. 3–4)

Reuben, in his longing for Tirzah, is a prey to doubts. A description of the nations contracting as they see him is followed by a statement of the position of fallen man now that the split has taken place:

> Hand stood between Reuben & Merlin, as the Reasoning Spectre
> Stands between the Vegetative Man & his Immortal Imagination
> (36 [32]. 23–4)

By the intervention of the Spectre between them, vegetative Reuben and imaginative Merlin are both diminished. In the general disruption, the four Zoas are displaced from their true stations to the four elements, where they become fairies of air, genii of fire, nymphs of water and gnomes of earth; dominance in this Lockean universe belongs to length, breadth and height.

The following plate is dominated by its illumination (fig. 23) which shows, at the top, the figure of Jesus actually receiving the body of the fallen Albion and, at the bottom, the spectre hanging, bat-like, over the sleeping emanation. The upper design takes place in the realm of eternity: a winged sun of vision supports the scene, which is set between an oak-tree and a palm, the Body of Jesus providing its illumination. The lower

takes place on the sea of time and space, a sun and moon repeating the spectre-emanation motif. The text itself is short.
Los stands forth for a moment in indignation, his spectre being
called up to contend with the reasoning spectre of Albion and
to threaten it with a death of eight thousand years. But when
he sees the signs of death in Albion his indignation changes to
compassion.

Albion himself continues to harden and turn away from
Universal Love. The Saviour, however, follows him, pleading
the cause of humanity. Against Albion's warlike demeanour,
he pleads that true warfare consists of the wars of life—where
intellectual spears make wounds of love, and the long winged
arrows are arrows of thought. Humanity should not only
contract, to perceive the great multitude of men, but also
expand—to see all men as one, the one man being revealed
fully in Jesus, the embodiment of imagination.

London in its spiritual form takes up the cry—its houses are
thoughts, its inhabitants affections, but its vegetated self is
devoted to the furnaces of Los and the Mills of Satan (one of
Blake's rare direct references in this poem to industrialism). The
plate concludes with a long visionary picture of England seen in
its inward form: the sublime cities of Verulam and Canterbury,
the Gothic beauties of York and Edinburgh. This beauty is the
'Gate' which leads to a country removed from the world of
moral law—a country visible to the emanation but invisible to
vegetating man. In London it succours the victims of justice:
it stands between Hyde Park and Tyburn to receive the souls of
justice's victims. It is a Gate (not unlike the door of Sanctuary
in churches) which the watch-fiends of Satan can never find.
Outside it the mills of the moral law and intellectual analysis
are everywhere, but they in their turn know nothing of human
beauty and mercy. The illumination shows the analytical
watch-fiends of Satan, mounted and armed, their bows and
arrows aimed ready: beneath them the sun of Vision is setting.

As Albion reaches the gate, ready to disappear into the world
of Law, he speaks to Los, 'the friend who most lov'd him. In
Cambridgeshire / his eternal station' (a reference, probably, to
the supreme architectural beauties of Ely and Cambridge).
He tells him that he is dying in loneliness, forsaken by God,

accompanied by no man. He desires a companion who will be a ransom for him. Los replies by questioning the idea of atoning death, declaring that wisdom and mercy do not endure atonement—on the contrary, the very moral severity presupposed by such a doctrine destroys mercy in its victim.

The whole earth mourns the dying Albion; for chaos would ensue were Albion to be finally swallowed up. But the Divine Family is merciful and weeps over him in the form of the various Gothic cities of England, culminating in Bath—which, by its own Gothic and neo-classical architecture, symbolizes the mingling of benevolent and corrupting elements in its civilization. Originally a place of healing fountains, it has reached its peak as a city of devotion to appearances. It is both physician and poisoner, the Babylon of Blake's England.

Meanwhile there remains one point of vision, corresponding to the Gate of Los. It is the 'Grain of Sand' in Lambeth, at first sight only hard and gritty but (like the grain in 'Auguries of Innocence') capable of revealing eternity. It is closely related to sexual experience—particularly, perhaps, to the moment of free, instinctive pleasure which always subsists at its heart, however hard the pressure of the moral law to make it secret and shameful.

Apart from this one atom of hope, however, the scene is dark and the Zoas look on in self-containment, absorbing everything into themselves like complacent spectators at the theatre—

> . . . as at a trajic scene.
> The soul drinks murder & revenge, & applauds its own
>   holiness . . .
>
> (41 [37]. 29–30)

(Blake's satiric side-glance at the life of his day also makes a shrewd psychological point). The plate is half-filled by a picture of Man in a state of contraction, locked in himself, with a scroll carrying in reverse the inscription

> Each Man is in his Spectre's power
>   Untill the arrival of that hour,
> When his Humanity awake
>   And cast his Spectre into the Lake

Albion is now 'in his spectre's power', and this leads him to
reproach Los for exercising mercy instead of justice. In reply
Los expounds the doctrine of the limits of Opaqueness and
Contraction (that is, of Satan's loss of light and Adam's loss
of expansive generosity). The limiting of contraction in Adam
involves the creation of Eve, that man may continue to exist in
his children and the opportunities for selflessness and vision be
renewed in each generation.

> . . . there is no Limit of Expansion! there is no limit of Trans-
>   lucence.
> In the bosom of Man for ever from eternity to eternity . . .
>   (42. 35–6)

Los, refusing to destroy the 'little ones', turns away to weep
for Albion: Albion calls on the powers of Hand and Hyle to
seize him. But these 'Spectres of the Dead' are ultimately
powerless: inwardly they are themselves groaning for release.

The key to their liberty is held by Jerusalem, who shortly
afterwards offers her own account of the situation, telling how
Eden, the place of human exchanges, was caught up with the
sun of heat and turned into contention and war; and how the
continent of Atlantis, place of vision, was caught up with
the moon—becoming, like it, an opaque globe lit by faint
beams.

> The Visions of Eternity, by reason of narrowed perceptions,
> Are become weak Visions of Time & Space, fix'd into furrows of
>   death;
> Till deep dissimulation is the only defence an honest man has left.
>   (49. 21–3)

So the ideals of vision and forgiveness are hardened and contracted

>   to become One Great Satan
> Inslavd to the most powerful Selfhood . . .
>   (49. 29–30)

She concludes with an injunction to the Daughters that they
should learn to distinguish the essence of humanity from the
various states in which they see it around them.

In some of the following plates there are further interventions

from forces who retain the Divine Vision either fully or partially.
The dwellers in Eternity, for example, are surprised to see

> a Mighty-One
> Among the Flowers of Beulah still retain his awful strength . . .
>
> (55. 1–2)

(the appearance of Albion as the Divine Vision has created this
impression: normally the Eternals descend into Beulah only for
repose). Some resolve to descend and investigate, others are
fearful. They prefer their own happy state of perfect vision,
where the Eternal Man walks among them, calling them
brothers and friends. In the world below they see only

> . . . that Veil which Satan puts between Eve & Adam,
> By which the Princes of the Dead enslave their Votaries
> Teaching them to form the Serpent of precious stones & gold
> To sieze the Sons of Jerusalem & plant them in One Mans Loins
> To make One Family of Contraries: that Joseph may be sold
> Into Egypt: for Negation; a Veil the Saviour born & dying rends.
>
> (55. 11–16)

Their words are a résumé of the fall of man. When Eve is
created, the limit of human contraction is set up, for mortal
life can now at least be renewed in child-birth. But this involves
the creation of many separate selves—and therefore of Satan,
principle of self, whose energy hardens into the solid form of
jewels and gold. Equally, it involves the creation of families as
separate entities, so that men find themselves set one against
the other. And when contraries war against each other within
the family itself, the imagination which ought to bind family to
family is finally sold into the visionless tyranny of Egypt.

> Is this thy soft Family-love
> Thy cruel Patriarchal pride
> Planting thy Family alone,
> Destroying all the World beside.
>
> (27. 77–80)

In the cosmic struggle which follows, the seas lift up their
voices and the stars in their courses fight for Albion (as they
fought against the fallen Sisera[36]).

New interventions by the dwellers in eternity, who bring the
forces of the sublime to bear, are accompanied by activity on
the part of the Daughters of Albion, whose actions spring from

a complementary pathos. Los asks them for the secret of their
tenderness and they give a simple explanation. The sublimity
of sexual love was lost: when, instead, the dog of lust came and
wept at their door, they took pity on it, therefore. Instead of a
full visionary love, Gwendolen and Merlin, creatures of lost
vision, enact a second-best, basic love: that of the earthworm
burrowing in the clay, the physical sexual activity by which life
is maintained.

> O it was lost for ever! and we found it not: it came
> And wept at our wintry Door: Look! Look! behold! Gwendolen
> Is become a Clod of Clay! Merlin is a Worm of the Valley!
>
> (56. 26–8)

Los re-affirms his separateness and dominance, in spite of the
continued trilling of the daughters of Albion and the inade-
quacy of man. The daughters reply that it is for fear of the
light that they hide the Divine Vision 'with Curtain & Veil &
fleshy Tabernacle'. But Jerusalem, conscious that, in spite of
everything, she can discern the 'lineaments Divine & ...
Voice', asks him whether he is indeed alive for ever more (as
the Gospels assert) or a delusive shadow (as the Babel of Reason
insists). Confident of his existence, she makes a contrast between the analytic reason which sees the stars as manifesta-
tions of cold law and the vision which responds to the living
beauty of stars such as the Pleiades:

> The Stars of Albion cruel rise; thou bindest to sweet influences . . .
>
> (60. 60)

(In the Bible, Job's God asks out of the whirlwind: 'Canst thou
bind the sweet influences of Pleiades . . .?').[37] She declares her
intuitive belief that despite her sins and blasphemies, the
Divine Vision will recognize that she is deluded and pity her.
The Divine Vision in reply confirms his presence, and welcomes
her pity and love for the terror and woe that have arisen over
Albion, whom he has power to raise from death.

The glimmering vision of this moment is extended by the
plate (already discussed) giving Blake's version of the story of
Joseph and Mary; but it is not shared by Vala, who sees
humanity as merely a 'delusion'. Even when, in the following
chapter, she acknowledges her own cruelty, recalling how

Albion was slain by Luvah (her deluded male counterpart) and affirming the torture of her own separation from Jerusalem the harlot daughter, she still insists that if a 'Delusion' is found (in other words, if true humanity is re-established) woman must perish and the 'heaven of heavens' remain no more. In one sense, she is perfectly right. If Humanity awakens, woman will cease to be dominant and the fixed universe of natural religion will disappear: what she does not grasp is that they will not be missed, for they will be superseded by an order in which man and woman live contented upon an earth that is informed by the splendour of the divine vision.

Insistently she cries to the Lamb of God for pity, yet continues to ply her spindle, which consumes human victims in cruelty. Other victims are offered on serpent temples throughout the earth, where human energies are perverted into torment. Hand is victim of reason: Cambel, his counterpart, shines with delusive light, drawing him out fibre by fibre. Hyle is victim of moral law; Gwendolen, his counterpart, bends all his body to the service of 'self interest & selfish natural virtue'.

Cambel and Gwendolen discuss the best way of keeping their males in subjection. Gwendolen declares that she has devoted herself to her cruel warrior. For his sake she has refused Merlin, who offered imaginative love:

> He brings to me the Images of his Love & I reject in chastity
> And turn them out into the streets for Harlots to be food
> To the stern Warrior.
>
> (81. 3–5)

She attacks those elements of the male love that threaten her domination—natural, physical love (Reuben) and beautiful, imaginative love (Joseph):

> I have destroyed Wandring Reuben who strove to bind my Will
> I have stripd off Josephs beautiful integument for my Beloved,
> The Cruel-one of Albion: to clothe him in gems of my Zone . . .
>
> (81. 10–12)

Now natural love is no more than a weeping infant, imaginative love a cloud:

> Humanity is become
> A weeping Infant in ruind lovely Jerusalems folding Cloud . . .
>
> (81. 13–14)

The illumination to this plate is a commentary on her words. Gwendolen, a daughter of Jerusalem, is seen within her cloud, conversing with her sisters (one of whom covers her breasts and womb in a gesture of chastity) and pointing to the clouds and darkness beyond. Within the cloud, words are written;

> In Heaven the only Art of Living
> Is Forgetting & Forgiving
>   Especially to the Female

In the darkness beyond the cloud, on the other hand, more ominous and bitter words appear:

> But if you on Earth Forgive
> You shall not find where to Live

At the foot of the plate appear two more lines which interpret all that has been said on it:

> In heaven Love begets Love: but Fear is the Parent of Earthly Love!
> And he who will not bend to Love must be subdud by Fear.

Gwendolen's speech to the Daughters of Albion continues. They must bind the forms of men to their embrace in order that they may not be 'annihilated', their 'delusions' discovered. She declares proudly that her own work has been wrought without any 'delusion' of vision, so that her mighty Hyle has become a weeping infant. In her attempts to entice her sisters towards Babylon she even utters a falsehood, which yet turns out to be prophetically true. The falsehood consists of words which she heard Enitharmon say to Los, proclaiming the dominance of the Daughters of Albion and requiring the abandonment of Albion, together with the creation of the nations of the earth (except America, the one place where Albion might be free). The fury of man is to be exhausted in war, so that woman may remain permanently dominant. Humanity, the 'Great Delusion', is now changed to war and sacrifice; unable to live in its sight she would like it to be bound into her power, and since this is impossible she discloses the one thing really under her control, the wayward infant which was Hyle.

To her horror, however, when she shows him, she discovers that her attack on Vision has had the effect of destroying the humanity of her own infant, who appears simply as a winding worm, threatening her own beauty. (Humanity in its proper form alternates between the nature of the worm and the nature of the god, each being modified by the one's consciousness of the other; without vision, however, sense of the flesh as worm-like simply becomes related to the eighteenth-century fear of the churchyard worm—and so to Urizen's horrified sense that 'all life feeds on death'—hence Gwendolen's horror.)

The sisters of Gwendolen try to turn this vegetated human being into a form of love. Los, meanwhile, sees in these events a justification of his own being. He is confirmed in his belief that in his nature as Urthona, he is the true keeper of the Gates of Heaven and that, given a proper fulfilment of love, he could be restored to the Paradise Garden; but his continued separation from Enitharmon fills him with physical pain and keeps him from this state:

> I know I am Urthona, keeper of the Gates of Heaven,
> And that I can at will expatiate in the Gardens of Bliss;
> But pangs of love draw me down to my loins which are
> Become a fountain of veiny pipes . . .
>
> (82. 81–4)

This moment of self-knowledge on the part of Los is a turning-point in the last section of the poem. From now on he will affirm himself more and more strongly until his object, the awakening of Albion, is achieved. For the moment, however, he declares his intention of standing by Albion. Afraid that he may forget Eternity in the process of labouring against 'Patriarchal pomp and cruelty', he asks Enion and Tharmas to help him.

Because vision is not restored, Los's search for Jerusalem and union can, for the time being, only realize itself in a pursuit of Enitharmon and separation. Like Milton's Adam and Eve after the fall, they are not one person but two—

> Two Wills they had: Two Intellects: & not as in times of old.
>
> (86. 61)

Their separation results in an ambivalent relationship. They terrify each other and yet live in perpetual desire. But they will have nothing to do with the innocent state of unity that was lost in the murder of Tharmas; on the contrary, they reject even Tharmas's emanation Enion, who wanders Isis-like in quest of her lost lover,

> Repelling weeping Enion blind & age-bent into the fourfold Desarts.
>
> (87. 1–2)

The illumination shows the four circles of the full pattern. Los pursues Enitharmon, as she floats in front of him like Jerusalem, towards the realm of Luvah and the lost Albion. Enion, blind and age-bent, reaches out vainly to the two lovers from the world of dead Tharmas. In the fourth and last circle, Urizen, a blind Hercules, puts forth all his strength to preserve his own sphere separate and intact.

In spite of the apparent hopelessness of this cycle, however, Los's persistent energy begins to have its effect, as he continues to crush the work of his spectre and to proclaim the virtues of wisdom and intellect as opposed to the old virtue of 'moral goodness'. His forceful utterance is counterpointed by an illustration which shows man stretched between sublimity and pathos, linked on one side of his body to a symbol of the sun-like, golden fourfold vision, on the other to a fibre which ends in an ear of corn or a bunch of fruit.

Los now sees that all mankind is beginning to take refuge in Albion. Enitharmon, terrified, fears that if Albion is indeed present she herself is doomed, together with her power, for at one touch of his hand she will vanish away. Los immediately replies that she will indeed vanish, in the sense that all distinctions of sex will vanish ('for in the kingdom of heaven they neither marry nor are given in marriage'). Their separation will also vanish, however, and with it all crimes, punishments, accusations of sin, jealousies, revenges, murders and hidings of cruelty in deceit will disappear, to remain only as vague memories in a world dominated by mutual forgiveness.

In the next plate Enitharmon is shown rearing out of sleep and listening to the Accusers (related by an inscription to Anytus, Melitus and Lycon, the accusers of Socrates, and to Caiaphas, the accuser of Jesus). She calls aloud to Rintrah and Palamabron, sensing that her former servants are now rising in their own pride and ignoring her. Her speech makes it clear that her attempts to domination have, all along, been due to memory of the former times when her little ones and beloved ones were with her by nature, before the disruption which drew them away. As she ceases, Los takes up the speech, declaring his conviction that Albion is made one with him and that all shall be united in Jesus. If Bacon, Newton and Locke effectively deny eternal life and if the resulting natural religion leads to worship of mystery, that is, after all, the promised signal of apocalypse in the Bible.

The next plate begins with a description of Albion lying on his rock, storm-beaten and snow-covered, wrapped by the weeds of death, the famished Eagle of infinity screaming overhead, the wolf of famine howling near by.

But suddenly, in an abrupt transition, time is finished. The divine breath breathes over Albion; England awakes from her sleep of death on his bosom. She is immediately aware of previous nightmare states, in which she has done murderous acts in her mistaken dreams of chastity and moral law, playing the jealous wife.

Hearing her voice, Albion awakens—at first in pain. As the Divine Breath goes forth over the morning hills, however, he rises in anger. Like Ulysses returning to Ithaca, he seizes his bow and bends it. He compels the Zoas each to his proper task: Urizen to his furrow, Tharmas to his sheepfold, Luvah to his loom. In the background Urthona continues unwearied at his labours, in the shape of his spectre Los:

> Therefore the Sons of Eden praise Urthonas Spectre in songs
> Because he kept the Divine Vision in time of trouble.
>
> (95. 19–20)

England assumes her rightful place at Albion's side, a moon to his sun, reflecting his light. The illustration shows her clinging to a faded, aging man, restoring him. Blake (emphasizing the human relevance of his doctrine) describes her

> Rejoicing in his indignation! adoring his wrathful rebuke.

and comments,

> She who adores not your frowns will only loathe your smiles
>
> (95. 23–4)

With this reunion between Albion and his emanation, the inner myth completes its cycle and Albion can resume his total humanity. The place of the Zoas is here less prominent than in the former poem, however. Instead it is the rehumanization of the universe which is emphasized, as every object, freed from the laws which bound it down, assumes its own identity. Los, on the other hand, is given a prominence which corresponds to his more important part in the epic. He is now the acknowledged hero, the artist whose guardianship of the Divine Vision has made possible the awakening of Albion. Piers Plowman, in Langland's poem, eventually became Piers the Builder of the Barn; so Los now stands by Albion as the Good Shepherd. As elsewhere, Blake achieves one of his best dramatic strokes when he does not adhere too closely to the rules of his own mythology. Albion is left with a brotherhood that was not available on the same scale to the Eternal Man of *Vala*.

V   The renovation of vision

Just as the characters of *Jerusalem*, even more than those of *The Four Zoas*, reflect basic Blakean themes, so the over-riding note of visionary transformation is more marked. The final awakening of the Eternal Man is not here simply apocalyptic, it is prepared for throughout the poem by the nourishment of art and creativity. Sublimity and pathos, the states between which true vision operates, are therefore organizing ideas from the beginning: even the opening illustration (fig. 63), showing Blake in the form of Los entering a sublime Gothic doorway with a sun-like lamp of vision in his hand, bore at one time an inscription which included the monitory words,

His Sublime & Pathos become Two Rocks fixd in the Earth

The title-page which follows, *Jerusalem, the Emanation of the Giant Albion*, bears designs illustrating the complementary theme of pathos in the lost 'emanation'. Fairy-like figures float round a central woman who sleeps like an emergent chrysalis, with winglike representations of the sun, moon and stars spreading out from her. She is Jerusalem, the sleeping beauty of nature in its eternal form: the other figures watch and mourn, guarding her, fearful for her.

The dedication of the first chapter, 'To the Public', consists mainly of a defence of the form in which the poem is to be presented—both its metre and the prevailing enthusiasm. Like Milton, or Coleridge in his preface to *Christabel*, Blake proclaims a new theory of prosody; but where Coleridge had rediscovered the rhythmic possibilities of ballad and nursery-rhyme metres, Blake is occupied with the development of an 'instinctive' rhythm, one which will act like the powers of digestion or sleep in the human body. He is resolved to break the bonds of blank verse, even the developed forms used by Shakespeare and Milton, and to use instead a method by which variety of cadence will occur in every line. In point of fact the rhythm used is very like that of the Old Testament in the Authorized Version: it clearly owes much to reiterated reading of visionary passages such as those in the Book of Isaiah.

The first illustration to Chapter One shows the Earth-mother grasping out and trying to cover with her veil two men who are turning away from her. One is peering into the darkness of mental abstraction, the other looks towards some children caught up with their mother, who in her turn points to a vision hidden from his sight: that of the moon and stars, with the motto *Μονος ὁ Ιεσους*—idiosyncratic Greek for 'Jesus only'. Vegetated men, when not wholly captivated by nature, can look only towards the darkness of single vision or towards the tenderness of threefold vision, each of which, however, contains hidden clues to the nature of the fourfold.

In traditional epic fashion, Blake begins by proclaiming his subject:

Of the Sleep of Ulro! and of the passage through
Eternal Death! and of the awaking to Eternal Life.

Just as the discussion of the prosody reflects Milton's discussion before *Paradise Lost*,[38] the form of the opening directly reflects Milton's 'Of Man's First Disobedience...' The Miltonic note continues, the lines

This theme calls me in sleep night after night, & ev'ry morn
Awakes me at sun-rise . . .

being a direct reminiscence of the lines

> while thou
> Visit'st my slumbers Nightly, or when Morn
> Purples the East. . . .

When Blake records the words which are dictated to him (a call to Albion to awake), another echo occurs. The Saviour is reproaching Albion because his Emanation is hidden:

> the Divine Vision is darkend:
> Thy Emanation that was wont to play before thy face,
> Beaming forth with her daughters into the Divine bosom . . .

This recalls Milton's description of the Muse Urania:

> Thou with Eternal wisdom didst converse,
> Wisdom thy Sister, and with her didst play
> In presence of th'Almightie Father, pleas'd
> With thy Celestial Song.[39]

The Almighty Father of Milton's poem has become the Eternal Man of Blake's, it is true, but the content of the vision remains very much the same. The harmony at the heart of Creation is a play of feminine beauty, reflecting his light back to the creating genius and so helping to preserve and restore his art. Blake's next lines picture the disruption in that harmony, as Albion, 'the perturbed man', turns away from the exhortation, declaring that the 'Saviour' is simply a phantom of the overheated brain, a shadow: man, he says, can live only by demonstration. He will not be bound by love, therefore, but will bind his mountains to himself and establish there his 'Laws of Moral Virtue'.

So Albion assumes selfish possession of his mountains (emblems of the lost sublime) and hides his emanation on Thames and Medway, 'rivers of Beulah' (emblems of lost pathos). To the Saviour's call for constant forgiveness, he replies with nothing but jealousy.

As a result, the cities of England which are associated with intellectual and imaginative virtues are darkened. Cambridge, Oxford and London, homes of learning, are now given over to analytical reasoning; Ely, Lincoln and Norwich, cities where Gothic architecture once triumphed, are in danger of being swallowed up.

Blake next inserts a personal passage, declaring that in this situation it is his task

> To open the Eternal Worlds, to open the immortal Eyes
> Of Man inwards into the Worlds of Thought: into Eternity
> Ever expanding in the Bosom of God, the Human Imagination
> (5. 18–20)

This declaration is followed by a prayer for the spirit of meekness and love and for the annihilation of selfhood.

Having attuned his reader to the dominant note of his poem, Blake moves directly into a description of the despair of Los, separated from his emanation and left wrestling with his spectre. Yet Los is soon forced to recognise the grounds that remain for hope. If the sons of Albion are trying to give mathematical definition to their beliefs, that very action by its positiveness gives body to what is false and so enables men to recognize and reject it. Works of charity, too, have their value: Blake's description of their construction becomes an allegory of compassion comparable to those which appear from time to time in *The Pilgrim's Progress*:[40]

> What are those golden builders doing? where was the burying-
> place
> Of soft Ethinthus? near Tyburns fatal Tree? is that
> Mild Zions hills most ancient promontory; near mournful
> Ever weeping Paddington? is that Calvary and Golgotha?
> Becoming a building of pity and compassion? Lo!
> The stones are pity, and the bricks, well wrought affections:
> Enameld with love & kindness, & the tiles engraven gold
> Labour of merciful hands: the beams & rafters are forgiveness:
> The mortar & cement of the work, tears of honesty: the nails,
> And the screws & iron braces, are well wrought blandishments,
> And well contrived words, firm fixing, never forgotten,
> Always comforting the remembrance: the floors, humility,
> The cielings, devotion: the hearths, thanksgiving:
> Prepare the furniture O Lambeth in thy pitying looms!
> The curtains, woven tears & sighs, wrought into lovely forms
> For comfort. there the secret furniture of Jerusalems chamber
> Is wrought: Lambeth! the Bride the Lambs Wife loveth thee:
> Thou art one with her & knowest not of self in thy supreme joy.
> Go on, builders in hope: tho Jerusalem wanders far away,
> Without the gate of Los: among the dark Satanic wheels.
> (12. 25–44)

The light of Blake's compassion shines through the imagery of these lines; the central point is the same as that in his poem, 'The Mental Traveller'.[41] In the retreat from vision, men create buildings devoted to pity and charity: these, in an imperfect world, are praiseworthy, even if they are static forms which would not be necessary in the energized state of vision, where actions of pity and charity would flow forth naturally everywhere.

A long description of the gates of Golgonooza, the omnipresent city of creative energy, follows. As the fourfold city, it is foursquare and has four gates in each direction, opening out upon the four levels of man's vision: Ulro, Generation, Beulah and Eden. Within the city the same pattern is repeated. In each house all the pots and vessels and garments and utensils are fourfold but in each there is a third Gate closed with a threefold curtain of ivory, fine linen and ermine (symbols of the mild threefold vision) while in the centre of the city stands Luban, with the palace of Los and the golden looms of Cathedron surrounded by a moat of fire. This is the sphere of generation and twofold vision. Ulro, of course, has no place within the city but lies around it; it consists of two elements: the 'Vegetative universe' reaching out to the Mundane Shell (positive but ineffective energy) and the Satanic Wheels (abstract and negative vision)

> The Vegetative Universe. opens like a flower from the Earths
> center:
> In which is Eternity. It expands in Stars to the Mundane Shell
> And there it meets Eternity again, both within and without,
> And the abstract Voids between the Stars are the Satanic
> Wheels . . .

$$(13. 34-7)$$

The symbolism of this becomes clear as soon as we grasp the antithesis involved. The Vegetative Universe exists between the two limits of Eternity. Eternity can be traced either at the heart of a flower or in the realm of light beyond the regions of the stars. Calculators and reasoners may go on measuring to the utmost limits of human perception in either direction, but Eternity will lie always just beyond them: they are worshipping the mechanism of the flower instead of its heart, the abstract voids between the stars instead of the light of the stars them-selves. Their diagrams to analyse the courses of the planets become Satanic wheels which bind humanity.

But while the pathos of the flower and the sublimity of the stars are lost to man, to Jerusalem, the beautiful emanation, they are not. One illustration shows her lying like a hill open to the stars, while far below her men wander and struggle, locked in by caves of the earth; the next (fig. 48) shows the divine Vision as a crescent moon (like the moon-ark which Blake had engraved in his youth)[42] resting upon the waters beneath which lie Albion's children.

It is not until the second half of the poem, however, that sub-limity and pathos can come into their own as creative forces: in Chapter Three Los grieves over Albion and then his grief is transformed into creativity. First his grief is described—in language which echoes the gospel narrative that begins, 'But Mary stood without at the sepulchre weeping':

> But Los, who is the Vehicular Form of strong Urthona
> Wept vehemently over Albion. . . .
>
> (53. 1–2)

Like the exiles in Babylon he sits by the river—in his case the Thames. Because the curse of Albion remains upon him, he is constantly in the furnaces of twofold vision, which rage without restraint. Yet he goes on building. The direct link between twofold and fourfold vision means that in the midst of all his raging and fury he can build the city of Golgonooza, which Blake identifies with 'the Spiritual Fourfold / London: con-tinually building & continually decaying desolate!' But Los follows Albion in being cut off from his Emanation:

> Man divided from his Emanation is a dark Spectre
> His Emanation is an ever-weeping melancholy Shadow
> But she is made receptive of Generation thro' mercy
> In the Potters Furnace, among the Funeral Urns of Beulah
> From Surrey hills, thro' Italy and Greece, to Hinnoms vale.
>
> (53. 25–9)

The valley of Hinnom was the place where child sacrifice was carried out. Jeremiah prophesied against it by holding up a

vase which he presently broke in pieces. Blake seems to have
connected this with the Greek and Etruscan funeral vases,
which were objects of great interest in his time. He once copied
the Portland Vase, the designs of which he probably interpreted
as showing man 'dying', cut off from his emanation and 'rising
again', reunited with her.[43] Such vases he would regard as emblems of the constant victories of Art over the fear of death in
the human mind. The breaking of a vase by Jeremiah emblematized and condensed the destruction of the divine image involved in child sacrifice.

If this is obscurely presented, the passage at the head of the
next plate makes the point with clarity:

> In Great Eternity every particular Form gives forth or Emanates
> Its own peculiar Light, & the Form is the Divine Vision
> And the Light is his Garment. This is Jerusalem in every Man
> A Tent & Tabernacle of Mutual Forgiveness Male & Female
> Clothings.
> And Jerusalem is called Liberty among the Children of Albion
> $(54. 1-5)$

This is the heart of *Jerusalem*. In the Divine Vision all becomes
translucent to man as he expands to perceive it: his vision of his
world is crowned by his vision of humanity, shining through
every individual member of the human race. This state, moreover, by bringing about constant forgiveness, is the only state
in which true liberty can be found. Any other pretence of liberty will founder on the rock of human separateness and visionlessness.

The 'Eyes of God', elected to look after humanity in its
separateness, are a force against such lack of vision: in electing
them the Eternals proclaim the virtues of generosity and mag-
nanimity, declaring that if men, instead of continually contracting into separateness, would also expand into vision, if they
would allow their bodily organs to exist both as worms and
as gods, alternating between pathos and sublimity, insistence
upon chastity would disappear. Time and Space would be no
more a static sea; instead, Space would be a green and fertile
earth, Time the Son of the Morning in his Chariot (cf. figs. 71,
78). Against such forces the 'Ulro Visions of Chastity' would

be no more than dust on the plough or dregs of the wine-press:

> for tho we sit down within
> The plowed furrow. listning to the weeping clods till we
> Contact or Expand Space at will: or if we raise ourselves
> Upon the chariots of the morning. Contracting or Expanding
>   Time!
> Every one knows, we are One Family: One Man blessed for
>   ever . . .

$$(55. 42-6)$$

In a world that has been usurped by Urizen, the Eyes of God must remain for the time being largely impotent. But Los goes forth as their champion and awakens the Daughters of Albion to remembrance of lost vision. Their voices are soon joined by those of all the cities of England, expressing an even more power-ful yearning and a further protest against the human attitude which distinguishes between a church and a theatre or between a wife and a harlot.

The illumination shows two women rising over London, not hindered by their roots from mounting among the stars of vision, while below a star rests by the form of Jerusalem, still sleeping in the earth. But Albion, like Los, refuses to listen to reasoning which asserts the superiority of humanity over the states through which it passes. He is ploughed into the earth by the Zoas (which are in reality his own energies), while his spectre rises 'over the starry pole' (probably Arcturus, the constellation in the form of a man by the Plough[44]).

Although the following two plates are among the obscurest in the poem, their drift is clear. Now that Albion is ploughed into the ground, civilization is in chaos. The Daughters of Albion dance in cruelty; Forms are destroyed by jealousy and pity; Rational Philosophy and Mathematic Demonstration are made to exist in isolation; finally, the Contraries are hammered into existence by Los to become the rocky world of Urizen, 'dark Rocks among the Stars of God'. In addition, the veil of Vala, the barrier to Vision which Albion cast into the Sea of Time and Space, begins to 'Vegetate & Petrify'. But creativity cannot be thwarted: Los, working at this material too, turns it into the Mundane Shell—a place for spectres of the dead to

inhabit but also the place where man will be redeemed and
awake again into eternity. It remains now, a solitary Form in
the midst of Four Chaoses—and Blake emphasizes its loneliness
by recalling the former glory of the Zoas and their fall from a
world of vision and desire:

> But when Luvah assumed the World of Urizen Southward
> And Albion was slain upon his Mountains & in his Tent.
> All fell towards the Center, sinking downwards in dire ruin,
>
> In the South remains a burning Fire: in the East, a Void
> In the West, a World of raging Waters: in the North: solid Dark-
> ness
> Unfathomable without end: but in the midst of these
> Is Built eternally the sublime Universe of Los & Enitharmon
>   (59. 15–21)

Their sublime work includes the labours of Los's daughters,
who labour continually to create life and love, ignoring all
discouragements. Others create the beauties of sexual attraction in order that Rahab and Tirzah, their representatives, may
live and breathe and love (although, by the predicament of all
the Zoas in their fall, they will exist for themselves alone).
Others create 'the Silk-worm & the Spider & the Catterpiller'
(which have in common the property of creating fine 'fabrics')
and the 'wooly Lamb & the downy Fowl'—to teach mankind
pity and compassion. Since the pathos and sublime of these
realms have been destroyed the only Human powers that are
left are those of sexual desire and pity. Sexual desire, therefore,
assumes a disproportionate importance while yet remaining,
basically, an unfulfilled little yearning, a 'weeping infant'. In
woman, for example, only the maternal instincts are active,

> The Cities & Villages of Albion become Rock & Sand Unhuman-
> ized
> The Druid Sons of Albion & the Heavens a Void around un-
> fathomable
> No Human Form but Sexual & a little weeping Infant pale
> reflected
> Multitudinous in the Looking Glass of Enitharmon, on all sides
> Around in the clouds of the Female, on Albions Cliffs of the Dead
>   (63. 18–22)

The illustration at this point reiterates in feminine form the general pattern of the previous page:[45] the bound head is replaced by a bloody moon, around which revolve clouds bearing a similar plumage: beneath lies the body of Jerusalem, surrounded by a winding worm. The interpretation of the illumination is emphasized directly by the words surrounding it:

above,

Such the appearance in Cheviot: in the Divisions of Reuben

below,

When the Cherubim hid their heads under their wings in deep
    slumbers
When the Druids demanded Chastity from Woman & all was lost.
                                                    (63. 24–5)

(the moon and plumed clouds represent the cherubim of Vision hiding their heads, the winding worm Reuben, or vegetative love, and the woman the law of chastity). The true sublimity of man and woman is lost:

    . . . they refuse liberty to the Male; & not like Beulah
Where every Female delights to give her maiden to her husband
The Female searches sea & land for gratifications to the
Male Genius: who in return clothes her in gems & gold
And feeds her with the food of Eden. hence all her beauty
    beams . . .
                                                    (69. 14–18)

The verse continues with one of Blake's finest descriptions of the limited but blissful married state, in which the woman creates space, the male time and variation:

She Creates at her will a little moony night & silence
With Spaces of sweet gardens & a tent of elegant beauty!
Closed in by a sandy desart & a night of stars shining.
And a little tender moon & hovering angels on the wing.
And the Male gives a Time & Revolution to her Space
Till the time of love is passed in ever varying delights . . .
                                                    (69. 19–24)

But when Beulah is the highest form known to man, it becomes dominated by the secrecy of single vision. As in Blake's poem 'The Crystal Cabinet', the male who remains in the world

of Los is then fated to sink from the delights of love to the bondage of vegetation.⁴⁶

> . . . thence in Beulah they are stolen by secret amorous theft,
> Till they have had Punishment enough to make them commit
>   Crimes.
> Hence rose the Tabernacle in the Wilderness & all its Offerings,
> From Male & Female Loves in Beulah & their Jealousies
> But no one can consummate Female bliss in Los's World without
> Becoming a Generated Mortal, a Vegetating Death . . .
>
> (69. 26-31)

Nevertheless, if the spectres of the Dead have been raised,
creating mutual hate, deceit and fear, if the veil of secrecy has
been created in the temple of the female, the advent of the
Jesus of fourfold imagination will rend the veil from top
to bottom. The false holiness associated with sex will give
place to a free relationship that opens the whole body to embraces:

> For the Sanctuary of Eden. is in the Camp: in the Outline,
> In the Circumference: & every Minute Particular is Holy:
> Embraces are Cominglings: from the Head even to the Feet;
> And not a pompous High Priest entering by a Secret Place.
>
> (69. 41-4)

This vision of true sexual relationship, touched again by the
shrewd phallic wit of the 'pompous High Priest', gives place to
a picture of the threefold Hand, whose three heads are constantly set to devour Albion's body in its three dead regions.
The point is illustrated by an illumination showing the threefold trilithon imprisoning a moon, darkened except for a small
sliver of light. The complement of Hand is Rahab, who, as
Abstract Philosophy, lies deep within Albion. She too exists
threefold, so that the man or god who embraces her is met by
the threefold embrace of mind, heart and loins—everything, in
fact, except the immortal power of imagination which would
make her love fourfold and infinite, liberating her lover. Without this, she at once delights and destroys her lover by establish-
ing her power over him.

Yet above Albion's land is still seen the 'Heavenly Canaan'—

the reality and image of the true paradise within man. All beauty in creation is a part of this Canaan for it is all human in quality—

> For all are Men in Eternity. Rivers Mountains Cities Villages,
> All are Human & when you enter into their Bosoms you walk
> In Heavens & Earths; as in your own Bosom you bear your
>   Heaven
> And Earth, & all you behold tho it appears Without it is Within
> In your Imagination of which this World of Mortality is but a
>   Shadow.

(71. 15–19)

' . . . tho it appears Without it is Within In your Imagination . . .' We are back at the foundations of Blake's vision. He follows this enunciation by presenting a complete vision of England, one town after another, trying to suggest the imaginative life of each. Though tedious if read as a catalogue, the passage comes to life if the reader allows the imagery of light and music to saturate it as Blake intends.

In his vision the cities are seen mostly as static, but a few contain within them the dynamic power of change: for example, the positive figures of Rintrah, Palamabron, Theotormon and Bromion are active in the centres of intellectual life—the four provinces of Ireland; the Universities of Scotland; Oxford, Cambridge and Winchester.

All this is an ideal vision. In each case, Los's chief aim is to prevent Albion from finally turning his back on the Divine Vision and falling into eternal Death. The illumination shows the sleeping figure of Jerusalem set against the sinister bird (the stooping, female-breasted swan of his plate 11, now with spectre wings) which, possessing the wings of vision, but in spectrous form, threatens her existence.

On the next page (fig. 38) the image of the sun, the serpent and the wings reappears, now in disintegration. The serpent crawls at the foot of the page with the reproachful comment (written backwards), 'Women the comforters of Men become the Tormentors & Punishers': energy is corrupted when cut off from the context of its proper activity. In the midst of the plate, winged angels backed by flames weep (for wrath and pity are their alternate functions) over a rocky universe. This rock, all that remains of the sun-like universe of love, is inscribed with the words

> Continually Building. Continually Decaying because of Love & Jealousy

The text of the plate includes a catalogue of the nations of the earth within which this universe is constantly growing and decaying. There follows an account of Los, building the inward imagination of Man in the limited form of the 'Mundane Shell' which reflects the world that he perceives. In order that the world shall not utterly perish in vegetation, however, a gate is kept open between Beulah and Eternity (just as Bunyan's Beulah was near the Gate of Heaven[47]). This gate is guarded by those who have contributed to the perennial tradition of sexual mysticism, where human love is seen as a symbol of the divine.

> And a Son of Eden was set over each daughter of Beulah to guard
> In Albions Tomb the wondrous Creation: & the Four-fold Gate
> Towards Beulah is to the South   Fenelon, Guion, Teresa,
> Whitefield & Hervey, guard that Gate; with all the gentle Souls
> Who guide the great Wine-press of Love . . .
>
> (72. 48–52)

The next page (fig. 46) contains a magnificent vignette of Los at work. Infinity, to quote Stanley Gardner's phrase, is on the anvil: the blows of his hammer prevent it from escaping into indefiniteness—instead, he beats it into the body of the sun, the orb of which lies shining beneath his blows. The text describes his work, which gives actuality to all the potencies of the world—creating weapons of destruction, creating, also, all the forces of nature from wild animals down to rocks, and finally fixing the limits of opacity and contraction in Satan and Adam (later to reappear in the pairs Peleg and Joktan, Esau and Jacob, Saul and David[48]). Voltaire (declares Blake) insinuates that all this work is the work of a cruel Christian God and mocks him. In fact, however, Jesus is the remover of limits, and is the resurrection from the dead. It is Voltaire who is wrong, for he actually sets up cruel kings in the holiness of the 'Natural Religion' which he preaches, whereas Los creates them simply in order that they may be revealed and so demolished. When such tyrants are created in Ulro Los creates round them the great visionary figures who preserve them from eternal death—Adam, Noah, Abraham, Moses, Samuel, David, Ezekiel. And even while the Spectres of the Dead are howling for the destruction of Albion, Los is ministering to *them*: feeding them, clothing them, giving them pleasure. He cannot restore them, but he can prevent them from destroying others.

The next plate dwells on the nature of the spectres of the dead, reinforcing all that has been said previously and emphasizing their opposition to true art. As Los drives the sons and daughters of Albion from their ancient mountains they become the twelve gods of Asia, opposing the divine Vision

> by Harmonies of Concords & Discords
> Opposed to Melody. and by Lights & Shades, opposed to Outline
> And by Abstraction opposed to the Visions of Imagination . . .
> (74. 24–6)

Their dominion is temporary, however, limited to the period until the nature of art and Christianity are better understood. Blake begins his final chapter with his own view of the matter. 'We are told to abstain from fleshly desires that we may lose no time from the Work of the Lord', he begins. His agreement with the injunction involves, of course, a silent reinterpretation. If 'abstention from fleshly desires' meant abstaining from anything connected with Art or Science, he would not accept it. The Work of the Lord, to his mind, consists in the *exercise* of the Imagination: and to this end the Arts and Sciences are necessary means.

> I know of no other Christianity and of no other Gospel than the liberty both of body & mind to exercise the Divine Arts of Imagination   Imagination the real & eternal World of which this Vegetable Universe is but a faint shadow & in which we shall live in our Eternal or Imaginative Bodies, when these Vegetated Mortal Bodies are no more.

The building of Jerusalem consists in cultivating these arts, learning from the vegetable mortal bodies which shadow forth the eternal, but never becoming enslaved to them. Even Heaven and Hell are related to this vital distinction. 'What is the Joy of Heaven but Improvement in the things of the Spirit? What are the Pains of Hell but Ignorance, Bodily Lust, Idleness &

devastation of the things of the Spirit?' He deplores those who refer to the mental gifts of others as 'pride & selfishness & sin'; on the contrary, they are the energies which build Jerusalem.

The preface now continues in verse, with a vision of Religion as a Wheel of Fire. The decline of the Divine Vision in a previous passage is repeated here: the flame of fire becomes a wheel round the heavens which gradually eats up all the elements of vision and desire till sun and moon are no more than orb and faded globe, while man vegetates into a little root a fathom long. To the question 'Is this the law of Jesus . . . ?' a Watcher replies that it is not. Jesus strove against this wheel of anti-vision; its protagonist was the Caiaphas who delivered him to be crucified. The gospel of Jesus is a gospel of freedom and happiness.

Finally comes a simple lyric, calling on England to receive Jerusalem again and foreseeing a time when 'London's towers' will

> Recieve the Lamb of God to dwell
> In Englands green & pleasant bowers.

The poem is resumed with a picture of fallen Albion at his lowest point. The Spectres of Albion's sons try to devour, once and for all, the Sleeping Humanity their father. Los is reduced to walking round incessantly, smashing the rocks of self-righteousness. Jerusalem is shown in her desolation, lamenting her condition and recalling her former happiness amid fertile gardens, love and music. Only the illumination to this page (fig. 43) offers hope. The visionary, with human body and eagle head, sits on the rock of desolation, gazing over the sea of time and space to a distant sun rising in splendour.

Los's guardianship of vision is in fact a key to the new hope in this chapter. He hears the daughters of Albion singing of the past, when Albion possessed his land and the daughters of Beulah were seen on its green mountains. This was before Hand and Hyle fled away, leading Jerusalem after them. Now they are forced to build Babylon instead of Jerusalem, while the true London wanders the streets of his own city as a beggar, led by a child. (The illumination to the plate illustrates this. The sinister, commercially symbolic 'golden bowl' of St Paul's dome is seen dominantly established within the gates of a Gothic city, while a dark sun sets and an old crippled man is led forward by a child. The last detail suggests a reminiscence of the story of the infant Samuel and Eli:[49] 'there is no open Vision'.) The Daughters go on to sing of further destruction as Hand gains power in the East in Egypt, India and finally Tartary (still the apotheosis of cruelty and terror for Blake's contemporaries). They call to Los for help. As they do so, they take the falsehood, the 'winding worm' which Gwendolen hid, and create a place of threefold vision which can include it—

> a Space & an Allegory around the Winding Worm
> They namd it Canaan & built for it a tender Moon . . .
>
> (85. 1–2)

When this space of pathos has been created, Los plays his part by giving it 'Time and Revolution', thus raising it to the prophetic status of 'Divine Analogy'. Then he calls Jerusalem to the fulfilment of this prophecy—she must cease rending herself apart for the building of an earthly kingdom of pride, oppression and delusion, and emerge in her beauty. The illumination shows the beautiful Jerusalem, lit by the sun of eternity, drawing forth fruit and fertility from a male who, hardly able to bear her, turns back towards the star and half-veiled moon of incomplete vision. Los's poetry is some of the finest in the book, drawing imagery of the Apocalypse into a larger, sensuous pattern.

> I see the River of Life & Tree of Life
> I see the New Jerusalem descending out of Heaven
> Between thy Wings of gold & silver featherd immortal
> Clear as the rainbow, as the cloud of the Suns tabernacle
>
> (86. 18–21)

His song is followed by an account of his sons and daughters at work and then by a passage which reiterates the point of 'The Crystal Cabinet'. Those who consummate threefold vision without awareness of fourfold will fall automatically through twofold 'generation' to the darkness of single vision.

> Nor can any consummate bliss without being Generated
> On Earth; of those whose Emanations weave the loves
> Of Beulah for Jerusalem & Shiloh, in immortal Golgonooza

Concentering in the majestic form of Erin in eternal tears
Viewing the Winding Worm on the Desarts of Great Tartary
Viewing Los in his shudderings, pouring balm on his sorrows . . .
(86. 42–7)

Los cries out to Enitharmon, asking her to enact the function
(portrayed in the previous illumination) of drawing forth fruit
and fertility from the male:

> . . . sieze therefore in thy hand
> The small fibres as they shoot around me draw out in pity
> And let them run on the winds of thy bosom: I will fix them
> With pulsations. we will divide them into Sons & Daughters
> To live in thy Bosoms translucence as in an eternal morning . . .
> (87. 7–11)

Enitharmon refuses, declaring that she will weave his 'fibres' to
her own will.

> Let Mans delight be Love; but Womans delight be Pride.
> In Eden our loves were the same here they are opposite . . .
> (87. 16–17)

She mistrusts his love for Jerusalem and is jealous of it.

Los replies by extolling the human relationships of Eternity,
where the brotherhood of man is realized and made possible by
the union of each man with his emanation.

> When in Eternity Man converses with Man they enter
> Into each others Bosom (which are Universes of delight)
> In mutual interchange. and first their Emanations meet
> Surrounded by their Children. if they embrace & comingle
> The Human Four-fold Forms mingle also in thunders of Intellect
> But if the Emanations mingle not; with storms & agitations
> Of Earthquakes & consuming fires they roll apart in fear . . .
> (88. 3–9)

Enitharmon refuses to listen, declaring that this is 'Woman's
World' and that she will create secret places, a female tabernacle for the moral law, so that those who love Jesus will
loathe female love until even God himself becomes a male
enslaved to the female.

Hearing her words the Spectre (who is the veil that caused
their separation) smiles sullenly and explains his mode of
working. The lack of true sexual vision creates an opening for

meanness and cunning. The sexual organs become themselves associated with the meaner scavenging functions of the body, while sexual disharmony creates family feuds and feminine jealousy.

Undismayed, Los continues to create:

> The blow of his Hammer is Justice. the swing of his Hammer
>   Mercy,
> The force of Los's Hammer is eternal Forgiveness; but
> His rage or his mildness were vain, she scatterd his love on the
>   wind
> Eastward into her own Center . . .
>
> (88. 49–52)

The consequence of her action is an overwhelming vision of the Covering Cherub, the Selfhood, which appears as a hermaphroditic form in which Luvah and Vala combine in an orgy of lust and war—the corrupted form of the winepress of Luvah.

The selfhood is revealed first as a figure of selfish holiness, containing the pomp and hypocrisy of Pharisees, Sadducees and other religious orders. Its monstrous form contains in its head the land of anti-vision—Egypt as opposed to Eden—with all its tyranny and brick-kilns; in its bosom are all the enticing religions described in the Old Testament (cults of sensuality without vision) and in its loins the Babylon and Rome of the tyrannizing moral law. Jerusalem, the guiding vision, exists only in the devouring stomach, hidden away. The power that is seen is that of the Double Female, 'a Dragon red & hidden Harlot', religion hid in war, who appears also in *Milton*.[50] This is the ultimate luring and consuming Antichrist.

The following plate describes the state of separation more fully, emphasizing again the relation between masculine and sublime on the one hand, feminine and pathos on the other:

>   . . . no more the Masculine mingles
> With the Feminine. but the Sublime is shut out from the Pathos
> In howling torment, to build stone walls of separation, com-
>   pelling
> The Pathos, to weave curtains of hiding secrecy from the torment.
>
> (90. 10–13)

The sons of Albion find themselves commingling with Luvah in his love, rage and suffering, hardened into a jewel-like furnace,

> For the Male is a Furnace of beryll: the Female is a golden Loom
> (90. 27)

Los's reply touches new heights of prophetic vision. He declares that the ultimate sin of the individual lies in appropriating to himself eternal states. States such as David or Eve, the Woman or the Lord, Reuben or Benjamin, all exist validly: but it is the task of the individual to pass through them, not to rest in them. To rest in one particular state is to create a selfhood. Above all, he abominates the setting up of a Christ who is bound down to flesh and a woman who is a Virgin Mother.

> A Vegetated Christ & a Virgin Eve, are the Hermaphroditic
> Blasphemy, by his Maternal Birth he is that Evil-One
> And his Maternal Humanity must be put off Eternally
> Lest the Sexual Generation swallow up Regeneration
> Come Lord Jesus take on thee the Satanic Body of Holiness
> (90. 34–8)

Imagination, in other words, must inhabit the frigid body of Holiness and inform it with everchanging vitality. In so far as Christ is bound down to natural and moral law, he is nullified.

As Los's cry goes forth, the sons of Albion themselves are united by their mingling with Luvah into a single figure, the great Satan.

In another burst of prophetic vision, Los summarizes the fall of man as a similar process: when man appropriates universality (Luvah assuming the world of Urizen) he divides into male and female: and when the male and female become individuals, they enter the world of death (Luvah kills Tharmas, Cain kills Abel). He comments on the acute irony of a situation in which those who enslave with cruelty compel their slaves to worship a God of mercy.

The Giants of Albion are ashamed at Los's words, but set up rocking stones which symbolize their state of nodding hypocrisy:[51] publicly they conspire together to affirm themselves Deists and worship Nature and the Natural Law, but their true state is one of opacity, mocking the ideas of God and Eternal Life.

Los's firm adherence to his prophetic rôle is bringing its final reward however: Albion begins to awaken in pain and to see him as Jesus the Good Shepherd. As Albion perceives that his selfhood has been marching against this true Jesus, who proclaims that Man cannot exist 'but by Brotherhood', he glimpses the 'sublime honour' of Los and becomes lost in a complete forgetfulness of his own self, which causes him to throw himself in the Furnaces of Affliction; as he does so they become fountains of living waters flowing from the 'Humanity Divine'. The Four Zoas unite with him and he stands fourfold among the visions of God, calling upon Jersualem to awake. Finally, he seizes his bow—and because he is fourfold man, four men seize their bows:

<blockquote>
for bright beaming Urizen
Layd his hand on the South & took a breathing Bow of carved
    Gold
Luvah his hand stretch'd to the East & bore a Silver Bow bright
    shining
Tharmas Westward a Bow of Brass pure flaming richly wrought
Urthona Northward in thick storms a Bow of Iron terrible
    thundering.
</blockquote>

(97. 7–11)

The bow is pictured as common to both sexes, with arrows of love as its children. Albion has awoken to sublimity. Beneath the description of the drawing of the bow, the illumination shows him thrusting down the spectre sun, and rising in a world where the moon and giant star of vision have long foreshadowed his return.

At the drawing of the bow the Druid spectre vanishes and Bacon, Newton and Locke appear in heaven in their true sublimity, accompanied by the masters of poetic vision, their united vision containing, instead of destroying, the sexual.

<blockquote>
The Druid Spectre was Annihilate loud thundring rejoicing ter-
    rific vanishing
Fourfold Annihilation & at the clangor of the Arrows of Intellect
The innumerable Chariots of the Almighty appeard in Heaven
And Bacon & Newton & Locke. & Milton & Shakspear &
    Chaucer
A Sun of blood red wrath surrounding heaven on all sides around
Glorious incomprehensible by Mortal Man & each Chariot was
    Sexual Threefold.
</blockquote>

(98. 6–11)

Albion stands up fourfold, the Body of Death destroyed and the
lineaments of Man revealed,

> rejoicing in Unity
> In the Four Senses in the Outline the Circumference & Form, for
>   ever
> In forgiveness of Sins which is Self Annihilation. it is the Covenant
>   of Jehovah
>
> (98. 21–3)

The state of true humanity is revealed by the 'exchanges'
between men in eternity.

> And they conversed together in Visionary forms dramatic which
>   bright
> Redounded from their Tongues in thunderous majesty. in Visions
> In new Expanses, creating exemplars of Memory and of Intellect
> Creating Space, Creating Time according to the wonders Divine
> Of Human Imagination, throughout all the Three Regions
>   immense
> Of Childhood, Manhood & Old Age & the all tremendous
>   unfathomable Non Ens
> Of Death was seen in regenerations terrific or complacent varying
> According to the subject of discourse. . . .
>
> (98. 28–35)

All men are one man in their common vision: all animals
humanize under the spell of forgiveness, including the 'all
wondrous Serpent clothed in gems & rich array'. They inquire
among themselves concerning the nightmare states which they
dimly remember—states of natural religion, of the tree of good
and evil, of the oppression of nations, of Albion taxing the
nations into desolation. The illumination counterpoints this
by showing the small creatures of earth at play: even the serpent, its fire subdued, is now benevolent.

In this visionary condition all forms are 'identified' in the
Blakean sense: they possess their true identity, going forth in the
sublime light of fourfold vision and returning in the restful light
of threefold:

> All Human Forms identified even Tree Metal Earth & Stone. all
> Human Forms identified, living going forth & returning wearied

> Into the Planetary lives of Years Months Days & Hours reposing
> And then Awaking into his Bosom in the Life of Immortality.
>
> And I heard the Name of their Emanations   they are named
> Jerusalem.
>
> (99. 1–5)

The illumination to these final lines, which shows Jerusalem embraced by an aged Albion, is based on an engraving by Martin de Vos, showing the Prodigal Son embraced by his father.[52] The source points the meaning of the plate. As always in Blake, both sides lose by separation: God loses as well as Satan when Satan is cast out; the Father needs the Prodigal Son as the Son needs the Father; Albion and Jerusalem are equally diminished by separation. Only when the flame of energy in time rushes to restore the fading light of eternity in man can human Vision be renewed.

The final illumination of the book, a full-page design (fig. 60) brings us back to the present. Los is standing before the stone-circle and serpentine avenues of eighteenth-century reason, caught in the midst of his labours—his hammer a phallus, his tongs a more creative form of the Newtonian compasses. On either side of him are emblems of his inspiration: to the left his spectre, no longer hostile, soars aloft, bearing the sun on his shoulders, towards fourfold vision; on the right his threefold emanation, her eyes fixed on him, unwinds the beauties of nature, spinning from her hank a moon of light to shine among giant stars of imagination. It is a vision of twofold creativity, restrained by the limitations of a civilization that is devoted to law and single vision, yet still working heroically to restore man to his fuller and freer condition.

So ends *Jerusalem*. The concluding pages confirm its thematic coherence: the accounts of Man in his primal paradisal state, Man restored to that state at the end of the poem, and Los guarding the vision throughout the period of its eclipse are all part of a single, dominant theme, that of the loss and renewal of Vision.

The constant suggestion of a detailed plot where none in fact exists, is somewhat misleading. So far as there is a guiding statement, it is at the opening of the poem:

> Of the Sleep of Ulro! and of the passage through
> Eternal Death! and of the awaking to Eternal Life.

This is less a plot than a reiterated theme, however, expressed against different forms and in different contexts.

Another source of confusion lies in the symbolism, with its constant changes of level. On the other hand, even when one is least expecting it, Blake is always reaching out to some new inspiration. Not all the plates are fully coherent, but there is hardly a plate without some lines that communicate a new idea or a fresh and direct emotion. These are the final justification of a detailed commentary, which establishes the basic pattern of visionary ideas and shows that if Blake's poetry sometimes seems to be an eddying rather than a progression—the restatement of one basic pattern in different forms—that is because the central pattern is at once desperately important to him, yet difficult to communicate in any single form. So it becomes possible for the reader to pass quickly through such passages as the catalogues of English counties, where the initial attraction of a welcome concreteness is delusive, demanding illumination from elsewhere in the poem. The subtlety of Blake's mind lies not there, but in short passages which, though at first they bewilder by juxtaposing symbolism drawn from varying sources, open to reveal the poet's emotion and central concern.

Another point has emerged. It is profitable to look at the shape of individual plates as well as at the pattern of the whole poem. Blake, filled with enthusiasm by some new way of expressing his central beliefs, would often set to work to engrave a single plate or a brief sequence, which he subsequently wove into the whole. The poem as a whole is therefore best viewed as a succession of inter-related visions, geared to a compulsive and obsessive pattern of ideas.

Yet there *is* a homogeneity to the poem, as one might guess from the homogeneity of its illuminations. The more one reads in it, the more the inward force of Blake's vision becomes apparent. Despite lapses to obscurity, the poem begins to exist as a vast expression of the groaning and travailing of creation towards the life and visionary forms of eternity. It is as though a photographer had taken many scenes from the life of a city, by day and by night, from many angles, in order to suggest an impression which he could never convey by a simple panoramic view. In so far as this method succeeds, Blake justifies the motto which he attached to the preface of his last chapter:

I give you the end of a golden string,
    Only wind it into a ball:
It will lead you in at Heavens gate,
    Built in Jerusalems wall.

And the more one penetrates Blake's themes of sublimity and pathos in this poem the more one sees how perfectly the idea of Jerusalem, as expressed in the Book of Revelation, matched his own preoccupations. The double conception of Jerusalem as 'heavenly city' and 'a bride adorned for her husband' fitted the dimensions of his visionary universe, where in moments of pathos humanity could be seen in the form of a single human being whose 'minute particulars' criticized the defects of policies based on an abstract 'general good', and in moments of sublimity humanity could be visualized as a 'heavenly city' which expressed the energies of all while respecting the identities of each.

Jerusalem as woman was the embodiment of Blake's conviction that human sexual love, though grounded in pathos, also at its heights reached, 'between two moments', a god-like sublimity, the worm-like phallus being then transformed into the sceptre of that sovereignty. Jerusalem as city, on the other hand, was a place of human sublimity which would give meaning to man's creative instinct while also allowing rest from labour in the nearby pastures of Beulah. The contracting, tender beauty of Jerusalem the bride and the expansive, radiating beauty of Jerusalem the city were for Blake the ultimates to which his art and poetry aspired.

8 An Informing Vision

Blake's achievement in *Jerusalem* did not lie in the creation of an ultimate, ordered mythology. There is good myth-making in the poem, as we have seen, but the ideal of creating a complete mythological interpretation of the universe eluded him as it has eluded every Romantic writer. To his credit, however, he was, at a certain point, willing to cease the attempt and to put together a thematically allied body of poetry in four symmetrical sections. This stroke was the expression of his final conviction that imaginative vision mattered, independently of any success or failure in using it to explain the detailed course of human history. Once he had realized this he could allow the book to exist within the homogeneity of his own organizing vision both as a general statement and as a series of linked statements about the central importance of such an organizing vision within our world. The result is the illuminated book that we know: highly idiosyncratic, bewildering in some details, convincing in the whole and, visually, one of the most beautiful books in the world.

Blake had come to acknowledge that the most important point about his visionary universe was not that it was a universe but that it was visionary. The acknowledgment corresponds to a development in his own thought. During the composition of the writings which culminated in the unfinished 'Vala', Blake had been possessed by two main ideas. One was that it might be possible to come at the truth behind the universe by reinterpreting the myths and traditions in the Bible and in classical mythology; the other that it might be possible to achieve the fourfold vision by way of twofold—that the exploration of desire and energy might give *permanent* experience of the infinite. The presence of the first idea can be traced in the much-revised pages of *Vala*, the presence of the second, perhaps, in the phallic drawings with which Blake decorated some of those pages.

The decisive change in Blake's art comes after his abandonment of the second idea. In the end, he acknowledged something which had always been implicit in the structure of his mythology: that threefold vision was a better key to the nature of the infinite than twofold: that light, rather than heat, love rather than desire, were at the heart of his universe. He recorded the change in a letter of 1804 which concluded with the words:

> . . . excuse my enthusiasm or rather madness, for I am really drunk with intellectual vision whenever I take a pencil or graver into my hand, even as I used to be in my youth, and as I have not been for twenty dark, but very profitable years . . .[1]

This new development was accompanied by a return to some of the themes and images of his youth. Although Blake was turning his back on some of the explorations of his middle years, it is equally true to say that he was now realizing more fully elements that had always been present in his art. This is more clear as we look at the development of his visual art.

From his earliest period, Blake always saw his subject through the transforming lens of his own visionary interpretation, so that his illustrations may sometimes surprise the reader. *Hamlet*, for instance, is interpreted in his illustration (fig. 7) as if it were a variant on *Paradise Lost*. Hamlet himself is not unlike Blake's Satan, and his encounter with the armed ghost resembles that between Satan and Death. Blake reads Shakespeare, like other authors, allegorically.[2]

In the year 1795 Blake began a long series of illuminations to Young's *Night Thoughts*. It has been noticed that this work was roughly contemporaneous with the composition of *Vala*; that the division of Blake's poem into nine 'Nights' follows the arrangement of Young's work; and that some of the later pages of *Vala* were actually written on proof sheets of Blake's published engravings for Young.[3] These associations should not, however, distract us from the fact that the central relationship between the two works is one of contrast rather than resemblance. Blake is setting out to supersede Young's loose meditations on 'Life, Death and Immortality' by a highly worked out mythological narrative. The division into Nights is in fact one of the more formal and mechanical features of his poem.

When he was actually illustrating Young, it is true, he was remarkably faithful to the text before him. Although his own symbolism is at times evident in the illustrations it never finally takes precedence over Young's meaning. His relationship with the earlier poets, in fact, combines agreement and criticism. The whole point of Young's poem is to recall a young man, Lorenzo, to thoughts of Eternity, the light of which will one day blaze into this universe bringing with it the Last Judgment. Blake is equally urgent that men should remind themselves of Eternity—but affirms that Eternity is constantly manifest here and now in this world. He is thus led to value states of vision which are ignored by the orthodox, and to see the world as a place where Eternity is constantly being revealed rather than to dismiss it in favour of a narrow asceticism. In illustrating Young he constantly stresses his own more positive assertion of Eternity.

The illustrations are worked in a novel manner, completely surrounding the letter-press of the page and so drawn as to suggest that the scene continues behind the page. On each page, a particular line or lines (indicated by a cross) provides the subject of the illumination.

Several times, Blake uses his own distinctive idiom in order to illustrate one of Young's sentiments. For instance, to the line, 'thy Pleasure is the promise of thy Pain' (addressed to a young person), he attaches a design showing a small family in which the child is clutching at a butterfly while near by his father lies encircled by a serpent.[4] The meaning is clarified as soon as we remember his stanza,

> He who binds to himself a joy
>   Doth the winged life destroy
> But he who kisses the joy as it flies
>   Lives in Eternitys sun rise[5]

The child clutching at a butterfly is symbolizing his desire for the possession of joy; the man, through constant pursuit of the same desire, has become throttled and enslaved by his own energies.

Again, when Young writes, 'The Thought of Death shall, like a God, inspire,' Blake depicts a man clutching at two apples from a tree while winged figures float around, one with bow and arrow, another with an axe to hew down the branch.[6] Here,

Blake is using the Miltonic incident of Man's eating the apple in order to become like a god; the moral, however, is inverted—Man actually secures divinity from the thought of death.

In other cases, symbols from the Prophetic Books reappear. When Young devotes a Night to Nature, Blake decorates the appropriate title-page with the vast and glittering coils of a serpent.[7] When he writes, 'Wit, a true Pagan, deifies the Brute,' Blake shows a man adoring a coiled serpent which is stooping down from a tree.[8] When he writes, 'Great Ill is an achievement of great powers.' Blake depicts a figure falling, a sun in each hand—the fall of true Genius.[9] For the line, 'Reason is Man's Peculiar; Sense the Brute's', Blake's design is fairly conventional, showing a man reading, while a dog kills a rabbit near by.[10] When, on the other hand, Young glorifies the idea of Death with the words 'And Sense and Reason point the way', Blake brings in an unusual image: Eve and Adam are pointing to a Gothic archway containing the gate of vision.[11] Similarly, when Young writes of Shame,

> This instinct calls on Darkness to conceal
> Our rapturous relation to the Stalls,

Blake shows Adam and Eve lying in shame, as he depicted Har and Heva at the beginning of *Songs of Innocence and of Experience*.[12] Blake evidently associated Adam and Eve with unfallen Reason and Sense respectively.

Although some of the early designs for *Night Thoughts* were engraved by Blake and subsequently published, the greater number of the illustrations were never used. In all he produced 537; of these less than a hundred have since been reproduced. Until the complete series is published, it can be seen only by visiting the Print Room of the British Museum, where it is housed in many volumes. Although an examination of the full series might at first be disappointing, the extensive view lends impressiveness to the achievement. Motifs of design recur at intervals and reinforce each other; one becomes attuned to the scale of the undertaking and the effects of its proportions upon individual designs; more important still, one becomes accustomed to the homogeneity of Blake's style in the series. Few things are more striking about Blake than his ability to develop a peculiar style for an individual series of designs or illuminations and to create the whole series within that same style. To look at all the illustrations to Young is to learn another of his artistic dialects.

Blake's flexibility of mind is shown at its best in his dealings with Young. His constant emphasis is on the points which they have in common; but the *atmosphere* is constantly different, and on a closer examination of certain designs Blake's idiosyncratic attitude becomes apparent. Both share a firm belief that eternity is more real and important than time. But whereas Young holds this belief within the tradition of eighteenth-century pietism, eternity sitting in judgment on the productions of time, Blake holds it within his own world-view, where eternity is in love with the productions of time. Young sees the impending irruption of eternity as a reason for denying oneself the sensual joys of this world; Blake sees the enduring presence of eternity as a reason for enjoying the revelation which they afford—but not for attempting to seize or bind them to oneself in any way.

Another series of illustrations in the same manner was executed to surround the text of Gray's *Poems*. As we have seen, Blake used one of the poems as the excuse for a light-hearted display of his doctrine of the spectre and emanation.[13] For the most part, however, he follows Gray closely. His own verse inscription exhibits his attitude:

> Around the Springs of Gray my wild root weaves
> Traveller repose & Dream among my leaves.[14]

H. M. Margoliouth, noticing the less iconoclastic tone of Blake's later references to religion, supposed that Blake must have undergone some sort of religious crisis at the end of the eighteenth century which turned him into a Christian.[15] This theory will not do as it stands, however, for Blake not only displayed great sympathy for Christianity in his early works, but also voiced criticisms of it in his later. The structure of his mythology changed little; but within that structure he moved away from the whole-hearted advocacy of social, political and religious freedom which had characterized some of his earlier poems.

Whatever his attitude to Christianity, however, Blake always returned to the Bible for inspiration. Whether or not it was still the 'Bible of Hell', it remained the most visionary document known to him. Almost all the incidents which he chose to illustrate express the theme. Obvious examples are 'David and Goliath' (innocent boyhood vision versus the twisted energy of giant strength); 'Abraham and Isaac' (Abraham turned away from his determination to obey the instruction of God by sacrificing his son, in favour of the ram—that familiar symbol in Blake for the organized innocence which is humanity's defence against the inhuman rigour of the Law); or 'Babylon' (the innocent inhabitants of Jerusalem forced to hang up their harps in a land filled with people and objects symbolizing commercialism and tyranny).[16] 'The finding of Moses' by Pharaoh's daughter is the discovery of a hidden visionary humanity;[17] 'The Sealing of the Stone' shows the Pharisees and soldiers taking care to seal every chink of the entrance to the cave where Jesus, the visionary human being *par excellence*, has been thrust in darkness.[18] With 'Jacob's Ladder', Blake is able to depict the 'exchanges' of true humanity, as they ascend and descend between earth and heaven, greeting each other in passing.[19] 'Samson', on the other hand, expresses Blake's old feeling for this Old Testament figure as a representative of humanity in its sublimity and splendour.[20] He is shown on the knees of Delilah, his shorn head reminiscent of the many figures in Blake whose hairlessness is an emblem of their enslavement to analytic reason (cf. fig. 20) while she beckons to the warlike Philistines to enter and complete his enslavement. In his youth, as we have seen, Blake had written of the young Samson, son of an angel from the fields of light, destined to deliver Israel;[21] now he completes the picture by making the fallen Samson an emblem of Man in the toils of rational analysis.

As always, however, his attention remains firmly riveted on the two great moments of the Bible: the Creation and the Incarnation. A late scheme for illustrating Genesis contains most succinctly his version of the Fall and its various stages:

Chapter I   The Creation of the Natural Man
Chapter II   The Natural Man divided into Male and Female &
               of the Tree of Life & of the Tree of Good and Evil

The chapter subjects might be summarized in terms of the main
protagonists as follows: God and Adam; Adam, Eve and Satan;
Adam and Eve with Satan triumphant; Cain and Abel. The
stages in Blake's earlier mythology have evidently played their
part in evolving this view of the Creation and Fall as a series of
steps, culminating in the establishment of the fear of death:
this is coupled with Blake's favourite but heretical view that
the brand of Cain was in fact the sign of God's forgiveness.

Throughout his life, Blake was particularly fascinated by the
Book of Job. In his first drawing, painting and engraving of the
subject (1785–93) he showed Job, his wife and the comforters.[23]
In 1800 he produced two further paintings, showing Satan
smiting Job with boils and God answering Job out of the whirlwind.[24] In both these designs a degree of symbolic organization
is present: Satan's fiery form shows that he represents the rise
of Energy against Job's faded Vision; God in the whirlwind, on
the other hand, represents Job himself in his visionary form,
surrounded by the energies of angels.

This idea was not fully developed until much later in Blake's
life, when it became the subject of a longer series of illustrations.
Several sets of these designs are extant, culminating in the well-
known series of engravings.

In many of the designs, Job is on earth below and God in
Heaven above. In each case, it is important to observe that
both God and Job possess the same features: the heavenly scene
exists simply to present the earthly one in its full visionary context. The first design,[25] which is not so divided, shows Job in
his prosperity under an oak tree. On the left, one can see the
sublime architecture of a gothic city: the rising sun is inscribed
with the words 'Our Father which art in Heaven &c'. On the
right the moon and a single star are shining over the pathos of a
pastoral landscape, in which tents are prominent. Job, in the
centre, is surrounded by his shepherd sons and his family,
while in front his rams and sheep lie peacefully asleep, even the

sheepdog resting with an expression of wise innocence upon his face. On the laps of Job and his wife lie open books which they are not looking at; the family is praying. Only two things signify the danger which lurks in the background. The first is that the musical instruments of Job and his children are not in use, but hang neglected above their heads; the second is the inscription which appears in the middle of the engraving: 'The Letter killeth / The Spirit giveth Life'. By neglecting art, Job and his sons are in danger of substituting the letter for the Spirit.

In the second design, the danger has increased, by the further separation of vision from energy. At the top of the design, God is seen, his book on his knees, against the wan light of a faded sun. Before him runs the Satanic spirit of Energy, his force contrasting with the etiolation of the Father. This represents the scene where the sons of God present themselves before the Lord. Below, a similar separation of Vision from energy is evident in the scene of the first design. The single oak, the Tree of Life, has been replaced by several trees of Good and Evil: the serpents wound round their stems represent the danger of separating the one from the other. The sheep now look more foolish, while in a chest, shut away from them, lies the sleeping dog who ought to be guarding them; at his side are several volumes. The family of Job is also now divided into 'good' sons and daughters and others, who are engaged in scholastic dispute. The letter has triumphed.

The third scene represents the scene in which Job's sons are killed by the destruction of the house in which they are feasting. The design shows Satan, now spectrous, destroying the house, while Job's loyal son, rising with his child (like Los in the design at the end of *Europe*) is powerless to prevent the destruction. The fourth design (fig. 65) shows the messenger telling Job of the catastrophe. The city of vision survives in the distance, but Job is sitting by pillars which resemble the trilithon of Stonehenge except for a gap in the upper stone. In the next (fig. 66), a complete trilithon stands near by while Job gives a stone instead of bread to a passing beggar (in his own form) who is leaning on a crutch which resembles the phallic hammer of Los in *Jerusalem* and who is led by a dog which is equally starved. Above,

God is shown drooping, while Satan pours his phials of corrupted energy downwards, to enter the head of Job. The starvation and subsequent corruption of energy, especially sexual energy, are here hinted at.

In the following design (fig. 67) this last theme is brought to a climax, with Satan pouring his poison over the whole body of Job, who lies diseased; his wife laments at his side. Even the trilitha are now ruined. The three comforters enter (fig. 68). They, too, possess the features of Job, but their lineaments of woe contrast with his patient resignation. Finally, with wife and comforters alike hiding their faces, Job lifts up his hand and curses the day on which he was born (fig. 69).

In the next three designs the comforters do their work. They are the 'Accusers' of other Blakean works, the figures who judge the just man on the grounds of a supposed lack of 'holiness'. So in the first of these designs the upper, 'visionary' part of the design shows Job rearing up in bed, his hair standing on end as he sees the God of earlier designs pass before his face. This God is surrounded by the pale ghostly light of holiness, and it is his *purity* which terrifies Job ('Shall a Man be more pure than his Maker?' he cries). In the next design, Job ignores the pointing accusing hands of his comforters and insists upon his righteousness. The inscription at the foot of the engraving explains his defence: 'Man that is born of a woman is of few days & full of trouble / He cometh up like a flower & is cut down he fleeth also as a shadow / & continueth not / And dost thou open thine eyes on such a one and bringest me into judgment with thee.' His insistence on the essential harmlessness of the human condition only brings him into worse torments: he is next seen lying on a mat, where devils strive to pull him down into the flames and chain him with his own energies, while over him hovers an ambiguous God who, with terrifying visage and snaky selfhood coiled about him, points behind himself to the tables of the law.

This torment, however, marks the nadir of Job's agony. In the next design (fig. 70) he is back by the trilithon, now heavily built up, and imprisoning within its narrow aperture a single star. But overhead the night is full of stars; before Job stands a young man, Elihu, who points towards their light and recalls Job to Vision. 'I am Young & ye are very Old wherefore I was afraid', runs the inscription: in the margin two angels comment, 'Lo all these things worketh God oftentimes with Man to bring back his Soul from the pit to be enlightened with the light of the living.'

The young visionary's words of inspiration are followed by Job's vision of the Lord speaking to him out of the whirlwind, and this in turn by a vision of the creation (fig. 74) in which Job and his companions look up from their darkness to see God stretching forth his hands above the chariot of the morning and the chariot of night. A young sun-god drives the glorious horses of visionary Reason in the one, a moon-goddess guides the serpents of energy in the other. Above God stand his Sons, their arms and wings outstretched to each other against the starry height. The main inscription reads, 'When the morning Stars sang together, & all the Sons of God shouted for joy.'

In this design, only the Sons of God are fully visionary. God himself is separated by clouds both from them and from Job: his earthly powers involve a separation of vision from energy, of day from night. The following designs explain the position further. God sadly points down past Job and his wife to the forces of Behemoth and Leviathan (Behemoth the symbol of obtuse brutal energy, Leviathan—as in *The Marriage of Heaven and Hell*—symbolizing the coils of Reason in the Sea of Time and Space). In the next design, he shows how this state of misused power came about. Satan and his crew, who have been cast down in flames below the earth, are about to be turned from ministers of flaming fire into monstrous and perverted energies like Behemoth and Leviathan. Finally, as the comforters turn away in shame, the Lord himself appears before Job and his wife to bless them. His light, though faded, still beams with a certain beauty.

Subsequent plates display the response of Job. Of the stones of the trilithon he makes an altar, on which a large coloured flame ascends towards the pale but vast light of his Lord. Before this flame his companions kneel. In the next design he is once again sitting beneath a tree while crops grow nearby and representatives of honest humanity (resembling Joseph and Mary, or Los and Enitharmon) draw near, each offering a piece of money. Next he is seen in restored prosperity, surrounded by his daughters ('There were not found Women as fair as the daughters of Job'). He stretches out his hands towards designs on the walls of the room, showing scenes from his experience.

In the final design of the series[25] we are restored to the scene of the first, under the oak tree. But now Job and his sons and daughters are on their feet, playing their harps and instruments and singing praise to God. Against the rising sun (now on the right of the design) the prayer 'Our Father which art in Heaven' (which can, in Blake's eyes, soon be perverted into the worship of an absentee God, a deity distanced into holiness) is replaced by the song 'Great & Marvellous are thy Works Lord God Almighty...' The Night of absence from vision is passed.

Blake's version of the Book of Job is not orthodox. For the Job who professes blind faith in a holy God despite all the injuries and calumnies he suffers, is substituted a figure asserting the rights of humanity against the demands of so-called holiness, until he is granted a vision of the universe which, in explaining the presence of evil by the decline of energy, reveals beneath its temporary, second-best order the hope of restoration to a more glorious state, where Vision and Energy are reintegrated and where the morning stars sing together and all the Sons of God shout for joy. The God of this world, as thus revealed, is not the tyrant that he sometimes seems, but a figure of faded vision, whose benevolent legalism is a desperate attempt to maintain order in a universe where the insistent irruptions of his own rejected energy threaten him constantly with chaos. He is not humanity's tyrant, but humanity's selfhood; humanity must either learn to live with him, therefore, or replace its selfhood by a more visionary identity which, like the Job of the final plate, lives by brotherhood and music rather than by law.

In these designs, Blake achieved a new mastery of his medium. In the works of his early prime he had concentrated on the lines of energy. The engraving of *America*, which is chiefly notable for this feature, represents a high-water mark in his early art. But this was not what he himself now wanted to achieve. He had become more interested in creating an art where even the lines of energy are in subordination to the radiance of vision.

So, in these later works, the visionary element in his art becomes steadily more important: there is a struggle between the demands of vision and the demands of line. Communication is not always immediate: sometimes one must share Blake's vision in order to enjoy the painting. His art is teaching the language by which it is to be understood. Even in the production of the various versions of *Job*, advances in technique towards this end are evident, and are carried on into other work. The designs for *The Pilgrim's Progress*, for example, carry on the general style of one set of the Job illustrations. What has just been said about Blake's art is supported in the preface to these illustrations, where no less a Blake scholar than Sir Geoffrey Keynes confesses that when he first looked at the designs he found them disappointing; yet returning to them some years later he was surprised by their beauty.[26]

At the end of his life Blake occupied himself with a series of designs to illustrate the vision of Dante. In the *Pilgrim's Progress* illustrations there is hardly any symbolism that does not derive from Bunyan; here there is slightly more reference to his personal mythology.

Blake was never altogether enthusiastic about Dante the man. While making the designs he had several conversations with Henry Crabb Robinson on the subject. One of his observations is fairly neutral—Robinson asked him whether Dante was morally pure when he wrote and Blake replied that he did not think that there was any purity in God's eyes. A later one is more telling: Blake remarked, 'Dante saw Devils where I see none. I see only good.' And on December 17th, 1825, Robinson records his opinions as follows:

'(Dante) was an "Atheist", a mere politician busied about this world as Milton was, till in his old age he returned back to God whom he had in his childhood.' I tried to get out from Blake that he meant this charge only in a higher sense, and not using the word Atheism in its popular meaning. But he would not allow this.[27]

Blake certainly did not exempt the *Divine Comedy* from

criticism. Indeed, he was at pains to set down his own contrary opinions on several of the designs. On one he wrote,

> Every thing in Dantes Comedia shows That for Tyrannical Purposes he has made This World the Foundation of All & the Goddess Nature . . . Memory is his Inspirer & not Imagination the Holy Ghost.

On another,

> It seems as if Dantes supreme Good was something Superior to the Father of Jesus for if he gives his rain to the Evil & the Good & his Sun to the Just and the Unjust He could never have Built Dantes Hell nor the Hell of the Bible neither in the way our Parsons explain it   It must have been originally Formed by the Devil Him self & So I understand it to have been.

Another comment on the same design makes a further charge (echoing a passage from *Jerusalem*):

> Whatever book is for Vengeance for Sin & whatever Book is Against the Forgiveness of Sins is not of the Father, but of Satan the Accuser & Father of Hell.[28]

Why, then, did Blake spend so many months in illustrating Dante's writings? The answer may be found in another of the conversations, when Crabb Robinson tried to discover whether Blake thought Swedenborg and Dante alike.

> As far as I could collect, he does. *Dante* he said was the greater poet. He had *political* objects. Yet this, though wrong, does not appear in Blake's mind to affect the truth of his vision.[29]

In saying this, Blake is evidently referring to one of his favourite beliefs. All truly creative artists have access to the Divine Vision; and this fact is not affected if some whose minds are open to it interpret what they see falsely. The structure of Dante's vision is true even if his own attitudes, as revealed in personal comments, are wrong.

This belief can be seen at work within Blake's designs.[30] As with his designs for *Paradise Lost*, he finds a point of contact with his author by assuming that what he regards as evils are in fact perverted energies. He has an immediate opportunity for working at this idea in the incident that opens the *Divine Comedy*: Dante's meeting with the three beasts. Blake makes it

clear from his representation of the animals that they symbolize human passions. His idea of Hell, likewise, makes it
a place where men are tormented by misuse of their own
energies.

Dante himself is depicted like the poet in *Milton*, or the
Pilgrim in *The Pilgrim's Progress*, a figure travelling in the mild
light of vision. From his encounter with the beasts, he flees
towards the descending figure of Virgil, represented as like
himself: Virgil is the guardian of his visionary form. With this
guide, Dante can set forth to explore the circles of Hell and
see the torments of the strong. Penetrating the forest of error,
they come to the entrance of Hell, which is this world under the
dominion of Law. On either side of the entrance sit figures
tortured in flames: on the left a bald man, suffering from the
bonds of the natural law, on the right a strong man, his hands
shackled, suffering from the bonds of the moral law. By the
left-hand figure are the three beasts, still fairly benevolent in
feature, but beginning to show the dangerous side of their
natures. Over the entrance a great figure stretches forth his
hands: Blake has placed by him a note: 'The Angry God of
this World'. Before him kneels a figure representing all forms
of power in this world. He wears a spiked crown of violence and
swings a censer of religious mystery.

These are the two presiding spirits of the world that we know;
between them and the captives, however, float four figures
representing the innocent elements of nature—earth, water, air
and fire. The earth-figure sits by a spinning wheel, like
Enitharmon. These forces remain essentially uncorrupted by
the perversities of a human world.

Descent into the circles of Hell brings the two poets to a
cliff-edge below which the ancient poets can be seen. As one of
them sleeps Homer is seen advancing, a sword in his hand. The
detail, which appears in the original Dante, is used by Blake to
express the first decline of the bardic vision: even Homer sings
of wars. In the next design, Homer and his companions are
shown, still bardic, among the trees of error, while above them,
but still shut off by clouds from full vision, an aged figure
ministers to a large flame on an altar (exactly like Job). His
devotion (that of an Old Testament poet?) is accompanied by

the presence of floating figures, all representing the innocence of threefold vision.

After the decline of bardic vision, the decline of love. In one of his most celebrated designs, Blake shows the Circle of the Lustful. In a sun at the right of the design, Paolo and Francesca are seen at the moment of their embrace. This moment of infinite desire is succeeded to the left by a sweeping flame in which the two lovers are seen again, their faces now caught in the uncontrolled lineaments of lustful desire; in the stream of the whirlwind which occupies the entire left of the picture appear all the torments of love when pursued for its own sake.

Lower energies are seen: gluttony, the pursuit of wealth, anger and, finally, the 'Goddess Fortune'. From this low point, Dante and Virgil sail to the City of Dis, which shows a still further decline. Here the angel who opens the gate, his wings spread like those in the Egyptian hierogram, is greeted by a gorgon-like figure of anti-vision, from whom serpents spit forth poison. It is the old mistaken opposition between vision and energy.

Inside the city the human beings who are being tortured— self-murderers, blasphemers, usurers, seducers, flatterers and so on—are more fully in the bonds of their Selfhood. A witty drawing shows Fucci 'making the figs' against God. The gesture is echoed by a serpent's tail behind the uplifted finger of one hand, and a serpent wreathed round the other arm, its head forming the same shape as the hand: the domination of the Selfhood is neatly suggested. In the background one serpent is swallowing another—the logical conclusion of devotion to the Selfhood. The theme continues in the next design, which shows Agnello Brunelleschi being attacked by the six-footed serpent. The position which is shown in the design, with the serpent swallowing his head from behind, while it still remains attached to his body, is anatomically impossible, and evidently intended to express the inward state of a man devoured by his Selfhood. Subsequent designs show scenes of transformation, Brunelleschi being partly transformed by a serpent towards devilhood, Donati fully transformed into a serpent and Guercio Cavalcanti retransformed from a serpent into a man. There follows the Pit of Disease, and then primeval giants sunk in the soil.

Nimrod is a fallen energy; in the background his archetype, Human Power, with orb and sceptre and spiked crown (the frozen residuals of wisdom, love and visionary reasoning) has shrunk into a tiny doorway, shaped like the trilithon, beneath the ruins of the Tower of Babel. Finally comes a vision of three Titans. Aged Energy on the one side and Youthful Vision on the other gaze ruefully at the central figure, who could unite them if he were not bound in chains. After the Circle of Traitors, the imprisoned Ugolino and the spectrous Lucifer who presides over this solidified universe, Dante and Virgil emerge to see, once again, the rays of the sun.

In Purgatory they meet Cato, a figure representing all that was most good and evil in the ancient world. While Virgil points both up and down, however, Cato points down only, in judgment. And now, with Cato looking on by his still-tended flame, an angelic boat arrives to waft the souls for purgation. This 'moon-ark' of vision, which has often figured in Blake's art, is inhabited by a winged angel (fig. 50). There follows the ascent of the mountain. In the daytime Dante and Virgil ascend by the light of a pale visionary sun, at night Lucia, a moon-like radiance behind her, carries the sleeping Dante. Within the gate of Purgatory, the ascent of the mountain continues and the two pilgrims pass designs sculpted in the rock. In Dante the three designs which are mentioned, the Annunciation, the Recovery of the Ark, and the story of Trajan and the Widow, are all intended to teach humility. Humility was a virtue which Blake distrusted; he uses only the first two designs, which can also be seen as emblems of vision. In the one, the ark of twofold Vision goes forward beneath the wings of the cherubim; the King of Israel dances before to the harp, while behind Uzzah, who has dared to touch the ark,[31] falls back, struck by lightning; in the background, Michal, David's wife, looks down at him with contempt. The other design, by contrast, shows Mary receiving the angel of the Lord in all his splendour. Vision is here humanized and fourfold: Pathos is wedded to the sublime.

As they ascend higher, beyond the circle of the Proud, Dante and Virgil pass into the flames (emblems again of twofold vision) and sleep beneath a mighty moon in which appears Dante's dream of Rachel and Leah. Once again, Dante's own interpretation—that these two figures represent, respectively, the lives of passive contemplation and active labour—is sidestepped: Blake is more interested in suggesting the dangers of self-contemplation and 'vegetation', the errors which keep human beings locked in the sphere of threefold vision which they were intended to use only for repose.

A series of paradisal visions follows. First Beatrice appears in her chariot, drawn by a visionary-eyed gryphon whose head resembles that of the figure portrayed at the beginning of the last chapter of *Jerusalem*. The chariot itself displays a vision of Nature in its glory: Beatrice is Vala transformed into Jerusalem. A vortex of serpentine energy, filled with eyes and human faces, represents the fusion of vision and energy. Above it, wings filled with eyes support the symbols of the evangelists, the heads of a bull, a lion and an eagle (which, by contrast with the three beasts at the opening of the series, are energies transformed to the service of vision), and the head of the Son of Man. In the middle stands Vala, now crowned and robed as the bride Jerusalem.

After another version of the Harlot and the Giant, the figure of a forgiving Christ beams forth on the adoring Dante, to be followed by a design of circular stairs (recalling Blake's version of Jacob's Ladder) and a vision of the Recording Angel, with a star of Vision shining brightly in the gothic sweep of his upfolded wings. Dante and Beatrice pass into a sphere where they can contemplate the Divine Image in each other, amid flowery cycles of flame. Ageing Energy descends to them in the form of St Peter, offering them the key of Heaven. He in turn is joined by the figure of Ageing Innocence, in the form of St James. Finally these two, who, when they arrived, were contending against one another, are joined by St John the Evangelist, the figure of vision who unites them. Reconciled, they look on in rapt contemplation while he descends to Dante and Beatrice.

His descent introduces the final revelation of the sequence. First the nine spheres are accompanied by the ages of man; in them the sun passes from its rising, through intensities of energy to the heat of Mars and 'Mental fight' with warrior heads on either side, and then on, to be finally lost in a vision of

Humanity, with the 'young-eyed Cherubim' beneath an ageing Father. After this, Dante is seen drinking from the River of Light, which flows down from the sun-fountain in the heavens and includes within itself a glorious vision of the whole Creation.

Having entered fully into Dante's vision at this point, however, Blake establishes his own position against it in a further elaboration. After Dante has drunk from the river of light, he beholds the abode of the Blessed rising like a great rose from the sea of light and his attention is drawn towards the figure of the Virgin, surrounded by a host of angels. Blake's illustration to this castigates the world to which Dante the man paid court. The Virgin is indeed presiding over the rose, but with a sceptre of hardened innocence in the one hand and a looking-glass of self-contemplation in the other. Around her lie the Old and New Testaments chained down, with the words 'Thrones' and 'Dominions' above them: near by, on the other hand, Homer and Aristotle lie open. When religion is used as an instrument of dominion, the sublime revelation in the Bible is replaced by Homer's war-epics and Aristotle's analytics. The consequences are also shown in the design. Various figures representing the energies of Nature are seen, either bound or rearing up before the figure of Vala, whose domination in the foreground relies upon that of the Virgin behind.

But, there is also a steady ambiguity in the design, which presents the potentialities of humanity as well as the actuality. The Virgin could be the Bride; a visionary reading of the Bible could reveal its true glory, still leaving Homer and Aristotle their due place; the energies of nature could flower to the light of eternity. And with this final ambiguity, presenting the ultimate choice before mankind, Blake closes his last attempt to interpret another man's vision.

Blake's own comments on his designs for Dante, together with the deliberate alterations by which he suggests Dante's errors and brings out the 'vision within the vision', help us with a problem that arises in considering his later work as a whole. How far was he willing to go in order to be faithful to his author? If his designs for Milton seem to conflict with his comments in *The Marriage of Heaven and Hell*, does this reflect a change in his own beliefs or a concession to the text before him?

The comments on Dante suggest that in so far as Blake had moved, it was away from an advocacy of political and social freedom within the present world towards an assertion that man always enjoys the possibility of freedom, spiritual and physical, if he will only awaken to it.

Time is a refraction of Eternity. Any suggestion of 'other-worldliness' in such a belief is tempered by the fact that the Eternal Man is always present within each individual. Worldly pleasures are only attacked by Blake so far as they are hindrances of the Eternal Man, that sublime in him which is his greatest pleasure. The balance is clearly suggested in the inscriptions to his engraving of the Laocoön group, which he took to be an emblem of man in his fallen state, the two sons who are wrestling with serpents being 'Adam' and 'Satan' respectively.[32] In these Art is made the key to Christianity, the Imagination being identified as the Jesus who could reconcile the struggling energies of Adam and Satan. It is Art, too, that reconciles Time and Eternity. So Blake does not repudiate pleasure, but declares, 'For every Pleasure Money is Useless.' On the other hand he does repudiate Chastity and Abstinence as 'the Two Impossibilities . . . Gods of the Heathen'. And as soon as he has declared that the True Christian Charity is not dependent on Money he hastens to mention in parenthesis that Money is, however, 'the lifes blood of Poor Families'.

His remarks on Homer and Virgil,[33] engraved about the same time, emphasize his distinction between that generous love of the world which is shown in Art and that love of the world which drives men towards possession and dominion.

Nowhere is Blake's ambiguity of attitude more marked than in his treatment of the Bible. Despite his early promise to present the world with the 'Bible of Hell', and his near-identification of Jesus with the negative Theotormon in *The Song of Los*, we find him from an early age producing illustrations of biblical episodes which are immediately acceptable to the most devout Christian. Does this point to a basic inconsistency of attitude, or is there some reconciling thread?

Such inconsistency as may exist is inherent in Blake's ambiguous attitude towards the energies of desire. Despite his persistent refusal to believe in positive evil or to regard the devils as anything but perverted energies, he was, with the passing of time, less willing to write in favour of free indulgence of desire. He had not abandoned his belief that the perfection of humanity would consist in a marriage of vision with desire, but he had become conscious that in the present world such a state was unlikely to be reached on the general scale that would alone permit universal freedom.

At the same time, other elements in the Bible retained their importance for him. Even in *The Marriage of Heaven and Hell*, his most antinomian work, he wrote with approval of the prophet Isaiah, and the sublimity and pathos of his writings.[34] Isaiah's promised revelation of the glory of God and his prophecy of peace to all men remained for Blake the heart of the Bible. So far as the biblical devotion to law was concerned, he reconciled his own antipathy to it with his belief in virtue by invoking the New Testament principle of forgiveness. So in a manuscript poem he wrote,

> & Throughout all Eternity
> I forgive you you forgive me
> As our dear Redeemer said:
> This the Wine & this the Bread[35]

In the case of the Bible we have, in addition to the various illustrations, a late piece of work written by Blake *in propria persona*. 'The Everlasting Gospel' is a series of verse fragments which present his developed view of Christ.[36] In a pencilled prose paragraph, he indicates the specific value of the New Testament above the other writings of the ancient world.

> There is not one Moral Virtue that Jesus Inculcated but Plato & Cicero did Inculcate before him   what then did Christ Inculcate. Forgiveness of Sins.   This alone is the Gospel & this is the Life & Immortality brought to light by Jesus. Even the Covenant of Jehovah, which is This   If you forgive one another your Trespasses so shall Jehovah forgive you That he himself may dwell among you but if you Avenge you Murder the Divine Image & he

cannot dwell among you because you murder him he arises
Again & you deny that he is Arisen & are blind to Spirit

The forgiveness of sins, a constant feature of Christ's teaching
and a pivotal element in the Lord's Prayer, reaches its fullest
expression in his words from the Cross, which Blake sees as
reverberating through all human history, whenever any man is
accused of sin.

Then Jesus rose & said to Me
Thy Sins are all forgiven thee
Loud Pilate Howld loud Caiaphas yelld
When they the Gospel Light beheld . . .

The Moral Virtues in Great fear
Formed the Cross & Nails & Spear
And the Accuser standing by
Cried out 'Crucify Crucify . . .'

The 'Cross & Nails & Spear' may well be intended to stand
as antitypes of the bow of gold, the arrows of desire and the spear
which arm the protagonist of 'mental fight'; the point to be
emphasized, at all events, is that the crucifiers are attacking
forgiveness and protecting Law. As in *Jerusalem*, it is Christ's
forgiveness from the cross, not any supposed atoning virtue in
the sacrifice itself, that makes the crucifixion an emblem of
redemption.

From this central point, Blake radiates his case that the
Christ normally offered as a pattern for mankind has no existence in the gospel record. Blake finds there not a figure of
universal benevolence (—after all, 'Caiaphas was in his own
Mind / A benefactor to Mankind') but a visionary:

The Vision of Christ that thou dost see
Is my Visions Greatest Enemy
Thine has a great hook nose like thine
Mine has a snub nose like to mine
Thine is the friend of All Mankind
Mine speaks in parables to the Blind. . . .

Against the popular conception of a 'gentle Jesus' (even if
'gentle' is interpreted in the sense of 'gentility') Blake sets the
record of a Christ so thoughtless of others as to leave his parents
for three days, and then disclaim allegiance to them.[37] This,

the main incident recorded from his childhood, is one of disobedience. Blake continues, ironically,

> Obedience is a duty then
> And favour gains with God & Men

When Satan called for obedience, moreover, Christ came out
in open revolt against him—

> And bursting forth his furious ire
> Became a Chariot of fire
> Throughout the land he took his course
> And traced diseases to their source
> He cursd the Scribe & Pharisee
> Trampling down Hipocrisy
> Where eer his Chariot took its way
> There Gates of Death let in the day
> Broke down from every Chain & Bar. . . .

Blake always refused to sanction the *physical* violence in the
Bible, however, Speaking to Crabb Robinson on one occasion,
he remarked that Christ ought not to have resorted to force in
cleansing the Temple—'he took much after his mother (the
Law)'.[38] So here he is careful to view the incident allegorically:

> He scourgd the Merchant Canaanite
> From out the Temple of his Mind
> And in his Body tight does bind
> Satan & all his Hellish Crew

At this point, the concept of 'vegetation' reappears, as Blake
declares firmly that Christ in his energy had nothing to do with
the basic deadness of the flesh:

> And thus with wrath he did subdue
> The Serpent Bulk of Natures dross
> Till he had naild it to the Cross
> He took on Sin in the Virgins Womb
> And put it off on the Cross & Tomb
> To be worshipd by the Church of Rome

Only the golden form of the Eternal Man has any reality, and
this has as little to do with humility as with overweening pride.
Jesus acts with 'triumphant, honest pride':

> If he had been Antichrist Creeping Jesus
> Hed have done any thing to please us

Gone sneaking into Synagogues
And not usd the Elders & Priests like dogs . . .

He did not die with Christian Ease
Asking pardon of his Enemies
If he had Caiaphas would forgive
Sneaking submission can always live

God does not ask humility from man: on the contrary, he
demands recognition of the divinity in the human and the
human in the divine:

If thou humblest thyself thou humblest me
Thou also dwellst in Eternity
Thou art a Man God is no more
Thy own Humanity learn to adore . . .

Humility involves a failure to recognize one's own eternal
identity and so leads to doubt:

Humility is only doubt
And does the Sun & Moon blot out . . .

The resulting single vision 'distorts the Heavens from Pole to
Pole'. Moreover, natural religion leads to moral cruelty. Jesus,
on the other hand, does away with the curses of the moral law,
the contentions of 'good' and 'evil'. He breaks all the 'commandments'. His nature is shown clearly in his treatment of
the woman who was found in adultery and condemned by the
law of Moses to be stoned to death:

What was the sound of Jesus breath
He laid His hand on Moses Law
The Ancient Heavens in Silent Awe
Writ with Curses from Pole to Pole
All away began to roll
The Earth trembling & Naked lay
In secret bed of Mortal Clay
On Sinai felt the hand Divine
Putting back the bloody shrine
And she heard the breath of God
As she heard by Edens flood
Good & Evil are no more
Sinais trumpets cease to roar. . . .

Abstinence has too long been elevated to the rank of a virtue by
the cult of a 'holiness' so pure that in its sight even Heaven

becomes impure. The worshippers of such 'holiness' actually lose the true revelation by neglecting the physical roots of love—

That they may call a shame & Sin
Loves temple that God dwelleth in
And hide in secret hidden Shrine
The Naked Human form divine
And render that a Lawless thing
On which the Soul Expands its wing. . . .

Nevertheless, Blake is further from affirming sexual freedom than he was when he wrote *Visions of the Daughters of Albion*. Forgiveness, not indulgence, is his theme. When he looks at life, the controlling dialectic of lost vision which was present even in his most enthusiastic early prophetic books is seen to be still at work, but there is less hope than before that the dialectic can be resolved in this life:

Do what you will, this Life's a Fiction
And is made up of Contradiction.

—a statement similar to that which occurs in the last version of *The Gates of Paradise*.[39]

From Blake's vision of Christ as a figure of infinite energy, judging the world in his chariot of fire, we may turn to the view of the Bible which he presented in one of his late tempera paintings. This painting (fig. 75) sometimes called 'The Spiritual Condition of Man', can be characterized more accurately.[40] It was presumably painted for Butts, who bought many of Blake's biblical paintings; Blake would therefore be concerned to keep the orthodox element of his beliefs in the foreground.

The painting is organized in an unusual manner. Down the left-hand side, and up the right-hand, appears a succession of biblical incidents, some of which Blake had illustrated elsewhere. Those on the left include the expulsion from Eden; the Ark; the Covenant of Noah; the judgment of Solomon; the captivity in Babylon; and the crucifixion; those on the right the Empty Tomb; Pentecost; John's vision of the Martyr's Crown in Revelation; the Spectre cherub (the Beast: 'Religion hidden in War'); the Last Trump; and Christ in Judgment.

These motifs represent moments of the Bible which are, in

differing ways, important for Blake's own interpretation. The vision is no longer possessed after the expulsion from Eden but is nevertheless guarded by Noah: the ark and the rainbow on the waters are its emblems. It beams out still in the human wisdom with which Solomon identifies the true mother of a child by her selfless love, but is now under a pressure which, strengthened in the Captivity, intensifies to a climax in the Crucifixion. After the Resurrection, vision revives in the disciples, and their inspiration, reaching a new intensity in the Revelation of St John the Divine, will eventually be crowned by the glorification of humanity, the true revelation of Christ, triumphing over the alliance between priests and warriors.

So far we have dealt only with the two sides of the design; the designs in the centre are more prominent, and are organized by Blake's 'levels of vision'. At the foot, in the foreground of a plain, stand three figures which can be identified by their respective symbols as Faith, Hope and Charity. Charity, crowned, stands in the middle. Above her head floats another woman surrounded by young children and babies; she clearly represents the expression of charity by human kindness. Finally, above this sphere of threefold vision (which suggests the practical charity of the Epistle of St James), comes the fourfold Revelation: an adoring human being kneels before the orb of full vision, while on either side stand a man and woman (Adam and Eve, Los and Enitharmon, the Spirit and the Bride) who are singing and praising the Vision. The ascent of Charity, via human kindness, to vision is thus at the centre of the design. There seems, however, to be a further significance in the organization of the design. The position of Faith, Hope and Charity is between the incidents of the Cross (which is facing away from the spectator) and the Tomb. Do they represent the Vision which was crucified and then rose again? It is more likely that Blake, positive as usual, is presenting his conception of the value of the Church, while insisting that it has missed the point of its own revelation. It has not seen that the importance of the gospel narrative lies not in the cross and empty tomb, but in the fact that the Christ to whom these things happened was living an allegory of the life of the Eternal Man in each individual. Whether on the other, hidden side of the cross or sealed in the tomb, the true Christ still remains, a potential revelation within the lineaments of each human being.

Nevertheless, although the Church has missed this central revelation, worshipping a Christ who sacrifices himself in humility instead of the Jesus who revealed himself in 'triumphant, honest pride', it cannot be dismissed out of hand. St Paul may not, in Blake's eyes, have grasped the central significance of the life of Christ, but he did see the importance of faith, hope and charity—virtues which, honestly pursued, can bring men, by way of love for their fellows, to that full charity which is a part of true vision. The figures of Faith, Hope and Charity are not those of Blake's best women: certainly, they do not possess 'the lineaments of gratified desire'. But they still guard the important realm of threefold vision above and help to indicate the vision which they refract obliquely. The best title for the picture as a whole would therefore be 'A Vision of the Bible and the Church.'

A more complicated design of the same sort is to be found in the tempera painting which was discovered at Arlington Court some years ago (fig. 78). Several attempts have since been made to determine the subject of the picture. Titles which have been proposed for it include 'A Vision of the Cabbala', 'The Circle of the Life of Man', 'The Sea of Time and Space' and 'Regeneration'.[41] Miss Kathleen Raine has suggested that it is 'a pictorial statement of the metaphysical theme developed by Porphyry in his *Cave of the Nymphs*, with certain details added from Blake's own study of the *Odyssey*'.[42]

As will be seen from the reproduction, the picture is complicated in design. The various elements in it may be characterized as follows. In the foreground flows a river with flames proceeding from it. Just above, four figures are writhing together in a confined space, some of them clutching at a rope which is unwinding from a long hank. To the right of this a flight of steps leading up from the river is flanked on either side by tall trees, the branches of which intermingle above. A figure at the foot of the steps carrying a pail from the river is gazing at a figure who stands by the trees at the left holding a ball of thread, the skein of which is held by another figure outside the trees. Two figures on the right hold ropes and nets, while below them a third, slumbering, lies partly submerged in the river. Further up the steps appear three more figures who have emerged from the flames beyond them and hold shuttles aloft in their hands. At the top of the design, in a cavern, several figures are walking serenely with pails on their heads, gazing at a visionary scene in the top left-hand corner.

The scene so far described occupies the right-hand half of the picture. To the left it is dominated by a man and woman on an isthmus beyond the great roots of the tree. The male is crouching towards the sea, holding his outstretched hands over it. Out at sea, four horses are plunging side by side in the waves, with a naked figure leaning upon them. A wreath of cloud connects this scene with another in the sky, which is hidden from the people on the shore by further clouds. A chariot of fire stands there: four horses which are harnessed to it are being held back and groomed by women. In the chariot the chariot-eer lies asleep, surrounded by an aureole of glory: attendant maidens wait near by.

The woman on the isthmus, dressed in simple but beautiful clothing, stands at the man's side, her right hand indicating the writhing figures below, her left pointing to the visionary scene above. Behind her can be seen various slopes down to the sea on which figures are reclining: one of them holds a vessel from which a stream of water flows down the hillside. Trees and a temple are visible.

In the course of his discussion, Mr George Wingfield Digby has discussed[43] several parallels in Blake's art and poetry which help to interpret the symbols involved; in most cases, however, his interpretation can be taken a stage further. He points out that the male figure on the isthmus bears a marked resemblance to the portrayal of Jesus in the designs for *Paradise Regained* and suggests that he is either Jesus or Albion. We may suggest that in these late designs Blake's idea of Jesus on earth is not unlike his conception of Los, guardian of vision—the enduring Spirit of Man. The female figure at his side, suggests Mr Digby, is Jerusalem or Vala: we may go further and suggest that she is, specifically, the Jerusalem described in the Book of Revelation, 'prepared as a bride adorned for her husband'.[44]

Mr Digby also points out that the 'chariot of fire' appears

several times in Blake's work. Apart from his well-known 'Bring me my chariot of fire!' in the preface to *Milton*, he depicted Jehovah judging Adam from a static chariot, and in 'The Everlasting Gospel' described Christ's battle with Satan as follows:

> And bursting forth his furious ire
> Became a Chariot of fire
> Throughout the land he took his course
> And traced diseases to their source
> He cursd the Scribe & Pharisee
> Trampling down Hipocrisy
> Where eer his Chariot took its way
> There Gates of Death let in the day
> Broke down from every Chain & Bar. . . .[45]

There is a *prima facie* case, therefore, for identifying the sleeping figure in the chariot as Christ in his eternal identity, always ready to break through as Fourfold Vision into the world of Space and Time.

The horses and female figures out at sea help this identification. Mr Digby refers to the *Job* plates, on which Blake was working during the same years, and reminds us that in the plate 'When the Morning Stars sang together', (fig. 74) the Lord is shown in the centre of his creation, with the sun-god riding off on four horses (exactly like those in the present picture) on one side, while the moon-goddess drives a pair of snakes on the other. In the present picture, it is a female figure that is resting by the horses. Once again we may move on from Mr Digby's point and argue that in bringing together these two elements from the design, Blake intended to represent the visionary potentiality in nature. In other words, the woman, Vala, represents the light of the moon (but not the passions of the night, normally hidden energies in our universe) while the horses represent the power of the sun (but not the lost god of light). The light and the heat, juxtaposed, image the light and power of the lost sun which will be restored only when the Fourfold vision breaks through in his chariot. If we take the sea here to be the Sea of Time and Space, the point is strengthened, for, according to *Revelation*, the sea will be no more when the New Jerusalem descends—and there will be no more need

of sun and moon, since the Lord God Almighty and the Lamb
will be sufficient light.[46] So we may take it that the figure of
Vala with the horses of light, floating on the Sea of Time and
Space, present the visionary beauty of nature: they are an
eternal prophecy of the Divine Vision which, breaking through
the clouds, establishes that beauty for ever with the reign of
Humanity in its full sublimity and pathos. It is appropriate,
therefore, that they should be linked to the sleeping, waiting
charioteer who represents that intervention.

There is another link with Jerusalem, the heavenly city. Mr
Digby points out that the figure with the ball of thread inside
the trees may well be related to the idea expressed in the lines
that prefix the last chapter of *Jerusalem*:

> I give you the end of a golden string,
>   Only wind it into a ball:
> It will lead you in at Heavens gate,
>   Built in Jerusalems wall.

The existence of this verse (including the oblique reference to
dawn revelation furnished by the Shakespearean context of
'Heaven's gate')[47] encourages a comparison of the whole of the
right-hand side of the picture with a description in Blake's
Vision of the Last Judgment:

> The Temple stands on the Mount of God from it flows on each
> side the River of Life on whose banks Grows the tree of Life
> among whose branches temples & Pinnacles tents & pavilions
> Gardens & Groves display Paradise with its Inhabitants walking
> up & down in Conversations concerning Mental Delights   Here
> they are no longer talking of what is Good & Evil or of what is
> Right or Wrong & puzzling themselves in Satan's Labyrinth
> But are Conversing with Eternal Realities as they Exist in the
> Human Imagination We are in a World of Generation & death
> & this world we must cast off if we would be Painters Such as
> Rafael, Mich Angelo & the Ancient Sculptors . . .[48]

The scene described is palpably *not* the one in the present
design; but the individual elements correspond so closely as
to suggest a community of theme. The figures on the steps
appear to have emerged from tribulation by fire and are perhaps, like the figures in the peaceful scene above them, 'walking
up & down in Conversations concerning Mental Delights'.

The writing figures beneath are evidently in the 'World of Generation & death'; if the rope which preoccupies them corresponds with the thread elsewhere in the design as a symbol of 'vegetated' life, it is clear that, unlike those who possess life as a means to vision, they are possessed and bound by it.

Sir Geoffrey Keynes has pointed to a similarity between the four latter figures and the figures representing the three Fates in one of Blake's illustrations to *Il Penseroso*. If so, however, they represent a development of that idea rather than a repetition of it. They could well represent four ways of becoming ensnared by 'the World of Generation and death'. The figure in front is grasping what Keynes describes as a 'huge phallic coil of rope shaped like a distaff'.[49] Behind him, his hand is on a vessel from which a flood of liquid is flowing—often in Blake a symbol of poison. This might refer to the vial with which one of the angels of wrath poisoned the river of life in the Book of Revelation. The figure could then stand for the distortion of sexual energies into vice. The second figure is examining one strand of the rope intently: she would seem to stand for that habit of minute analysis which concentrates on the particular at the expense of life in its fullness. A third figure, who has masculine features with feminine breasts, reminds one of certain traditions in sorcery. The figure at the extreme left carries, like Atropos, a pair of shears with which she is about to cut the rope: in some sense or other she evidently represents murder.

The river flowing past the figures has been variously identified as the river of life, or oblivion, or death: we may tentatively think of it as the river of *mortal* life—bearing in mind that this in itself may involve 'oblivion' (the sleeping figure on the right) or 'death' (the figures on the left). The figure at the bottom of the steps, her scale-covered pail filled with water is more difficult to identify; it is probable that, although still tainted by the water of this life, she is protesting her right to enter between the trees. In that case, the figures above, bearing plain pails upon their heads, can be regarded as similar figures, who have entered and passed through the realms of fire and enlightenment, to reach the heights of true vision.

The picture is also organized in the levels of vision to which we have become accustomed. The soul rising from the various dangers of immersion in the waters of mortality must pass through the world of energy, here symbolized in the furnaces from which the figures re-emerge carrying shuttles—a combination of the worlds of Los and Enitharmon. It must also enter into the spirit of Vision, as symbolized by the earthly figures on the isthmus and the vision on the waters of Time and Space. So it may come to the pleasant land beyond both, corresponding to the land of Beulah in Blake's mythology, a land from which the fourfold vision may be apprehended but not possessed, and in which the temple and waters of life foretell the paradise which that vision will restore.

But there is a more specific organization in the design. We have noticed, throughout our discussion, parallels with the Book of Revelation: and in one particular passage of that work may be found focused the following elements of Blake's picture:

The figure rising from the river and claiming entry to the flight of steps.

The gateway of trees above the steps.

The writhing figures, which could represent sexual vice, devotion to reason, sorcery and murder, respectively.

The revelation within nature on the Sea of Time and Space.

The connected revelation of the true Son of the Morning, Jesus, asleep in his chariot above.

The human form of Jesus and the bride Jerusalem on the isthmus.

The figures by the streams of an earthly paradise.

The presence of all these elements forces one irresistibly to the conclusion that the picture represents Blake's interpretation of a passage from the last chapter of Revelation:

I am Alpha and Omega, the beginning and the end, the first and the last.

Blessed are they that do his commandments, that they may have right to the tree of life, and may enter in through the gates into the city.

For without are dogs, and sorcerers, and whoremongers, and murderers, and idolaters, and whosoever loveth and maketh a lie.

I Jesus have sent mine angel to testify unto you these things in the churches. I am the root and the offspring of David, and the bright and morning star.

And the Spirit and the bride say, Come. And let him that heareth say, Come. And let him that is athirst come. And whosoever will, let him take the water of life freely.[50]

Several of Blake's idiosyncratic interpretations occur here. The 'idolaters' are those who fall down before the deity of analytic reason; the 'angel' which testifies to the churches is the revelation of eternity in the beauty of nature.

The weight of evidence concentrated within these lines makes them compelling as a source. The picture as a whole may be described as Blake's vision of the Book of Revelation, as miniatured within these verses. Moreover, after I had reached this conclusion, confirmatory evidence proved to be at hand. It turned out that the first rough pencil sketch for the centre of the design bore on its back the pencilled inscription, 'The Spirit and the Bride say "Come".'[51] The connection between this inscription and the completed painting had been previously thought to be too tenuous to warrant attention, but the weight of concealed evidence makes it clear that whoever pencilled the words knew the mind of Blake. Whether interpreted as religious mythology or psychological symbolism (and by now the close relationship in Blake's mind of the two modes is apparent) the completed painting represents his most complex and concentrated attempt to render a vision of human life under the hidden but impending apocalypse of that glory which gives eternal significance to its temporary forms.

A much simpler design of Blake's expresses the same theme at its barest. The parable of the Wise and Foolish Virgins (fig. 77) evidently attracted him considerably: he illustrated it several times.[52] The design in each case is simple. The ten virgins stand in the foreground, five with their lamps burning, five with their lamps empty, while overhead flies an angel blowing the trumpet of the Last Judgment. The symbolism is equally clear. The oil in the lamps represents the light of Vision: some human beings renew it constantly by the exercise of imagination and desire, others allow it to die. According to their action, so they are perpetually judged. But as in the *Canterbury Tales* design,[53] wise and foolish virgins alike possess the features of 'the human face divine'. It is only the emotions depicted on their faces that betray the sense of fulfilment in the one group, of loss in the other. The most striking quality of the painting, however, is its consummate success as an immediate visual experience. In some other paintings, Blake is in danger of losing his audience by relying on a symbolic organization which can be approached only by way of an inward response from the observer. Here, although the inward response, and an acquaintance with Blake's other representations of the human face, are as valuable as before, there is also immediate communication: the mastery of line in this painting would make it striking even if one had seen no other work by Blake. It is one of the high occasions in his art where vision and design are perfectly fused.

Blake's apocalypse is not merely an event at the end of time, but one which is constantly realized in the moments of human inspiration. There is a certain justice, therefore, in the fact that while some designs present the impending Apocalypse, and others the Last Judgment itself, this, the only one which presents the actual apocalyptic moment, the moment, suspended between 'time' and 'eternity', to which humanity perpetually returns, is also one of his finest achievements in purely artistic terms.

9 Epilogue: The Achievement

Blake's devotion to Dante, Bunyan and the Bible in his later work rounds the cycle of his development. By the time that he wrote *Jerusalem* the vehemence of his early prophetic books had already disappeared. Indignation, protest, anger had given place to the belief that one force only could redeem mankind: the indwelling light of imaginative power which would release in men delight in creative power and a compassionate forgiveness.

As Blake had become possessed by this belief he had returned to the emblems which fascinated him in his youth. In *Jerusalem* we meet again the Druids, the Druid temples and the contrast between the trilithon of mathematically organized reason on the one hand and the pathos and sublime of the true Gothic style on the other. In that work, too, he uses again the emblem of the sun, the serpent and the wings to present the dynamic relationship between vision, desire and love.

At the end of his life, however, Blake's use of symbolic utterance dwindled. In *Jerusalem* he had carried myth-making to the limits of communication; in the illustrations to Job and in his picture 'The Spirit and the Bride' he had shown how far he could go in organizing visual symbols into an intricate pattern. The art of his final period is in this respect more straightforward, an attempt to allow the light of his vision to illuminate scenes from Bunyan or Dante that were already familiar to his audience; symbolism, though still present, is here more direct and obvious.

In dealing with Blake's visual art I have been largely concerned with its meaning. It would of course be possible to make a different evaluation by dealing with the art in terms purely of visual design. The two modes are not mutually exclusive, however. We have rightly revolted against the 'literary' art of some Victorian painters, where the moral point bears only a tenuous relation to the visual effect of the picture. But in the case of a 'visionary' painter the problem is more intricate, since the symbolic meaning is a guide to the internal organization of the design. The picture actually changes for us as we learn what it is about.

It is the same with Blake's poetry. Purists might object that an investigation of the sort that has been carried out in these pages does violence to the poetry as poetry. Blake, it might be said, is made to seem more and more a moralist, less and less a poet. This, however, is only a primary and superficial effect. One is reminded of the similar argument that critical analysis destroys poetry. To know Blake's meaning does not take us away from the poetry; it simply shows us one of the ways in which the poetry is organized. And the effect of that knowledge is that, in time, the music of the poetry is released. Because we are no longer interrupted by irritating questions of meaning, we are free to respond to the verse, and its meaning, more completely.

One effect of our investigation is to make us more familiar with the visionary background of Blake's longer prophetic works. His is one of the most heroic attempts to define man's moral and psychological state by projecting a symbolic and interpretative landscape. The wastes and horrors which at first sight loom large in the prophetic books become more comprehensible as one sees that they always contain within themselves the presupposition of a different, paradisal landscape that has been lost. Blake's preoccupation here springs partly from his concern with the waste lands that were being created, physically, in England during his lifetime. When he looked at the bleakness of contemporary civilization and the heartlessness of its industrial centres, he interpreted it in terms of the activity of Tubal-Cain and his sons, who tried to turn to positive use the visionless energies which were otherwise employed by men in mutual destruction. When, in turn, he looked at the tendency towards destruction, he saw at its heart the image of Cain himself, whose murder of an innocence once alive in the pastoral flocks and lands of Abel was prompted, paradoxically, by his own horror of death. And when he looked into this pervasive horror of death among human beings, he saw as its cause the decline of vision from awareness of eternity to analysis and doubt. At the heart of *that* decline lay the failure of the sexes to fulfil themselves, imaged in the failure of his Adam and Eve. And that failure in its turn was due to the ultimate failure of man to exist in his true human glory—to be the god-like Man walking in his Garden, radiant, generous and self-giving.

Every man alive, according to Blake, is a work of degeneration, in which, behind the façade of reason, guile and self-interest, can be traced a series of ruined positives—the visionless creativity of Cain and his sons, the murdered innocence of Abel, the sexual failure of Adam, the visionary failure of the divine Man. The failures are in an ascending order, the final one containing the others. Unfallen humanity, on the other hand, would exist positively in all four spheres. At the heart of the Garden the Tree and Fountain of Life would be the centre of abounding energies (the animals of Eden). Around them would rise the Gothic buildings of a new Jerusalem, a city of joyful industry surrounded in its turn by pastures of innocence and rest. On the mountains beyond would shine the palaces of light, beaconing the true exercise of reason, while caverns in the distance would resound to a groundbass provided by the sustaining, basic rhythms of energy. From the inhabitants of this land there would rise, night and morning, the music of praise and joy.

Blake's many lapses into diffuseness and obscurity cannot affect the status of this, his central vision. The biblical reference here is no dead letter: it is linked throughout to a psychological interpretation of the nature of humanity as the starlit, ruined, wasted landscape where a sublime, illuminated man might walk in a paradisal garden.

Exploration and interpretation of Blake's work has led us naturally to treat it as a complete corpus, looking for the lines of development and for indications of internal self-consistency. Both are present, demonstrably so, but the danger of reprojecting Blake's visionary universe on such a scale is that it may begin to seem self-contained and distanced from its creator. It is time to remind ourselves of the strong expressive element in his work, the degree to which his idea of the creation was always being actively revised and renewed.

Blake's expressionist leanings, rare for his time, were part of his own conception of creation; they were also encouraged by the unusual intensity and realism of his visionary experiences. When he speaks of having seen the design 'The Ancient of Days' hovering above the staircase at Hercules buildings[1] he seems to be speaking in a very literal sense; and those who saw him executing his visionary heads in later years said that he drew as if a model were physically sitting to him.[2] At such times the visionary experience was not (as for many people) an intriguing interlude but an absolute visitation: it had a reality which continued to dominate his consciousness after the experience itself had ceased.

I argued earlier that the paradigm of four levels of vision was created by Blake from his reading of Boehme at an early stage; whether or not this is so it is clear that this paradigm, too, corresponded in an important way to the structure of his own psyche. If the visionary experience, when it visited him, possessed him absolutely, other moments in his experience were, correspondingly, absolute. Most people with strong imaginations find some difficulty in understanding how their fellow men can be content to pass their lives in the way that they do; for Blake the absoluteness of his visionary sense could involve also at times a sense of absolute alienation:[3]

> O why was I born with a different face
> Why was I not born like the rest of my race
> When I look each one starts! when I speak I offend
> Then I'm silent & passive & lose every Friend

The last two lines, describing in turn the faults of his active and passive states, follow a revealing piece of self-examination which occurs in the same letter:

> It is certain! that a too passive manner inconsistent with my active physiognomy had done me much mischief . . .

It is clear that the alternations between extreme active and passive states which he describes here were a strong feature of his personality from early youth, when his 'unbending deportment' caused him to become *persona non grata* in Mrs Mathew's circle.[4] But the same alternations which made him feel a misfit in polite company gave him the dimensions of his personality as an artist: they were the contraries out of which his threefold and twofold vision were made.

His concepts of the 'emanation' and the 'Spectre' spring from the same source. I earlier discussed the possible relationship of these concepts to ancient mythologies and to the idea of light in the Newtonian universe, but it is clear that for him they were effective criticisms of Newton because they were also firmly grounded in his own experience. If the 'emanation' bears a strong resemblance to Jung's 'anima', equally, it has deeper roots, in Romanticism. Blake's depiction of it in *Jerusalem* in the form of a butterfly reminds us that the link between butterfly and the Greek 'psyche' was re-emphasized in his time, along with the rediscovery of the myth of Cupid and Psyche,[5] and proved a valuable emblem for those who were asserting the importance of the feminine sensibility in man. The idea of a feminine element in the human personality, asserted both in Coleridge's ideal of androgyneity[6] and in Shelley's concept of the 'epipsychidion',[7] remained a potent force throughout the subsequent century and gave a certain colouring to nineteenth-century idealism.

The idea of the 'spectre', on the other hand, is Blake's tribute to the moral ambivalence of what is given in human personality. In the creative artist this is the daemonic energy which all too easily bows itself to the spirit of the age and produces works to that limited taste, but can also, when necessary, defend the vision of the artist himself—even if its only weapons are an outright rudeness. And if the emanation is evanescent to the eye of sense, as real and yet as unseizable as the flight of the butterfly, the spectre has the advantage of bringing with him his own strong charge of reality. When Blake is in full discursive play as an artist he creates Urizen, both placing him accurately and allowing his emanation to understand and pity him as an ineffective form of the good: he is pictured sometimes as a stern being leaning down to create in the darkness, sometimes as a kindly ancient figure, unable to understand the world in which he has created his forms, pitying the results, but still convinced that his own repressive measures are necessary to restrain natural cruelty.

In the notebook epigrams, on the other hand, where the

guardian Spectre takes over, Urizen is demoted to 'Nobodaddy'. Kindly understanding is replaced by straightforward abuse:[8]

> Then old Nobodaddy aloft
> Farted & belched & cough'd,
> And said I love hanging & drawing & quartering
> Every bit as well as war & slaughtering
> Damn praying & singing
> Unless they will bring in
> The blood of ten thousand by fighting or swinging

Blake's 'active physiognomy' is very present in verses like this. But it is also present, unobtrusively yet more positively, in a good deal of his writing, giving to individual lines and phrases their power to strike the reader forcefully. It is this quality which makes him 'dam' good to steal from' (Füseli's phrase[9]) and results in individual phrases being quoted by modern writers for their gnomic quality.

When Blake allows his spectre to speak he achieves an extraordinary directness of utterance. But in the major part of his work the relationship between active and passive is just as important, bringing into play more subtle effects. The very dualism which could make him either aggressive or taciturn among other people works for the good of his art. In some of his later visual work, for example, it is as if he has first drawn and coloured his subject in passive, threefold vision and then engraved it in the energy of twofold. Both versions are necessary for the full effect.

The lonely directness of the spectre's utterance is matched by a hidden yearning to the emanation: they form the parts of a broken dialectic. In the fullness of true fourfold vision the two activities would be integrated. Perception would be directly communicant; the stars would have their spears again. While separation persists, on the other hand, reason and pity are the only positives: in Urizen's domain the stars flee away into separated points of light and water heaven with tears of pity, leaving energy raging in its own destructive isolation.

Blake has found his own way to escape from Urizen's world. Moments of social despair like those quoted above are matched by assertions of energy in his creative work. His prose often shows the assertiveness in action: it moves from a rational statement of the situation to a sudden 'It is true!' or 'It is certain!'—changing the tone from rationality to an enthusiasm which for Blake creates its own sense of reality.

Awareness of this helps us to deal with an important issue. In what sense did Blake present his mythology as 'true'? This is a particularly hard question to answer—the more so since the territory which he was exploring was itself so uncharted. At times he gives the impression that he is coming to the key of all mythologies—the inner meaning of all ancient myths and traditions, the recorded interpretations of which he felt often to disguise rather than reveal their true content. At other times he seems to suggest that he is simply using traditional mythical figures in order to transmit ideas of his own which, he feels, transcend, while including, the ideas in earlier religions and mythologies and which give a deeper insight into human nature.

I am inclined to think that Blake himself was unsure of the exact status of his mythology, and that we have a very clear presentation of the shape of his own thinking on the subject in a passage at the beginning of Chapter Two of *Jerusalem*, discussing the possible convergence of the British and Hebrew mythologies: 'Jerusalem the Emanation of the Giant Albion! Can it be? Is it a Truth that the Learned have explored? Was Britain the Primitive Seat of the Patriarchal Religion? If it is true: my title-page is also True, that Jerusalem was & is the Emanation of the Giant Albion . . .'

After this, all doubts swallowed up in excited affirmation, Blake breaks into exclamations of rejoicing at the truth of his identification. He points out that the Jewish ancestral figures Abraham, Heber, Shem and Noah, with their patriarchal pillars and oak groves, must have been Druids and that the Jewish cabbalistic tradition of Adam Kadmon, the Man who 'anciently containd in his mighty limbs all things in Heaven & Earth' corresponds to his own Albion.

The passage begins with questions which might equally have been put (though in a slightly different tone of voice) by Urizen; but whereas Urizen would have continued with a weary shake of the head, Blake goes on to press the positive possibilities until they take fire in an 'It is true!' As soon as this happens Blake is possessed by his own vision and is able to link himself with all the traditions that he had pursued excitedly as a young man. The greatest example of this assertiveness in action is in the famous passage where he contrasts the two ways of seeing the sun—the Urizenic, which sees it shining in separation like a golden guinea, and the Blakean, which sees an innumerable company of the heavenly host singing 'holy holy holy is the lord of hosts'. The second way lives by creating the song in the per- ceiver as well as the perceived. The only vestige of this imme- diacy of vision which Blake finds in the world around him lies in the human instinct to rhythm, which has the same ability to fuse the perceiver and the perceived in the moment of per- ception. It is for this reason that he speaks of Los as dwelling in the 'auricular nerve'. Rhythm is the one form of direct vision that remains; for the rest, it must either be encircled and glimpsed in the assertion of energy or perhaps descend, unbidden, in the lawful time of repose which follows that exertion.

Blake was not content to be the sole inhabitant of his universe, however. He believed not only that all men were potential citizens of his city but that all men actually belonged to it, whether they wanted to or not, at particular moments of their existence. His vision may be nursed in isolation but his art is not the art of a man who has isolated himself; it is the art of a man who has walked the streets of London gazing intently in the faces of the people that he meets for signs of their 'visionary' selves. At the moment when he is most intent on pursuing the arts of law and commerce a man may show the vestiges of a radiance that betrays a different nature; another man, exerting his energies in physical labour, may suggest to an observer the existence of other dimensions to his psychic existence. Keats (another intent observer of this kind) remarked that though a quarrel in the streets was a thing to be hated, the energies dis- played in it were fine,[10] while Blake observed that whores, unlike many lawful matrons, always displayed the 'lineaments of gratified desire'.[11] Many of Blake's visual effects spring from this direct observation of his fellows: his mannered renderings of the human face, for example, are often attempts to catch some particular expression or set of lineaments which he has seen in one human being or another—the momentary badge of his secret citizenship.

There is a sense, of course, in which some of Blake's ideas look back to the eighteenth century rather than forward to the twentieth. It would be possible, for example, to see his idea that all things have their ground in an original concord as a development from Leibnitz's pre-established harmony or Pope's account of the creation in his 'Essay on Man'. ('All discord harmony not understood; / All partial evil, universal good . . .'.) The difference, of course, is that he sees no beneficence in nature itself. His acute sense of human suffering and isolation preserved him from the foolishness of thinkers such as Soames Jenyns[12] and he is quite clear in his mind that the perfection which exists at the heart of his visionary universe has little relationship with the processes of the natural one. In her own workings nature remains an inscrutable, self-contradictory blind force, indifferent to man—whose perfections are always momentary; it is only by connecting these moments of perfection in his imagination that man discovers another universe which explains his own humanity to him without reference to Newtonian laws and, by making him see that he is 'made for joy and woe', enables him to develop those resources of himself that correspond to the extremes of the human condition. If the slender strand of his ultimate, guarded optimism links Blake to the eighteenth century, the whole content of that optimism is based on a rejection of 'the Delusive Goddess Nature and her Laws'[13] —a rejection which would have been utterly alien to the Augustans.

Blake's concern with freedom, equally, is of the period that produced the French Revolution; but his thinking on the subject moves steadily further away from political commitment; it ends, indeed, in the belief that true freedom is a 'Freedom from all Law of the Members' in 'The Mind in which every one is King & Priest in his own House'.[14]

Because Blake's art is so involved with his own identity as a man and an artist, he has been most readily understood by later artists with similar preoccupations. His most important nineteenth-century heir is, of course, Yeats, whose interest in his symbolism was fostered by work on one of the earliest editions.

The effect is felt through the rest of his work: one thinks not only of his Blakean stanza,[15]

> Locke fell into a swoon;
> The Garden died;
> God took the spinning-jenny
> Out of his side.

but of the moment in his late poem 'An Acre of Grass' when Blake's vision of 'The Ancient of Days' hovering above the staircase becomes a central paradigm for the man who continues to batter away for truth in old age.[16]

Where Yeats came to Blake in youth through his own interests in symbolism and the status of the human imagination, Lawrence, who was more taken by Blake's statements about the importance of human energy and desire, was attracted, if anything, still earlier in life. Jessie Chambers records an adolescent conversation:[17]

> As we walked through the wood he talked to me in his rapt way about Blake, telling me what a wonderful man he was, quite poor, who taught himself everything he knew; how he made pictures and wrote poems that were interdependent, and did the printing and engraving himself, in fact producing the book entirely by his own hands . . .

The influence of Blake's work runs deeply in Lawrence's, but more often in general themes than in particular echoes. Lawrence evidently found ingredients of his own 'prophetic' style in Blake's: the two writers in fact form the major expressive tradition in modern English literature. His insistence on the importance of acknowledging and accepting desire is very Blakean, while his attacks on the domination of the female will in Western society may owe something to lines such as 'O Albion, why didst thou a Female Will create?'[18] The last two words of his story, 'The Christening': 'But his daughters shrank, sullen', echo a phrase in *The Song of Los*:[19]

> The sullen Earth
> Shrunk!

For the more general and important debt we turn to an essay such as 'The Crown',[20] where the dialectic between the Lion and Unicorn, seen as symbols of contrary states in man, seems to be a direct development from the dialectic between the lion of experience and the lamb of innocence in Blake.

Later writers have approached Blake in an even more complimentary way. Following, perhaps, in the tradition of Aldous Huxley, whose citations of Blake always carry an implicit charge of approval, certain novelists have used Blake and his writings to express a particular form of human consciousness. The most extended example is Joyce Cary's *The Horse's Mouth*, where he presents an artist-hero who is also a Cockney visionary, alternating his Londoner's speech with his quotations from Blake. In so doing he is able to suggest a consciousness which is too imaginative to find expression solely in the language of the streets, but which also by-passes the normal language of polite, middle-class society.

Blake himself is mentioned frequently in *The Horse's Mouth*; later novelists have felt free to adopt a more oblique approach, simply incorporating lines of his work in their text with the clear assumption that the reader will recognize their authorship. In Saul Bellow's *Herzog*, for example, an interior monologue by the hero concludes,[21]

> ... he had not forgotten the odor of his mother's saliva on the handkerchief that summer morning in the squat hollow Canadian station, the black iron and the sublime brass. All children have cheeks and all mothers spittle to wipe them tenderly. These things either matter or they do not matter. It depends on the universe, what it is. These acute memories are probably symptoms of disorder. To him perpetual thought of death was a sin. Drive your cart and your plow over the bones of the dead.

and in Iris Murdoch's *The Time of the Angels*, an autodidact servant's stream of consciousness is expressed in a similar way:[22]

> ... A train passes beneath and jolts everything in the house a millimetre or two and jolts Pattie's heart with a little reminder of death. She murmurs the poetry which takes the place of the poor defeated magic of her childhood. Turn away no more. Why wilt thou turn away? The starry floor, the watery shore, is given thee till the break of day.
>
> She goes into the kitchen where the strawberry blond is waiting to take her to see his father.

Blake's influence on a variety of later writers is clear and acknowledged. We are still left asking, however, whether his larger, organizing ideas have general validity.

In some respects Blake's attacks on the Newtonian universe are outdated by the advance of science itself. Advances in physics have long left behind conceptions of matter which rested on the presupposition of the indivisible atom at one extreme and of endless space at the other; or a study of the stars which found its chief focus in the orbitings of the planets. So far as these ideas remain a part of popular conceptions of nature, however, Blake's questionings retain their validity: and in spite of many intelligent accounts of the rôle of the creative imagination in scientific work, there is still room for discussion concerning the *kinds* of imagination involved: is there, in other words, a 'scientific' creative imagination which differs from the 'humanized' creative imagination of artists like Blake? At the very least it seems possible to argue for the existence of an 'objective' imagination, which organizes on the basis of the perceived structure of the outside world, and a 'subjective' imagination which organizes mainly on the basis of what is given from within the human psyche.

A similar argument can be mounted concerning the study of mythology in Blake's time and ours. We now know that in attempting to link his ideas to those of antiquarians like Bryant and Stukeley Blake was mistaken. Their ideas of early history, largely based on a biblical cosmology, were hopelessly simplified and distorted. At the same time, the spread of similar emblems and myths throughout the world remains an intriguing and rather mysterious phenomenon, not fully explained by fertility rituals or Jungian archetypes. Blake's interpretations are too privately based to be considered with full seriousness as historical explanations, nor did he, except in moments of enthusiasm like the one mentioned above, claim for them more than the authority of his own vision. But they do leave a sense of mystery which more 'scientific' explanations will not allow.

For our own century, nevertheless, Blake's dealings with ancient mythology are less rewarding than his attempts to provide symbolic expression of man's own inward nature and energies. Here, it seems to me, his claims as a prophet of modern thinking ought not to be exaggerated. He sometimes anticipates

Freud, for example, notably in his sense of the relationship between sexual frustration and aggression, but these moments do not loom large in his work as a whole. There is a stronger correlation between his thinking and Jung's (we have already commented on the resemblance between his 'emanation' and Jung's 'anima') but here again one is soon brought up against essential differences. It is unwise, for example, to link his Four Zoas with Jung's four 'Psychological functions', for the principles of organization are different. The Zoas are rooted in Blake's own version of human nature which moves out from the energies of head, heart and genitals to the expressive actions of hands and feet. Jung's four functions, thinking (or intellectual cognition), feeling (or subjective evaluation), sensation (or perception by the sense organs) and intuition (or perception by the unconscious) do not fit this pattern: they are more inward.[23] Nor does Jung's idea that the Christian Trinity should really be a Quaternity[24] correspond to Blake's fourfold scheme. His ideas are always firmly his own: if they look strikingly modern when compared with those of his contemporaries they also refuse to settle comfortably into the moulds made by men with different basic concerns.

If his assertion of an 'active universe', one of his most controversial and suggestive ideas, also has a prophetic ring, here again he turns out to be enlarging a trend in the thought of his own time. In his recent study of that title,[25] H. W. Piper has shown how the idea, developed largely in France, entered intellectual life at the end of the eighteenth century, finding a place in the speculations of poets like Wordsworth and Coleridge. Blake's version, like other elements in his Romanticism, differs by going further. It is not simply the phenomenon of organic life which is central to his universe, but the whole inward life of man as mediated by his imagination—which is given not only important status but eternal existence. It is one thing to organize one's thinking about the world around the facts of biological life, quite another to proclaim the existence of the 'Real Man, the Imagination', who is 'stronger & stronger as this Foolish Body decays'.[26]

This development makes art, rather than 'life', the central process in creation: it therefore allows for a creative principle which is more than a life-urge. It also makes possible some of Blake's most interesting speculations, such as his idea that time and space are created not as an ultimate framework but as an act of mercy, since human beings would otherwise be exposed to an infinite energy which would be totally unbearable. (The idea, which has been held by some mystics, appears also in Coleridge's poetry and thinking.[27]) This leads him naturally to his idea of the creation itself—not a raising of forms out of nothingness at the beginning of time but the perpetual containment of an energy and light that would otherwise be unendurable.

Blake always returns to the human, however. His concern is less with the problems of physics than with the state of man. His thinking leads back to the idea that the ultimate truth of things lies ready to be discovered not in the immensities of outer space but in the human beings around us. It is not simply a living universe that Blake wants to restore us to, but a human and visionary one.

Blake's concept of the human cuts across some of our received categories. One of the most important twentieth-century developments has been the revolt against the Victorian ideal that a man should possess a fixed 'character' (however subtly defined) and the movement instead towards the ideal of developing a many-sided and flexible 'personality' (the 'human adjustment' of the psychologists). Blake would no doubt have been more sympathetic to the second ideal than the first, but he was also equipped to perceive the dangers of an absolute flexibility—'the Divinity of Yes & No too The Yea Nay Creeping Jesus' as he put it.[28] His own concept involves the existence not of 'character' but of 'characters'—a series of states through which the human being must be continually passing without remaining in any one. Flexibility of personality for him is expressive rather than adaptive: it is a series of changing *forms* that contain and express the imaginatively organized energy of the individual human being.

Blake's most subtle and potent idea (which brings the artistic and the human still closer together) is the same idea that works through his extended myth-making: the idea that the reason and pity of eighteenth-century society were reduced and fixed forms for what should be a more dynamic human state—expressed for example in the expansions and contractions of the human blood. He took two contemporary words which were in danger of degenerating into cant terms, 'sublimity' and 'pathos', and rescued them from their respective associations with Gothic melodrama and the sentimental sensibility by relating them back to actual operations of the human body.

This conception of the way that energy operates when humanized is astonishingly perceptive—the more so because once formulated it appears so obvious. Any normal child in the emotional life of a single day demonstrates the process several times by the alternations of his moods. The first movements towards language sometimes seem to take the same form, expansive assertive noises alternating with contracting quiet ones. Although the necessity of these alternations is quietly allowed for in the latitude of expression that is given to young children, however, it is hardly noticed in larger ideas of education. As a result emotional development is channelled into more restrictive channels and in the end the imagination itself (which should be nourished from such sources) is slowly starved. In this respect, as in others, we have still not caught up with Blake.

It is when he expresses the humanized movements of energy, whether expanding to the confluence between vision and desire that is the human sublime or contracting to the compassionate sense of particular identity that is true pathos, that Blake still moves us most. His whole work expresses his belief that art does not exist until nature is seen in these terms. His own art exists not to imitate the natural world on its own terms but to recreate it in a form which appeals also to the dynamics of the imagination—conceived of not as an inward retina of the eye's memory but as an index of the whole marvellous inward nature of man. His individual works of art are not therefore icons to remind us of an agreed reality; they are attempts to render an intense vision of the world which he recognizes to be idiosyncratic yet claims to be also at least potentially, universal. 'All men partake of vision, but it is lost by not being cultivated.'[29] A cultivation of it, according to him, would cure many human evils by curing them at their source. Human beings, instead of vainly pursuing states of permanent pleasure, would become responsive to the thin dancing line of joy within themselves ('Under every grief & pine / Runs a joy with silken twine')[30] and would allow it to guide them through the states of human experience without any irritable quest for permanence.

Blake's visionary universe is the product of a lonely, independent, pugnacious man, raising his voice in a society where the growth of industry, the spread of commerce and the establishment of a great empire abroad had produced an unprecedented increase in wealth. His indignation, vividly expressed, was directed partly against the dark side of that civilization: the ignorance, disease and poverty which a society founded on individual enterprise allowed to flourish unchecked.

Blake's indignation still moves us as it moved humanitarian thinkers like George Eliot a hundred years ago. But he, no more than George Eliot, would have been content with social reform alone. Men need a pattern against which to live: Blake's mythologizing was an attempt to furnish a pattern which would be more energetic than the fashionable pietism of his day, more generous than the prudential maxims by which his contemporaries ordered their existence. His mythology has, as we have seen, many limitations; yet when its limitations have been numbered it remains an extraordinarily successful attempt to state the case for a view of humanity which recognizes its potentialities of generosity, compassion and illumination. In the later prophetic books it is this indirect communication which is important, and in so far as the creation of a visionary universe is necessary for this communication we value its creation.

It is one of the more cherished illusions of contemporary criticism that only the single, direct artistic creations of our civilization ought to be valued and taken seriously as positive achievements. In a civilization which contains as a necessary part of its own existence the fragmentation of those things that go to make the complete artist, such achievements will necessarily be rare. And we shall hardly understand even them unless we are willing to look also at some of the important failures—for it is those that show us their creators as allegorical figures, containing within themselves the fragmentation of our nature, yet deprived by their age of a direct mode of communicating the fullness of their own humanity.

Blake has left enough passages of superb direct utterance in verse and prose to convince us of his high status as an artist. It is when we move into contemplation of his wider achievement, his attempt to create a visionary universe in his art and his later prophetic books, with all the failures and successes that are inextricably intertwined there, that we begin to sense his full significance as an allegorical figure. If his belief in his own genius led him constantly to excess, it was also the driving force behind a heroic endeavour: the attempt to convey his vision that human experience in all its forms was richer than his contemporaries supposed. By being true to all the facets of his own experience he created a memorable body of art in an age that was more than usually prone to blinker itself with the tenets of a narrow utilitarianism. But his relevance cannot be tied down to his own time: he succeeds in reminding us, too, of the imaginative and emotional resources which are neglected and wasted by any civilization which bases itself merely on commercial values, scientific analysis and the rule of prudence.

Appendix One

Blake's Interpretation of Shakespeare: a Reconstruction

'But Shakespeare in riper years lent me his hand.' Blake's enigmatic statement in the lines of 1800 describing his 'lot in the heavens'[1] suggests a powerful and important influence; yet the references to Shakespeare in his work are few and scattered. It is only when they are brought together and examined carefully with his illustrations that hints of a detailed and rather subtle interpretation emerge. Some of the elements are, predictably, idiosyncratic. Although the basic interpretation is coloured by his own obsessional ideas, however, the details can be supported to a surprising extent by Shakespeare's text and are by no means unilluminating. If I am right Blake saw many things which later critics have come to only with difficulty. (I do not, of course, fully share all the ideas about Shakespeare that are presented in this appendix, but it would be difficult to establish continual discriminations without making the discussion tedious.)

Blake's reading of *A Midsummer Night's Dream* demonstrates the pervasiveness of his own preoccupations when reading Shakespeare. When he found that another reader had inscribed in his copy of Swedenborg's *Heaven and Hell* the lines 'And as Imagination bodies forth yᵉ forms of things unseen—turns them to shape & gives to airy Nothing a local habitation & a Name' he wrote an angry rejoinder underneath: 'Thus Fools quote Shakespeare   The above is Theseus's opinion not Shakespeare's   You might as well quote Satans blasphemies from Milton & give them as Miltons opinions'.[2] He made a similar observation to Gilchrist about the lines in later years.[3] The sentiment is at first sight surprising if one remembers that Blake used the same lines to describe the work of the sons of Los in *Milton*;[4] he evidently felt, however, that 'giving to airy Nothing a local habitation and a Name' was a work of rescue in Urizen's domain, whereas the Imagination worked with eternal forms. Theseus, by giving this patronizing account, was displaying the decline of his own vision. And when Blake illustrated the play (in a design (fig. 10) tentatively dated 1785)[5] he showed Oberon and Titania as figures rather like Har and Heva, looking on in impotence and faded beauty while before them Puck, a figure with the lineaments of lustful energy, cavorted in front of a group of dancing fairies who ran in a visionary circle. The figure of Puck can be related to that of the lustful figures in *The Gates of Paradise* or of Satan rearing himself before God in the Job illustrations:[6] he illustrates the dangerous insurgence of energy when vision is fading. The danger is here averted however by the work of imagination (represented by the fairies) which prevents it becoming actual. The threat is contained as a 'Dream'. 'Queen Katharine's Dream', by contrast, is a direct vision of the sovereignty of Genius.

The evidence from sources such as these that Blake read Shakespeare as human allegory is reinforced from internal evidence of a different kind. Mr A. J. Fichter first pointed out to me the resemblance between some of the language used by Tharmas in *Vala* and that used by Othello and Hamlet.[7] It suggested to me that in fashioning his dramatic epic poem Blake was consciously drawing on a reading of Shakespearean tragedy which would see each of the four main heroes as groping in a universe which, because he has lost the secret of true humanity, he does not understand.

One of Blake's rare direct comments on Shakespeare supports this view. In a discussion of Chaucer he wrote[8]

> By way of illustration, I instance Shakspeare's Witches in Macbeth. Those who dress them for the stage, consider them as wretched old women, and not as Shakspeare intended, the Goddesses of Destiny; this shews how Chaucer has been misunderstood in his sublime work. Shakspeare's Fairies also are the rulers of the vegetable world, and so are Chaucer's; let them be so considered, and then the poet will be understood, and not else.

This suggests that he thought of the Weird Sisters as creatures whose energies figure the sublime, their 'fair is foul and foul is fair' superseding the conventional categories of moral value; they offer Macbeth a vision of his own ambiguous destiny. As with all human beings his true destiny is to realize the royalty of his own nature ('that shall be king hereafter'). But emerging from a battle where his energies have been wholeheartedly devoted to destruction, he thinks only in terms of force and death. If he is to be king hereafter, that must mean that he will succeed Duncan: he therefore hears the message of the Sisters as an invitation to murder.

As he contemplates the deed, however, the nobility of his heart argues against it; his fancy, in support, invokes a visionary world in which the highest virtue known to his military nature, pity ('. . . like a newborn babe striding the blast') pleads against him. The image shows his impoverished state. Only a humanity which has lost touch with a true sublime would make *pity* stride the blast (cf. fig. 8). In the sublime state man himself rides aloft on the chariot of his own

genius: the proper place for the newborn babe is in the complementary realm of pathos, which exists for rest from the sublime, not
as an end in itself.

The remainder of Macbeth's discourse betrays the poverty of his
mental universe still further. His argument is carried out wholly in
terms of the Law ('this even-handed justice' . . . 'He's here in
double trust . . .'): he cannot raise the level of his argument because
he lacks a true sense of the human. His couriers of the air are
sightless.

Lady Macbeth understands him through and through: her first
speech would be seen by Blake as showing great insight into his
nature. She knows that Macbeth's nature contains a strong sense
of human pity ('It is too full of human kindness'); she knows, too,
his essential legalism ('. . . what thou wouldst highly, / That
wouldst thou holily; wouldst not play false, and yet wouldst wrongly
win'). If he is to become king, therefore, he must be won from his
pity and his sense of the law, which alike impede him from 'the
golden round, / Which fate and metaphysical aid doth seem / To
have thee crowned withal'. The tragic irony of these last lines, on
Blake's interpretation, is intense. Lady Macbeth too has an image
of men in his sublimity, the 'golden round' of majesty. But, like her
husband, she sees no way to it except by way of an earthly crown.

Her arguments are cunning: they knock away the prop of Macbeth's reduced sense of pathos, leaving him hooked on his basic
legalism:

> I have given suck, and know
> How tender 'tis to love the babe that milks me:
> I would, while it was smiling in my face,
> Have pluck'd my nipple from his boneless gums,
> And dash'd the brains out, had I so sworn as you
> Have done to this.

Macbeth, deprived of female support for his precarious sense of pity
and convinced that a subject's promise to kill his king is more
binding than the general bond of trust between host and guest,
begins to think simply in terms of success or failure.

Duncan, as all his speeches testify, is a figure of ripeness and
innocence: surrounded by peace and fertility, his only fault is a
failure of insight, an over-credulous willingness to believe that a
man's face corresponds to his mind. Even Lady Macbeth is
inhibited from action against him by her sense of his goodness ('Had
he not resembled my father as I slept I had done it') while Macbeth
grasps in the moment of action that he is killing something more
than a man: he is killing innocence, with its accompanying peace
and fertility and all its fruits in human nature ('Methought I heard

a voice cry "Sleep no more!" to all the house: "Glamis hath mur-der'd sleep and therefore Cawdor shall sleep no more: Macbeth shall sleep no more" '). He even glimpses something further, as we see from the imagery which steals into his lying speech after the murder (rather as if the very act of making his fancy work at full stretch prompted his imagination to slip in some wisdom of its own):

> Here lay Duncan,
> His silver skin, laced with his golden blood,
> And his gash'd stabs look'd like a breach in nature
> For ruin's wasteful entrance . . .

For a moment Macbeth has had a different vision of human blood, seeing it as the gold of man, the wealth which can give him true sublimity. He has seen the real sovereignty of Duncan—not that of the earthly king who rules with a silver rod in his hand and a golden bowl on his head, but that of the human being who allows the gold of his energies to shine through the innocent silver of his wisdom.

This is only a momentary glance at the truth, however. It is swallowed up by Macbeth's own account of his killing of the grooms, and by his staggering hypocrisy immediately afterwards:

> who could refrain,
> That had a heart to love, and in that heart
> Courage to make 's love known?

—so true an account of the way that human nature ought to act (and of the way of acting that gives man his true sublimity) that Lady Macbeth is overcome and needs to be helped away. But Macbeth, now an accomplished hypocrite, is becoming also the complete 'man of blood'. Blood is no longer an energy of life; it is the emblem and means of death.

The changed state of affairs is evidenced by the old man whose report of strange events in nature suggests a lost and disordered sublimity: the falcon 'towering in her pride of place' has become the prey of a mousing owl; the horses of Duncan 'beauteous and swift, the minions of their race' have turned wild and eat one another.

These events image Macbeth's own state. The forces of sublimity have all become objects of fear and terror. The Weird Sisters, on the other hand, speak out of energy itself: they meet after battle, or in thunder, lightning or rain; their characteristic habitat is the tem-pest, their characteristic cry 'I'll do, I'll do, and I'll do'. Their prophecies, too, demand the operation of energy: the burning fire and the bubbling cauldron into which they throw pieces of energetic living things—from snake, newt and frog, via blaspheming Jew, Turk and Tartar to goat, tiger and baboon. When Macbeth asks them what they do, their answer is precise—'a deed without a name': they are ministers of unorganized energy. And Macbeth in a sense understands, for he speaks of them in terms of untied winds that raise the waves of the sea, engulfing navigation, or lodge bladed corn, or blow down trees or even destroy castles, palaces and pyramids. It is typical of his state of mind that energies for him automatically mean destructive energies; within these limitations he understands them.

The later prophecies of the Sisters are equally ambiguous: each can be read in a Blakean manner. First the armed head, emblem of an outraged justice which must now inexorably take its course in the shape of Macduff ('Thou hast harp'd my fear aright', says Macbeth); next the 'bloody child', emblem of the innocence murdered by Macbeth, telling him to be 'bloody, bold and resolute' for 'none of woman born / Shall harm Macbeth' (—none can, according to Blake: if a man is bold and resolute in the power of his own blood and his own innocence he cannot be harmed in his eternal nature); and then the child crowned, with a tree in his hand, emblem of organized innocence restored, who tells him that he shall never be vanquished until Birnam wood (emblem perhaps of innocent nature) comes to Dunsinane hill. Finally, at Macbeth's insistence, the whole line of kings is seen, figuring a 'sovereign' life that is infinite. Macbeth, who is already entrenched in the realm of death cannot bear the sight. He misunderstands each of the prophecies, in fact: he sees the armed head as an injunction to murder Banquo, he hears the bloody child's message as a guarantee of his own physical inviolability and he understands the crowned child's message as a further guarantee that he will not be vanquished in battle. When he reads his own preoccupations into the line of kings however, seeing in each the features of Banquo, his hopes turn to despair.

In the end, of course, Macbeth is paid in his own coin; the prophecies are fulfilled literally. He is slain by Macduff, who was not 'born' in the normal sense, and whose soldiers have camouflaged themselves with the foliage of Birnam wood.

By the time that justice is done, however, Macbeth is beyond the reach even of fear, that final vestige of his lost sense of sublimity ('The time has been, my senses would have cool'd / To hear a night-shriek'). He has forsaken even the ambiguous vision offered by the Sisters ('no more sights!') and murdered Macduff's wife and children. The reality that he knows now is the reality of blood—blood against blood. 'I am in blood / stepp'd in so far that, should I wade no more, / returning were as tedious as go o'er'—Macbeth's legalistic reasoning has now cozened him into envisaging as a river what is in fact a sea.

The necessary remedy is a re-establishment of innocence—which can no longer be the unsuspecting innocence of Duncan. Malcolm finds it necessary to dissemble in the other direction, to put on a mask of villainy in order to reassure himself of Macduff's good faith. Only when he has heard Macduff's outraged response to his black picture of himself can he reveal himself as one who is in fact innocent and who delights 'no less in truth than life'. And immediately afterwards the Doctor comes in to report on the powers of the king of England—his ability to heal the 'strangely-visited people / All swoln and ulcerous', hanging a golden stamp about their necks; his powers of prophecy; the blessings that hang about his throne. This is an emblem of the way that true sovereignty operates in human nature and it is followed immediately by the successful campaign against Macbeth.

Macbeth and Lady Macbeth are by now locked in a realm of despair and death. Lady Macbeth's attempts to cleanse her hands speak out of a consciousness that her human creativeness is muddied at the source; Macbeth, even his fear gone, lives in a Urizenic world which is dominated by his sense of death. Yet his heart is still inviolable: 'The mind I sway by and the heart I bear / Shall never sag with doubt nor shake with fear'. His chief anger is directed against a servant whose white face betrays no trace of the heart's operation ('cream-faced' . . . 'goose' . . . 'lily-liver'd' . . . 'linen cheeks' . . . whey-face'). Seeing in him no trace of the blood that is now his one reality he tells him, 'Go prick thy face and over-red thy fear' and girds himself to act resolutely with the energy of his own heart. Yet these actions all take place within a consciousness of death; the poverty of his imagination is revealed when news of his wife's death is brought to him—a death which he can now see only as part of an endless chain of death stretching throughout the universe ('She should have died hereafter; / There would have been a time for such a word'). His Urizenic preoccupation with time and space haunts him now with a sense of the endlessness of time ('tomorrow, and tomorrow, and tomorrow') and of the insignificance of human life ('a tale told by an idiot'). His heart has lost all human sublimity: it is that of a bear tied to a stake. He will not even allow himself the 'nobility' of falling on his sword: that would be foolishness. He will live to the end by blood alone.

At the end Malcolm can reduce the stature of Macbeth and his wife, distancing them before our very eyes as 'this dead butcher and his fiend-like queen'. But for Blake this distancing and deflation is dangerous. Like the naval officer at the end of Golding's *Lord of the Flies* who sees only an unkempt schoolboy before him and does not possess the more penetrating look that would carry him into 'the darkness of man's heart', Malcolm, dismissing the dead Macbeth so peremptorily, does not see that he is dealing with the perpetual tragedy of man's heart, which again and again misunderstands the nature of its own energies and devotes to destruction what might have made human life sublime.

For Blake, I suggest, *Macbeth* was more than a statement about the origins of evil or the way that tyrannies establish themselves: it was an exhibition of the slavery of the heart under the laws of Urizen, where the tyranny of analytic reason turns human sublimity into destructive fear, and human pathos into helpless pity. And when (probably in 1795), he made two illustrations of *Macbeth*[9] it was precisely these two topics that engaged him: in one, 'Pity' (fig. 9), he showed a woman reaching down to a baby from the sightless couriers of failed sublimity, looking down apprehensively at the body of a woman on the earth who represents lost innocence and pathos, while behind her a Urizenic figure stretches out his darkness over the earth; in the other (fig. 8) he showed Hecate surrounded by forms of animal life—the donkey, the owl and the bat, for example—which combine in forms of horror. Two of Hecate's faces hide themselves, the third looks ambiguously into the central animal countenance, that of a serpent's head which bears the lineaments of energy. In Urizen's kingdom the human heart confronted by energy can respond only by a despairing pity or a desperate fear. Yet in these movements, did the heart but know, lies the key to true pathos and sublimity.

Blake's other illustration to the play, a pencil-drawing,[10] is a straightforward rendering of the feast, with Banquo's ghost (fig. 10). In this case he shows Macbeth starting before a figure which stares at him from the lineaments of a visionary humanity.

If *Macbeth* is to be seen as demonstrating the manner in which the human heart, murdering its own innocence, establishes the tyranny of Urizen, *King Lear* would emerge as a drama set in the heart of Urizen's kingdom. The latter play, of course, appealed particularly strongly to the Gothic taste of the late eighteenth century and the indications are that Blake's own response to the play was shaped by his own version of the Gothic. His readiness to quote from the play later on suggests the impact it made on him in his youth. In 1798 his hostile annotation to a passage where Bacon states 'it is greater blasphemy to personate God and bring him in saying, "I will descend, and be like the Prince of Darkness" ' includes the comment 'The Prince of Darkness is a gentleman and not a man: he is a Lord Chancellor'.[11] Part of the inscription on one of his illustrations to Dante runs: 'As poor Churchill said Nature thou art my Goddess'.[12] And his very last letter, with its prayer to

be preserved from 'the divinity of yes and no too' is a direct reminiscence of Lear's bitter reflection: 'To say "ay" and "no" to every
thing that I said! "Ay" and "no" too was no good divinity.'[13]

The response is, of course, at its intensest in 'Tiriel', where the
appearance of Tiriel with the dying Myratana recalls the entry of
Lear with Cordelia dead in his arms, while the curse on his sons—
'Serpents, not sons!'—mirrors Lear's curses on his 'serpent' daughters and echoes, in the actual verbal form, Albany's 'Tigers, not
daughters . . .'. Tiriel, a figure of self-deception and hypocrisy, has,
like Lear, lost all sense of reality; for him, however, there is no hope
at all. His final state, stretched out at the feet of Har and Heva 'in
awful death' is in direct (and no doubt intentional) contrast to the
Lear of Blake's illustration (fig. 4) stretched at the feet of Cordelia
in the lineaments of a regained innocence.

Lear is only partly relatable to Tiriel himself, however: Gloucester's blindness in the world of experience aligns him more closely
with this figure, whereas Lear is nearer to Blake's innocent Har.
Like Har, Lear has never faced experience. He knows nothing of the
realities of poverty or hunger suffered by his humbler subjects and
this ignorance is matched by a lack of self-knowledge. 'He hath ever
but slenderly known himself': his readiness to be duped by hypocrisy
bears out the accuracy of Regan's observation.

Like Har also, Lear thinks primarily in terms of simple arithmetical calculations. This is shown from the first scene of the play,
where, having already planned a division of the kingdom on terms
so equal that no one can find fault, he initiates the formal charade
by which this division will ostensibly be made in direct proportion
to the quantity of love protested by each daughter. Blake's 'Aged
ignorance' is here seen in action: Lear's wordplay on the word
'nothing', though no doubt intended to demonstrate his wit, displays
only this same enslavement to arithmetical logic. It also further
inhibits the tongue-tied Cordelia, so that she can reply only in a
nobler form of the same legalistic language ('I love your majesty
According to my bond; nor more nor less').

The dispute with the daughters is organized with similar numerical exactness around the number of retainers that he is to keep; and
when Goneril halves their number Lear halves the number of his
remaining daughters ('Yet have I left a daughter . . .'). His innocent habits of calculation leave him perilously exposed, however,
when he enters a world where calculation means negotiation for
power. When he says to Regan, 'I gave you all' she can reply 'And
in good time you gave it'. Since calculation is the only wisdom that
either world, Lear's or Gloucester's, recognizes as valid, Regan
scores.

Unlike Blake's Har, who simply grew old and foolish in his law-dominated paradise, Lear's late entry into the world of experience means that he must suffer the consequences of his failures. His refusal to listen to the voices of honesty, Kent and Cordelia, coupled with his uncritical acceptance of the other daughters' flatteries, has precipitated a sequence of actions which is to culminate in the exile on the heath, where he faces the facts of human suffering and the energies of nature in their most uncompromising form.

The etiolated Innocence of Lear's world is matched by the unenlightened Experience of Gloucester and Edmund. Although Gloucester has a superstitious view of the world, Edmund an un-superstitious one, their basic attitude to nature is the same: that of a sharp knowingness, an assumption that everything can be understood by observing Nature closely. The only difference is that Edmund's attitude, being attuned to the actualities of human behaviour rather than to supposed influences from the stars, makes it easier for him to manipulate affairs to his advantage.

In action, on the other hand, the two men are completely different. The purity of Edmund's self-interest makes him, like Blake's tiger, a being of energy isolated from any context of human compassion—a being of

> More composition and fierce quality
> Than doth, within a dull, stale, tired bed,
> Go to the creating a whole tribe of fops,
> Got 'tween asleep and wake . . .

who sees everything that separates him from his interests as 'the plague of custom'. He is both attractive and terrifying. Gloucester, on the other hand, maunders in a perpetual state of misunderstanding. It is only when he is physically blinded that he gains some insight into the true meaning of the universe and begins to feel that, in another sense, he has gained vision ('I stumbled when I saw'). But his regained vision impels him towards death rather than life. Even when he has been prevented from killing himself and has resolved to endure in future, he cannot say more to Edgar's 'ripeness is all' than 'And that's true too'—his last words in the play.

Lear, Gloucester and Edmund are alike devotees of Nature. Edmund's very first words are a declaration of allegiance: 'Thou, nature, art my goddess', while Lear prefaces his cursing of Goneril with the words, 'Hear, nature, hear; dear goddess, hear!' But Edmund, the accomplished Machiavel, is destined eventually to be outwitted and to perish by the same sort of stratagem that has served him in seeking his own ends. His opportunism is as self-defeating as

Lear's more innocent devotion to Nature. With the names changed Blake's words in 'Tiriel' would fit this world too:[14]

> Thy laws, O Lear, & Edmund's wisdom, end together in a curse.

Such are the fates of all who give themselves to Nature, and their fates are inter-related. Where innocence means Lear, experience is likely to mean Edmund.

There are other voices of experience in the play, however, both of them, by the standards of Lear and Edmund, foolish. The first is that of the Fool, who expresses throughout a wisdom of the flesh that Lear has never known. Sometimes it is the voice of simple folk wisdom—which, even in prudential terms, often works better than Lear's dead calculations:

> Have more than thou showest,
> Speak less than thou knowest,
> Lend less than thou owest,
> Ride more than thou goest,
> Learn more than thou trowest,
> Set less than thou throwest;
> Leave thy drink and thy whore,
> And keep in-a-door,
> And thou shalt have more
> Than two tens to a score.

Lear's reliance on *exact* numerical calculations are a sign that he has lost the golden crown of his own human sublimity ('thou hadst little wit in thy bald crown, when thou gavest thy golden one away' the Fool tells him).

Just as Lear's sense of pathos has never extended beyond self-pity, so his sublimity has never been more than a sense of the majesty of his own self. The two can alternate with absurd rapidity. his

> You see me here, you gods, a poor old man,
> As full of grief as age; wretched in both . . .

being followed only seven lines later by

> I will do such things—
> What they are yet I know not, but they shall be
> The terrors of the earth.

He has settled his emotions on himself because he cannot conceive of a nature which is not fixed and can find no nature which is so fixed as his own. Even when he is beginning to repent of his actions to Cordelia he still complains that her fault of duty

> wrench'd my frame of nature
> From the fix'd place . . .

Kent has some inkling of Lear's mistake. When Lear, after the rejection of Cordelia, turns on him with the words

Now, by Apollo,—

Kent replies

> Now, by Apollo, king,
> Thou swear'st thy gods in vain.

Lear's limited view of nature has automatically exiled him from the sublime world of Apollo and left him in the universe of a harsher god, a god of experience. When Lear refuses to believe that Kent can have been put in the stocks by his daughter and exclaims

By Jupiter, I swear, no.

Kent can turn the point back on him with the words

By Juno, I swear, ay.

Kent recognizes the nature of this world of experience—the world of tyranny and jealousy where Jupiter and Juno are perpetually at strife.

Only the fool sees further into human nature. When Lear asks angrily,

Dost thou call me fool, boy?

he replies,

All thy other titles thou hast given away; that thou wast born with.

and Kent comments,

This is not altogether fool, my lord.

It is not: every baby is born a worm, a 'fool in the flesh': this is the pathos of the human condition. But Lear's Fool also knows of human sublimity. In one of the profoundest exchanges in the play Lear asks him

Who is it that can tell me who I am?

and the Fool replies

Lear's shadow.

Lear's shadow, like every other man's, sees him always surrounded by radiance from a hidden light—it sees him, therefore, in his human sublimity. But Lear pays no attention to the Fool—he simply continues his monologue:

I would learn that; for, by the marks of sovereignty, knowledge and reason, I should be false persuaded I had daughters.

For him the only marks of sovereignty are knowledge and reason: he could hardly declare his allegiance to Blake's Urizen more unequivocally.

Lear's failure of experience is not confined to the world of human suffering; his language throughout betrays the fact that he has never faced the realities of sexual experience which would have given him a human sense and a context for dealing with suffering and energy.

His failure is shown in his readiness to disclaim his legal bond with Cordelia ('all my paternal care, / Propinquity and property of blood') and to curse Goneril's fertility—as if these were not basic, given realities but simply pawns in his hand. It is also shown in his conventional attitude to sin and crime, still active when he first enters the storm:

> Tremble, thou wretch,
> That hast within thee undivulged crimes,
> Unwhipp'd of justice: hide thee, thou bloody hand;
> Thou perjured, and thou simular man of virtue
> That art incestuous . . .

and his own complacent appeal to the same tribunal: 'I am a man / More sinn'd against than sinning'. It is only after he has passed through the vortex of experience that he sees the truth: that the superior and inferior are equally guilty—

> Thou rascal beadle, hold thy bloody hand!
> Why dost thou lash that whore? Strip thine own back;
> Thou hotly lust'st to use her in that kind
> For which thou whip'st her . . .

The language of his new insights betrays the limitations of his advance in knowledge, even now. If he has learned about illusion in human society, his conception of sexual energy is unchanged. This comes out strongly in his madness:

> The fitchew nor the soiled horse goes to't with a more riotous appetite. Down from the waist they are Centaurs, though women all above: but to the girdle do the Gods inherit, beneath is all the Fiends. There's hell, there's darkness, there is the sulphurous pit; burning, scalding, stench, consumption . . .

When Lear says in the same sentence 'good apothecary, sweeten my imagination', we can be sure that Blake would have endorsed his plea.

It is too late, however. Lear's perception of the universality behind the hypocritical categories of righteousness and sin simply leaves him exposed to a vision in which death is the only reality ('Then kill, kill, kill, kill, kill, kill!'). The attraction of this magnetic

force is so powerful that it renders the ceremonies of sexual generation farcical by comparison, and he can comment

> I will die bravely, like a smug bridegroom.

Lear has faced experience in its harshest form, but his lack of
'organized innocence' has meant that experience must be for him
not a womb but a vortex. He has his reward, nevertheless. Because
he *has* faced reality he can be restored to a state of original innocence. He refuses Cordelia's invitation to re-enter the world of
experience ('Shall we not see these daughters and these sisters?') with
a speech that shows him repossessed of the childlike vision that can
transfigure the harshness of reality: 'Come, let's away to prison: / We
two alone will sing like birds i' the cage'. (One of the entertain-
ments in the unenergized paradise of Blake's 'Tiriel' was to 'hear Har
sing in the great cage'.[15]) Lear's innocence is renewed, but he is too
old to incorporate within himself the sort of spontaneous and
instinctive wisdom that he might have found by attending to his
phallic consciousness.

In this play the voice of phallic wisdom is the voice of the Fool.
Phallic wisdom lives in the moment; it knows nothing of rational
consistency or of quantitative measurement. For this reason Lear
has always feared it and as far as possible ignored it. The force of the
phallic lives on in him as the 'hysterica passio' of a man who has
never learned how to organize it; he betrays the status he has given
it when he speaks to it as if it were a dog:

> Hysterica passio, down, thou climbing sorrow,
> Thy elements below!

Soon it becomes disguised as the heart,

> O me, my heart, my rising heart! But down!

but the Fool recognizes the real nature of Lear's malady:

> Cry to it, nuncle, as the cockney did to the eels when she put 'em i' the
> paste alive; she knapped 'em o' the coxcombs with a stick, and cried
> 'Down, wantons, down!'

Lear cannot admit the Fool's sayings but he cannot altogether
exclude them either. Since this is the wisdom of the flesh he will
never escape its voice so long as he is in the body. But if he cannot
ignore the wisdom that speaks from below the dead-level line of his
reasonings he can ignore the wisdom that lies above it—and this he
does when he banishes Cordelia.

It is a part of Blake's tragic vision that in Western civilization the
focus is always on that which can be measured quantitatively. The

Fool's voice can never be heard except as a peripheral voice, trying to get a word in edgeways and, when it succeeds, stealing a momentary recognition that is immediately forgotten in the organized scheme of human perceptions. Cordelia, similarly, can rarely express herself positively. An extraordinary number of her speeches are negative speeches—paradoxically, the one moment when she can actually say, firmly, that she is acting out of her love is when she marches against her native country. Her negative becomes a part of the play's emotional effect, indeed: it achieves its own pathos when the 'nothing, my lord' of her first scene is transmuted into the 'no cause, no cause' of her last—for this time Lear knows what she means.

In one sense the fool's chatter is as far below Lear's mind as Cordelia's love is above it; in another, both are superior to him. They express between them the organic energy and the steady vision which would both be necessary to Lear if he were to achieve that state of organized innocence which is the proper human condition. In the event, only one character achieves it—Edgar, whose 'ripeness is all' expresses what he has learned. Lear, as we have said, only achieves one element: the restored innocence which Cordelia's vision gives him. But his apprehension of the further possibilities is shown in the brilliant stroke by which, in his last speech, he talks of Cordelia as his 'fool'. It is his tribute to a fuller human experience that he is too old to learn.

What is a sub-theme in *King Lear* is at the centre of *Othello*, which confronts Blake with the tragedy of man's genital life under the law. Othello seems full of energy; he has all the nobility of a great heart and all the frankness of a man who lives by action. 'The Moor is of a free and open nature, / That thinks men honest that but seem to be so,' remarks Iago; as with Duncan, it is a generous fault.

Othello has a further failing, however, without which Iago's poison could not work. Like Macbeth, he is a slave to legalism. His case against Desdemona, and his judgment, are both made in the terms of a devotion to law ('It is the cause, it is the cause, my soul: Let me not name it to you, you chaste stars! / It is the cause') which also involves a delusion of holiness, and enables him to speak even of 'putting out the light' of nature without checking his action:

> . . . but once put out thy light,
> Thou cunning'st pattern of excelling nature,
> I know not where is that Promethean heat
> That can thy light relume.

Othello's vision is closed; if it were not, Iago's deceit would lead nowhere; because it is, deceit becomes poison and Othello's genital energy is turned to destruction. He murders Desdemona because he has already murdered his own innocent vision, leaving himself innocent only in gullibility—and a natural prey to the naked reasonings and isolated energy of Iago.

This play gives us a third component in Blake's human tragedy: it shows us also the birth of that jealousy which for him is the natural results when moral law works in the unenlightened self.

If *Macbeth* is a tragedy of the human heart, *Lear* a tragedy of the human head, and *Othello* a tragedy of the human genitals, *Hamlet* completes Blake's pattern of decline. Hamlet is creative man as he is left after this threefold loss: fit for action ('the courtier's, soldier's, scholar's, eye, tongue, sword') yet with no identity to act from except that of a trained reason which has learnt its lessons well in Urizen's school at Wittenburg. This reason leads not to integrated action but to drooping despair: Hamlet is 'sicklied o'er with the pale cast of thought'. Yet his own nature still calls him to action.

As with the other murders in the tragedies Blake would see a symbolic significance here. Hamlet's father is more than a murdered king: he is murdered genital innocence, corresponding to something which is murdered in Hamlet himself. The comparison is made overtly when Hamlet thinks of the relationship between his father and Claudius as that of 'Hyperion to a Satyr'. His father was the slain Adonis, the lost Ancient Man of Blake's mythology. ('He was a man,' says Hamlet simply, 'take him for all in all, I shall not look upon his like again'.) And Hamlet finds himself confronted by the Ghost of this innocence, an innocence which normally has no part in his philosophy. That his father's voice is not merely that of a father crying out to be avenged, but the voice of a genital innocence that has been destroyed would be clear to Blake from his account of the murder:

> 'Tis given out that, sleeping in my orchard,
> A serpent stung me; so the whole ear of Denmark
> Is by a forged process of my death
> Rankly abused: but know, thou noble youth,
> The serpent that did sting thy father's life
> Now wears his crown.

A clear version, Blake would say, of the universal lie by which men think of sex as Satanic instead of seeing that it is innocent, murdered by the power of a legalistic tyranny. And he would see in the account of the murder itself a description of the processes by which law and analytic reason together poison the genital life:

> Sleeping within my orchard,
> My custom always of the afternoon,
> Upon my secure hour thy uncle stole

> With juice of cursed hebenon in a vial
> And in the porches of my ears did pour
> The leperous distilment; whose effect
> Holds such an enmity with blood of man
> That swift as quick-silver it courses through
> The natural gates and alleys of the body;
> And with a sudden vigour it doth posset
> And curd, like eager droppings into milk
> The thin and wholesome blood: so did it mine;
> And a most instant tetter bark'd about,
> Most lazar-like, with vile and loathsome crust,
> All my smooth body.

With this murder man is delivered to the 'lazar-house' of Adam's vision in *Paradise Lost* (which Blake once painted with a jealous God waving a phallus overhead[16]) or the 'prison-house' of Hamlet's ghost.

For Hamlet the vision is disturbing; yet the only equipment he has to deal with what he has heard lies in his own analytic reason. As his jesting with Ophelia shows, he is a man of phallic wit rather than genital sublimity; his touchstone for behaviour is always that of reason:

> . . . a beast that wants discourse of reason
> Would have mourn'd longer . . .

In this he is abetted by the full man of reason Horatio, who warns him against responding to the ghost too fiercely since it might draw him to the flood or the summit of the cliff;—or might it not

> assume some other horrible form
> Which might deprive your sovereignty of reason
> And draw you into madness?

Yet Hamlet is not entirely persuaded. When he insists on following the ghost, for example, he feels himself transformed:

> My fate cries out
> And makes each petty artery in this body
> As hardy as the Nemean lion's nerve.

and Horatio comments apprehensively

> He waxes desperate with imagination.

Hamlet is more ready than Horatio to trust his imagination; he is not a straightforward rationalist. His own energy gives him a serpentine cunning which enables him to survive at crucial moments. But his honesty is not matched by penetration. He misunderstands the Ghost, mistaking the garment for the man. As the opening of the play makes clear, old Hamlet, however beautiful he may have been, had devoted his energy to military adventures. Although not unprovoked they have left their mark. His reappearance clad in armour is a sign that he is not organized innocence, but its Spectre: the cry for revenge comes from this armoured spectral form.

Like the Weird Sisters, the Ghost is a figure of the hero's ambiguous destiny. Hamlet, like Macbeth, misunderstands. The Ghost is a monitory figure, showing to Hamlet the results of not making peace with the earth (Hamlet half sees this when he thinks of the Ghost as working in the earth like a mole, or cries 'Rest, rest, perturbed spirit!'—it is his own spirit, as well as his father's, that he is addressing[17]). But Hamlet has not the penetration to see this fully: he becomes what he beholds and takes literally the Ghost's cry for revenge.

Hamlet's tendency to be trapped by his own legalism is shown by the way in which he refrains from killing Claudius at his prayers for fear that he will go to heaven in a state of repentance (the right action for a foolish reason) or fills his monologues with irrelevant weighings of the moral law. He sees that the nature of the Ghost is somehow relevant to the nature of his own existence ('To be, or not to be, that is the question . . .') but the militaristic terms of his discourse ('whether 'tis nobler in the mind to suffer / The slings and arrows of outrageous fortune, / Or to take arms against a sea of troubles, / And by opposing end them') betrays his limited cast of mind. In the same way, his killing of Polonius (that figure of unorganized innocence) provides only the socially accurate but morally bizarre reflection, 'I took thee for thy better'.

Limited by the mental universe in which he has been brought up (the legalism of Elsinore, the rationalism of Wittenburg) Hamlet cannot quite see that his task is not to embark on a course of revenge which will simply repeat his father's military adventures but to achieve true sovereignty. He cannot come to terms with his own energies. He admires the energy of the player who can create an entire passion in himself for the sake of the play he is acting in and is angry that he cannot act with similar passion; yet he says to Horatio,

> Give me that man
> That is not passion's slave, and I will wear him
> In my heart's core, ay, in my heart of heart,
> As I do thee.

He arranges the theatricals to catch the conscience of the king symbolically, without in fact achieving anything more than a symbolic call for lights from the king. He sets upon his mother with the picture of his father, a perfect image of the lost Eternal Man

> Hyperion's curls, the front of Jove himself,
> An eye like Mars to threaten and command;
> A station like the herald Mercury
> New-lighted on a heaven-kissing hill . . .

but his reproaches to her are based largely on the moral law ('O shame! where is thy blush?') and become a form of attack which reduces her humanity. His description of sexual pleasure ('the rank sweat of an enseamed bed,/stewed in corruption, honeying and making love') betrays the deprivation of his own imagination and raises once again the armed spectre of the Ghost to incite him to revenge. (His mother, who retains her sexual innocence, cannot see him.) At the end his mother's heart is, she says, 'cleft in twain', but the moral battering from her son has created nothing in her: she is simply left without 'life to breathe / What thou hast said to me', and as a 'sick soul'. Hamlet's encounter with the Captain, which again shows his uncomprehending admiration of energy concludes with the mistaken reflection that

> Rightly to be great
> Is not to stir without great argument,
> But greatly to find quarrel in a straw
> When honour's at the stake.

and with the dangerously Macbethian resolve,

> O, from this time forth,
> My thoughts be bloody, or be nothing worth!

Meanwhile Ophelia, a more pathetic victim of the moral law, is left uttering speeches which hide nothing of their origin in disturbed sexuality.

In the graveyard Hamlet reflects on the universality of death with a wit that shows him once again to be, though not free, not altogether a slave in Urizen's kingdom. The energy which he then displays against Laertes is a foretaste of the final act by which he kills Claudius. He acts, as he thinks, honestly; but he leaves Denmark in a negative state: it has the prospect of honest and rational government at the hands of men such as Fortinbras and Horatio, but the basic problems posed by the inadequacies of human nature are no nearer solution.

Hamlet *is* honest as well as rational and for that he seems to have Blake's approval. Even the rational Horatio, after all, is moved to unaccustomed poetry when Hamlet dies:

> Good night, sweet prince,
> And flights of angels sing thee to thy rest!

and Fortinbras comments that

> he was likely, had he been put on,
> To have proved most royally . . .

He has not 'been put on'. Honesty and energy alone are not enough in the struggle to achieve human sovereignty. Hamlet never passes beyond the limitations shown in his encounter with the Ghost: and Blake's illustration (fig. 7) which shows the prince looking with horror at this mailed figure of his own destiny suggests that he saw the encounter as the central fact of the play.

Blake's reading of Shakespeare takes us through the four tragedies from the central one, Macbeth's murder of innocence, to the gropings and thrusts of Hamlet in a world where his attempts to kill a tyrant ignore the real tyranny under which he and Claudius and all men live. It would not be difficult to extend Blake's reading to other Shakespearean plays: *Coriolanus*, for example, would show the tragedy of the isolated head, while the tragi-comedy of Falstaff could be seen as that of the isolated heart ('The king has killed his heart' the hostess says with strangely perceptive ambiguity; and later, 'Ah poor heart'; while her final comment that he is 'in Arthur's bosom' would have seemed neither more nor less than the truth to the Blake who saw in Arthur the very image of the Ancient Man). But we need only look at one more play, in which Blake could see his Eternal Man, potential in every man but usually lost through legalism and the murder of genital innocence, vividly portrayed. If the four great tragedies give us four views of the loss of the Eternal Man, *Antony and Cleopatra* displays him rediscovered. In this play hero and heroine are enabled to move through a relationship which seems to their soldiers and courtiers to be no more than lust on a high level (and 'dotage' in a general) by their consciousness that they are enacting human experience as it should be ('The nobleness of life is to do thus'). Antony's extravagance is the direct antithesis of Cordelia's inhibition:

> CLEO. If it be love indeed, tell me how much.
> ANT. There's beggary in the love than can be reckon'd.
> CLEO. I'll set a bourn how far to be belov'd
> ANT. Then must thou needs find out new heaven, new earth.

This generosity and prodigality are a mark of genital liberation. It relates everything that Antony and Cleopatra do to eternity and infinity: so that Cleopatra can say,

> Eternity was in our lips and eyes,
> Bliss in our brows' bent, none our parts so poor
> But was a race of heaven.

while she herself is 'infinite variety'. Under the light of this energy everything takes on a new life of its own: Antony and Cleopatra walk the streets at night to 'note the qualities of people' and Cleopatra works a magic by which everything that lives becomes holy:

> for vilest things
> Become themselves in her, that the holy priests
> Bless her when she is riggish.

If the exercise of energy nourishes vision, desire at this intensity creates sublimity. Antony, in Cleopatra's eyes, is transformed eventually into a figure of Man in his sublime form, corresponding to the cosmic Man of Blake's mythology. Her lament, 'The soldier's pole is fallen', may even have given him a clue for his idea of Man as the true pole of the universe, his visionary head replaced by the 'starry pole' of the astronomers when vision fades, his sublime phallus replaced by the pole of the military standard when life-giving sexuality is replaced by death-dealing militarism.[18]

Antony, for Cleopatra, becomes in retrospect an incarnation of vision and desire reunited: her final vision of him makes him no less than Blake's Ancient Man, who 'contain'd in his mighty limbs all things in Heaven & Earth'[19] (Dolabella's first attempt to intercede with her mistress is taken up into, and becomes a part of the paean):

> His face was as the heavens; and therein stuck
> A sun and moon, which kept their course, and lighted
> The little O, the earth.

DOLA.   Most sovereign creature,—

CLEO. His legs bestrid the ocean: his rear'd arm
> Crested the world: his voice was propertied
> As all the tuned spheres, and that to friends;
> But when he meant to quail and shake the orb,
> He was as rattling thunder. For his bounty,
> There was no winter in't; an autumn 'twas
> That grew the more by reaping; his delights
> Were dolphin-like; they show'd his back above
> The element they lived in: in his livery
> Walk'd crowns and crownets; realms and islands were
> As plates dropped from his pocket.

DOLA.   Cleopatra,—

CLEO. Think you there was, or might be, such a man
> As this I dream'd of?

DOLA.   Gentle madam, no.

CLEO. You lie, up to the hearing of the gods.
> But if there be, or ever were, one such,
> It's past the size of dreaming: nature wants stuff
> To vie strange forms with fancy; yet to imagine
> An Antony, were nature's piece 'gainst fancy,
> Condemning shadows quite.

The final passage would be for Blake Shakespeare's culminating vindication of the imagination—his assertion that while fancy may be another form of dreaming, the true sublimity of imagination carries its own self-authentication and creates a reality which could not be justified from nature alone.

Cleopatra, through the transformation of her energy into desire and of her fancy into vision, has gained the sovereignty of nature which Macbeth, Lear, Othello and Hamlet all missed. At the end of the play she can say with justice 'Give me my robe, put on my crown; I have / Immortal longings in me'; where Macbeth, under his destructive vision of blood, had become more and more possessed by the sense of death, her own sense of the blood's sublimity enables her to demonstrate her liberation from the fear of death by applying the worm to her own bosom.

As I said at the outset, Blake's view of Shakespeare, though stamped initially by his own preoccupations, is surprisingly successful in accounting for certain features of the plays. The imagery of blood in *Macbeth*, for example, remarked on by various commentators, assumes a more organic connection with the play if the drama itself is seen as more literally a 'drama of the human heart'. The ghost in *Hamlet*, equally, a feature of the play almost impossible to explain consistently (as Mr H. A. Mason has recently shown[20]), loses part of his enigma if we suppose that he reflects back to Hamlet one form of his own nature—the armed selfhood that demands revenge. It is not surprising that his mother, who loved the Hyperion in her husband, cannot see the ghost.

The most striking congruence with the view of Shakespeare suggested here is to be found in John Danby's book *Shakespeare's Doctrine of Nature*—which I had not in fact read when I first formulated my reconstruction. Danby sees the structure of ideas in the play as a dialectic between 'nature' as conceived by the house of Lear and 'nature' as conceived by the house of Gloucester. The limbs of this dialectic are straightforwardly related to current philosophies of the time: the reverence for custom and ancient law displayed by writers in the tradition of Hooker and the fascinated worship of the processes of nature in action which culminates in Hobbes. Danby, in other words, gives historical context to a dialectic which Blake sees in more universal terms.

In one sense it is not surprising that Danby should agree with Blake, since his own work shows traces of Blake's influence. When he comes to write of Cordelia, for example, he compares her firmly with the little boy of 'A Little Boy Lost' in *Songs of Experience*,[21] and in giving her the status of the 'true' nature which lies behind the Lear's stale legalism and Gloucester's knowing observations, he finds it fitting to use the metaphor of 'Jerusalem' to describe her.[22] Blake would, I think, have endorsed this: he would have seen Cordelia as the true 'emanation' of Lear, just as he would have seen Kent as Lear's honest 'spectre'. Danby stresses the theme of Honesty in the plays and shows Shakespeare's preoccupation with the situation created by the 'machiavell'—the man who succeeds in counterfeiting good so completely that no-one can tell the difference. Blake's own preoccupation with the same theme is evident in his 'Argument' to *The Marriage of Heaven and Hell*.

In one respect Danby's interpretation differs from the one that I have attributed to Blake. In his discussion of the Fool he actually points to the resemblance between the Fool's sayings and some of Blake's more gnomic verses, but his view of the Fool is that he simply 'stands for the unillumined head', his salvation being that he does not follow the counsels of self-interest which he consistently offers. In drawing this conclusion Danby dwells on the large number of speeches in which the Fool is the mouthpiece for straightforwardly prudential advice—even to the extent of urging the king in the storm to capitulate and ask his daughter's blessing. This last Danby describes as 'a nadir of negated humanity'.[23]

It seems to me, however, that to discuss the morality of the Fool is a contradiction in terms: it is like discussing the morality of Papageno in *The Magic Flute*. If the Fool's speech represents simply the 'wisdom of the flesh' it can have nothing to do with moral thought; we should not look for rational consistency in it. Every speech of the Fool is organized simply by the perceptions of the moment; it is therefore useless to compare one speech with another or to bring our own organized judgments to bear. What should be recognized is that in its totality the Fool, who possesses the single virtue of negative capability, making his mind a thoroughfare for all thoughts and not a select party, is able to present to Lear a form of wisdom, ranging from the prudential to the sublime, which he has largely disregarded and that Lear needs this wisdom as much as he needs Cordelia's.

The more one examines the relationship between the two writers the clearer it becomes that Blake was for some time closely engaged with Shakespeare's thinking and poetry, and that the highly-wrought working of his ideas under the influence of that mental encounter provided a powerful underswell in his own creative art. The debt, I would suggest, goes far deeper than is possible to demonstrate by simple parallels, since the creative encounter often seems to take place beneath the surface of the finished product. A simple example of what I have in mind could be found by reading 'The Sick Rose' in the context of Hamlet's consciousness. Ophelia recognizes that Hamlet formerly the 'rose of the fair state', is now sick: his sickness, we learn later, springs from a disgust which is prompted by his mother's behaviour, and voiced in an imagery of unorganized experience:

So Lust, though to a radiant Angell link'd
Will sate itself in a Celestiall bed, and prey on Garbage.

At a certain point, however, this type of encounter must be left to the reader's own literary intuitions.

Blake's great tribute to Shakespeare appears in a letter of 1800, and groups him at the beginning with Milton, Ezra and Isaiah; but the phrase 'in riper years' (an echo, possibly, of Edgar's 'ripeness is all') gives little clue. Any dating must be very tentative, but the evidence that we have suggests an account on the following lines:

(1) An early reading in the context of Elizabethan poetry. (He is said to have read the *Sonnets, Venus and Adonis* and *The Rape of Lucretia* at an early age.[24]) The results here would be found in *Poetical Sketches*, particularly the drama 'Edward III'.

(2) A reading of the plays in the mid- to late 1780s in connection with the themes of Innocence and Experience. This is suggested both by the structure of 'Tiriel' and by the use of quotations from *Hamlet* ('Rest, rest, perturbed Spirit' and 'O that the Everlasting had not fixed / His canon gainst self slaughter') as epigraphs for drawings which, in *The Gates of Paradise*, portray the despair springing from dependence on reason.[25]

(3) A further reading of the plays in connection with the theme of energy, associated with Blake's quadripartite vision of human energy in terms of the sublimity of the head, the pathos of the heart, the beauty of the genitals and the proportion of the hands and feet. This could be connected both with illustrations to *Hamlet* and *Macbeth* of 1795 and with the evolution of the idea of the Four Zoas, forming an essential part of the creative ferment which is an attractive feature of his first epic attempts.

In the 1790s Blake was in danger of over-commitment to energy as a way of life: he often comes dangerously near to such a commitment in *The Marriage of Heaven and Hell*. I have argued both here and in my previous study that he was preserved from the dangers of an unwary surrender by the survival of his 'fourfold' vision, which from childhood onwards had placed the 'human' poles of sublimity and pathos as guardians of his humanized universe, keeping energy within a field of proper exercise beneath them. If this is so, and if my estimate of the relationship is correct, it is clear that Shakespeare's profound human vision was one of the chief forces in keeping Blake on this path.

Appendix Two

Blake's use of earlier sources in 'Tiriel'

Despite the fact that the poem was not altogether successful and was left in manuscript, 'Tiriel' is more than usually important as an allegorical Blakean 'primitive'. The details of the allegory lie closer than usual to the surface of the poem and therefore show the workings of Blake's mind more clearly.

The recent edition of the poem by G. E. Bentley Jnr[1] has brought together for the first time the manuscript and most of the illustrations (which are dispersed in various collections). Although his editorial work is extremely valuable, however, Professor Bentley's interpretation of the poem is disappointing, since he insists on pursuing the details of the narrative at the expense of its significance. Discussing the parallels with Lear and Oedipus, for example, which other critics have mentioned, he simple notes that the textual parallels are somewhat meagre.

In dealing with Blake 'source-hunting' of the normal type is always unrewarding: the scholar must be prepared to make the imaginative leap which enables him to see the *allegorical* point which Blake (rightly or wrongly) found in the source and which he allowed to work in his own narrative. Professor Bentley's most important contribution to the discussion lies in his observation of the parallels between the story of Tiriel and the story of Joseph, but here too the allegorical point slips through his fingers. Joseph sold into Egypt was always for Blake an emblem of the human imagination enslaved by a mathematical and commercial civilization: Tiriel is the sort of slave that is left at the end of such a process. The pyramids of the illustrations reinforce this 'Egyptian' element in the poem.

Two critics who have shown themselves more ready to see the degree of allegorical organization are Professor Robert F. Gleckner and Miss Kathleen Raine.[2] Professor Gleckner's point of departure is to regard the poem, basically, as an exploration of the states of innocence and experience. Tiriel he sees as the tyrannizing priest-father-hypocrite whose oppression falls like a blight across the pages of *Songs of Experience*. Har and Heva, he says, have imbued Tiriel their son with a law which he in turn has visited upon his sons: terrified by such a progeny they have fled back in search of the innocence that they have lost. He quotes the later account of the flight of Har and Heva and draws attention to the lines which immediately follow it:

> Thus the terrible race of Los & Enitharmon gave
> Laws & Religions to the sons of Har binding them more
> And more to Earth: closing and restraining:
> Till a Philosophy of Five Senses was complete . . .[3]

Har he thus sees as the 'rational self'.

Professor Gleckner's discussion of Ijim is particularly valuable. He points out that in his annotations to Lavater, Blake drew a distinction between superstition and hypocrisy.

> no man was ever truly superstitious who was not truly religious as far as he knew
>> True superstition is ignorant honesty & this is beloved of god and man
>> I do not allow that there is such a thing as Superstition taken in the strict sense of the word
>> A man must first decieve himself before he is thus Superstitious and so he is a hypocrite.
>> Hipocrisy. is as distant from superstition. as the wolf from the lamb.[4]

The distinction, it is suggested, lies behind the confrontation of the hypocritical Tiriel and the superstitious Ijim.

This is, I think, an important element in the poem and reflects a constant concern of Blake's during these years. When hypocrisy has learned to mime honesty to perfection, what is the honest man to do in reply? And how are *we* to know him? He no doubt learned from Shakespeare's concern with the question in plays such as *King John*, *Richard III*, *Othello*, *Hamlet* and *Lear* (Professor Danby has some excellent chapters on the subject)[5]. It would also form part of his interest in Spenser: the theme of 'duplicity' is prominent in *The Faerie Queene*. There is a particular striking resemblance between the account of the guileful Malengin changing himself into various disguises when pursued by Talus[6] and Ijim's account of the various disguises assumed by Tiriel.

In Blake, however, the question of honesty is always resolved ultimately by asserting the supremacy of Vision: and this too he would find in Spenser. Indeed, Spenser's allegorizing has many points of contact with Blake's. Duessa, figure of deceit, is close to Blake's Vala, the deceiving vision of nature, while Una, with her lamb and lion, closely parallels Blake's idea that honesty must necessarily keep company with both innocence and experience: Una's lamb being a good emblem of the innocent 'emanation', her lion well representing the defending 'spectre'. Blake would no doubt have read other elements of Spenser's allegory in his own terms— the lovers turned into trees in Book One could be seen as emblem -

tizing his belief that love turned inwards becomes 'vegetated'; Una's encounter with the lion in the same book provides a model for 'The Little Girl Lost', as I have noted elsewhere.[7] Damon has produced a list of further parallels between Blake and Spenser which suggest the degree to which Blake drew on the earlier poet.[8]

For Blake, Spenser was a major figure both because he saw the difficulties of man in apprehending truth and because he saw that the truth, once discovered, would be imaginatively more satisfying than falsehood. This is true of his own treatments of the problem of honesty as well, and for this reason the imaginative approach to Blake's sources adopted by writers such as S. F. Damon, Northrop Frye and Kathleen Raine carries us furthest towards the full meaning of a poem like 'Tiriel'.

One notable feature of the poem is that whereas in later works Blake's names are usually either obvious or fictitious, here they can all be traced to further sources. The poem may well have been composed while Blake was still in a first flush of excitement over some of his ideas and eagerly reading works which might throw light on them.

Tiriel in Cornelius Agrippa's *Three Books of Occult Philosophy* is the name which signifies 'the Intelligence of Mercury' (S. F. Damon).[9]

The name of *Har* may contain the suggestion of a faded version of Hercules (see above, p. 43). In Mallet's *Northern Antiquities* he is the lowest of three kings who answer the traveller, Ganglier, when he comes (concealing his identity like Tiriel) to enquire concerning the nature of the creation. When a question is asked concerning the nature of God,

> Har replies, He lives for ever; he governs all his kingdom; and directs the great things as well as the small. Jafnhar adds: He hath formed the heaven, the earth, and the air. Thridi proceeds, He hath done more; he hath made man, and given him a spirit or soul. . . .[10]

Miss Raine, who quotes this information, goes on to indicate three levels in all. Har teaches only a natural religion; Jafnhar is also aware of the celestial world; and Thridi, alone, knows of an eternal world.[11]

Mnetha 'owes her name to a combination of *mnemosyne* (memory) and perhaps Manethon the Egyptian chronologist, and Athena' (Kathleen Raine and Northrop Frye).[12]

Hela is the goddess of death in Scandinavian mythology (Kathleen Raine).[13]

Ijim comes from Swedenborg's *True Christian Religion*:

> Diabolical love is the Love of Self. . . . In hell this love causes its lusts to appear at a distance like various wild beasts. . . . These are the

ochim, tziim, and ijim, mentioned by the prophets of the Old Testament, where they speak of the love of dominion from the love of self.

(Northrop Frye)[14]

Zazel, like Tiriel, comes from Cornelius Agrippa's *Three Books of Occult Philosophy*:

> The flesh being forsaken, and the body being defunct of life, is called a dead Carkass; Which as say the divines of the Hebrews, is left to the power of the demon *Zazel*, of whom it is said in the Scripture, *Thou shalt eat dust all thy daies*; and elsewhere, *The dust of the earth is his bread*.

(Kathleen Raine)[15]

These exact sources for names indicate some of the books that were in Blake's mind when he wrote his poem. Other sources also suggest themselves. The relationship with *King Lear* has been discussed in the previous appendix. Miss Kathleen Raine has pointed out that there is an equally strong resemblance to Oedipus, who in *Oedipus Tyrannus* is banished from Thebes, and in *Oedipus Coloneus* curses his sons. She mentions that a new translation of Sophocles had appeared in 1788.[16]

David Erdman felt that the model for Tiriel was George III, the tyrant who had lost his kingdom in the west (Myratana was once 'Queen of all the Western plains'; in a later poem the tyrant Bromion declares to Oothoon, 'Thy soft American plains are mine').[17] Miss Raine accepts this, but with the reservation that 'Blake's use of myth gives history a spiritual context, relates it to the human soul and the daimonic powers . . . that move mankind to action.'[18]

This modification of Erdman's position seems to me justified. It was always one of Blake's claims that he was less interested in particular historical events than in the forces which move beneath all history, constantly reproducing the same patterns and so giving mankind the opportunity of dealing with the future by properly interpreting the past.[19] 'Tiriel' is likely to be less a commentary on current political events than an attempt to relate those events to a wider pattern.

At the same time, it seems to me that in some cases Miss Raine's criticisms must also be levelled at her own conclusions. For example, she goes on to seek detailed parallels with the Oedipus plays. There can be little doubt that Blake's mind had played over Sophocles, as over Shakespeare, before he wrote the poem: there are strong resemblances, as she shows, to their language and imagery. But Blake's chief preoccupation was with his own patterns of interpretation: he was interested in these poets mainly because they were dealing with themes that mattered to him. To say, baldly, that the curse which Tiriel pronounces and suffers from is the curse of the House of Cadmus is to lay oneself open to the objection that Tiriel does not kill his father or marry his mother. It is likely, on the other hand, that the name 'Cadmus' reminded Blake of Adam Kadmon, the primitive Man of the Cabbala, and so set him thinking about the curse on Adam and his sons—the curse, that is, that lies upon all men. And this would lead him on to the reflection that the two sins of Oedipus were extreme forms of the love of self. Destructive energy is seen in its purest form in parricide, the murder of the man to whom one is linked most closely by bonds of blood; possessive love, equally, is purest in the desire to regain, in sexual love, the absolute self-gratification of the infant at the breast of its mother.

Similarly, our discussion in the previous appendix suggests that Blake read *King Lear*, another favourite of the 'Gothic' school, with an eye to its universal significance. Was not Lear a man under the domination of the self, until, through the stresses of experience, he was brought back to the innocence which he had rejected in the person of Cordelia?

In dealing with Har and Heva, Miss Raine draws attention to the fact that they appear elsewhere in Blake—at a point when 'Eternity was obliterated & erased':

> that dread day when Har and Heva fled.
> Because their brethren & sisters liv'd in War & Lust;
> And as they fled they shrunk
> Into two narrow doleful forms:
> Creeping in reptile flesh upon
> The bosom of the ground:
> And all the vast of Nature shrunk
> Before their shrunken eyes.[20]

As she points out, this has an evident connection with the story of Cadmus and Harmonia in Ovid's *Metamorphoses*.[21] The resemblance between 'Cadmus' and Adam Kadmon, it may be added, would focus Blake's attention all the more closely on this story of two divine figures who were transformed into harmless serpents: was this another diffracted version of the story of the Fall? Miss Raine also points out that, when he had slain the serpent and was watching it wallow in its own poison, Cadmus heard an oracle proclaim that he was in fact looking at what he himself should become. This she relates to Blake's doctrine that man 'becomes what he beholds'. She does not pursue the point, however, beyond remarking that Har and Heva, for all their harmlessness, are not proof against evil.

Finally, Miss Raine uses Ovid's *Metamorphoses* again in dealing with the various forms in which Ijim declares that he has seen Tiriel.[22] All these forms, she says, appear in the successive metamorphoses of Proteus as described in Ovid, with the exception of the tiger (which she would trace to Agrippa) and the toad, which she would trace to Satan's appearance in that form as he first tempts Eve with evil dreams. Following this last hint, she points to the affinity between Tiriel and Satan, brought out by the reference to himself as 'subtil as a serpent in a paradise' at the end of the poem. She concludes her article with a brief interpretation of 'Tiriel', in which she declares that imaginative wisdom is ever-young and its symbol is the Child: angels appear in the form of a child, Satan only as old and experienced.

> Thus Tiriel stands as the symbol of all bodies of tradition, kingdoms, and institutions that seek perpetuity in Mnetha's kingdom, where records of the past are preserved like papyrus and mummies in the dry sands of the spiritual Egypt. But the long continuance of the temporal never leads to eternity; is, indeed, only an obstacle to the realization of that world of imagination that man can enter only by becoming 'as a little child'.[23]

The conclusion is admirable in its affirmation, but in spite of all the many valuable pointers given in the article, some sections of the poem are hardly accounted for by it. Both Miss Raine and Professor Gleckner miss the high degree of organization which, for better or worse, characterizes this particular poem of Blake's. And they both miss the most important clue of all: Tiriel's blindness.

Nevertheless, just as Professor Gleckner's study has the virtue of taking Blake's ideas seriously, Miss Raine's indicates the intense attention which Blake paid to some individual books, especially during this period. It becomes possible to read them with Blake's eyes and to sense his mind at work. One can see, for example, how the three answers of the three kings quoted above from the Scandinavian mythology would strike him as representing ascending levels of vision: Har seeing the world as bound by law, Jafnhar taking in man's response to the beauty of the world and Thridi crowning all with a sense that the very existence of man is the most important and revealing fact in the universe.

In the same way, as one turns the pages of Cornelius Agrippa one senses that the universe of 'Tiriel' may owe something to Agrippa's theory of the three elements as earth, sulphur and mercury. Zazel, as we have seen, is specifically associated by Agrippa with earth and Tiriel with mercury; Ijim, with his fiery nature, would make a natural intelligence of sulphur which, in alchemy, 'coagulates the Mercury and fixes him at last',[24] as Ijim holds Tiriel. The three figures together would thus represent elements warring in Chaos, exiled by the failure of Har from the humanized paradise where they would exist together in harmony. Under his lawbound dominion fiery energy turns into selfish destruction (or at best honest indignation), the mercurial powers of the mind, (properly exercised as wisdom) turn into hypocrisy, poisoning the whole of existence, and the fertile earth, alienated, becomes a cold realm of worms and death.

Such speculations are more for the devotee than for the general reader perhaps, but they reinforce one's sense of his pertinacious intelligence. T. S. Eliot once compared his thought to that of a man who has put together an ingenious piece of home-made furniture from odds and ends about the house.[25] This is too patronizing. A better image might be that of a magpie, looking for the brightly shining myth or image which would suit the pattern of his own organization, but this still would not do justice to the range and subtlety of Blake's achievement. In a period when language did not exist for ideas which have since become part of the normal equipment of psychological interpretation he was forced to evolve his own set of terms for a highly perceptive view of human nature: the books that he read therefore became a necessary food for the development of his ideas. Viewed in this way Blake's reading at the end of the eighteenth century is a source of endless fascination.

Appendix Three

'Vala, or The Four Zoas' : Text and Illustrations

The original manuscript of 'Vala, or *The Four Zoas*' is by no means a straightforward document: it is rewritten and over-written in many places. In my discussion, however, I have referred to these changes only where they seemed relevant to the argument being advanced. It seems to me that they usually reflect Blake's detailed difficulties in creating the ordered poem that he wanted rather than any changes in his *basic* ideas and purposes. The recent edition by G. E. Bentley Jnr, which contains lithographic reproduction of all the manuscript pages, enables the reader to see some of the problems for himself.[1]

H. M. Margoliouth attempted to clarify the situation by printing the text as Blake at one time numbered it.[2] Unfortunately, however, he then undermined the principle of his edition by relegating part of the numbered text to an appendix. This act, an attempt to take the text a stage further back, is an implicit confession that extracting the 'numbered text' had not clarified the poem as much as he had hoped. One would not arrive at a coherent poem by isolating that, or any other state, since there was no stage at which Blake created, even for a time, a coherent form which he afterwards rejected. The process of revision was constant; any new orderings always shaded off into new growth.

Nevertheless, examination of the manuscript reveals certain facts about its growth in Blake's mind which explains some puzzling features, including the illustrations. The designs throughout the manuscript form a particularly interesting group among Blake's visual work since, apart from a few obvious illustrations, they seem at first sight to bear little or no relationship to the text. All the commentators who have examined the text, including G. E. Bentley Jnr, have decided that only some designs are relevant (though Margoliouth declared in his edition that more of the drawings illustrated something in the text than had been previously realized).[3] At one time I shared the general view and thought that at least the manuscript pages written on blank spaces in the midst of proof pages containing engraved designs for Young's *Night Thoughts* could not normally be related to the engravings, particularly since on several occasions versions of the same proof were used more than once.

I have gradually come to realize, however, that the connection between virtually all the designs and text in the manuscript is a close one. Examination of the designs actually engraved for Young's *Night Thoughts* shows that many contain Blakean motifs which extend beyond the authority of Young's text. At first one may be deceived by the series of explanations at the end of the printed edition, which in every case explain the relevance of the designs to Young's text and meaning. One soon comes to realize, however, that these explanations were inserted because the designs were so obviously *not* straightforward illustrations. There is a beautiful ambiguity in many of them: while they can fairly claim to illustrate the point which Young is making, they also incorporate an implicit criticism of his attitude as a whole.

To grasp this ambiguity is to see the engravings themselves in a new light. When read purely against the printed explanations they have a dark menacing quality, many of them illustrating the terrors and imminence of death. But the Death who haunts and strikes in many of the designs is also depicted, behind his terror, as a blind, benevolent old man. In Young's world there is a very real horror awaiting the man who has not accepted the doctrines of religion, but in Blake's the fear itself is largely an illusion, created by the fact that Urizen's world is dominated by time and fate. When Young writes of a dwelling on human grief Blake's design shows the self-absorptions of the man of reason; the 'truth' which Young finds in religious consolations Blake finds in the potentialities of vision. Blake takes the energy and sublimity of Young's conceptions and follows those at the expense of the more pietistic reflections which betray Young's surviving allegiance to Urizen.

Although the proofs on which the text of 'Vala' is written form the larger part of the complete manuscript, they are used only for the later pages. The earlier text, up to page 42 (Night III, 108), which is designed on blank sheets, forms a separate group of its own. The designs here, which are normally at the foot of the page, but some-times extend up into the side margins, are of importance to the interpretation of the poem as a whole, since they make clear that the phallic significance which one senses from time to time is really a part of the poem. As each of the Zoas is depicted in turn he is given the lineaments which Blake detects in those whose phallic existence is in some way deprived. Enion's pitted and hollow features are ample testimony of her privation; Tharmas's rugged features show the displacement of his sexual energy. Urizen is little more than a draft for a human being, made up of lines rather than lineaments; his only remaining human features are his eyes. Ahania, his emanation, is a shadowy figure, Vala is at once attractive and elusive. Los and Enitharmon are more visionary children, but their creative radiance, undirected by any fuller human vision, is bent into scorn and enmity. Luvah appears either as a suffering Christ bearing his body through flames of fire, or as an Orc-figure (child or man) whose full and wanton features show the ambiguity created by unorganized sexual drive.

Elsewhere Luvah's nightmares are depicted—dreams of sexual distortion which show that the failure of the Eternal Man was involved with a failure of sexual sublimity. At one point the phallus itself is shown, turned into a foolish toy; at another Los and Enitharmon look on with prurient fascination at a reclining figure who, in the original drawing, evidently had an erect phallus.

Even in the agonies of the Zoas, however, they always retain a suggestion of their lost beauty; further drawings in the manuscript suggest the sublimity of the human form which they have lost.

Drawings such as these are not confined to the early sheets; they often appear on the textual pages which appear on the backs of *Night Thoughts* designs; but it seems clear that Blake thought the phallic significance of the poem to be particularly relevant in the early Nights, where the disorder of the Zoas is being explained, and towards the end, when the Eternal Man is awakening.

The process of construction may be followed further. The fact that the sheets on which the early Nights are written contain many passages which are written out in Blake's best copperplate handwriting suggests that they were copied from an already existing draft. The copperplate passages disappear once he begins using sheets from the *Night Thoughts* engravings. The theory which suggests itself, therefore, is as follows.

About 1795 Blake was engaged on a small prophetic book, which was perhaps designed as a sequel to the *Book of Los* and might even have been called at first *The Song of Eno* (the original manuscript of Vala began first 'This is the Dirge of Eno', then 'This is the Song of Enitharmon'; in *The Book of Los* Eno sings the opening song that recalls the 'times remote' of generosity and love). This, we may suppose, would have been concerned with the fall from sexual sublimity and the subsequent larger human privations reflected, for instance, in the songs of Enion in Night the first and Night the Second.

The theme, once sown, would grow. The relationship between the lapse which deprived Enion and the delusive view of nature caused by inadequate vision would suggest something longer than the early prophetic books if it were to be worked out in detail: 'The Book of Vala', perhaps.

At the same time, from 1794 to 1796 Blake was at work on his illustrations to Young's *Night Thoughts* in which, as we have said, drawings presented in illustration of Young's text turn out also to criticize some of Young's basic attitudes. The process can be seen in action still further if we look at some of the engraved proofs now incorporated into the text of 'Vala', where, at a stage before the writing in of the poem, Blake would sometimes turn over his engraved design and draw on the back a contrasting or counter-pointing design, the confrontation between terrified man and terrifying energy for Young being backed by a drawing of energy organized, for example, or the failure of the sun-charioteer for Young by a vision of time as a restored son of the morning.[4]

At some stage (perhaps a long time after) Blake realized that this process of inner interpretation could be extended, this time poetically. If the illustrations of Young were, in a deeper sense, a visual commentary on aspects of life in Urizen's world, they could be used as a loose framework for the second part of his epic poem, which was to portray that world in action. After the early nights had presented their successive accounts of the lapse of the Eternal Man, and after Ahania's crowning account had been rejected in anger by Urizen, the way would be open for the main action of the poem: the establishment of Urizen's tyranny, the struggles of the Zoas and the final awakening—incorporating on the way some 'mythological' segments from previous books. On the back of the engraved proofs, if no pencil design existed already, more specific drawings could portray the successive states of the Zoas.

This process can be seen mirrored in the manuscript as it now stands. The first group of sheets, with text written on paper supplied for the *Night Thoughts* engravings but not used, contains a large number of pages in Blake's copperplate hand, suggesting that he is copying from poetry already written; it ends with Ahania's account of the lapse of the Eternal Man and Urizen's angry refusal to accept it, an illustration below showing the teaching of sexual shame. This is followed immediately by the first of the *Night Thoughts* pages, showing the God of the Old Testament as a god of thunders. The remaining designs contain similar ambiguities; the further meaning is always related to Blake's text at that point. In several cases the same design is used more than once, if further relevance occurs. This suggests either that Blake had already decided that this poem would be his own private epic and that he would keep it for himself, unpublished (as David Erdman has suggested)[5] or that he wanted to compose it quickly as a long poem and would then have decided which visual themes to retain in his final engraved text.

Although 'Vala' is, as I have argued in Chapter Six, an integrated whole, the main ideas of which remain constant through Blake's various revisions, the changes both in text and illustration towards the end of Night the Third result in the most important stage in the development of the poem and help to explain some features of the text—the fact, for instance, that some of the best lyrical passages, such as the song of Enitharmon, are grouped closely together in the first part of the poem, appearing at rarer intervals from Night the Fourth onwards. Blake's constructional decision here may be compared with George Eliot's in welding two originally separate stories together to make *Middlemarch*; the idea is enlarged, the work gains in complexity of suggestion—but, to the critical observer, some of the joins still show.

A few drawings are too generalized for profitable comment; the following is an attempt to indicate the symbolic significance of the others:

1   An angel descending with trumpet to awaken the Zoas, sunk in sleep.
2   The artist, also asleep, but only as 'rest before labour'.
3   Vala (with eyes like Newton's in Blake's representation of him).
4   A phallus bridled and turned into a snaky toy; its cherub reversed into an accusing angel aiming his arrows ('stern demands of Right & Duty instead of Liberty').
5   An angel buried in reasoning study on the waves of the sea (Tharmas bent to create a world of time and space dominated by Destiny: 'in darkness & solitude forming Seas of Doubt & rocks of Repentance').
6   Winged Tharmas in repose.
7   The snaky spectre of Tharmas rising up in flames.
8   Los and Enitharmon as babies on the breasts of Enion ('Infolding the bright Infants from the desolating Winds').
9   Los and Enitharmon as inspired children, desolate Enion following ('He could control the times . . . she . . . the spaces').
12   Los as a fencer attacking Enitharmon ('Los now repented that he had smitten Enitharmon').
13   A sleeping serpent, representing a temporary harmony of energy ('Not long in harmony they dwell').
14   Serpentine energies awake again (the singers at the feast).
15   Urizen analyzing a rope into its several strands ('the Human Form is no more').
17   Enion turned into a spirit of pity.
18   A predatory form swooping (corresponding to imagery of preying in text).
19   A vegetated cherub and desolate woman (perhaps intended originally as a plate to sum up the content of Night One as a whole).
20   A male-female form, with penis and vagina, wrapped in serpentine coils (another summing-up plate?)
23   Man darkening into fallen reason ('Man called Urizen and said Take thou possession . . .').

24 Urizen falling with his rope of analysis into the deep while his female counterpart stands neglected ('pale he beheld the Abyss').

25 A figure working at a loom-like machine created by phallic shapes ('Vala fed in cruel delight! the furnaces with fire').

26 Monstrous forms of distorted sexual energies (the nightmares of Luvah in the furnace).

27 Urizen as a skeletal figure of self-enclosed death, with the attractive Vala whom he both yearns after and holds in thrall
　　　(Luvah: 'O Urizen my enemy I weep for thy stern ambition
　　　But weep in vain O when will you return Vala the wanderer').

28 Vala resting by her lover after his agony ('Then were the furnaces unseal'd').

29 A figure sewing the nets of Urizen's world ('many a net is netted').

31 Vala weeping before Luvah ('The King of Light beheld her mourning among the Brick kilns . . . Luvah in vain her lamentations heard').

32 Prostrate figures; a male and female meeting under the law of chastity ('spirits mournd their bondage night & day').

35 A woman carrying wares for sale; labourers harvesting in a field ('Wisdom is sold in the desolate market where none come to buy / And in the witherd field where the farmer plows for bread in vain / It is an easy thing to triumph in the summers sun . . .').

36 Ahania falling through space ('drawn thro unbounded space / Onto the margin of Non Entity').

37 Ahania before Urizen ('O Urizen look on Me, like a mournful stream / I embrace round thy knees . . .').

38 A deadened Los leaning on an alarmed Enitharmon ('Vala shall become a worm in Enitharmon's Womb / . . . And Luvah in the loins of Los a dark and furious death').

39 Los and Enitharmon as children look in prurient amazement at a reclining figure (an erasure probably showed originally the erect phallus of the Eternal Man in his sleep: 'When Urizen slept in the porch & the Ancient Man was smitten').

40 A male and female figure, perhaps in coitus; behind them a little winged figure: the recording cherub of false holiness judging sexuality ('To his own Shadow words . . . uttering / O I am nothing when I enter into judgment with thee').

41 A female figure leaning back towards another (the erasure on which was probably originally a large phallus) (Vala abandoned as the Eternal Man turns away).

42 A woman with the children Los and Enitharmon, looking at Los's genitals; another chasing away a bat-winged phallus (the teaching of shame).

43 Jehovah as god of thunders (Urizen arising as tyrant).

44 The agony and rage of phallic Tharmas (a crowned figure of female chastity nearby).

45 Jesus (as the good Samaritan) ministering to a young man, the despairing victim of rationalism (counterpointing Tharmas's complaint that rage and mercy have become alike to him).

46 Tharmas's horror at the evanishing of Enion.

47 The sun-charioteer riding into dark clouds of reason as suffering figures look on (Tharmas riding on the dark abyss).

48 A figure with pierced heart (the wounded Luvah whose failure makes possible the contentions between Los and Enitharmon).

49 A man asleep in the coils of his snaky selfhood, while his child reaches out to catch a bird (lack of vision leading to destructive possessiveness: the growing jealousy of Los).

50 Enion in her privation, a cloud emerging (Los issuing as 'A shadow blue obscure & dismal from the breathing Nostrils / Of Enion').

51 The writing on the wall at Belshazzar's feast (Tharmas: 'What can I now behold but an Eternal Death?').

52 Los arising to recreate the ruined furnaces, Enitharmon rejecting him.

53 Death as terrifying bellman (Los begins to bind Urizen as a protection against death).

54 The globe as created by Los.

55 Visionless humanity led by the renewal of vision in Christ ('The daughters of Beulah saw the Divine Vision they were comforted').

56 Figure with the eye of single vision (the limit of opacity, or Satan) looking at a figure of human energy (the limit of contraction, or Adam) (Urizen with his fallen vision looking at a Los who has the lineaments of Orc).

57 A hunting satyr with phallic spear and phallic dogs of destruction (Los's energy turned into the lust and destructiveness of Orc).

58 Woman giving birth to a figure of Christ in glory ('from (Enitharmon's) heart rending his way a terrible Child sprang forth').

59 Christ with pierced hands and feet walking through flames (the sufferings of Luvah in the world of Los and Enitharmon under Urizen's restraining jealousy).

60 Los in jealousy sees Orc embracing his mother.

61 A figure looking down on the world (Orc's expansive and contracting vision).

62 Los and Enitharmon visiting Orc bound.

63 Joseph (a figure like Los as servant of Urizen) measuring out his baby with the span of his hand.

64 An immortal looking away from humanity in dark vision and creating a Urizenic net (Urizen's memory of his lapse).

65 Man confronted by terrifying energy (Urizen aware of Orc).

66 A vision of organized energy and vision.

67 Eve and Adam pointing up to the Gothic arch of a doorway and down to the earth (NT text: 'Sense and Reason point the way') while visionless man turns away from the sublimity and pathos that they offer ('Urizen . . . explord his dens').

68 The fallen emanation of Urizen's world (Urizen curses his daughters).

69 The figure of cruel justice in Urizen's world ('What & who art thou cold Demon . . .?').

70 A crocodile as monstrous energy (the terror of energy under Urizen).

71 Death the bellman (=53) ('Urizen fell & death Shut up his powers in oblivion').

72 Figures under a poison tree (Urizen's world of death).

73 A figure escaping from the coils of a serpent (Urizen's momentary vision of the world of eternity).

74 Urizen exploring with his globe of fire.

75 The failure of the sun-charioteer of intellect (the creation of Time in Urizen's world).

76 Time restored as a son of the morning.

77 A serpent-coiled man (=49) ('Los felt the Envy in his limbs . . .').

78 Orc lying on the rock.

79 Heavenly figure descending with a message to a man shut up in woe (Orc speaking to Urizen).

81 Death striking his dart at the sun (the despair of Los).

82 A woman revolving a starry circle (Enitharmon devoting herself to mystery).

83 A shadowy angel brooding over representatives of humanity swept to oblivion in a stream (mystery elevated).

84 A spectrous figure looking up ('the Spectre is in every Man insane brutish Deformd . . . but my Eyes are always upon thee O lovely / Delusion').

85 Man of Reason turning away from humanity (Los under the domination of his Spectre) (NT text: 'If angels tremble, 'tis at such a sight').

86 Enitharmon as emanation ('my lovely Enitharmon').

91 Man, thorn-bound, reading a book while a small figure of female charity looks on ('Knowing the arts of Urizen were Pity & Meek affection').

92 Drooping figures (the triumph of Urizen).

93 Drooping figures at a banquet while death with his dart descends on them (the cult of sensuality created by the fear of death).

94 Despairing figure (? the despair of Tharmas).

95 An old man on spectrous chair teaching children to count while a more visionary child looks on from his mother's lap (education in the empire of Urizen).

96 Figures bowing before a disguised phallus ('That whosoever enterd into the temple might not behold / The hidden wonders allegoric of the Generations Of secret lust . . .').

97 Christ as the Good Samaritan ministering to Tharmas-figure (Pity, the 'crystal form' of Tharmas, created when he was divided, returning to him).

98 A serpent with priestly head (the Prester Serpent).

99 Caricature figure of face, wings and hooves (humanity as created in threefold vision, without the fourfold sublimity that gives human form: 'the Vegetated bodies which Enitharmon wove / Opend within their hearts & in their loins & in their brain / To Beulah').

101 Death swooping on mother and child (Urizen's war destroying three-fold vision ('Thus Urizen in self-deceit . . .')).

102 The Shadowy Female enduring Urizen's destruction.

103 Man tippling, a dark clad woman looking on recording (the Shadowy Female looking at 'he who assumed Luvah's name') (NT: sensual man and his conscience).

104 Woman pushing a largely hidden wheel consisting of eyed serpent body (=Mystery) ('The Lamb of God Descended thro Jerusalems gates / To put off Mystery . . .').

105 Trumpeter descending to rouse a skeleton (= man stripped of his perceptions by the cruel Daughters).

106 Prostrate woman ('the female death').

107 The man of reason asleep and dreaming of beautiful forms (Urizen's fitful vision).

108 A woman crying in anguish; a wingless cherub, with bow reversed, nearby (Ahania crying aloud at the suffering and the deprivation of sexual pleasure in Urizen's world).

109 The figure of Truth (NT) bursting out in lightnings (Enion's prophetic reply to Ahania, promising the coming of the bridegroom).

110 Woman reaching out over space (Jerusalem weeping over the sepulchre for two thousand years).

111 Pierced Christ walking through flames (the sufferings of human energy in the Christian era).

112 Man with a woman who is crying out in rage and indignation (the voice of human indignation during the Christian era?).

114 The triumph of Christ.

115 The sufferings of Christ.

116 The triumph of Christ (a pencil drawing resembling 114).

117 Angels descending and ascending (the Last Judgment).

118 Man of energy and man of single vision leaning towards a woman (Orc and Urizen struggling for the favours of Vala—whom both misapprehend).

119 Man in air with finger on the world (counterpointing Urizen's mourning for a world exiled from his).

120 A figure (male or female?) with compasses hovering above ('The Eternal Man sat on the rocks . . .').

121 Figures breathing life into supine man (Urizen, 'anxious . . . to reassume the human').

122 Supine woman (Jerusalem).

123 Singer with harp ascending despite manacled foot (The release of imprisoned humanity into fourfold vision).

124 Vegetated women (grave) and a crippled rational man (cavern) ('Urizen drove his plow / Over the graves and caverns of the dead').

125 Man of reason inspired by winged beings (Urizen reunited with his emanation).

126 A fearsome warlike figure ('fierce Orc').

127 Time averted, showing his wings ('O Sun thou art nothing to me now / Go on thy course rejoicing').

128 A sleeping woman with labourers at work on stones and a musician playing (Vala's dreams of delight and sexual consummation).

129 Jesus as good Samaritan (=45) (Vala's vision of Tharmas's deprivation and Luvah's ministry).

130 A Man struggling to awake (the growth of Enion and Tharmas as renewed children awakens the Eternal Man).

131 Figures breathing life into prostrate man ('the Spirits of Men beneath / Cried out to be delivered').

132 Figure of energy standing over a figure of single vision, Vala looking on (the triumph of Luvah).

133 Death striking his dart at the sun (Urizen with his flail?)

134 Strange monster with cherubs on back ('Lo how the Pomp of Mystery goes down into the Caves').

135 Time as reaper sweeping away hosts of humanity including visionless old man with book ('Attempting to be more than Man we become less').

136 Human face in the midst of cherub wings (the ambiguity of natural beauty: mystery or revelation? (the animals in the furnaces)).

137 Human figures wrestling (the struggles of Urthona and Tharmas).

138 The awakening of Vala.

139 The rising of man to his eternal stature.

In some cases, as in the last pages of the eighth and ninth Nights, the designs seem to illustrate the general shape of the action as much as particular events on that page. My interpretations also range from those that are obvious to some which are necessarily tentative; none is arbitrary, however, though brevity often precludes the full explanation or defence for a particular identification. In the case of the two Night VIIs, I have followed Margoliouth in treating both as part of the full text of the poem, though it is possible that either may have been intended to replace the other. I have made little attempt to enter on the vexed question of the dating. G. E. Bentley Jnr points out that on page 48 there is a right to left impression of part of the last page of Hayley's first Ballad (pub. 1 June 1802). If we accept that this is *under* Blake's writing, it is tempting to think that the summer of that year may have marked the time when he made the decisive change; it could even be that bringing Hayley's ballad in contact with one of his old proofs made him aware of the superiority of his own writing and prompted him to resume composition, with the proofs as a stimulus. The reader who wishes to pursue these vexed problems further should consult the discussions by Margoliouth, Bentley, W. H. Stephenson[6] and David Erdman.

Notes

Place of publication is London unless otherwise stated; details of publication are given at first entry.

Chapter One

1 I have discussed briefly the question of Blake's 'sanity' in my *Blake's Humanism*, 1968, pp. 2–4. There can be no doubt that about 1797–1803 some sort of crisis took place (including some paranoid overtones), which was followed by a remarkable reintegration during the remaining years of his life. Any judgment of this, however, must take account of the remarkable intelligence, insight and organization of his work throughout both periods, and it is on this that I have found it important to dwell.

Chapter Two

1 NB 14; NC 10; E 408.

2 Mona Wilson, who mentions these, also includes in her list Gray, Collins, Thomson, Percy and Ossian. *Life of William Blake*, 1948, p. 7.

3 NB 8; NC 6; E 404.

4 Young, *Night Thoughts*, I, 16 (Album 14 in British Museum Print Room collection).

5 NB 99; NC 184; E 465.

6 NB 3; NC 1; E 400.

7 'An Imitation of Spenser', NB 18; NC 14; E 412.

8 Reproduced, John Milton, *Poems in English* with illustrations by William Blake (ed. G. Keynes), 1926. See also my *Blake's Humanism*, pp. 194–6 and figs. 45, 53, 54.

9 'Mad Song', NB 12; NC 9; E 407. (Cf 'Infant Sorrow' NB 76; NC 217; E 28.)

10 J. T. Smith, *Nollekens and his Times*, 1828, II, 457–8.

11 Mona Wilson, *op. cit.*, 2–4.

12 J. Bryant, *A New System, or an Analysis of Ancient Mythology*, 1774–6, III, 601.

13 According to Blake's inscription in ink on the first state of the engraving, the 'old Italian drawing' was by Salviati. (See G. Keynes, *Engravings by William Blake : The Separate Plates*, Dublin, 1950, p. 4.) It seems more likely that he copied it from an engraving by Beatrizet (fig. 56), however. David Erdman argues that the later, engraved inscription was produced in the period 1809–20 (*Philological Quarterly*, 1952, XXXI, 337–43). See also G. Keynes, *Blake Studies*, 1949, pp. 45–6.

14 W. Stukeley, *Stonehenge, A Temple Restored to the British Druids*, 1740; *Abury, a Temple of the British Druids*, 1743. The best account of contemporary interest in the Druids is to be found in A. L. Owen's *The Famous Druids*, Oxford, 1962.

15 Wordsworth, *The Prelude*, xiii (1850 ed.), ll. 343–9. (1805 ed., xii, 348–53). Ed. E. de Selincourt, Oxford, 1950, pp. 466–7.

16 J. Toland, 'Specimen of the Critical History of the Celtic Religion and Learning, containing an Account of the Druids', *Collection of Several Pieces*, 1726, I, 48–9.

17 Will Brangwen. D. H. Lawrence, *The Rainbow*, ch. vii (1955, p. 199).

18 NB 10; NC 7; E 405.

19 NC 620; E 143.

20 William Stukeley, *Letter to Roger Gale*, 1726–7. Quoted, W. Hutchinson, *History of Cumberland*, Carlisle, 1794, I, 241–2.

21 J. Bryant, *op. cit.*, plate VIII, facing I, 488 (p. 478 in British Museum copy). See above, Note 12.

22 *Europe*, ll. 21–2. NB 216; NC 241; E 62. See my *Blake's Humanism*, p. 126.

23 *Jerusalem*, pl. 100. First discussed by R[uthven] Todd. See below, p. 374.

24 *Milton*, plate 4. E. J. Ellis and W. B. Yeats, *Works of William Blake*, London, 1893, vol. III.

25 *Marriage of Heaven and Hell*, plate 4. NB 182; NC 149; E 34.

26 *Op. cit.*, I, plate VIII; II, plate IV. The right-hand illustration of the second plate has been reproduced by Giorgio Melchiori in *The Whole Mystery of Art* (1960, p. 168). It was originally discovered, and tentatively attributed to Blake, by Geoffrey Keynes (*Blake Studies*, 1949, p. 44). Melchiori's discussion is devoted to Yeats's use of the image, which he found in Blake and elsewhere, and is mainly important for students of Yeats. Melchiori, following Keynes (*Blake Studies*, 1949, p. 167) also points out that Blake might have come across the image in Erasmus Darwin's *Botanic Garden* (1789–91), to which he contributed illustrations and which contains a reference to 'The Egg of Night, on Chaos hurl'd' which 'Burst, and disclosed the cradle of the world'. As always with Blake, the chief importance lies in what he himself made of such sources.

27 See 'There is no Natural Religion' (1st Series). NB 147; NC 97; E 1.

28 Letter of 12.9.1800. NB 840; NC 799; E 680.

29 *Blake's Humanism*, pp. 23–34.

30 Jacob Boehme, *Works . . . with figures, illustrating his Principles, left by the Rev. W. Law. 4 vols., 1764–81*, plate, 'The Constituent Parts of Man'. In different copies the plates are bound variously. Since the impression is sometimes given that these designs were made by William Law himself, it should be pointed out that some, if not all, appear in earlier German editions.

31 *Ibid.*, plate, 'The Tree of the Soul'.

32 Bunyan, *The Pilgrim's Progress*, 1678, pp. 217–18.

33 *Milton*, 35, 22–5. NB 422; NC 525; E 134.

34 *Milton*, 30, 1–2. NB 415; NC 518; E 128.

35 *The Marriage of Heaven and Hell*, plates 17–20. NB 189; NC 156; E 41.

36 For Egyptian mythology see, e.g., Plutarch, *De Iside et Osiride Liber*, ed. S. Squire, Cambridge, 1744 (ii), pp. 41–3. The relationship between Plato's 'four levels' and Blake's is discussed by T. F. Gould in his forthcoming book, *The Sun, the Line and the Cave*. The general importance of the four levels for Blake is also brought out by Harold Bloom in his *Blake's Apocalypse*, 1963; my own investigation, though largely in agreement with his, was carried out independently.

37 Letter to Butts, 22.11.1802. NB 861; NC 818; E 693.

38 E. J. Morley, *Henry Crabb Robinson on Books and their Writers*, 1938, I, 327.

39 See below, pp. 244, 249, 374 etc.

40 See, e.g., 'A Descriptive Catalogue' (1809). NB 596; NC 567; E 523–4 and my *Blake's Humanism*, pp. 193–4.

41 *The Protestant's Bible*, 1780, at Gen. xxxvii, 28. The design is wrongly inscribed 'after Rubens'.

42 S. Gardner, *Blake*, 1968, pp. 62–3. A handsome set of engravings of Raphael's designs was published in 1772–7.

43 D. Figgis, *Paintings of William Blake*, 1925, plates 59 and 60.

44 NB 44; NC 37; E 434.

45 NB 133; NC 748; E 516.

46 *Jerusalem*, 91. 37–8; NB 558; NC 738; E 249.

47 See 'The Crystal Cabinet', NB 116; NC 429; E 479, and my *Blake's Humanism*, pp. 88–9. See also p. xv above, for a source in Vaughan.

48 See *Europe*, 10. 10–11. NB 216; NC 241; E 62.

49 I Sam. iii. 1.

50 Judges xiii–xvi. Cf. *Milton*, 22. 50.

51 Judges iv.

52 II Sam. i. 25.

53 Judges v. 20.

54 *Jerusalem*, 59. 16.

55 Gen. xxviii. 11–12.

56 D. Figgis, *op. cit.*, plate 80.

57 Gen. xxviii. 16–17.

58 Lev. xxvi. 19.

59 Daniel ii. Blake used a similar figure in his illustrations to Dante. See A. S. Roe, *Blake's Illustrations to the Divine Comedy*, Princeton, 1953, pp. 83–4.

60 Daniel iii.

61 Lucifer was the name given by Isaiah to the King of Babylon. It was applied to Satan by the early fathers (e.g., Jerome and Tertullian) and in the Middle Ages became common in this sense. (See Schaff-Hertzog, *Encyclopaedia of Religious Knowledge*, 1910, s.v.)

62 The prologue was added to the later edition, entitled 'For the Sexes: the Gates of Paradise'. NB 569; NC 761; E 256.

63 Num. xxi. 6–9. Blake painted this incident; see G. Keynes, *Blake's Illustrations to the Bible*, 1957, plate 45. Christ's use of the same image (John iii. 14–15) would also fit into his interpretation.

64 N. Frye, *Fearful Symmetry*, Princeton, 1947, pp. 137–9.

65 Ezekiel xxviii. 13–14.

66 *Paradise Lost*, x, 504–16.

67 NB 579; NC 771; E 266.

68 NB 670; NC 42; E 438.

69 G. Grigson, *Samuel Palmer: the Visionary Years*, 1947, p. 20.

70 *Paradise Lost*, iv, 453–76. The idea that the sin of Psyche was to 'fall in love with love' might perhaps be regarded as a further refinement on this theme. (See Thomas Taylor, *Cupid and Psyche*, 1795, p. viii.)

71 Young, *Night Thoughts*, VI. (Blake's illustration is in the British Museum Print Room, Album 25, VI, 23. It is also reproduced in the Harvard selection of Blake's illustrations to Young.)

72 The term 'emanation' is actually used to describe post-Newtonian theories of light: see L. Euler, *Letters to a German Princess*, 1795, I, 72–82.

73 'A Vision of the Last Judgment', NB 652; NC 617; E 555. Blake's quotation amalgamates Isaiah vi. 3 with Rev. iv. 8.

74 From a notebook. NB 105; NC 415; E 467.

75 See *William Blake's Designs for Gray's poems*, with an introduction by H. J. C. Grierson. Oxford, 1922.

76 NB 585; NC 780; E 269.

77 Shelley, *Prometheus Unbound*, Act I, ll. 107–305.

78 NB 639; NC 606; E 545–6.

79 NB 609–10; NC 578; E 534.

80 A. Sammes, *Britannia Antiqua Illustrata*, pp. 142–3.

81 J. Toland, 'History of the Druids', *Collection of Several Pieces*, I, 70 f.

82 E.g. 'Babylon with cruel OG, / With Moral & Self-righteous Law . . .' *Jerusalem*, 27. 22–3. NB 464; NC 650; E 170.

83 Sammes, *loc. cit.*; 'Tiriel', 2. 35; 3. 25. (NB 152–3; NC 101–3; E 275–6.)

84 Sammes, *op. cit.*, pp. 127–8.

85 NB 37–9; NC 31–3; E 428–30.

86 See his *Philosophical and Mathematical Commentaries of Proclus*, II (1788), 294–309nn.

87 Now in the British Museum. Reprod., *The Blake Collection of W. Graham Robertson* (ed. K. Preston), 1952, plate 24.

88 After describing Chaucer's Reeve and Manciple as characters of 'the most consummate worldly wisdom' he says, 'The Shipman, or Sailor, is a similar genius of Ulyssean art; but with the highest courage added.' (NB 601; NC 571; E 527); and in a letter he writes that Mr Johnson's 'aggravating letters' . . . 'would have called for the sceptre of Agamemnon rather than the tongue of Ulysses' (NB 894; NC 847).

89 Plates 97–8.

90 Annotation to Boyd's Dante. NC 412; E 623.

91 'On Virgil' (NB 583; NC 778; E 267). Cf. Laocoön Inscriptions (NB 581; NC 777; E 272).

92 See 'Descriptive Catalogue', ii, NB 594; NC 565; E 522.

93 *Ibid.*

94 Annotations to Reynolds's *Discourses*, VII, 195. NB 805; NC 473; E 647.

95 Letter of 6.7.1803. NB 869; NC 825.

96 *Milton*, 22. 53. NB 402; NC 506; E 117.

97 *Last Judgment*. NB 638; NC 605; E 544.

98 'On Homer's Poetry.' NB 582; NC 778; E 267.

99 'Descriptive Catalogue', ii, *loc. cit.* For Ovid, cf. *Last Judgment*. NB 640; NC 607; E 546.

100 NB 594; NC 565; E 522.

101 Isaiah vi, 1–7.

102 NB 583; NC 778; E 267.

103 *Jerusalem* 98. 46. NB 567; NC 746; E 256.

104 Reproduced by Geoffrey Keynes in his *Bibliography* (1921) and in his *Engravings by William Blake: the Separate Plates*, Dublin 1956, plate 37. Also in E, plate 3. Inscriptions alone, NB 580–2; NC 775–7; E 270–2.

105 A copy can be seen in the British Museum Print Room.

106 *Aeneid*, ii, 40–56; 199–249.

107 Ophiucus is also a constellation, and there are signs that Blake at some stage saw traditional names of constellations as signs that his 'mythology' had once been universal. Thus Orion, with his phallus turned sword, would become an image of Adam turned into Cain, while Ophiucus would be the serpent-holder whose serpents turn into strangulating reasonings: 'The Kingdom of Og is in Orion: Sihon is in Ophiucus' (*Milton*, 37. 50). The Plough pointing to the pole becomes an image of Urizen, whereas 'The Plowman of Chaucer is Hercules in his supreme eternal state' ('Descriptive Catalogue'). Arcturus is the lost Arthur or Eternal Man (ch. vii below).

108 'On Virgil' and 'On Homer's Poetry'. NB 582–3: NC 778; E 267.

109 *Ibid.*

110 'Descriptive Catalogue', v. NB 608–12; NC 577–81; E 533–6.

111 NB 595–606; NC 566–75; E 523–31.

112 NB 610; NC 579; E 535.

113 See *Middlemarch*, chs xxi–xxii. Symbolic references are clearly at play in these chapters.

114 'Descriptive Catalogue', xv. NB 617; NC 585; E 540.

Chapter Three

1 Füseli's remark about Blake. See A. Gilchrist, *Life of Blake*, ch. vii, 1863, I, 52.

2 NB 655, 663; NC 539, 556; E 497, 496.

3 See, e.g., F. W. Bateson's remark in *Essays in Criticism*, 1961, XI, 163.

4 NB 667–8; NC 40–1; E 437.

5 The best discussion of this group occurs in G. M. Harper's *The Neoplatonism of William Blake*, Chapel Hill, 1961, pp. 37–43.

6 NB 688; NC 60; E 453.

7 NB 689; NC 61; E 454.

8 NB 684; NC 56; E 450.

9 W. H. Auden, 'A Mental Prince', *The Observer*, 17.11.57. See also the ensuing correspondence, 24.11.57 and 1.12.57.

10 J. Middleton Murry, *William Blake*, 1933, pp. 39–40, 45–6.

11 See F. A. Lea, *John Middleton Murry*, 1959, pp. 99–103.

12 A. Gilchrist, *op. cit.*, I, 59.

13 N. Frye, *Fearful Symmetry*, Princeton, 1947, p. 243.

14 D. Figgis, *Paintings of William Blake*, 1925, pl. 94.

15 Cf *The Tempest*, I, ii, 343–62.

16 In his illustrations to Young's *Night Thoughts*, Blake uses Adam and Eve pointing at a door to illustrate the lines, '*Sense*, and *Reason* show the door, / Call for my Bier, and point me to the Dust' (IV, 10). The drawing is in the British Museum Print Room, Album 19. Cf. p. 266 below.

17 The same figures reappear in the title-page to *Songs of Innocence and of Experience*: the flames of experience are shown sweeping over the bodies of Har and Heva, who have tried to remain in innocence.

18 In *A Voyage to Laputa*.

19 See above, p. 48.

20 Coleridge, *Poems* (ed. E. H. Coleridge), Oxford, 1913, I, 289.

21 See N. Frye, *op. cit.*, pp. 242–4.

22 See Appendix I.

23 See S. F. Damon, *William Blake, his Philosophy and Symbols*. Gloucester, Mass., (1924) 1958, p. 308 (cf. p. 72 and Frye, *op. cit.*, p. 245).

24 The river Adona is probably intended to indicate a more innocent form of Milton's river Adonis (discussed below) and also of the occult quality Adonai. Similarly 'Mne Seraphim' is an 'innocent' version of the occult 'Bne Seraphim' (cf. S. F. Damon, *A Blake Dictionary*, 1965, s.v.) the change of letter indicating the dominance of Mnetha. Blake's use of occult names at this time is further discussed in Appendix II and notes.

25 J. G. Davies, *The Theology of William Blake*, Oxford, 1948, p. 44, quoting *The True Christian Religion*, p. 387.

26 Bernard Blackstone, *English Blake*, 1949, p. 41.

27 *Paradise Lost*, i, 446–52.

28 E. Young, *The Complaint, or Night Thoughts on Life, Death and Immortality*, V, 48–51.

29 'Auguries of Innocence', ll. 105–6. NB 120; NC 433; E 483.

30 *Jerusalem*, 64. 22–3. NB 515; NC 699; E 213.

31 See A. S. Roe, *Blake's Illustrations to the Divine Comedy*, plate 28.

32 S. F. Damon, *op. cit.*, p. 312.

33 'The Little Girl Lost and Found' in *The Divine Vision* (ed. V. de Sola Pinto), 1957, p. 20.

34 NB 5; NC 2; E 401.

35 NB 160n; NC 109; E 736. The next line, 'Can wisdom be put in a silver rod or love in a golden bowl?' is also deleted, to reappear as the motto to *Thel*.

36 In *Aeneid*, vi, 893–901, Aeneas returns to the world through the Gate of Ivory: this too may have worked in Blake's imagination.

37 David Erdman, *Blake: Prophet against Empire*, Princeton, 1954, p. 107, fig. 3 (Erdman is using the similar design from *America*, plate 13). The last plate of *Thel* is evidently later than the others, which suggests that it may replace an earlier, deleted version. Without such a version, however, one can only say that the style of this plate seems to be moving towards that of *America* and *The Marriage of Heaven and Hell* but does not necessarily represent any change in the basic conclusion as first conceived.

Chapter Four

1 Coleridge, *Collected Letters* (ed. E. L. Griggs), 1956, I, 397.

2 Reproduced in my *Blake's Humanism*, figs. 32, 33; cf. also p. 256.

3 'Auguries of Innocence', ll. 59–60. NB 119; NC 432; E 482.

4 NB 570–1; NC 762–4; E 258–9. See my *Blake's Humanism*, figs. 7–11 and pp. 233–7.

5 See, e.g., A. Blunt, *The Art of William Blake*, 1959, plate 11a, and Milton, *Poems in English* (ed. G. Keynes), 1926, I, plate facing p. 48.

6 NB 652; NC 617; E 555.

7 See, e.g., *Antony and Cleopatra*, II, vii, 26–7.

8 Blake seems to be equating the rock with the tablets of the law in order to establish his connection with Mount Sinai.

9 *Paradise Lost*, ix, 1099–1110.

10 'Contemplation'. NB 44; NC 37; E 433.

11 *MHH* 14. NB 187; NC 154; E 39.

12 NB 16on; NC 109; E 736.

13 NB 165; NC 130; E 6. Quoted above, p. 68.

14 In some important work on the romantic conception of music, shortly to be published, Professor John Hollander draws attention to the importance of the shell-image at this time, as suggesting a correspondence between the physical shape of the inner ear and the sense of echoing sound. (The popular romantic image of the shell held to the ear and supposedly making the sound of the sea brings the two elements together perfectly). Blake's image of the ear and the whirlpool in *Thel* (which Professor Hollander mentions) could be said to extend this idea by introducing Blake's conception of infinity. It can be related to his design in *America* (fig. 26) where an idea also found in *Europe* ('Thought chang'd the infinite to a serpent') is expressed by a man peering down into a serpent, its coils arranged like the revolutions of a whirlpool, and to plate 15 of *America*, where a coiled shell by the body of visionless man at the bottom of the sea illustrates the hardening of his senses. His use of the voluted scroll in other designs may be an extension of the idea; where the book represents knowledge made finite and ordered, the scroll (where at any point the page being read is exposed between two volutions) could suggest the reading of the imaginative man, for whom everything that he reads has an infinite resonance.

15 NB 216; NC 241; E 62.

16 NB 212; NC 237; E 58. The last line is a hit at Johnson's belief in 'the general'. Cf. *Rasselas*, ch. x.

17 See my *Blake's Humanism*, pp. 120–2.

Chapter Five

1 NB 372; NC 380; E 763–4.

2 NB 185; NC 152; E 37.

3 See my *Blake's Humanism*, pp. 108 and n, 122–4.

4 *Ibid.*, pp. 120–32; 228.

5 See his *Three Principles of the Divine Essence*. Boehme, *Works*, I(ii), 204–28.

6 This idea seems to be used by Blake in the 'Argument' to *The Marriage of Heaven and Hell*. NB 181; NC 148–9; E 33.

7 Daniel iii.

8 Daniel iii, 31–5.

9 George Herbert, 'The Elixir'. *Works* (ed. F. E. Hutchinson), Oxford, 1941, p. 184.

10 *The Four Zoas*, III, 209–11. NB 285; NC 297; E 324.

11 John Smith, *Select Discourses*, 1660, pp. 102–3.

12 *Milton*, 28. 16–17. NB 411; NC 515; E 124–5 (cf. *Europe*, 14. 15–20; *Song of Los*, 3. 28).

13 See Appendix Three.

Chapter Six

1 Annotation to Richard Watson's *Apology for the Bible*, p. 14. NB 761; NC 392; E 606–7. The nature of the political content in 'Vala' is discussed by David Erdman (*Blake: Prophet against Empire*, Princeton, 1954). The

chronology involved is further examined by G. E. Bentley Jnr in the preface
to his edition (Oxford, 1963).

2 See his note to Berkeley's *Siris*. NB 818; NC 773; E 653. Cf. Northrop
Frye, *Fearful Symmetry*, Princeton, 1947, p. 135.

3 Cf. 'Tiriel', I, 9. NB 150; NC 99; E 273.

4 *Paradise Lost*, iv, 977–9.

5 E.g. *Paradise Lost*, iii, 80–134.

6 See above, p. 101.

7 NB 203; NC 198; E 52.

8 *William Blake's 'Vala'* (ed. H. M. Margoliouth), Oxford, 1956, p. 3,
conflated with Erdman's text (E 296).

9 NB 571; NC 764; E 259. (Cf. my *Blake's Humanism*, pp. 233–7.)

10 See my *Coleridge the Visionary*, 1959, pp. 236–41.

11 *Paradise Lost*, iv, 128–30.

12 The line is a conflation of two excerpts from the eleventh chapter of
St John's Gospel: 'Thy brother shall rise again' (v. 23) and 'Said I not
unto thee, that, if thou wouldest believe, thou shouldest see the glory of
God?' (v. 40).

13 'Blake's "Cupid and Psyche" ', *The Listener*, 21.11.57, pp. 833–4.

14 From 'Auguries of Innocence'. NB 119; NC 432; E 482.

15 *Paradise Lost*, i, 670–798.

16 Joshua ii, 1–3; 6; 17–25; Isa. ii, 9. Cf. my *Blake's Humanism*, p. 209.

17 See below, pp. 269–73.

18 *Paradise Lost*, v, 656–72.

19 See above, pp. 24–5. With l. 149 cf. *Paradise Lost*, i, 242.

20 Cf. the morning hymn of Adam and Eve in *Paradise Lost*, v, 197–9. The
association of dawn with music was reinforced in Blake's time by the account
of the Temple of Memnon, where the first ray of the morning sun was said
to cause a musical string to vibrate. The image is used in Akenside's
Pleasures of Imagination, I, 109–24.

21 II Kings iv, 35.

22 *Paradise Lost*, i, 771–92.

23 *Paradise Lost*, v, 663–707.

24 Cf. the illustration to page 7 of *America*. Reproduced, Ellis and Yeats,
vol. III.

Chapter Seven

1 J 27, para. 2.

2 Three illustrations of Joseph and his Brethren are now in the Fitzwilliam
Museum, Cambridge. Reproduced in G. Keynes, *William Blake's Illustrations
to the Bible*, 1957, pp. 6–11. Others are at Windsor Castle and elsewhere.

3 Spenser, *The Faerie Queene*, II, x, 11 and IV, xi, 15–16.

4 'Arthur was a name for the constellation Arcturus, or Boötes, the keeper
of the North Pole.' NB 608; NC 577; E 533.

5 Most of the identifications were made by Herbert Jenkins in a paper,
'The Teaching of William Blake' (*Blake Society*: *Papers read at the first meeting*,
Olney, 1913, p. 26). Kox was Trooper Cock, Schofield's friend and ally;
Kwantok was John Quantock, J.P., and Peachey was John Peachey, J.P.,
the two magistrates at Chichester; Brereton was William Brereton, J.P., on

the bench when Blake appeared at Petworth; and Bowen probably T. B. Bowen, who practised on the Home circuit and Sussex sessions.

6 David Erdman argues in favour of identifying Hand with Leigh Hunt, whose editorial signature was a printer's fist, an accusing 'indicator'. (*Blake*: *Prophet against Empire*, p. 423). Hunt's *Examiner*, in spite of its liberal principles, had attacked Blake's exhibition and would therefore stand as an apt symbol of impotent desire. Hyle's domination by the female will is probably the key to his identification with Hayley, while Skofield, the John Schofield who accused Blake, is the meanest form of human life.

7 Ezekiel i, 15–16; x, 8–14, etc.

8 Cf. Genesis iv, 16–24.

9 Paul Miner's 'William Blake's London Residences', *Bulletin of New York Public Library*, 1958, LXII, 535–50, has an illustration of Willan's farm, showing the cows in the foreground. In his recent study (*Blake*, 1968, pp. 142–5) Stanley Gardner argues that the verses carry no pastoral nostalgia, since the country north of London was already laid waste by industrialism. He argues that Blake is expressing approval of new building such as Nash's terraces in Marylebone and the development of the 'extensive waste' that was Paddington. Although it may be accepted that the verses are not a simple nostalgia for a childhood countryside, however, it should be pointed out that all the places mentioned were country walks for Londoners in Blake's boyhood—and many of them for long afterwards. Most were hardly spoilt; in the case of Paddington, Blake's phrase, 'mournful, ever-weeping Paddington' (a reference perhaps to the number of springs in that area) suggests his own disquiet. The imagery suggests to me not an en-thusiasm for contemporary building, but a description of a landscape seen in a moment of vision—perhaps from Hampstead. From there Blake might have looked down on sunlit fields between Islington and Marylebone, with Primrose Hill and St John's Wood in the foreground, Kentish Town and St Pancras further left and Paddington to the right. Beyond the fields rises the city itself.

10 See above, pp. 38–42.

11 The proper name of 'Bedlam' was the Hospital of St Mary of Bethlehem.

12 *Areopagitica.*

13 Boehme's list is almost exactly the same. For Adam he has 'Abel'; he ends with 'holy Noah'. *Works*, 1764–81, I, 11.

14 See, e.g., *Vala, or The Four Zoas*, ii, 72–213; vi, 316–25. NB 269–73, 309; NC 282–5, 319–20; E 310–14, 345.

15 Since writing this I discover that Giorgio Melchiori has discussed this plate with the same idea in mind (*The Whole Mystery of Art*, 1960, p. 143). He notes that Yeats also probably read the design as a representation of the Swan and Leda, since this is the interpretation offered in the commentary which he prepared with E. J. Ellis. Melchiori's account offers many illus-trations of the resonances of the theme in Yeats's mind; in the case of Blake, however, I would maintain that the use of the myth must be referred directly to his preoccupation with the inter-relation between the visionary universe and the universe of nature. The myth fits his theme that where the relationship is denied, nature is likely to be 'raped', cruelly, by the infinite energies that are thus excluded.

16 St Mark ix, 44, 46, 48.

17 No one seems to have identified the English source from which Blake discovered the tradition of Adam Kadmon, but cabbalistic knowledge was constantly present in England in the eighteenth century. The best discussions of the subject occur in D. Saurat, *Blake and Modern Thought*, 1929, pp. 98–106, and Desirée Hirst, *Hidden Riches*, 1964.

18 See above, p. 89.

19 Cf. Luke ii, 47.

20 John xi, 24; Job xix, 26.

21 Matt. xiii, 24–30.

22 Gen. xxii, 1–13.

23 The phrase 'concursus fortuitus' is found in Cicero, but the use with reference to atoms seems, as one would expect, to come first in the seventeenth century. N.E.D. gives the first usage as by Henry More in his *Antidote to Atheism*, 1653.

24 See D. Figgis, *The Paintings of William Blake*, 1925, Pl. 93.

25 NB 73; NC 215; E 25.

26 *Paradise Lost*, x, 504–84.

27 II Kings v, 27.

28 Jonah iv.

29 This pre-Freudian insight may well have been stimulated by the similar story in Swift's 'Digression on Madness' (*A Tale of a Tub*, ed. D. Nicol Smith, Oxford, 1958, pp. 163–5).

30 Blake's illustration to Gray's 'Ode on a distant Prospect of Eton College' conveys a feeling for the schoolboys enjoying their temporary pleasures which adheres closely to Gray (*Designs for Gray's Poems*, 1922).

31 *Vala, or The Four Zoas*, ix, 100–13. NB 350; NC 360; E 374.

32 Compare Coleridge's comments on the 'sudden charm' diffused by moonlight, in *Biographia Literaria*, ch. xiv (ed. J. Shawcross, Oxford, 1907, II, 5).

33 See S. F. Damon, *William Blake, his Philosophy and Symbols*, Gloucester, Mass. (1924), 1958, p. 277. Blake placed this statement in his painting 'Epitome of Hervey's Meditations among the Tombs'. Reprod. M. Butlin, *Catalogue of Works of William Blake in the Tate Gallery*, 1957, plate 39.

34 Marlowe, *Doctor Faustus*, V, ii, 191 (ed. F. S. Boas, 1932, p. 173).

35 Daniel iii. See above, p. 36.

36 See above, p. 34.

37 Job xxxviii, 31.

38 The note on the Verse, which appears before the opening of Book One, was first added in the edition of 1668.

39 *Paradise Lost*, vii, 28–30; 9–12.

40 E.g., the interpreter's house and the House Beautiful (the one is inhabited by Innocence, the other by Discretion, Prudence, Piety and Charity). Bunyan's allegory has more to do with Faith than Blake's, which stresses the importance of works of compassion; it is only in the general atmosphere and descriptive touches that the resemblance is caught.

41 Cf. ll. 29–40. NB 111; NC 425; E 476.

42 See above, pp. 15–16; 34.

43 In 1791. See Geoffrey Keynes, 'Blake and the Wedgwoods', *Blake*

Studies, 1949, pp. 67–75. Cf my *Blake's Humanism*, p. 254 and figs. 26, 27.

44 See above, pp. 175–6.

45 See above, p. 190 (and fig. 36).

46 ll. 25–52. NB 111–12; NC 425–6; E 476.

47 Bunyan, *Pilgrim's Progress*, 1678, p. 225. The Gate of Heaven also has a way to Hell, of course (*ibid.*, p. 232).

48 In each of these pairs Blake sees a similar contrast: a figure of energy but lost vision on the one hand (Esau the hunter; Saul the black-tempered), a more visionary figure contracting to meanness on the other (Jacob the deceiver for gain, David who sends Uriah to certain death to gain his wife). Peleg and Joktan, the most mannered version of this contrast, are hardly mentioned in the Bible (Genesis x. 25 is the central place). But since Peleg means 'division' and Joktan 'he is made small', and since their appearance at an early point in Genesis suggested the possibility of a mysterious significance, Blake evidently seized on them as his first examples of a visionless energy facing a contracted humanity.

49 I Sam. iii.

50 *Milton*, 37. 43; 40. 22. NB 425, 426; NC 528, 532; E 137, 140.

51 According to John Toland ('History of the Druids', *Collection of Several Pieces*, I, p. 136) the rocking of the stones was caused by skilful hollowing-out of the interior, organized by the Druids to create the illusion of supernatural assent to their verdicts of guilt.

52 See A. Blunt, *The Art of William Blake*, 1959, plate 49, a and b.

Chapter Eight

1 Letter of 23.10.'04. NB 899–900; NC 851–2; E 703 (cf. letter of 4.12.'04). Cf. *Blake's Humanism*, pp. 188–90.

2 For further discussion of Shakespeare illustrations, see Appendix One.

3 H. M. Margoliouth argues for a date subsequent to the completion of the *Night Thoughts* illustrations for the major effort of composition, but makes it clear that the whole issue is in considerable doubt. (*William Blake's Vala*, Oxford, 1956, xxiii–xxv). See also Appendix Three.

4 British Museum Print Room: Album 14 (Young I, page 22); engraved edition, 1797, p. 12.

5 NB 99; NC 184; E 465.

6 *Op cit.*, Album 17 (III, 22).

7 Album 16 (III, title-page and verso).

8 Album 21 (V, 8). Reproduced in the Harvard edition of the illustrations (Cambridge, Mass., 1927), plate 4.

9 Album 25 (VI, 15).

10 Album 31 (VII, 70).

11 Album 19 (IV, 10). (Engraved edition, 1797, p. 72.)

12 Album 28 (VII, 25).

13 See above, pp. 40–1.

14 NB 104; NC 414; E 473.

15 H. M. Margoliouth, *William Blake*, 1951, pp. 124–5.

16 D. Figgis, *Paintings of William Blake*, 1957, plates 67, 79–84.

17 *The Blake Collection of W. Graham Robertson*, 1952, plate 26. Blake also illustrated the 'Hiding of Moses'. See Keynes, *Blake's Illustrations to the Bible*, 1957, plates 33, 34, 35.

18 G. Keynes, *Blake's Illustrations to the Bible*, 1957, p. 43, plate 145. For the rolling away of the stone, see D. Figgis, *op. cit.*, plate 49.

19 D. Figgis, *op. cit.*, plate 80.

20 *Ibid.*, plate 82.

21 NB 44–8; NC 37–40; E 434–6. See above, p. 32.

22 Mona Wilson, *Life of William Blake*, 1948, pp. 313–4; E 667.

23 *Illustrations of 'The Book of Job' by William Blake* (Introd. by Laurence Binyon and Geoffrey Keynes), New York, 1935, pp. 4–5.

24 *Ibid.*, pp. 6–7. Reprod. also D. Figgis, *op. cit.*, plates 61–2.

25 *Ibid.*, vol. ii. For commentary, I draw on the set of water-colours executed for Thomas Butts; the other water-colours and engravings will be found to differ occasionally, but in general Blake makes few significant alterations so far as symbolism is concerned. The inscriptions are taken from the engravings, which are reproduced in vol. i.

26 *The Pilgrim's Progress by John Bunyan, 1626–1688*, illus. by Blake and ed. G. B. Harrison with new introduction by G. Keynes, New York, 1941, p. xix.

27 A. S. Roe, *Blake's Illustrations to the Divine Comedy*, Princeton, 1953, pp. 32–3.

28 NB 700–701; NC 785; E 669. For the last extract, cf. *Jerusalem* 52; 'Every Religion that Preaches Vengeance for Sin is the Religion of the Enemy & Avenger; and not of the Forgiver of Sin, and their God is Satan, Named by the Divine Name' (quoted Roe, p. 31).

29 A. S. Roe, *op. cit.*, p. 32.

30 The complete set is reproduced in A. S. Roe, *op. cit.*

31 This detail is referred to only very obliquely by Dante, but is a favourite episode with Blake. See, e.g., NB 727, 113; NC 82, 427; E 585, 477; and cf. my *Blake's Humanism*, p. 93 and n.

32 See above, pp. 47–9 and nn.

33 NB 582–3; NC 778; E 267. See above, pp. 49–50.

34 See, e.g. NB 181; NC 149; E 34.

35 NB 106; NC 417; E 468.

36 NB 129–43; NC 748–59; E 510–16 and 792–6.

37 Luke iii. 41–51.

38 E. J. Morley, *Henry Crabb Robinson on Books and their Writers*, 1938, I, 342–3.

39 ll. 11–12. NB 577; NC 770; E 265. The locution follows Benjamin Whichcote's *Aphorisms* (1753 ed., no. 281): 'Sinners are made up of Contradictions'.

40 Kerrison Preston, *The Blake Collection of W. Graham Robertson*. 1952, plate 28. Mr Preston also discusses it in his pamphlet, published by the Fitzwilliam Museum, Cambridge, entitled *The Spiritual Condition of Man*.

41 By Joseph Wicksteed, Geoffrey Keynes, Kathleen Raine and George Wingfield Digby respectively. (See *Studies in Art for Belle da Costa Greene*, Princeton, 1954, p. 205; *ibid.*, 202–8; *The Divine Vision* (ed. V. de Sola Pinto) 1957, p. 19; G. W. Digby, *Symbol and Image in William Blake*, Oxford, 1957, pp. 54–93.)

42 *Loc. cit.*, Miss Raine's interpretation is developed in an article in the *Journal of the Warburg and Courtauld Institutes*, 1957, XX, 318–37. See also correspondence in the *Times Literary Supplement*, 24.1.58 and 31.1.58.

43 *Loc. cit.*

44 Rev. xxi. 2.

45 NB 134; NC 749; E 515.

46 Rev. xxi. 1; 23; xxii. 5.

47 *Cymbeline*, II, iii, 21.

48 NB 647; NC 613; E 552.

49 G. Keynes, in *Studies presented to Belle da Costa Greene*, Princeton, 1954, p. 206.

50 Rev. xxii. 13–17.

51 G. Keynes, *loc. cit.*

52 A good version occurs in D. Figgis, *Paintings of William Blake*, 1925, pl. 54. Others are in Geoffrey Keynes, *William Blake's Illustrations to the Bible*, 1957, plates 130, d and e.

53 See my discussion, *Blake's Humanism*, pp. 193–4.

Chapter Nine

1 J. T. Smith, *Nollekens and his Times*, 1828, II, 478 and n.

2 Mona Wilson, *Life of William Blake*, 1948, p. 271.

3 Letter of 16.8.1803. NB 873; NC 828; E 702.

4 J. T. Smith, *op. cit.*, II, 457.

5 See, e.g., W. Jones, 'On the Gods of Greece, Italy and India', *Asiatic Researches*, 1788, I, 223; Thomas Taylor, *Cupid and Psyche*, 1795.

6 Coleridge, *Table Talk*, 1.9.1832 (1835, II, 96) (cf. my *Coleridge the Visionary*, p. 283). For Shelley's word see J. A. Notopoulos, *The Platonism of Shelley*, Durham, N.C., 1949, pp. 280–1. He also traces the idea to Shelley's essay 'On Love': 'we dimly see within our intellectual nature a miniature as it were of our entire self . . . a soul within our soul'.

8 NB 102; NC 185; E 490 and n.

9 A. Gilchrist, *Life of Blake*. Quoted above, p. 54.

10 Letter of 19.3.1819. *Letters of John Keats* (ed. H. Rollins), Cambridge, Mass., II, 80.

11 NB 99; NC 178; E 465.

12 Soame Jenyns's *Free Inquiry into the Nature and Origin of Evil*, 1757, was reviewed in biting terms by Dr Johnson (*Works*, 1792, viii, 23–61).

13 Letter of 12.4.1827. NB 927; NC 879; E 708.

14 *Ibid.*

15 'Fragments'. *Collected Poems*, 1950, p. 240.

16 *Ibid.*, p. 347.

17 'E.T.', *D. H. Lawrence: A Personal Record*, 1935, pp. 62–3.

18 *Jerusalem* 56:43 (cf. 34: 26–31).

19 NB 250; NC 248; E 68. D. H. Lawrence, *Tales*, 1934, p. 183.

20 D. H. Lawrence, 'Reflections on the Death of a Porcupine' (reprinted in *Phoenix II*, 1968, 460–74).

21 Saul Bellow, *Herzog*, New York, 1964, p. 33.

22 Iris Murdoch, *The Time of the Angels*, 1966, pp. 10–11.

23 C. Jung (*Psychological Types*, 1923, p. 547), states that he claims no more for his four types than that they work: his concentration on the number four springs mainly from his experience of the mandala and the fourfold diagrams produced by his patients.

24 Avis M. Dry's *The Psychology of Jung*, 1961, contains (pp. 203–8) a good discussion of the limitations of Jung's quaternity theories. She points out that there is some uncertainty whether Jung is proposing to include evil or the feminine principle as the fourth member along with the other members of his Trinity.

25 *The Active Universe*, 1962.

26 Letter of 12.4.1827. NB 926; NC 878; E 707.

27 See his *Biographia Literaria*, II, 207–8.

28 Letter of 12.4.1827. NB 927; NC 878; E 707.

29 Edith J. Morley, *Henry Crabb Robinson on Books and their Writers*, 1938, I, 330.

30 'Auguries of Innocence'. NB 119; NC 432; E 482.

Appendix One

1 Letter to Flaxman of 12.9.1800. NB 840; NC 799; E 680. Quoted above, p. 23.

2 E 590; O* 939.

3 A. Gilchrist, *Life of William Blake*, 1880, I, 364.

4 *Milton*, 28. 3. NB 411; NC 514; E 124.

5 M. Butlin, *The Works of William Blake in the Tate Gallery*, 1957, plate 2.

6 E.g. *Gates of Paradise*, engravings 6–8, NB 572–3; NC 765–6; E 260–1; 'There was a day . . .' and 'Satan smiting Job with sore boils', engravings 2 and 6 from *Illustrations of 'The Book of Job'*.

7 Cf., e.g., his 'O fool fool to lose my sweetest bliss' (*Four Zoas*, 3. 168) with Othello's 'O fool! fool! fool! (*Othello*, V, ii) and his 'O I could tell thee tales / That would enrage thee' (*Four Zoas* 4, 114–5) with Hamlet's father's 'I could a tale unfold . . .' (*Hamlet*, I, v).

8 *Descriptive Catalogue*, NB 599; NC 569; E 526.

9 M. Butlin, *op. cit.*, items 17 and 18, plate 12.

10 G. Keynes, *Pencil drawings by William Blake*, (2nd Series), 1956, plate 3.

11 Annotation to Bacon's *Essays*. NB 768; NC 399; E 612.

12 NB 700 (*variatim*); NC 785; E 668.

13 Letter of 12.4.1827. NB 927; NC 878; E 707. Cf. *Lear* IV, vi.

14 'Tiriel', 8. 8. NB 160; NC 109; E 281.

15 *Ibid.*, 3. 21.

16 See 'The Lazar House' in the Fitzwilliam Museum, Cambridge.

17 Blake used this quotation in his notebook as an epigraph to the drawing later reproduced as 'Earth' in *The Gates of Paradise*. See my *Blake's Humanism*, pp. 236–8.

18 See the 'Introduction' to *Songs of Experience* (NB 65; NC 210; E 18) and my discussion in *Blake's Humanism*, pp. 79–80.

19 *Jerusalem* 27. NB 463; NC 649; E 170.

20 H. A. Mason, 'The Ghost in *Hamlet*'. *Cambridge Quarterly*, 1968, III, 127–52.

21 John Danby, *Shakespeare's Doctrine of Nature*, 1949, pp. 117–20.

22 *Ibid.*, pp. 125–6, 166.

23 *Ibid.*, p. 109.
24 B. H. Malkin, *A Father's Memoirs of his Child*, 1806, Preface.
25 See above, note 17.

Appendix Two
1 Oxford, 1967.
2 R. F. Gleckner, 'Blake's *Tiriel* and the State of Experience', *Philological Quarterly*, 1957, XXXVI, 195–210; Kathleen Raine, 'Some Sources of *Tiriel*', *Huntington Library Quarterly*, 1957, XXI, 1–36.
3 *The Song of Los*, 4. 13–16. NB 248; NC 246; E 66.
4 NB 718; NC 75; E 580.
5 John Danby, *Shakespeare's Doctrine of Nature*. See esp. Part II chs i, iv, v.
6 See *The Faerie Queene*, V, ix, 14–19.
7 *Blake's Humanism*, pp. 83–4.
8 See his art. 'Spenser' in *A Blake Dictionary*, Providence, Rhode Island, 1965, p. 383. One may also compare Phaedria's self-blame (*FQ*, II, vi, 32–4) with Leutha's (*Milton*, 11. 35–13. 6).
9 S. F. Damon, *William Blake: his Philosophy and Symbols*, p. 306. I suspect that Blake's mind worked through an identification of Mercury the Greek god with the qualities of mercury the substance to create an image for the human self with the composite suggestion of the light-giving god who falls; who becomes as elusive as quicksilver in his metamorphoses; yet who remains the 'messenger of the gods', holding a key to the meaning of the universe. Tiriel's ultimate metamorphosis as a rock (4:60) might well reflect the tradition that Mercury, in northern Druid countries, was represented by a square stone, symbolizing the eternal stability and power of the Deity —this would provide a link with Blake's derogation of the trilithon. (See J. Toland, 'History of the Druids', *Collection of Several Pieces*, I, 135). The dualism between Har, contracted son of Adam, and Tiriel, a form of Lucifer, may well derive from the dualism between the 'son of Adam' and the 'genius' in Eastern tales (see, e.g., *Tales of the East*, 1812, 11, 341); in the form of 'Adam' and 'Satan' it remains a permanent feature of Blake's thinking, organizing much of the contraction/expansion imagery in the one case and of the light/opacity imagery in the other.
10 N. Mallet, *Northern Antiquities*, 1770, II, 7.
11 Kathleen Raine, *op. cit.*, p. 21.
12 Kathleen Raine, *op. cit.*, p. 19; N. Frye, *op. cit.*, pp. 243–4.
13 Kathleen Raine, *op. cit.*, pp. 21–4.
14 N. Frye, *op. cit.*, p. 242 (citing *The True Christian Religion*, 45).
15 Kathleen Raine, *op. cit.*, p. 25. It should be borne in mind, of course, that names like this from Agrippa might well be known to someone who dabbled in magic. *The Conjuror's Magazine* for October 1791, for example, gives a brief table, initiating its readers into common magical names, which includes Tiriel, Zazel, Adonai and Bne Seraphim.
16 *Ibid.*, pp. 4–5, mentioning the translation by R. Potter, 1788.
17 David Erdman, *Blake, Prophet against Empire*, Princeton, 1954, p. 122.
18 Kathleen Raine, *op. cit.*, pp. 1–2.
19 See his annotation to Watson, quoted above, p. 117.

20 Kathleen Raine, *op. cit.*, pp. 17–18, citing *The Song of Los*, 4. 5–12 (NB 248; NC 246; E 66).

21 *Metamorphoses*, iii, 95–8; iv, 563–603.

22 Kathleen Raine, *op. cit.*, pp. 33–4 (Ovid's *Metamorphoses*, viii, 732–7). Ovid's boar and bull are not used by Blake.

23 Kathleen Raine, *op. cit.*, p. 36.

24 T. Vaughan, *Works* (ed. A. E. Waite), 1919, p. 271 (cf. 'Tiriel', 4. 60–1).

25 T. S. Eliot, *Selected Essays*, 1932, p. 321.

Appendix Three

1 *Vala, or The Four Zoas*, ed. G. E. Bentley, Jr., Oxford, 1963. I am particularly indebted to this edition for some of the detailed descriptions of the drawings.

2 *William Blake's Vala: Blake's Numbered Text.* Ed. H. M. Margoliouth, Oxford, 1956.

3 *Ibid.*, p. xv.

4 Pages 65, 75. Other relevant pages are 85, 115, 125, 131, 140 and, less certainly, 46 and 111.

5 'The Binding of Vala (Et Cetera)', *The Library*, 1964, XIX, (rev. 1968), 125.

6 W. H. Stevenson, 'Two Problems in *The Four Zoas*', *Blake Newsletter*, I, 3, 15.12.1967, pp. 13–16, and no. 4, March 1968.

The Illustrations: a Commentary

While the illustrations which follow include many designs which are discussed in the text they also provide an opportunity for exploring further the relationship between Blake's visual symbolism and the images of earlier art.

That Blake was from childhood well acquainted with European art, particularly of the Renaissance, is clear from an account by B. H. Malkin (*A Father's Memories of his Child*, 1806, pp. xviii–xix) which may be quoted in full:

> (Blake) early had the common opportunities of seeing pictures in houses of noblemen and gentlemen, and in the king's palaces. He . . . attended sales at Langford's, Christie's and other auction rooms. At ten years of age he was put to Mr. Parr's drawing-school in the Strand, where he soon attained the art of drawing from casts in plaster of the various antiques. His father bought for him the Gladiator, the Hercules, the Venus of Medicis, and various heads, hands, and feet. The same indulgent parent soon supplied him with money to buy prints; when he immediately began his collection, frequenting the shops of the print-dealers, and the sales of the auctioneers. Langford called him his little connoisseur; and often knocked down to him a cheap lot, with a friendly precipitation. He copied Raphael and Michael Angelo, Martin Hemskerck and Albert Durer, Julio Romano, and the rest of the historic class, neglecting to buy any other prints, however celebrated.

Throughout my study I have assumed that Blake's knowledge of traditional iconographical interpretation of symbols was at best sketchy and that he came to previous art rather with a sense of mystery. As a result, particularly in youth, he searched it for correspondences of his own and for confirmation or illustration of his own reading of human nature. This is shown when one places engravings which he would have known against designs of his own showing similar forms or themes. Sometimes there is a visible influence from the engraving to the form of Blake's design: this is particularly likely to be so in his dealings with Raphael, whose work he admired intensely. At other times the interest lies in the different treatment which Blake gives to a similar theme in order to express his own emphasis.

Boehme's 'Tree of the Soul' (Fig. 1) serves as a good illustration of the last point: Boehme presents a pietistic scheme of fourfold vision. Reinterpreted by Blake that vision would rise from the world of reason, via the worlds of energy and love, to the fourfold vision where desire and vision are at one. For the normal human being, who may escape the shackles of reason but cannot hope, except in rare moments, to reach the fourfold state, life will normally consist in an alternation between the states of love and energy. These are Blake's states of innocence and experience.

Innocence and Experience
The world of innocence alone is not enough; to try to stay in it is to remain an inhabitant of Blake's Vale of Har after the manner of his Har and Heva, who never seek to leave their paradisal state but remain under the tutelage of their memory-guardian, Mnetha. (As it happens Blake's depiction of these three figures carries an extraordinary resemblance to corresponding figures in Piero della Francesca's fresco 'The Death of Adam' at Arezzo—which he could hardly have known.) Figure 2 shows them in their etiolated state, beautiful but without the lineaments of energy, bathing while Mnetha looks on; figure 3 shows them laid out in death; figure 4 shows Lear (a Har-figure forced too late by the consequences of his own lawbound actions to face experience—which therefore assumes its most terrible forms) reviving with the aid of Cordelia to a more visionary state.

The following figures explore the world of visionless experience. Blake may well have read the story of Aeneas, losing his wife in Troy while carrying his old father Anchises on his back, and that of Hercules stifling the giant Antaeus (5) as emblematic accounts of the eternal struggle between youthful energy and aged hypocrisy; certainly his depiction of Tiriel on the back of Ijim (that Esau-like figure of honest indignation) (6) follows the lines of these incidents. The encounter with old age is repeated in Blake's depiction of Hamlet (7), who sees in the armed ghost of his formerly beautiful father a terrible prophecy of his own fate in the world of experience.

In that world, energies are distorted and misunderstood. Pathos is slain, and above her body Pity, like a newborn babe, is forced to ride sightless couriers of reason (9) which resemble the sightless mare of Füseli's 'Nightmare'. Hecate, who has never known fulfilled desire, hides all but one of her three faces; with that one she looks at animal lineaments which terrify her (8). In the world of *A Midsummer Night's Dream* there is a less fearful encounter, as the Har and Heva figures of Oberon and Titania stand by a lustful Puck in a scene which is made harmless by the dancing of visionary fairies (11). For Macbeth himself, on the other hand, is reserved the most terrible encounter of all: imagining himself securely ensconced in his castle of non-vision and destructive energy, he is confronted by the vision of honest innocence in Banquo (10).

Blake traces some of the roots of this distortion of experience to the relationship within the family, where the father, jealous of the child who retains a visionary energy that he has lost and whom he sees as a threat to his own pride, binds him down until he enroots in the earth and achieves the same form. The illustration to *America* which shows Los and Enitharmon visiting their bound son (14) seems to owe something both to Salviati's design of Adam, Eve and Cain (which suggests jealousy in Adam) (12) and to the engraving in Boehme (13) which shows a fallen man (similar to Salviati's Adam) at the very moment when the peacock of pride in his breast is confronted by the descent of the dove in the heart, and he begins the slow movement away from the nadir of his jealous humanity.

The Loss of Vision

If the world of experience is at first sight a moral state, the descent into it is brought about also by the enslavement of reason. The orthodox picture of a God who creates by his own power in dividing light from darkness (as in Raphael's fresco (15)) is reordered by Blake according to his own idea, which separates the divine vision from the divine energy. So in the illustrations to *The Book of Urizen* Raphael's God of power in the clouds is replaced by a meaner withdrawing figure who still tries desperately to create in the clouds (16), while his power, separated from him, is a figure of running energy (see *Urizen*, plate 3 (= *Blake's Humanism*, fig. 32) and engraving 2 to *Illustrations of the Book of Job*). (Jean Hagstrum (*William Blake, Poet and Painter*, Chicago, 1964) has also noticed some visual resemblances between Raphael's creation designs and Blake's.)

The withdrawal of Urizen is followed by his return as lawgiver, as in the tradition of Ogmius or Og (17), the shrunken form of that Phoenician Hercules who was said to have discovered the Cornish tin-mines (thus initiating the reign of commerce) and to have brought knowledge of mathematics to the British inhabitants (the pillars, with a galleon in the background, would probably connect in Blake's mind with the splendid engraving of a galleon and pillars which adorns the title-page to Bacon's *Novum Organum*, 1620). Under Ogmius' law these benefits become cruel gods. In the moral version of the story Moses (who is for Blake alternately a figure of energy (a pillar of fire by night) and a figure of law (a pillar of cloud by day) withdraws into the mountain, converses with shadows dire and returns reduced, bearing the tablets of the moral law (18). In the English sequel the bald slaves of law set up their warrior-god (the ancient Haesus) and sacrifice victims to the law with knife and cup while humanity looks on in dismay (19). An illustration to Blake's *Europe* shows a similar bald figure of reason exerting a stranglehold on his victims (20) (the motif may be compared with Blake's interest in the Laocoön design (see pp. 47–8, above)), while a design in *Jerusalem* shows daughters of the Law dancing around their victims as they carry out the rites of knife and cup against a Druid landscape (21).

The 'cherubim' of ancient temples preserve emblems of the lost, nobler tradition, including the ancient hieroglyphs of the sun, serpent and wings in various forms (22). Blake reproduces the sun and wings in two forms in a plate for *Jerusalem* (23) while the serpent's egg of hardened vision and the released serpent of destructive energy (24, 25) are a constant poetic theme. The serpent of energy can be reduced to analytic coils by the man of reason (26) until he is swallowed up in the sea of Time and Space (27). But the serpents will return to plague men in a more insidious fashion (28, 29) (the Laocoön design is again relevant). Only the daughters of Jerusalem, who know nothing of the Law, can bring them back into precarious harmony (30).

Other myths can be used to describe the fall of desire. The Fall of Phaethon is for Blake a story of the failure of Desire under the Law: the traditional rendering of it (31) is matched by his own design (32) in which the fall of Desire is also the Fall of Vision to a state of impotent Reasoning ('It indeed appeared to Reason as if Desire was cast out, but the Devils account is, that the Messiah fell. & formed a heaven of what he stole from the Abyss'). In the new regime of chastity, the horses of the chariot of Desire are replaced by dogs of straining lust pulling the chariot of Diana (33); the new doctrines of Sin and Atonement result in a still more absurd chariot, where bull-like tyrants, caricatures of the sublime cherubim, strive desperately to draw a chariot consisting of serpents whom they have already reduced to immobility by their coiling analysis, while on their back solemn little recording beasts are all that are left of the wings; the rejected energy of the sun burns around both them and the fading figures of Albion and Jerusalem (34).

Subsequent designs show the hierogram of the sun, the serpent and wings in various forms: a human head is strangled by a dead serpent of energy and spectre wings (35); a human head is strangled by the rope of reason sprouting the feathers of an Indian warrior (36); wings of the cherubim weave forgiveness while beneath them the cog-wheels of analysis and law weave destructive war (38); and winged angels weep over all that is left of the sun of desire, a rocky world which, like the Osiris tended by Isis, is continually building and continually decaying ('because of Love and Jealousy') while underneath the serpent of energy, now left to run in isolation, complains that 'Women the comforters of Men become the Tormenters & Punishers' (37).

The theme of Isis and Osiris is repeated in the design which Blake takes over from Füseli, representing 'The Fertilization of Egypt' (39). Here, in a world where desire (Osiris) has been usurped by jealousy (Typhon) and art replaced by the foolish pyramid, the energy of fertility is cut off from vision and left to the dog. So the dog-priest Anubis lifts his hands towards the distant light of the dogstar Sirius, while in the background the jealous god Typhon covers with his wings the springs of the Nile. (Füseli's original sketch has most of these features, but Blake adds the features of Urizen to the waving wings, and the pyramid to the landscape; in his final engraving he also adds a sistrum which suggests the absent Isis). In his title page to *Visions of the Daughters of Albion* Blake repeats the motif in simpler form, showing the woman of liberated desire springing from the sea like Venus Aphrodite only to be greeted by the covering wings of jealous Urizen (40).

The cherubim wings of false holiness in these designs turn into more aggressive eagle-wings in the designs that follow. The myth of Prometheus, his liver devoured perpetually by Jupiter's eagle, or of the giant Tityus, who suffered a similar fate (41), becomes for Blake an emblem of the destructive power of false holiness, as in *Visions of the Daughters of Albion*, where Oothoon calls on Theotormon's eagles to rend her breast ((42): the motif is repeated in *America*, plate 13 and *Milton*, plate 38). But for Oothoon this is a gesture of despair: she knows that the proper action of the Eagle is to 'lift his golden beak to the pure East, / Shaking the dust from his immortal pinions to awake / The sun that sleeps too long'. The eagle-headed guardian visionary of *Jerusalem* (43), looking out at the rising sun, embodies the same knowledge.

The Survival of Vision

In the visionless world of Urizen, the guardian of vision is Los, who clings fast to the instruments of desire. He holds his phallus-like hammer and stands by his forge on the rectangular blocks of his lawbound world, inhibited from full creativity by the chain that binds down the bellows of his forge and the spectre-wings of jealousy that hover over him (44). Ghisi's engraving of Vulcan at his forge (45), where the smith is actively assisted by cherubs of desire, suggests the ideal which Blake has in mind here. Nevertheless Los is still necessary to Urizen's world, which would be destroyed altogether if he did not actively beat the energy of the sun into a restraining sphere (46).

Meanwhile the vision which Los guards but does not possess is imaged in the moon-ark on the waters of time (47–50). However emaciated rational man may become he can never quite lose the vision of tenderness which visits his unconscious in dreams when he is asleep (51). All nature and all human splendour are signs of its hidden glory: the triple crown of the Pope, which directs false worship to himself, is still a clue to the sovereignty available to every human being; the sun, moon and stars which are studied so closely by the eye of reason are nevertheless pregnant with vision, just as the motion of the sunflower can be fully understood only if it is seen to yearn towards the sun (52).

All tyranny and cruelty is a sign of the sleep of humanity. The Jesus who has been veiled by the Church (53) is still in his more splendid form the key to humanity. Which is the truer human being, however: the kingly warrior, or the man who bows his head near his chariot (55)? the executioners of St Peter, or the centurion who bows his head in the background (56)? yet in each case the representative of normal humanity does no more than close his eyes, like the Druid who clutches his book (57); otherwise the Druid would become the open-eyed Bard: the Joseph of Arimathea who preserved the Jesus of Vision, or the Gothic artist who built the great cathedrals (58).

As it is, the Druids shut up the sun serpent and wings of vision into the circle and serpentine avenues of their rocky temple (59); it is left to the creative Los to rebuild the universe of sunlike sublimity and moonlit pathos in their despite (60). (Ruthven Todd (*Tracks in the Snow*, 1946, pp. 47–50 and plate 14) was the first to notice the similarity of these motifs, though he seems to have missed their full significance for Blake). While the land is dominated by the trilithon-like enclosing vision of the rationalists (61–2), the artist (63) can still show humanity its true context of hospitable friendship and Gothic beauty (64). In general, however, humanity is likely to suffer with Job (65–69) unless it can listen to the visionary (70) who sees that the universe is not simply a rocky temple raised to a god of Law, but a world of energy and vision, the twofold chariot of the sun, with its horses of intellect (71) being matched by the free play of energy in threefold organized innocence (72, 73). If humanity can pierce the clouds of the universe's laws to look at the play of the universe's energies these will in turn reveal above them the supreme, fourfold vision, where the stars sing together and all the sons of the morning shout for joy (74).

In his later designs Blake often returns to this theme in relation to the Bible. He gives his own vision of the Bible and the Church, for example, suggesting that their peculiar virtue lies in the New

Testament emphasis on Love or Charity, which liberates the power of threefold tenderness exhibited by St James and opens a way to the supreme fourfold vision of Revelation (75). Or he illustrates the Book of Revelation itself, suggesting that the Spirit and the Bride who say 'Come!' are the Desire and Vision of his own writings, calling man to the exercise of twofold energy and threefold love in readiness for the awakening of fourfold vision (78). Or, very simply, he can use the parable of the Wise and Foolish Virgins to show man as perpetually under judgment—not by the moral law, but by his own nourishment or neglect of vision (77). Here, as in other designs (e.g. 13, 65–8) visionless man is seen against a background of geometric or neo-classic architecture, but the Gothic motif in this design lies not in any corresponding Gothic architecture (as in *Jerusalem*: fig. 76) but in the shapes of the flames in the lamps themselves and in the radiance of the faces above them. The ultimate point of focus in Blake's art lies, here as always, in the 'human face divine'.

Table of Passages from
'The Four Zoas' and *Jerusalem*

The table below provides an index to passages from 'The Four Zoas' and *Jerusalem* which are discussed in this book, enabling the reader both to use the book as a running commentary on these poems and to look up particular passages.

'Vala, or The Four Zoas'

The textual references in the first column are to Keynes (Nonesuch Variorum and Oxford Standard editions) and in the second to Erdman and Bloom (see p. xv above).

Keynes	Erdman (plates)		Section and Page of Commentary above
Night I			
9–11	3.4–3.6		116
24–231	4.5–9.18	II	125–7
232–242	9.19–9.29	V	159–60
243–259	9.30–10.8	II	127
260–305	10.9–11.18	IV	149–51
306–365	11.19–13.10	II	127–8
366–463	13.11–18.10	V	160–2
464–end	18.11–end	V	159
Night II			
1–8	23.1–23.8	II	125 & 149
7–286	23.7–33.36	III	139–41 (cf. p. 196)
287–349	34.1–34.63	V	162
349–end	34.63–35.19	II	128–9
Night III			
1–40	38.1–39.14	III	141–2
41–130	39.12–43.22	IV	151–3 (cf. pp. 224–5)
131–175	43.23–45.8	III	142 (cf. pp. 314 ff)
144–end	44.5–46.12	II	129–30
Night IV			
1–end	47.1–55.31	II	130–3
[111–16	50.28–34	IV	149 (cf. pp. 314 ff)]
Night V			
1–113	57.1–61.10	II	133–4
114–134	61.11–62.8	V	162–3
135–184	62.9–63.18	II	134
185–197	63.19–63.31	IV	153
198–201	64.1–64.4	III	146
202–end	64.5–65.12	IV	153–5

Night VI

1–end	67.1–75.34	I	117–19 (cf. p. 196)

Night VIIa

1–134	77.1–80.26	I	119–21
135–289	80.27–84.23	IV	155–7
267–end	84.1–90.67	II	134–6

Night VIIb

1–122	95.15–98.31	V	163–4
124–169	91.1–92.16	I	121
170–209	92.17–93.19	III	142–3 (cf. p. 191)
210–end	93.20–95.14	II	136–8

Night VIII

1–139	99.1–102.22	I	121–2
140–557	102.23–110.2	III	143–5
558–584	110.3–110.29	V	164
585–end	110.30–111.24	I	122

Night IX

1–90	117.1–119.23	I	122–3
91–193	119.24–121.32	III	145–7
162–230	121.1–122.26	V	164–5
230–77	122.26–123.32	I	123–4
278–357	123.33–125.39	V	165–6
358–457	126.1–128.27	V	166
455–558	128.25–131.21	II	138–9
559–649	131.22–133.33	V	167
650–91	133.34–135.3	I	124
692–845	135.4–138.40	V	167–9
844–8	138.39–139.3	I	124–5
849–55	139.4–139.10	III	147
846–end	139.1–139.10	V	169

Jerusalem
(In this table the variant references in the Erdman edition are given in square brackets).

Keynes-Erdman	*Section and Page of Commentary*	
(frontispiece)	V	239 (cf. p. 19)
(title-page)	V	239 (cf. p. 300)
3.1–5.26	V	240–1 (cf. pp. 260–1)
5.34–12.4	II	195–8
12.5–13.37	V	242–4
13.38–16.69	I	178–80
17.1–17.58	II	198–200
17.59–19.47	IV	218–22
20.1–20.41	II	200–1
21.1–49	IV	222
21.50–24.11	II	201–2
23–24 (illus)	V	245
24.12–26 end	IV	222–4

The fourfold Vision : 1 The four levels of vision in Boehme ('The Tree of the Soul')

Innocence and Experience: 2 Innocence untouched by Experience ('Har and Heva bathing') **3** Death of untouched innocence **4** Renewal of innocence ('Lear and Cordelia in prison')

2

3

4

Energy and Innocence: **10** Macbeth and Banquo's ghost **11** Oberon, Titania, Puck and fairies dancing (illustration to *A Midsummer Night's Dream*)

10

11

12

13

14

15

16

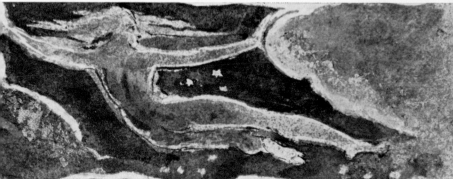

17

18

Cruelty under the Law: 19 Sacrifices to Haesus (detail) (in Sammes)
20 Lawbound man falling (*Europe*) **21** The rites of knife and cup (*Jerusalem*)

19

20

21

From Kæmpfer.

From Le Bruyn.

A Chinese Device.

From the Ruins of Naki Rust

From the Isiac Table.

Fallen Vision versus Energy: 24 Egg and Moon of lost vision **25**
Serpent and 'mundane egg' of residual vision (*Bryant*) **26** Reason reducing
serpent to analytic coils (*America*) **27** Death of analysed energy (*Marriage
of Heaven and Hell*)

24 & 25

26

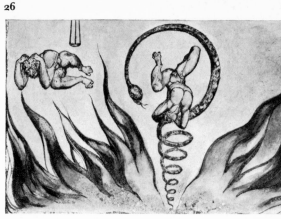

27

28

Energy versus Lost Vision: 28 (opposite page) Serpents attacking men (Ghisi) **29** Men gripped by spectrous energies (*Book of Urizen*) **30** Energies and vision reconciled (*Jerusalem*)

29

30

31

32

Energy under the Law: 33 Diana and chariot drawn by dogs (old engraving) **34** The chariot of the moral law (caricature of Sin and Atonement, *Jerusalem*)

33

34

Lost Vision under the Law: 35 Man strangled by spectre wings and dead serpent (*Europe*) **36** Man strangled by analytic reason (*Jerusalem*) **37** Winged angels and opaque world; serpent of lawbound energy below (*ibid.*)

35

36

37

The survival of Vision (from *Jerusalem*): **51** Rainbow and wings of beauty hovering over man in the sleep of non-vision **52** The ambiguous beauty of nature

51

52

53

54

Vision, lost and retained: **55** David victorious (after Raphael) **56**
Centurion at Crucifixion of St Peter (after Michelangelo) **57** British
Druid (in Sammes) **58** Joseph of Arimathea, 'Gothic artist' (Blake)

55

56

57

58

59

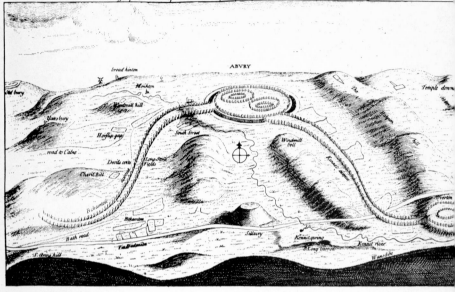

A Scenographic view of the Druid temple of ABVRY in north Wiltshire, as in its original.

60

Decline and renewal of Vision : 61 Trilithon of single vision (*Jerusalem*)
62 Trilithon of single vision and rocking stone of hypocrisy (*Milton*) **63**
Poet as gothic visionary (*Jerusalem*) **64** Gothic vision and Canterbury
Pilgrims (Blake)

61

62

63

64

Decline and renewal of Vision (illustrations to *Job*): **65** Gothic beauty threatened (messenger tells of destruction)   **66** Trilithon established (Job gives stone to a beggar)

65

66

Decline and renewal of Vision (illustrations to *Job*): **67** Sunset over elaborated trilitha (Job smitten with boils) **68** Dying light and ruined trilitha (Job and comforters)

67

68

Decline and renewal of Vision (illustrations to *Job*): **69** The trilithon triumphant in darkness (Job curses the day of his birth)   **70** The stars of vision renewed (Elihu as young visionary)

69

70

Vision and Desire Reunited: 71 Horses of the sun (Ghisi) **72** Energy bridled by innocence under the moon (*America*)　**73** Chariots of sun and moon (Ghisi)　**74** Chariots of intellect and Energy under supreme, fourfold vision ('When the Morning Stars sang together')

71

72

73

74

Index

Unless otherwise indicated, italicized items are literary or visual works by Blake. Indexing of common Blakean topics is often selective. Bold type indicates a central discussion, an asterisk that the topic is further discussed in *Blake's Humanism*, where the reader may also find (Appendix One) a summary, for reference, of Blake's early myth-making.